THE HANDBOOK OF *ASSET-BACKED SECURITIES*

THE HANDBOOK OF *ASSET-BACKED SECURITIES*

Jess Lederman
Editor

New York Institute of Finance

Library of Congress Cataloging-in-Publication Data

The Handbook of asset-backed securities / Jess Lederman, editor.
p. cm.
ISBN 0-13-372301-1
1. Asset-backed financing—handbooks, manuals, etc. I. Lederman, Jess. II. New York Institute of Finance.
HG4028.A84H36 1990 89-39387
658.15'224—dc20 CIP

This publication is designed to provide accurate and authoritative information in regard to the subject matter covered. It is sold with the understanding that the publisher is not engaged in rendering legal, accounting, or other professional service. If legal advice or other expert assistance is required, the services of a competent professional person should be sought.

From a Declaration of Principles Jointly Adopted by a Committee of the American Bar Association and a Committee of Publishers and Associations

Printed in the United States of America

10 9 8 7 6 5 4 3 2 1

New York Institute of Finance
A Division of Simon & Schuster, Inc.
2 Broadway
New York, New York 10004-2207

Contents

Chapter 19: Commercial Mortgage-Backed Securities

by Carl Kane

Preface

The asset-backed securities market is one of the most rapidly growing segments of the U.S. capital markets. It is also one of the most exciting and most profitable. Since its inception in the early 1980s, market participants have pioneered literally dozens of innovative structures designed to meet the changing needs of issuers and investors. Through asset securitization, corporate treasurers have reduced their funding costs and improved their financial ratios, commercial bankers and thrift executives have freed up capital and boosted earnings, and institutional investors have gained a new investment-grade instrument featuring attractive spreads to treasuries.

The Handbook of Asset-Backed Securities is the most comprehensive source of information ever compiled on the mechanics, economics, and critical issues associated with asset-backed securities. Part I provides a wide-ranging overview of asset securitization. Its nine chapters provide the nuts and bolts of securitization, covering legal, accounting, systems, credit enhancement, and management issues in detail. The 15 chapters in Part II offer an in-depth analysis of a broad variety of asset-backed securities, from the most commonplace (those backed by auto loans and credit cards) to the exotic (those backed by junk bonds, second mortgages, hotels, and leases).

Many thanks must be given to each of the contributing authors for the time and energy they took from their hectic schedules to produce a significant contribution to the existing body of literature on asset-backed finance. They are the driving force behind the dynamic market for asset-backed securities. I am also grateful for the help and support of the New York Institute of Finance, without which this project could not have been completed.

Jess Lederman
Cleveland, Ohio

About the Editor

Jess Lederman, chairman of the Asset Backed Capital Group, Inc. is widely recognized as one of the pioneers of the secondary mortgage market. He is a cofounder of two of the nation's major private mortgage conduits (private sector counterparts to the Federal National Mortgage Association and the Federal Home Loan Mortgage Corporation) and was the principal architect of the first Security and Exchange Commission's registered pass-through securities backed by adjustable-rate mortgages.

Lederman was formerly executive vice president of Bear Stearns Mortgage Capital Corporation and associate director of Bear Stearns & Co., Inc. Before joining Bear Stearns, he was vice president of sales and marketing for Sears Mortgage Securities Corporation and director of pricing and research for PMI Mortgage Insurance Co. in San Francisco.

Lederman graduated summa cum laude and Phi Beta Kappa from Columbia College in New York. He earned his M.B.A. at the Columbia University Graduate School of Business. He is a frequent speaker at industry seminars and has published numerous articles in leading mortgage finance journals. Lederman is also the editor and coauthor of *The Secondary Mortgage Market,* and *Mortgage Banking.*

Contributors

Joan A. Barmat runs the Asset Based Finance Group of Bear Stearns. Prior to this, she was managing director in the Investment Banking Group at Manufacturers Hanover Trust Co., where she was responsible for arranging asset-based finance and other funding transactions for U.S. financial institutions. She has an M.B.A. from Stanford University's business school, and has also worked in the international finance area of Morgan Guaranty Trust Company.

Russell B. Brewer II is managing director of Financial Security Assurance, Inc., where he manages the group responsible for providing surety bonds to support a wide range of nonmortgage asset-backed securities. Transactions completed to date have included securities backed by pools of computer leases, automobile loans, credit cards, trade receivables, time-share loans, bank loans, and high-yield securities.

Prior to joining Financial Security, Brewer was associate director in the Structured Transactions Group at Moody's Investors Service. In this capacity, he managed a team of professionals responsible for the development of credit standards in a variety of areas, including Moody's overcollateralization guidelines for mortgage-backed bonds and Moody's approach to rating receivable-backed securities. His group was also responsible for rating all mortgage cash flow bonds (CMOs) and receivable transactions (auto transactions, computer lease deals, and so on).

Brewer received his M.B.A. from New York University and a B.A. from Colby College.

Philip A. Brooks is associate director in the Income Property Department of the Mortgage Bankers Association of America (MBA) located in Washington, D.C. Among his responsibilities are the study and dissemination of information on agricultural credit to MBA's members. The MBA is the preeminent trade association for real estate finance, and its members include companies involved in all areas of commercial and residential real estate finance.

Robert W. Burke, Moody's Investors Services

Pat Cooper, Chemical Bank

William J. Curtin, Vice President, Mortgage Backed Securities Research, Drexel Burnham Lambert

Rodney S. Dayan is a senior partner in the New York law firm of Cadwalader, Wickersham & Taft, specializing in the area of structured mortgage and receivable financing. Cadwalader represents some of the largest issuers and investment bankers active in the national mortgage and asset-backed securities markets. Dayan received his undergraduate degree from Princeton University, did graduate work at Oxford, and received an LL.B. from Columbia Law School. He also holds a master's in law from New York University.

Charles M. Adelman, Maurine R. Bartlett, Barry J. Dichter, Bronislaw E. Grala, and John W. Osborn are also partners at Cadwalader, Wickersham & Taft, with extensive experience in structured mortgage and receivable financing. They specialize in tax law, bank and thrift regulatory law, insolvency, ERISA matters, and corporate/securities law, respectively.

Stephen H. Deckoff, Associate, Mortgage Backed Securities Research, Drexel Burnham Lambert

Karl P. Essig became a Principal of Morgan Stanley in 1987. He is responsible for the Asset-Backed Finance area of the firm. His department focuses on securitizing nonmortgage assets, including airplane leases, automobile loans, credit card receivables, home equity loans, franchisee loans, and trade receivables. He was a founding member of Morgan Stanley's currency and interest rate swap group and, from 1984 through 1986, he headed the swap unit in Tokyo. Essig received a B.A. from Stanford University and an M.P.P.M. from Yale University.

Harold H. Goldberg, Moody's Investor Services

Samuel Gordon, Moody's Investors Services

Thomas P. Hourican, Standard & Poor's Corporation.

Linda S. Iseley is vice president and a member of the Receivables Group at Financial Security Assurance, Inc., which provides credit enhancement for a wide range of asset-backed securities. She has primary responsibility for the marketing function within the Receivables Group. She heads the group's direct calling program for banks, thrifts, finance companies, insurance companies, and corporations.

Prior to joining Financial Security, Iseley was a marketing representative in the commercial finance department of Irving Trust. In this capacity, she was responsible for sourcing and structuring asset-based leveraged buyouts and traditional commercial finance facilities.

Iseley holds a B.S. in business administration from the University of North Carolina at Chapel Hill.

Carl Kane is managing director of Management Advisory Services in the New York office of Kenneth Leventhal & Company. In the last few years, he has focused on the securitization of commercial real estate. He led the Leventhal team that developed the Standard & Poor's Corporation rating system for commercial mortgage-backed securities. His work in this area has involved assisting numerous developers and financial institutions in evaluating, structuring, and executing commercial real estate financing transactions. He has also conducted strategic studies for major financial institutions on the impact of commercial real estate securitization.

Before joining Kenneth Leventhal & Company, Kane founded his own consulting firm, working primarily with smaller growth-oriented companies. Prior to that he practiced management consulting with Booz Allen & Hamilton, Inc., and Touche Ross & Co., where he was responsible for a wide variety of client assignments in banking, insurance, health care, publishing, and retailing.

Stuart Lewtan founded Lewtan Technologies, Inc. after a career in investment banking at The First National Bank of Boston. Lewtan Technologies, Inc. is committed to addressing the systems issues in asset-backed securities. The depth of their involvement in the securitization industry is evident in the line of software products and services that they have developed to facilitate the complicated structures required by asset-backed deals. The STARS line-up of products and services includes the STARS Servicing System, the STARS Trustee System, and the STARS Structuring System. The company's consulting services also include portfolio and prepayment analyses.

Victor M. Lopez-Balboa is a member of the Mortgage Finance Group at Goldman, Sachs & Co. The group's focus is on overall finance, trading, and sale coverage for the savings and loan industry, mortgage bankers, and governmental housing agencies, as well as on mortgage and nonmortgage asset securitization for commercial banks and finance and insurance companies. Lopez-Balboa devotes his time to general mortgage finance activities, collateralized mortgage obligations, and securitization transactions that involve nonauto retail installment sale contracts, closed-end consumer loans, variable-rate open-end second mortgages, closed-end fixed-rate second mortgages, and commercial equipment leases.

Lopez-Balboa joined Goldman, Sachs & Co. as an associate in August 1986. That same year he received his J.D./M.B.A. from the Law School and the Wharton School, University of Pennsylvania. He received a B.A. in economics and political science from Columbia University.

K. Jeanne Person is an analyst in the Bond Portfolio Analysis Group at Salomon Brothers. Prior to joining the firm in February 1987, she worked as the Washington correspondent for *Mortgage-Backed Securities Letter,* a weekly newsletter covering the mortgage securities market, and as an associate editor for *Bondweek,* a weekly publication covering the taxable U.S. and international bond markets. She has an M.S. from the Columbia University Graduate School of Journalism and a B.A. in economics from Princeton University.

Kenneth J.H. Pinkes, Moody's Investors Services

Raymond T. Sloane, Jr., is the partner in charge of the Litigation Consulting Services Department in the New York office of Spicer & Oppenheim.

Prior to heading the Litigation Consulting Practice, Sloane served as the partner in charge of the Technical Research and Review Department in New York, where he developed an expertise in highly complex, technical accounting and auditing issues. He also serves as an adviser to his firm's Senior Technical Committee on Accounting and Auditing Standards and is the firm-designated expert on the Securities and Exchange Commission.

A member of the American Institute of Certified Public Accountants and the New York State Society of Certified Public Accounts, Sloane is also an attorney and member of the American Bar Association and the New York State Bar Association. He has lectured on the subject of asset-backed securities at the Institute for International Research and is a contributing author to the *Attorneys' Handbook of Accounting.*

Daniel J. Smith, assistant vice president, joined Duff & Phelps Credit Rating Co. in September 1986. Smith is in charge of commercial real estate analysis within the Structured Finance Group. He is a member of the Duff & Phelps Credit Rating Committee as well. Prior to joining Duff & Phelps, he was a manager of financial guarantee analysis with CNA Insurance Companies in Chicago. There, he managed a staff of analysts who underwrote real estate projects using bond financing guaranteed by CNA. He was also responsible for structuring the financing of each transaction prior to closing and administering the CNA Financial Guarantee real estate portfolio. Prior to his four years in real estate, Smith was an actuarial analyst responsible for the projection of CNA's various liability reserves. He has also been a high school mathematics instructor.

Smith holds a B.A. from DePaul University.

Thomas A. Tranfaglia, Jr., is an audit manager in the New York office of Spicer & Oppenheim and currently handles several audit clients that are issuers of asset-backed securities. He has also served in the firm's National Office Accounting and Auditing Department, where he specialized in accounting for financial instruments.

Tranfaglia is a member of the American Institute of Certified Public Accountants and the New York State Society of Certified Public Accountants and has been a contributing author to *The CPA Journal*.

Peter J. Travers is a member of the Asset Securitization Group at Goldman, Sachs & Co. The group, which is a joint venture between Goldman, Sachs & Co.'s Mortgage Finance and Corporate Finance Groups, has completed numerous public and private offerings of securities backed by credit card accounts, auto loans, trade receivables, nonauto retail installment sale contracts, and closed-end unsecured consumer loans. Travers is currently devoting his time primarily to securitization transactions, including credit-enhanced auction preferred stock offerings that involve various types of consumer loans, variable-rate open-end second mortgage loans (home equity lines), closed-end fixed-rate second mortgage loans, computer and auto leases, and nonperforming assets.

Travers joined Goldman, Sachs & Co. as a vice president in April 1987. Prior to that, he worked on new product development for PaineWebber Capital Markets and practiced law for four years with Sullivan & Cromwell.

Travers received a joint J.D./M.B.A. degree from Columbia University and a B.A. in philosophy from the University of California, Berkeley.

Townsend Walker is a vice president in Bank of America's Corporate Finance Americas Group. For two years, he directed the Asset Finance

Group, which managed the structuring and sale of over $2 billion of Bank of America's consumer assets. The group is also responsible for marketing, originating, structuring, and placing consumer loans and trade receivables for the bank's customers.

Walker joined Bank of America in 1972 as a foreign exchange dealer and has worked in investment banking for the bank in San Francisco, London, and Paris. He received a B.S.F.S. from Georgetown University, an M.A. in economics from New York University, and a Ph.D. in economics from Stanford University.

M. Douglas Watson, Jr., Moody's Investors Services

PART I
ASSET SECURITIZATION

CHAPTER 1
Securitization: An Overview

Joan Barmat

INTRODUCTION

Pledging expected asset cash flow as the basis for raising funds is hardly a novel concept. However, the adaptation of this concept in the form of securitization has introduced a process that may significantly alter many premises of current financial markets.

Securitization is still new. The first large, public asset-backed debt issues of 1985 and 1986 have not yet matured, and significant uncertainties about loss experience, payment patterns, and structure remain. But powerful economic forces, such as disintermediation and the maturing of the mortgage-backed market, continue to encourage the growth of the securitization phenomenon, which from January 1985 to November 1988 totalled over $33 billion in public issue volume.

Unlike the mortgages that support most of the mortgage-backed security market, assets that back securities are nonstandardized in several key respects:

- Asset type
- Payor/cash flow source credit quality

- Servicing and processing procedures
- Payment patterns

This lack of standardization will limit, to some extent, the growth in size and efficiency of the asset-backed security market in the near term and, possibly, beyond that. Potential corporate asset-backed security issuers/asset sellers continue to face the difficulties and costs inherent in adapting internal systems to securitization requirements, while investors are still learning how to analyze the characteristcs of and risks associated with various asset types and how to differentiate among issues for a given asset type. In this light, driven by a variety of needs, asset-backed issuers to date are, in effect, pioneers of a new technology. The current phase of this effort can be seen as an exploration of boundaries in structure, price, and acceptability. Some preliminary standards emerged and created a degree of efficiency and liquidity in certain sectors of the securitization market, such as debt securities backed by automobile and credit card receivables. Yet, comprehensive standardization, which would allow for more rapid market growth, remains elusive and is likely to remain so for years to come.

WHAT IS SECURITIZATION?

In essence, securitization is the open market selling of financial instruments backed by asset cash flow or asset value. It is characterized by (1) the pooling of assets or asset cash flow, and division of the benefits among investors on a pro rata basis, by systematic risk assessment, and (2) its offering form as a security (rather than, for example, as a loan or a group of receivables). To some extent, securitization can be seen as the offering of asset-backed instruments to nontraditional purchasers—that is, beyond commercial banks and the factoring industry to securities investors at large. Several factors critical to achieving this wider acceptance are:

- An ability to quantify risk
- Extensive and repeated explanation of risk factors
- Assignment of credit ratings comparable to those assigned to other investment alternatives

WHY SECURITIZE?

There are many reasons that certain corporations choose to securitize assets. Not all of these reasons are immediately obvious. However, several of the most compelling reasons are:

- *Lower-cost financing.* Regardless of whether asset-backed medium-term debt, commercial paper, or preferred stock is used, the assets owned by a company can be used to structure a security of higher credit quality and, therefore, of lower market cost than the corporate entity could itself.
- *Equity saving.* When faced by leverage restrictions (or for financial institutions, by regulatory capital requirements), a securitization transaction that qualifies as a sale of assets for accounting purposes reduces the need for higher-cost equity. Securitization allows for a reduction in assets *without* the sale of a business franchise and often *with* retention of most of the earning power of the asset.
- *Matched funding/funding strategy.* Depending on the structure chosen, securitization can offer perfect matched funding by eliminating funding exposure in terms of both duration and pricing basis.
- *Earnings.* When structured as a sale of assets, securitization allows sellers to recognize for generally accepted accounting principles (GAAP) accounting a gain (or loss) on sale equal to the present value of any expected future cash flows payable to the seller that will be derived from the assets and that are known at the time of sale (except for regular servicing income to the seller, unless this is the asset sold).
- *Nondisclosure:* For privately held or non-U.S. companies, securitization of assets can provide a means of financing that does not require overall financial disclosure to U.S. regulatory authorities, rating agencies, or investors. The characteristics of the assets being securitized, as well as those of the asset service (which need not be the seller/securitizer) are key to the process.

Whereas all of these reasons to securitize assets can apply to financial institutions, regulatory requirements relating to capital for thrift institutions and to proportions of asset categories allowed to be held can add special impetus for securitization.

HOW TO SECURITIZE ASSETS: A JIGSAW PUZZLE

The process of securitizing assets can be among the most comprehensive of any financial instrument. Whereas a given company may have a primary reason for undertaking the process, many potential interdependent side-effects must be considered. The key pieces of a securitization transaction that must be assembled include:

- Structure
  —Tax impacts
  —Accounting impacts
- Credit risk assessment
- Rating agency review
- Cost/financing strategy
- Technical support

All of these pieces must fit together for the transaction to be effective for both the securitizer and the investor. The most important aspects of these transaction factors are described briefly here.

Structure

Assets may be used to back either a debt instrument or an equity instrument with debt characteristics similar to certain types of preferred stock. To a great extent, the nature of the asset and its attendant expected cash flow will determine the type of instrument used. However, one fundamental rule of any asset used in securitization is that its cash flow or value can be estimated. Estimates of expected asset cash flow can, for example, be based on schedules, contracts, or demonstrated historical payment patterns. Periodic cash flow, as well as variations due to prepayment, delinquency, or default, are all part of the cash flow expectation equation.

Whether the securitizing company wants to achieve a true accounting sale of assets for a given unit or for the consolidated corporation is often another key determinant of the type of asset-backed security used. Accounting and tax ramifications are critical to this decision. For example, the leveraging and capital-saving benefits of true sale securitization can be offset by the impact of a large one-time gain on sale disrupting earnings flows and, in some cases, creating a large tax liability (for example, when the asset tax basis is low).

There are three basic structures of asset-backed debt instruments, from which many variations have developed. These are:

- Collateralized debt
- Pass-through obligations
- Pay-through obligations

Collateralized Debt

Collateralized debt is the form most similar to traditional asset-based borrowing. The owner of assets borrows money and pledges assets to secure repayment. The assets pledged may be measured according to their market value upon sale or their ability to generate a cash flow stream. The debt instrument issued need not match the cash flow configuration of any of the assets pledged. Since the borrower is the corporate entity pledging the assets, shelf registration of public issues is possible.

In this structure, overcollateralization—pledging more assets than the face value of debt issued to insure repayment—is often the most practical means of credit enhancement. When asset value rather than cash flow is used to establish required amounts of collateral, this is usually done on a mark-to-market basis to ensure debt payment coverage. This method of payment coverage is also used in some asset-backed preferred stock issues.

Since the direct issuance of collateralized debt does not achieve any of the capital saving aspects of a sale of assets, this structure of asset-backed security is usually used to achieve a lower cost of debt or preferred stock than an issuer could otherwise achieve.

Pass-Through Obligations

The simplest way to securitize assets with a regular cash flow is to sell direct participations. This often involves the sale of assets to a grantor trust, in which investors purchase equity interest in the assets of the trust and in subsequent cash flows. This is diagrammed in Figure 1-1.

A basic premise of the pass-through structure is that reconfiguration of cash flows is not permitted, as it would cause the trust to be deemed a taxable entity. Thus, imputed or actual interest and principal payments from payors may not be recharacterized, as would be the case, for example, with discount or premium prices paid for loan pools. The interest portion of a payment stream may be divided among, for example, investors and the servicer or to support credit enhancement, but principal must be passed through to repay investors as received. Thus, in a pass-through security, the basic economic outline of the debt instrument issued is essentially the same as that of the underlying asset.

Pay-Through Obligations

Often similar to collateralized mortgage obligations (CMOs), asset-backed securities may be structured so that asset cash flows can be reconfigured to support forms of debt unlike those of the underlying assets. It should be noted that unlike the mortgage-backed market, the term "pay-through" can be used to refer to true sale transactions, in which a sale occurs between the asset seller and a special-purpose trust or corporation. This special-purpose entity then issues a debt security collateralized by the asset cash flows. Where there is debt, there must be equity for tax purposes. Thus, in pay-through structures, equity can be supplied in the form of ownership of residual cash flow, a seller interest, or direct equity investment. Required levels of equity for a given pay-through structure are usually determined according to tax considerations. A simplified pay-through structure is diagrammed in Figure 1-2.

Variations on a pay-through structure are used for CMO-type auto and other vehicle loan securitization, for credit card and other revolving debt securitization, and for various forms of asset-backed commercial paper.

Figure 1-1. Pass-Through Structure

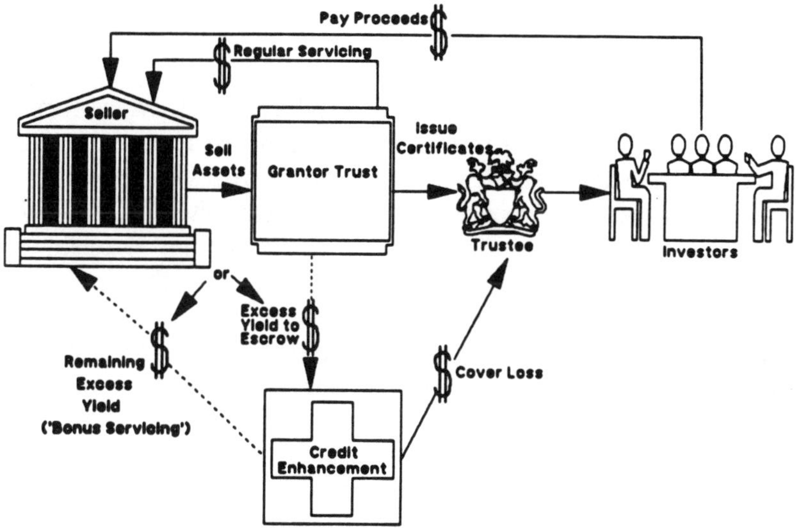

Figure 1-2. Pay-Through Structure

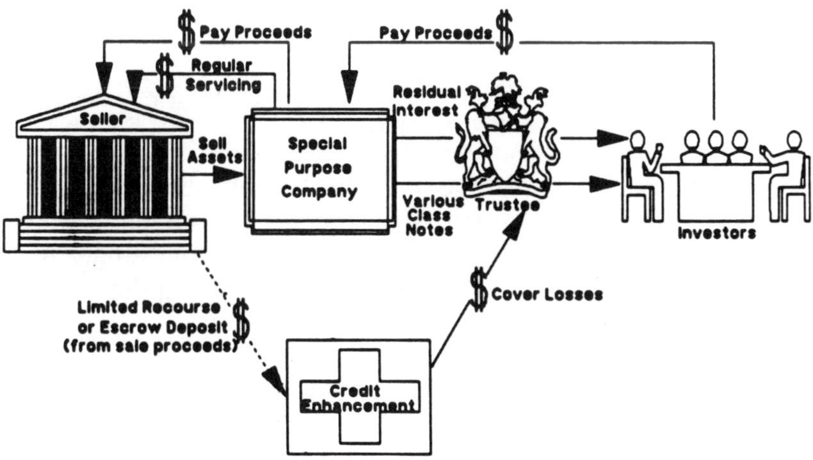

Credit Risk, Credit Enhancement, and Rating Considerations

Analysis of the risk related to assets pledged or sold in a securitization transaction can be divided into two main categories related to the characteristics of the assets themselves: a pool of a large number of relatively small-sized assets/receivables (typically consumer receivables) and a pool of a small number of relatively large-sized assets/receivables (commercial assets). In the first case, with large numbers of assets, risk analysis is based largely on historical loss and delinquency patterns (actuarial-type credit analysis). Included in this type of credit review is consideration of asset underwriting (credit-granting) criteria, of servicing characteristics and quality, and of historical or comparable asset loss and delinquency experience. Alternatively, the credit quality of each component in a pool would be analyzed to determine the pool's overall credit quality. In both cases, the nature of any general business or economic factors that could influence payment performance would also be carefully reviewed.

Once assessed, the perceived credit risks of a given asset pool can be reduced to achieve the lower market cost of securitization by obtaining additional sources of cash flow to cover expected losses and delinquencies. These sources of credit enhancement include:

- *Seller guarantee* of a portion of risk. This does not qualify as a true sale for U.S. financial institutions.
- *Subordinated interest* in the pool, which would absorb the first x percent of loss. To date, sellers have retained this interest, which creates, in effect, a form of seller guarantee. This would only qualify as a true sale for U.S. financial institutions if the subordinated interest were sold.
- *Overcollateralization* (separate from the yield/discount concept), in which the excess yield on assets is used to create a reserve against credit losses. This would only qualify as a true sale for financial institutions if the expense were taken up front.

- *Third party guarantee* from as little as 5 percent to as much as 100 percent of the face value of the collateral in the form of a bank letter of credit or insurance company surety bond. Generally, the third party guarantor is repaid by the seller or another credit enhancement source (for example, a reserve account or over-collateralization) up to an agreed-on percentage and to the extent that such other sources exist.

- *Reserve account* to cover a percentage of loss, which would be created from excess asset yield in premium collateral cases, from overcollateralization as above, or from a seller up-front deposit. Any amount that remains in such a reserve generally reverts to the portfolio servicer as bonus servicing income. This would only qualify as a true sale for financial institutions if the expense were taken up front.

These methods may be used alone or in combination, based on the parameters of a given asset portfolio and transaction structure, including accounting and tax considerations.

In addition to explicit loss protection, pool eligibility criteria used to screen the assets sold provide an additional way to control the credit quality of a securitized pool of assets. For example, choosing consumer assets with significant seasoning and little or no delinquency history would tend to provide a higher-quality credit pool. However, while in some cases, screening for higher-quality assets can be beneficial in saving credit enhancement costs, it is the predictability of loss rather than the absolute level of loss at a given point in time that is critical in the establishment of realistic credit enhancement parameters.

Accounting Issues in Credit Enhancement

A key issue for many companies that securitize assets is the accounting treatment of the various credit enhancement mechanisms with respect to sale treatment. Statement of Financial Accounting Standards No. 77 allows for a sale of assets with limited seller recourse if risk can be estimated and repurchase options eliminated. Most credit enhancement methods result in the creation of a credit reserve asset on the balance sheet of the seller, which represents limited recourse but does not allow for a 100 percent reduction in assets. However, it should be noted that U.S. financial institutions may not achieve a true sale of assets with any form of recourse for regulatory accounting (relevant for minimum capital guidelines). Thus, they are currently limited to using securitization structures with spread accounts, in which excess asset yield creates a cash reserve to support credit enhancement, if they want true sale treatment without recognition of a loss to create credit reserves.

Credit Rating

Unlike their role in assessing the risk in financial instruments of corporate issuers, credit rating agencies provide important input in the structuring of investment-grade asset-backed securities. For a given desired securitization issue rating, they will undertake extensive analysis of the assets to be used and of a broad array of attendant risks. Based on this analysis, they will, for example, assign a minimum level of required credit enhancement for a given rating. From the rating agency standpoint, all aspects of a securitization transaction must meet the overall issue rating (the "weakest link" approach). Thus, extensive quantitative and qualitative analysis is performed to determine risk parameters. Any that are not covered in a worst-case scenario by an adequately rated source must be covered by some form of credit enhancement. Thus, in many cases, factors such as servicing risk, cash account holder risk, and reimbursement risk must all be structured to meet a given rating criteria—in addition to conventional credit enhancement for credit loss risk.

Beyond basic risk analysis, rating agency counsel reviews asset-backed issue documentation for further potential risks. When a rating that is higher than that of the asset seller/issuer is sought for asset-backed securities (which is often the case), one critical legal document is the bankruptcy opinion of the seller/issuer's counsel. The purpose of this opinion is to provide support for the argument that in the case of seller/issuer bankruptcy, the assets sold or pledged will not be included in the bankrupt seller/issuer's estate. Rather, the assets will belong to investors either because they were truly sold or, if not deemed to be sold, because investors held a perfected security interest in the assets. Obtaining an acceptable form of bankruptcy opinion can pose some of the most difficult obstacles to arranging asset-backed transactions. Questions of title amendment; payment transfer fees; various state laws, including licensing issues; and custody of ownership documents are among the many that can be raised with respect to a bankruptcy opinion.

Cost/Financing Strategy

As mentioned earlier, the structure of an asset pool's cash flow or value will often dictate the pattern of its use in an asset-backed transaction. However, many variations are possible based on the asset holder's funding or capital strategies. For example, assets with revolving characteristics, such as revolving consumer loans or monthly trade receivables, may be used to back securities with short-term maturities (one to nine months), such as commercial paper. Alternatively, through reinvestment of monthly repayments, a medium- or long-term security backed by the same assets can be created. Thus a seller/issuer's funding strategy, such as whether to raise short- or longer-term money, can dictate how assets are used in asset-backed transactions, somewhat independent of the cash flow/ maturity characteristics of the assets themselves.

Another example of this concept can be found in the securitization of auto loans, in which the natural cash flow of the asset can be easily, directly securitized in the form of a medium-term debt instrument. However, auto loans have been used to back preferred stock on a revolving or revaluing basis, in which the maturity and cash flow characteristics of the security issued do not relate directly to the cash flow characteristics of a given pool of the underlying assets. In this case, the issuer's funding strategy required lower-cost capital through the issuance of preferred stock, and asset backing provided the means to achieve this end.

Technical Support

Execution of asset-backed transactions requires servicers of the underlying assets to have sound tracking and reporting capabilities. This aspect of an asset-backed transaction, which usually relies on a servicer's data processing capabilities, often determines overall feasibility and timing.

Generally, the functions that need to be performed for a cash flow–based transaction include:

- Marking records to identify assets sold
- Identifying periodic payments as belonging to sold assets (often on a daily basis)
- Transferring payments received on sold assets to a special account (in most cases)
- Reporting monthly on payments received, interest versus principal, losses, delinquencies, and prepayments, if applicable

In addition, special operational/reporting functions can be required for certain assets, such as the monthly reinvestment of principal, new account selection for revolving credit securitization, or frequent mark-to-market procedures for asset-backed transactions.

For example, Figure 1-3 illustrates the transaction support functions required for a standard consumer receivable–backed transaction.

The importance of technical support in asset-backed transactions cannot be overemphasized. However, it should be noted that once established, these procedures usually become routine and easy to expand to support similar repeat transactions.

ASSET-BACKED SECURITY ISSUANCE TRENDS

The first public issuance of asset-backed securities occurred in 1985 for Sperry Corporation; equipment leases were the assets used. Since that time to November 1988, there have been 105 public issues of various types of asset-backed securities, totaling over $33 billion in volume. Table 1-1 shows the annual volume of these issues.

Table 1-1. Annual Volume of Asset-Backed Securities 1985–1988

Year	*No. of Issues*	*Volume*
1985	7	$ 1,236.60
1986	17	10,026.75
1987	37	10,263.27
1988	44	11,632.52

It should be noted that privately placed asset-backed security transactions were performed prior to the first public issue and that they continue to be performed in large volume.

While the aggregate pattern of public issuance indicates overall growth, the underlying statistics better describe the subtleties of the development of the asset-backed market to date. Table 1-2 shows the types of issues and the new issuers of asset-backed securities since 1985.

Figure 1-3. Necessary Transaction Support Functions for a Standard Receivable-Backed Transaction

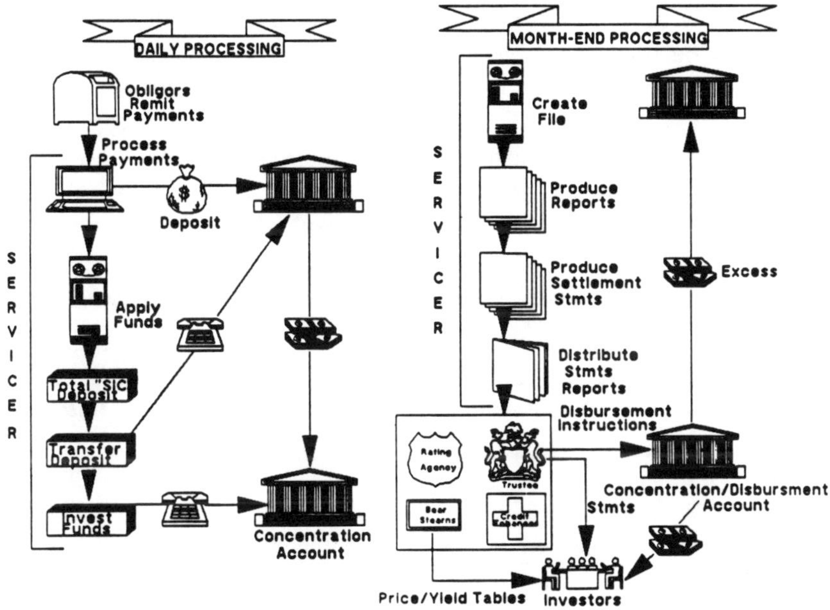

Table 1-2. Total Asset-Backed Security Issuance 1985–November 1988 Issuer Frequency Breakdown

Year	*No. of Issues*	*No of Issuers*	*1st-Time Issuers*	*Volume*
1985	7	6	6	$ 1,236.60
1986	17	9	6	10,026.75
1987	37	24	20	10,263.27
1988	44	27	15	11,632.52

As Table 1-2 shows, while aggregate issuance volume was essentially flat between 1986 and 1987, many new issuers entered the market in 1987. The reason for the large dollar volume in 1986 was GMAC's entry in the asset-backed security market with $8.3 billion in amount issued, or 83 percent of total market volume. GMAC issued only $2.4 billion of asset-backed securities in 1987 and has issued none to date in 1988. Thus, the apparent lack of increased volume between 1986 and 1987 is deceptive, as the growth in the number of issuers in this period—from 9 to 24—was explosive. Growth in the asset-backed security market between 1987 and November 1988 has been moderate, but a steady increase in the number of issues and issuers is apparent. Table 1-3 shows the composition of public asset-backed issues by type of asset used.

Table 1-3. Asset-Backed Security Issuance 1985–November 1988 Asset Type Breakdown

	Auto		*Credit Card*		*Other*	
Year	*No.*	*Volume*	*No.*	*Volume*	*No.*	*Volume*
1985	5	$ 898.60	—	—	2	$ 338.00
1986	15	9,646.30	—	—	2	380.45
1987	22	6,584.07	7	$2,409.50	8	1,269.70
1988	19	3,993.28	14	5,520.00	11	2,119.24

As indicated in Table 1-3, auto loan-backed securities dominated the market through 1987. However, during 1988, the volume of credit card receivable-backed issues was greater than that of any other type of asset-backed security. While the number of credit card receivable-backed issues was still less than the number of auto loan-backed issues, the doubling of the number of credit card receivable-backed security issuers in this period is significant.

In addition, one of the most important developments between 1987 and 1988, which is shown in Table 1-3, is the emergence of new asset types used to back securities issues. As shown in Table 1-4, which lists asset-backed issues not using auto and credit card assets, many types of assets have been used.

Table 1-4. Asset-Backed Issues, 1985–November 1988
Non-Auto, Non-Credit Card Issues

Offer Date	*Seller Servicer*	*Issuer*	*Type*	*Amount Issued ($ Mil.)*	*Collateral*
3/7/85	Sperry Corp.	Sperry Lease Finance Corp. Series A	Pay	192.00	Leases
9/12/85	Sperry Corp.	Sperry Lease Finance Corp. Series B	Pay	146.00	Leases
12/5/86	Goldome FSB	Goldome 1986—A Grantor Trust	Pass	206.00	Leases
12/17/86	Unisys Corp.	Sperry Lease Finance Corp. Series C	Pay	174.45	Leases
9/17/87	Mattel Inc. (preferred)	Mattel Funding Corp.	Pref.	62.50	Trade rec.
9/23/87	Union Carbide Corp. (preferred)	Union Carbide Finance Corp.	Pref.	249.00	Trade rec.
9/23/87	Imperial Savings Assoc.	Imperial Savings Assoc.		100.00	Corp. junk bonds
9/30/87	Green Tree Acceptance Corp.	Merrill Lynch Mortgage Investors Inc.		71.50	Loans for mfg. homes
10/2/87	American Airlines	American Airlines 1987—A Grantor Trust	Pass	92.62	Equipment
		Series A-1		3.45	notes
		Series A-2		6.52	financing
		Series A-3		9.93	leveraged
		Series A-4		7.88	leases
		Series A-5		1.71	for 6 jets
		Series A-6		19.95	
		Series A-7		43.19	

Table 1-4. Asset-Backed Issues, 1985–November 1988
Non-Auto, Non-Credit Card Issues (Continued)

Offer Date	*Seller Servicer*	*Issuer*	*Type*	*Amount Issued ($ Mil.)*	*Collateral*
10/8/87	Volkswagen of America	Volkswagen Lease Finance Corp.	Pay	150.00	Leases
11/12/87	Household Finance Corp.	Household Bk. Consumer Loan Series 1987A	Pay	432.08	Unsecured
		Class A-1		151.70	consumer
		Class A-2		280.38	loans
12/17/87	Green Tree Acceptance Corp.	Merrill Lynch Mortgage Investors Inc.		112.00	Loans for mfg. homes
1/7/88	Westfield Holdings Ltd.	Westfield Finance Inc.	Pref.	308.00	5 yr int-bearing notes
1/21/88	Empire of America FSB, Buffalo	EOA Auto Funding	Pref	225.00	Auto loans
3/24/88	Green Tree Acceptance Corp.	Merrill Lynch Mortgage Investors Inc. 1988E		106.00	Loans for mfg. homes
6/2/88	MEPC American Holdings	MEPC Capital Corp. II	Pref.	180.00	Comm. mortgage loans
6/3/88	Household Finance Corp.	Household Bk Consumer Loan Series 1988A	Pay	439.50	Consumer loans & installment
6/23/88	Green Tree Acceptance Corp.	Merrill Lynch Mortgage Investors Inc. 1988H		87.10	Loans for mfg. homes
9/12/88	SEC PAC Housing Svces Inc.	Merrill Lynch Mortgage Investors Inc. 1988J		106.66	Loans for mfg. homes

Table 1-4. Asset-Backed Issues, 1985–November 1988
Non-Auto, Non-Credit Card Issues (Continued)

Offer Date	*Seller Servicer*	*Issuer*	*Type*	*Amount Issued ($ Mil.)*	*Collateral*
9/12/88	American Airlines	American Airlines 1988—A Grantor Trust	Pass	60.28	Equipment
		Series A-1		2.51	notes
		Series A-2		2.77	financing
		Series A-3		21.83	leveraged
		Series A-4		33.17	leases for 4 jets
9/15/88	Chemical Bank	Chemical Bank Grantor Trust 1988-B	Pass	381.00	Marine loans
9/22/88	Green Tree Acceptance Corp.	Merrill Lynch Mortgage Investors Inc. 1988Q		104.50	Loans for mfg. homes
9/30/88	Western S&L Assoc.	Merrill Lynch Mortgage Investors Inc. 1988R		121.20	Loans for mfg. homes

As shown on Table 1-3, use of assets such as leases, manufactured housing, and boat loans demonstrate a significant broadening of the asset-backed market according to asset type. As investors become familiar with the various new assets used in securitization, this trend can be expected to continue.

ASSET-BACKED SECURITY PRICING PATTERNS

The pricing of asset-backed (debt) securities compared with that of other types of debt has evolved since the earliest issues. Initially, due in part to their novelty and similarity to certain types of mortgage-backed debt, the yield of asset-backed securities in terms of spread to Treasury bond yields was relatively high. As shown in Figure 1-4, these spreads have trended down since mid-1987 (except for a spike in response to plunging Treasury bond yields surrounding the October 1987 stock market crash), reflecting, among other things, increasing investor acceptance of this type of security.

Figure 1-4 also shows trading levels for other forms of comparable debt: CMOs and medium-term corporate securities. In essence, it shows that spreads on asset-backed securities have most closely followed the corporate debt market rather than the mortgage-backed market. This factor has been significant in determining which companies have become interested in using securitization as a financing tool. As the relative cost has come down as compared with A/AA-rated straight corporate debt, companies with these bond ratings have increasingly found cost savings in using securitization.

CONCLUSION

The use of securitization has grown significantly as structures and technology have become more routine, as the relative cost has become lower, and as investors have increased their understanding and acceptance of these structures. The implications of the potential further growth of securitization on U.S. debt markets, on financial analysis, and on many types of financial institutions have only begun to be felt.

Figure 1-4. Pricing Comparison Asset-Backed Issues versus Corporate Bonds: One- to Two-Year Average Life

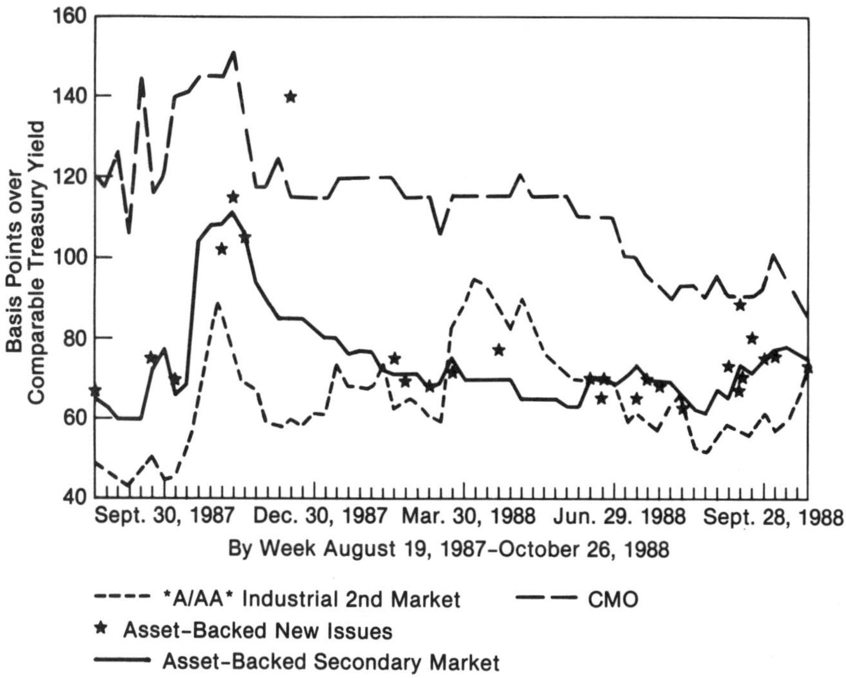

CHAPTER 2

Overview of Rating Agency Criteria for Asset-Backed Transactions

Thomas P. Hourican

INTRODUCTION

Standard & Poor's Corporation (S&P) applies the same basic rating approach to various types of asset-backed structured transactions, including credit card receivables, automobile receivables, and so on. The structure is analyzed, followed by assessment of the equity support that enhances credit quailty to the level desired by the issuer.

To analyze an asset-backed issue's structure, S&P evaluate:

- *Credit risk.* First, the originator's overall risk profile is examined. Then, portfolio quality is analyzed by various performance statistics and a review of the originator's credit and underwriting practices. In addition, the servicer and trustee are evaluated.
- *Cash flow.* Specific risks inherent in the payment structure are identified, and collateral is evaluated.
- *Legal issues.* Two key concerns in this area are the perfection of lien or asset ownership and the evaluation of risks as associated with the bankruptcy of the seller/servicer.

Credit analysis and legal analysis are closely interrelated. For this reason, when the seller of receivables is of sufficient credit quality, legal concerns relating to potential bankruptcy may be moderated. Once a transaction's risks in the above areas are identified, the final step is to assess the adequacy of equity support. Such supports include letters of credit, overcollateralization, and reserve funds.

EVALUATING CREDIT RISKS

The principal credit risk in asset-backed financings is the impairment of cash flows that results from delinquency or loss on pledged or acquired assets. Depending on the issue structure and the certificate contract, such impairment may cause liquidity risks if cash flows from receivables are insufficient to cover debt service or losses on a timely basis or if cash flows are ultimately insufficient to retire debt. Credit support, usually in the form of reserve funds, letters of credit, excess cash flow, or overcollateralization, mitigates these risks.

To determine the risks of delinquency or loss on the receivables, S&P uses a qualitative and quantitative approach supported by on-site management meetings. S&P evaluates the orignator's overall risk profile, underwriting standards, collection procedures, and pool selection process. This entails a review of the originator's historic and expected financial performance, organizational strengths and weaknesses, and competitive position and strategy in the business line from which assets are sold. S&P meets with management to review the underwriting, operations, and controls of the specific business unit. This involves a review of historic and current lending criteria; portfolio characteristics, including any relevant customer concentrations; historic and prospective value of the underlying assets backing the receivables; historic portfolio origination and repayment statistics; delinquency and loss statistics of the receivable portfolio; and audit procedures and accounting systems.

The process of selecting the pool from the portfolio is a critical step in the determination of credit risk. Care must be taken so that the pool represents either a random or superior sampling of the portfolio—not predominantly lesser-quality receivables left over from previous pool selections. How the selection process treats risk concentrations, lending criteria, current or historic delinquency, rewrites and extensions, and aging of accounts may also affect pool performance. S&P reviews the selection process for current financing, as well as for previous financings from the same portfolio. A conservative selection process in a previous financing may already have reduced portfolio quality.

S&P expects a wide disparity in portfolio performance based primarily on differences in underwriting, servicing, underlying asset protection, and the character and degree of risk concentration. Differences in the pool selection process are also expected to have a varying impact on receivable quality. As a result, credit support levels will vary significantly on an issuer-by-issuer basis, even for the same type of receivable.

PASS-THROUGHS AND PAY-THROUGHS

A primary challenge in rating receivable transaction is the assignment of accurate values to the receivables. In these structured financings, cash flows generated by receivables support certificates or note payments. Receivables must be valued so that their payments are sufficient to meet certificate or note obligations. The valuation of underlying receivables is similar in pass-throughs and pay-throughs, the two most common types of receivable transactions.

The pass-through structure essentially gives certificate holders an equity interest in the receivables. The structure establishes a grantor trust as the issuer, into which receivable collateral is sold. Certificate holders of the trust are entitled to all cash flows from the receivables.

A pay-through is the issuer's liability, for which the receivables serve as security. The cash flow of the receivables is the primary source of debt service. Pay-throughs can be structured as either single-class notes or as multiple-class notes. In a multiple-class structure, principal is repaid by class, beginning with the class with the earliest stated maturity.

Both pass-throughs and pay-throughs can use various methods to value the underlying receivables. Different discounting methods yield different values. These methods are not always acceptable from a ratings perspective, as discussed in the following section. Once the discounting method has been chosen, each receivable collateral piece must be valued. The sum of these values for the receivable collateral pool is the dollar amount of certificates or notes that are issued.

Collateral Valuation

Collateral for pass-throughs and pay-throughs is valued similarly, so that note holders are paid what they are promised. To ensure this, the note value of each piece of collateral must equal the lesser of:

- The principal amount of the notes that the collateral piece can support if it were to prepay
- The present value of the future scheduled cash flows (assuming no prepayments), discounted at the highest note interest rate

With premium collateral, the receivable collateral rate is greater than the rate on the notes, plus the servicing fee and other expenses. Notes must then be valued at the principal amount of the receivables (at par). Because the collateral is valued at par, receivable prepayments do not adversely affect the deal's cash flows. With a full prepayment, the amount paid is at least equal to the principal amount, plus one month's interest on the principal amount. With discount collateral, the receivable colateral rate is less than the rate on the notes, plus the servicing fee and other expenses. Notes can then be issued only at a discount. Without discounting, receivable payments would not meet the debt service obligations of the notes.

Valuation Assumptions

The assumptions behind the valuation method are extremely important. Any present-value method requires assumptions regarding the rate and frequency of discounting and the determination of what constitutes future scheduled cash flows.

In a multiple-class pay-through structure, the rate at which the cash flows are discounted must be the highest note rate of any of the bond classes. Discounting at the highest note rate is necessary because, with an ascending yield curve, the debt service requirement will increase as classes with lower rates are repaid. If, during the early years of the transaction, the higher-rate collateral were to

prepay, only the lower-rate collateral will be left to pay down the higher-rate notes, which will result in a potential shortfall.

The frequency of discounting must correspond to the frequency of note payment dates. This is the longest time period for which cash flow from the colalteral can be invested. For example, if notes are repaid quarterly, the cash flows must be discounted on a quarterly basis.

Future scheduled cash flows consist of:

- Cash flows net of servicing and other fees expected to be received if no prepayments occur
- Reinvestment income

If receivable collateral has a maturity longer than the notes' maturity, cash flow from the receivables expected after the notes' maturity cannot be included. For an AAA rating, the reinvestment income assumed to be received must be calculated assuming an annual rate of 4.5 percent for the first year of the transaction, 4 percent for the second year of the transaction, and 3 percent from the third year to the maturity of the notes (see Table 2-1 for reinvestment rate assumptions for other rating categories).

Table 2-1. Reinvestment Rate Assumptions

Rating	*Year 1*	*Year 2*	*Year 3 to Maturity*
AAA	4.5	4.0	3.0
AA	4.5	4.5	3.5
A	4.5	4.5	4.0
BBB	4.5	4.5	4.5

Instead of using the reinvestment rate assumptions in Table 2-1, some issuers negotiate a guaranteed investment contract that will lock in a higher reinvestment rate. Any guaranteed investment contract must be issued by an entity that has a rating at least equal to the rating desired on the transaction. The number of days of investment income that can be assumed is a function of when cash flow is remitted to the trustee. For example, if cash is remitted on the 20th of a month, reinvestment income can be assumed from the 22nd of that month to the next payment date. The two-day lag allows for delays incurred by remittance dates falling on weekends and holidays

Amortization of Collateral

Industry standards and accounting procedures provide different methods of amortizing receivable collateral. In particular, many automobile receivable contracts are amortized using the Rule of 78 method instead of the actuarial method, which is used to amortize most mortgages. Monthly payments due on a given loan are the same under both methods. However, these two methods allocate monthly payments to interest. As a result, the amortization of collateral is slower under the Rule of 78 method than under the actuarial method.

Under the Rule of 78 method, the interest portion of receivable payments might not match the notes' interest requirements. Without this match, a shortfall in cash flows is possible. To correct this mismatch, accounting systems are usually developed to convert the Rule of 78 method to the actuarial amortization method.

Additional Pay-Through Concerns

Pay-throughs usually create more concerns than do pass-throughs because of legal and structural differences. In particular, pay-throughs usually give rise to reinvestment risk, stated maturity determination concerns, and event of default/collateral sale restrictions.

Reinvestment Risk

Reinvestment risk arises when note payment dates are less frequent than collateral payment dates. The risk is that the collateral would be prepaid and then invested at a rate that is lower than the highest note rate (negative carry). Two options would cover this risk: First, a reserve fund could be established. Second, an interperiod call provision, enabling the notes to be called on dates other than note payment dates, could be written into the transaction documents.

If a reserve fund is used, it must be funded at an amount that would cover the worst-possible prepayment scenario. In that scenario, all of the collateral would be prepaid immediately after the transaction closed. As a result, the notes would not be paid out until the first payment date. For example, suppose that a transaction closed on the last day of December and the first note payment date were April 1 (note payment dates are quarterly). The reserve fund would then have to equal the cash available from all of the collateral prepaying on January 1, plus reinvestment income thereon at the assumed reinvestment rates to April 1, less debt service required on the notes on April 1.

If an interperiod call provision is used to cover reinvestment risk, the transaction documents must provide for a test to be performed by the trustee each month (other than months that include a note payment date). The test must show that cash flow received before the next note payment date, plus reinvestment income thereon, is greater than the debt service required to be paid on the next note payment date.

Stated Maturity Calculation

Stated maturity calculations must also include certain assumptions to ensure that notes will be retired by the stated maturity. Excess cash flow (cash flow above that needed to pay debt service on the notes) may be available to pay down notes. However, since the availability of excess cash is usually uncertain, it should not be used to determine stated maturities. The sources of excess cash flow are:

- Excess reinvestment income from investments that yield rates higher than those assumed or rates for more days of reinvestment than assumed
- Discounting at the highest note rate when determining note value
- Interest income from premium collateral
- Recaptured discount if the discount collateral prepays

As none of these sources is certain, excess cash flow cannot be used in the determination of the stated maturities of the note classes. To determine the stated maturity date, calculations must assume that only scheduled cash flows are received (no prepayments) and that only the change in note value is paid in principal on each payment date.

An exception to the foregoing is the stated maturity calculation for credit card receivable transactions. Credit card receivables are different from other receivable assets because their revolving nature creates new outstanding balances and, therefore, causes required minimum payments to fluctuate. S&P determines an assumed payment rate based on:

- Historical portfolio performance
- Industry trends
- Terms of the credit card agreement
- The desired rating

Cash flows based on this assumed payment rate and any credit enhancements must be sufficient to retire the notes on or prior to stated maturity.

Collateral Sale in Event of Default

Cash flow and credit criteria eliminate any concern that a monetary event of default would occur (a default in payment of principal or interest). Additionally, the single-purpose rating criteria and applicable legal opinions eliminate any concern about the issuer being involved in a bankruptcy proceeding either voluntarily or involuntarily. However, the rating criteria do not and cannot address the possibility of a technical event of default.

If a technical event of default occurs, the trustee can either sell the collateral (if the sale proceeds are sufficient to pay note holders the entire amount of principal and interest due or if 100 percent of the note holders approve of the sale) or continue to pay the notes in accordance with the terms of the documents as if no event of default had occurred (referred to as the optional preservation of the trust estate). The optional preservation of the trust estate election relies on collateral cash flow being sufficient to pay the note holders by the stated maturity of the notes. S&P's collateral valuation criteria assure cash flow adequacy, thereby enabling preservation of the trust estate to be a worthwhile option for the trustee.

Servicer/Trustee Evaluation

Both the trustee and servicer play integral roles in asset-backed receivable transactions. Through its analysis of the structure, S&P must feel confident that both entities are capable of performing their individual job functions. It is of utmost importance that their actions be in the best interests of the certificate holders.

The Servicer's Role

Several concerns must be addressed in the evaluation of the servicer in an asset-backed receivable transaction. The obligation of the servicer to manage and maintain control of the assets and the payment stream from the assets underlying the issue being rated is of utmost importance. Another crucial obligation of the servicer is its support of the transaction through a cash advance mechanism. S&P's review involves extensive analysis of these obligations, as well as the servicer's ability and willingness to perform various other functions.

The method of evaluating the servicer's capability to manage the assets depends on the actual role that the servicer plays in the receivable transaction. In most cases, the servicer is also the originator and underwriter of the receivables in the transaction. In such cases, S&P's evaluation of the servicer is part of the due diligence process and is reflected in the credit support required or the rating given the transaction. S&P's evaluation usually involves a site visit that includes an in-depth review of the company's operations and a meeting with management to discuss procedures, methodologies, past history, and future outlook. If the servicer is not also the originator or underwriter, S&P still completes a certain amount of due diligence on the servicer. In such cases, due diligence focuses more on management and company operations.

The servicer's role is also important to the protection of asset proceeds. If the servicer is not rated as high as the bonds, the servicer must remit cash flow to the trustee as soon as possible within a maximum of 48 hours. S&P perceives this time exposure as a risk. However, it is considered adequately maintained.

S&P's evaluation of the servicer's capabilities is inevitably limited in scope and duration. It is of utmost importance that a servicer support all of its representations and warranties and provide coverage against potential employee error. As a result, S&P requests the servicer to obtain error and omission insurance equal to 5 percent of the outstanding obligation or to demonstrate that other existing insurance is sufficient to cover the same inherent risks. Additionally, the servicer should not be allowed to resign until a suitable successor has been appointed. The servicing fee should be an amount within industry standards so as to ensure the willingness of a substitute servicer to step in should the original servicer withdraw for any reason. The servicer's fee, which should be a percentage of the principal balance outstanding, should be subordinated to the certificate holder's right to receive principal and interest. Payment of such fees should be demonstrated in the submitted cash flows. The pooling and servicing agreement or other applicable financing document should specify these points.

Depending on the legal structure of the transaction and whether the servicer is subject to the Bankruptcy Code, additional legal implications may arise and require additional analysis. For example, if the servicer is not a bank and sells with recourse or commingles funds, issues may arise. These concerns need to be adequately addressed in the structure set out in the financing documents and corresponding legal opinions (see the "Legal Issues" section following).

The method chosen to evaluate a servicer's ability to make good on a cash advance obligation depends on whether the servicer is rated or unrated. If the servicer is rated, its rating relative to that of the rated transaction is important. If a servicer is rated no more than one category below the proposed rating on the specified receivables transaction (without regard to pluses or minuses), S&P assumes that the servicer will be able to cover delinquencies with the degree of probability assumed by the rating on the transaction itself. If the servicer is unrated or is rated more than one category below the rating on the receivable transaction, S&P requires the servicer to obtain a surety bond letter of credit or other rated credit support.

Trustee Evaluation

The trustee also plays an important role in asset-backed financings. The trustee's function begins upon receipt of the asset proceeds from the servicer. In the financing documents, the trustee should be instructed to deposit the revenues immediately into the trust account designated for the transaction. The funds should not be commingled with the other funds of the trust department. The account should be held in trust for the benefit of certificate holders. If funds are to be invested, they should be held in permitted investments rated as high as the proposed rating on the transaction. Investments should mature no later than the date on which such funds are needed to pay certificate holders. Investing the funds in this manner alleviates the potential interruption of cash flow to certificate holders in the event of the bank's insolvency.

In addition to the trustee's role of passing through required payments to certificate holders, it is responsible for performing monthly calculations of payments received, as well as future cash flow. Such reports must be audited regularly. The complexity of the transaction will determine the frequency and scope of the independent audits, which should be completed at least annually. More complex transactions may require quarterly or semiannual audits.

Similar to the servicer, the trustee cannot resign without the prior appointment of a successor trustee capable of performing the trustee obligation under the documents. The trustee should be willing to take over the servicer's obligation in the event that the servicer withdraws or is unable to perform. Minimum capital and surplus requirements and experience with similar structures are suggested. Payment of the trustee's fees and expenses should also be provided, with such ongoing fees subordinated to payment to certificate holders. These fees should also be reflected in submitted cash flows.

LEGAL ISSUES

For purposes of this chapter, the term "debt" shall include certificates of participation and equity interests (other than preferred stock) in receivables.

Debt secured by nonmortgage receivables must satisfy essentially two legal concerns. Typically, this debt is secured by receivables sold by one company (the seller) to another company that issues the debt (the issuer). The financing must be structured to avoid the risks that:

- The seller's bankruptcy, which is generally assumed, could impair timely payment of debt service
- The issuer could become subject to a bankruptcy proceeding

Cash Flow Debt

Most of these financings are structured so that cash flow from the receivables is sufficient to pay debt service in a timely manner (cash flow debt). Others depend largely on a liquidity facility for payment (for example, commercial paper).

Borrowers Subject to the Code

For sellers that can become debtors under the Bankruptcy Code, transfer of receivables from seller to issuer must constitute an absolute sale—not a pledge. Otherwise, the receivables are likely to be viewed as collateral pledged by the seller. The automatic stay provisions of the code would then impair the timely flow of proceeds of the receivables to debt holders. Moreover, under Section 363 of the code, a court could permit the seller to use the receivables and proceeds thereof during its bankruptcy by providing a lien on other collateral to the issuer. Under these circumstances, the risk of the seller's bankruptcy and the likelihood that it would result in a default on the issuer's debt would be inconsistent with the highest debt ratings. Unless this concern is addressed, the rating on receivable-secured debt would not be higher than the seller's unsecured rating.

To address these concerns:

- Outside counsel to the seller should provide an unqualified opinion indicating that the transfer of the receivables by the seller to the issuer is sufficient to remove the receivables from the seller's estate for purposes of Section 541 of the code and that Section 362(a) of the code would not apply to receivables or proceeds therefrom in the event of the seller's bankruptcy.
- Collections of the receivables should not be commingled with funds of the seller in an account of the seller.
- There should be no recourse against the seller for defaulted receivables beyond a reasonably anticipated default rate based on a

historical analysis. Recourse for bad receivables against the seller on the part of pool insurers and providers of letters of credit must be limited to a reasonably anticipated default rate. Insurers or providers of letters of credit may, however, be subrogated to the issuer's rights against defaulting account debtors.

- Transfer of the receivables should be accounted for as a sale on the seller's financial statements.

Substantive Consolidation

Should such a subsidiary's assets and liabilities be substantively consolidated with those of a bankrupt parent, the receivables would be viewed as property of the bankrupt parent. As a result, timely payment of proceeds to debt holders would likely be impaired. Concern about substantive consolidation arises whenever the issuer is a subsidiary of the seller. As long as this risk exists, the debt could not be rated higher than the parent's unsecured rating.

To address this concern, the parent's counsel should provide an unqualified opinion indicating that the assets and liabilities of the subsidiary could not be consolidated with those of the parent in the event of the latter's bankruptcy. Additionally, the subsidiary should have a separate corporate existence with an independent officer and director, separate books and records, accounts that are not commingled with those of the parent, and appropriate meetings of the board of directors that are held to authorize corporate action.

Commingling

Purchasers of receivables must perfect their rights by complying with the Uniform Commercial Code. When the seller commingles proceeds of sold receivables with the seller's own funds, the rights of the purchaser of the receivables—that is, the issuer—may become imperfect. As a result, the issuer purchasing the receivables could be an unsecured creditor with respect to funds contained in such commingled account on the date of the seller's bankruptcy. Payments made from such a commingled account during the 90-day period preceding such bankruptcy might be recaptured as preferences.

These concerns may be addressed in any of the following ways:

- Proceeds could be collected by the issuer. In this event, the issuer may commingle proceeds of receivables not sold by the seller with proceeds of receivables sold by the seller and may remit the seller's proceeds to it.
- A bank could collect proceeds as an agent for the seller and for purchasers of receivables (including the issuer) as their interests appear. In this event, the bank should not be permitted to remit any proceeds to the seller without the written instruction of the issuer.
- The seller could collect proceeds of sold receivables in its own account provided that such account does not contain any of the seller's funds, including proceeds of receivables that the seller has not sold, and that the seller does not have a right to withdraw funds from such account.

Other Opinions

The seller's counsel should also opine that it knows of no other theory of law under which the receivables could be made available to the bankruptcy of the seller or its creditors or under which the bankruptcy of the seller could impair the timely flow of proceeds from the receivables to the seller or the debt holders. In rendering this opinion, counsel may assume that the issuer is not the subject of a bankruptcy proceeding.

Additional Disincentives

When the issuer is a subsidiary of the seller, a bankrupt seller might cause the bankruptcy filing of such subsidiary to attempt to appropriate the subsidiary's assets for the seller or its creditors. Such an attempt would be facilitated if the bankruptcy court in which the seller's case was pending had jurisdiction over the subsidiary. This concern derives from recent history of bankruptcies, in which bankrupt sellers caused seemingly healthy subsidiaries to file petitions under the code. During the subsidiary's bankruptcy proceedings, debt service could not be paid on the rated debt without a court order.

To address this concern, the board of directors of both the parent and subsidiary should adopt resolutions indicating that it is not the intent of either company to file or cause the filing of a voluntary bankruptcy petition with respect to the subsidiary, as long as the subsidiary is solvent and does not reasonably anticipate insolvency.

Moreover, the prospectus should disclose, in substance, the following:

- The financing is structured to assure purchasers of the debt that voluntary or involuntary application for relief under the code or any similar applicable law (insolvency laws) with respect to the seller will not result in a similar voluntary application with respect to the issuer, as long as the issuer is solvent and does not reasonably foresee becoming insolvent either by reason of the seller's insolvency or otherwise.
- Counsel has advised the issuer and its parent that, in counsel's opinion, the assets and liabilities of the issuer could not be substantively consolidated with the assets and liabilities of its parent in the event of an application for relief under the insolvency laws with respect to the issuer and/or its parent.
- In counsel's opinion, the transfer of receivables by the seller to the issuer constitutes a sale; therefore, such receivables would not be property of the seller in the event of the filing of an application for relief by or against the latter under the insolvency laws.
- Counsel knows of no other legal theory under which the receivables could be made available to the bankrupt seller or its creditors.
- After discussions with counsel, the issuer and its parent believe that, as long as the issuer is solvent and does not reasonably foresee becoming insolvent, the filing of voluntary application under the insolvency laws by the issuer for the purpose of transferring the issuer's assets to its parent or of otherwise making such assets available to its parent or its parent's creditors would be an inappropriate use of the insolvency laws, which could be successfully controverted by the debt holders.
- The issuer has no intent to file and its parent has no intent to cause the filing of a voluntary application under the insolvency

laws with respect to the issuer, as long as the issuer is solvent and does not reasonably foresee becoming insolvent.

Special-Purpose, "Bankruptcy-Remote" Criteria

Issuers that are eligible to become debtors under the code must satisfy special-purpose, bankruptcy-remote criteria. More precisely:

- The issuer's business must be restricted to the purchase of the receivables and the issuance of the rated debt.
- The issuer may not incur any additional debt other than debt that:
  —is rated the same as the rated debt;
  —is fully subordinated to the rated debt, is nonrecourse other than with respect to proceeds in excess of the proceeds necessary to pay the rated debt (excess proceeds), and does not constitute a claim against the issuer to the extent that excess proceeds are insufficient to pay such debt; or
  —Will not result in a reduction of the then-existing rating.

The above criteria are intended to provide certainty that the payment of proceeds from the receivables to the debt holders will be unimpaired by the seller's insolvency. As a general matter, if these criteria are not satisfied, the rating on the debt would not be higher than the seller's unsecured rating. However, circumstances might exist in which the likelihood of bankruptcy of a seller during the maturity of the debt would be sufficiently remote to justify non-compliance with certain of the criteria. This would be determined on a case-by-case basis. In such event, to avoid a downgrade due to deterioration of the financial condition of the seller, the documents should provide for compliance with such criteria if necessitated by such financial deterioration.

Issuers Not Subject to the Code

Issuers that are not subject to the code, such as banks and thrift institutions, are not required to satisfy S&P's true sale or special-purpose, bankruptcy-remote criteria. These entities may pledge—instead of sell—the receivables to the issuer or to the debt holders directly. Moreover, concerns regarding substantive consolidation and the filing of healthy subsidiaries are inapplicable. Nevertheless, the other criteria described earlier must be satisfied, and the following additional opinions are requested:

- That the debt holders' rights with respect to the receivables and proceeds thereon would be valid, binding, and enforceable notwithstanding the insolvency, receivership bankruptcy, or similar proceeding of the seller or pledgor of the receivables
- That the issuer or debt holders have, at least, a first perfected security interest in the receivables

Debt Dependent on Liquidity Facility

These ratings are based on both the receivables and the liquidity facility between the bank and the issuer, such as a revolving credit agreement. The need for a liquidity facility derives from mismatches between receivable maturities and debt maturities. For example, commercial paper might mature every 15, 30, or 90 days, while receivables might be paid every 120 days. Therefore, a liquidity facility is necessary to pay maturing commercial paper as it comes due.

Typically, the bank is required to lend to the issuer an amount equal to the amount of the receivable pool, less receivable defaults. The receivable pool must, therefore, be evaluated to determine that receivable defaults will not reduce the bank's obligation to fund maturing commercial paper below the amount of outstanding commercial paper.

As the rating disregards the ceditworthiness of the seller and the issuer, financing must be structured so that the insolvency or bankruptcy of either does not impair (1) the timely use of the liquidity facility to pay maturing commercial paper or (2) the ability of commercial paper holders to retain payments made to them.

The issuer's bankruptcy could result in two problems: First, it is uncertain whether, under Section 365(e)(2) of the Bankruptcy Code, the bank's obligation to fund would be enforceable in the event of the issuer's bankruptcy. Second, payments made by the issuer to commercial paper holders within the 90-day period (or within one year for commercial paper holders that are insiders) preceding the issuer's bankruptcy might be recaptured as preferences.

To address these concerns, financing should be structured to provide assurance that the issuer's bankruptcy will not occur for at least one year and one day after all of the commercial paper has been retired. The structure should also satisfy the following criteria:

- The issuer cannot incur any debt other than the commercial paper and the obligation to repay the bank for advances under the liquidity facility.
- The bank should be obligated to fund under the liquidity facility (up to the amount of nondefaulting receivables) in all events other than an issuer bankruptcy. A seller's bankruptcy should not excuse the bank from its obligations to fund.
- All of the issuer's creditors should enter into an agreement with the issuer and the depositary or trustee acting on behalf of the commercial paper holders that prohibits such creditors from filing an involuntary bankruptcy petition against the issuer for one year and one day after all of the commercial paper is retired.
- The depositary or trustee should be irrevocably instructed and have the right to draw on the liquidity facility on behalf of the commercial paper holders in the event that there are insufficient funds in the commercial paper account to pay the commercial paper holders or in the event that such funds are subject to a restraining order due to the seller's bankruptcy.
- No outstanding stock of the issuer should be owned by the seller. Instead, such stock should be owned by an entity, such as a charity or an affiliate of the commercial paper dealer, that has no incentive to cause the issuer to file a voluntary bankruptcy petition.
- The amount of the liquidity facility should not be reduced until receivable payments received by the issuer have been applied to the payment of commercial paper.

To address concerns regarding the seller's bankruptcy, a legal opinion that states that the liquidity facility is valid, binding, and enforceable notwithstanding the seller's bankruptcy should be provided.

CHAPTER 3

Legal Overview of Asset-Backed Securities

Rodney S. Dayan, Charles M. Adelman, Maurine R. Bartlett, Barry J. Dichter, Bronislaw E. Grala, and John W. Osborn[1]

INTRODUCTION

The securitization of assets often raises complex bankruptcy and tax questions, as well as issues under federal and state securities laws, the Employee Retirement Security Act (ERISA), and banking laws. This chapter provides a brief overview of some of the critical legal considerations raised in structuring asset-backed securities.

BANKRUPTCY AND INSOLVENCY CONSIDERATIONS

A primary goal of asset securitization is to obtain a credit rating for an issuance that is based primarily on the quality of the assets[2]

[1]The authors wish to thank Alan Parness of counsel and Richard Schetman, Dan Stolzer, and Eric Waxman for their assistance in the preparation of this chapter.

[2]The term "assets" will be used to refer both to assets that have been pledged to secure debt and to assets that have been transferred in a "true sale" from the originator to the issuer or purchaser.

(and any credit enhancements) backing the obligation,[3] without regard to the originator's[4] own creditworthiness. To accomplish this, the transaction must be structured so that the assets and their attendant cash flows will not be impaired by bankruptcy or insolvency of the originator of the assets.

Ordinarily, the rating of secured debt issued by a bankruptcy-eligible entity takes into account the rating of the borrower, regardless of the strength of the collateral. Thus, if a BBB-rated industrial corporation issued $1 million of debt secured by U.S. Government securities with a market value of $2 million, at first glance one might think that the debt could be rated AAA based on the collateral. However, in reality, it is unlikely that the collateral would improve the rating much beyond BBB+.[5]

The rating of the obligation at a level substantially below the quality of the security is explained by the effect that a bankruptcy or insolvency proceeding of the originator would have on the rights of creditors.

Bankruptcy-Eligible Entities

Upon the filing of a petition under the federal Bankruptcy Code, 11 U.S.C. Sections 101 *et seq.*, the rights of creditors, including secured creditors, are substantially impaired. For example, upon filing of a bankruptcy petition,[6] creditor actions to collect prepetition debt or to foreclose on collateral are automatically stayed under Section 362(a). Thus, a secured creditor would not receive timely payments and would be unable to realize on its collateral once a petition was filed.

[3]The term "obligation" will be used to refer both to debt and the obligation under a pooling and servicing agreement to remit principal and/or interest.

[4]The term "originator" will be used to refer to the entity that, directly or indirectly, originally owned the assets financed and that ultimately receives the proceeds of the financing. The originator or ultimate borrower is often not the issuer, as that term is defined for purposes of the securities laws.

[5]Neil D. Baron, "Innovations in Thrift Institution Surety-Type Mortgage-Backed Securities," *1985 PLI Course Handbook on Structured Mortgage and Receivable Financing* (New York: Practising Law Institute, 1985).

[6]The impairment of creditor rights is the same whether the petition is a voluntary one (filed by the debtor) or an involuntary one (filed by creditors).

In addition, as long as the creditor's interest is adequately protected, a debtor may use a secured creditor's collateral under Section 363(c) and may substitute collateral for the collateral originally pledged to the creditor—even if the substitute collateral is of a different type or quality—under Sections 363(e) and 361(3).

A debtor may also restructure secured debt as part of a plan of reorganization by changing the interest rate, the amortization schedule, the type of collateral, and the maturity date under Sections 1123(a) and 1123(b). A bankruptcy court may also allow the imposition of a lien that would be senior to existing liens against the collateral under Section 364(d) and may direct a secured creditor to relinquish its lien on collateral in excess of an amount reasonably necessary to protect the creditor under Sections 363, 506, and 542.

Banks and Thrifts

However, not all entities engaging in financing transactions are eligible for relief under the Bankruptcy Code. Among others, banks and savings and loan associations (thrifts) are not eligible for relief under the Bankruptcy Code. Instead, insolvency proceedings for banks and thrifts are governed by the statutes and regulations applicable to receiverships of the Federal Deposit Insurance Corporation (FDIC) and the Federal Savings and Loan Insurance Corporation (FSLIC) and by the policy pronouncements of governing regulatory agencies. Although receivers are not accorded the rights and powers of bankruptcy trustees, receivership proceedings can affect creditors' rights. For example, a receiver could seek an injunction against creditor actions. If granted, such an injunction would have an effect comparable to the automatic stay in bankruptcy cases. Also, counsel to the Federal Home Loan Bank board (FHLBB) has asserted that the FSLIC as receiver for an insolvent thrift institution would have the option either to accelerate a secured debt obligation or to assume and continue to perform a thrift's obligations.[7]

In addition, the FSLIC may enter into a "purchase and assumption" transaction, in which a large portion of the assets and liabilities of the insolvent thrift are transferred to a new entity. In such a

[7]See the "Bank and Thrift Regulatory Considerations—FSLIC and FDIC Receivership Considerations" section.

circumstance, the FSLIC may assert that default remedies that arise solely as a result of the insolvency are not enforceable.

Generally, however, in the rating of transactions that involve thrifts and banks, it is assumed that the impairment of creditors' rights that occurs when an entity becomes a debtor under the bankruptcy Code does not occur upon the appointment of a receiver for a bank or thrift.[8]

Structuring Methods

To achieve the goal discussed earlier—the rating of an issuance based on the quality of the collateral—the structure of the transaction must insulate payment of the obligation and the assets backing that payment from the effects of the originator's bankruptcy.[9] If the rights of the holders of the obligations would not be impaired in a bankruptcy of the originator, the rating for financing could be based exclusively on the creditworthiness of the assets.

Two basic methods are employed to achieve this result:

- The assets may be sold by the originator in a true sale to the holders of the obligation, instead of pledging them to secure a debt. Thus, the originator is not indebted to the holders of the obligation; if the originator acts as servicer, its obligation is to remit the pro rata portion of the principal and/or interest payments on the assets in accordance with the pooling and servicing agreement.
- The obligation may be issued and the assets owned by an issuer that is not likely to become the subject of a bankruptcy proceeding—a "bankruptcy-remote" entity. As noted earlier, thrifts and banks are not eligible for relief under the Bankruptcy Code.[10]

The two methods can be combined, as in a debt issuance by a special-purpose corporation that is secured by receivables purchased in a true sale from the originator.

[8]See letter of Norman H. Raiden, General Counsel to the FHLBB, December 16, 1983.

[9]As used in this section, the term "bankruptcy" subsumes both Bankruptcy Code and other insolvency-related proceedings.

[10]However, finance subsidiaries of banks and thrifts are eligible for relief under the Bankruptcy Code.

True Sale

The insulating effect of a true sale is derived from the principle that only debts of an entity that is a debtor under the Bankruptcy Code and assets that are "property of the estate" of the bankrupt debtor are subject to the impairment of creditors' rights that occurs upon the bankruptcy of a debtor. See, for example, Sections 362(a), 363, 541, 542, and 547.

A trustee in bankruptcy "stands in the shoes" of the debtor and succeeds only to the debtor's interests in property. If the originator has validly sold assets prior to its bankruptcy, those assets are not property of the estate and are not administered by the bankruptcy trustee. A true sale removes the assets from the estate of the originator so that the originator's bankruptcy would have no impact on the maintenance or disposition of the assets. Thus, the purchaser's rights in those assets are not impaired by the originator's bankruptcy.

An issue that often arises in rating a transaction structured as a sale is whether a court examining the transaction at the request of a trustee in bankruptcy or a creditor of the originator would recharacterize the transaction as a pledge of assets to secure debt or as a sale of assets. Notwithstanding the stated intent of the parties that a transaction be given effect as a sale of assets, the parties' labels do not control the legal characterization of a transaction; the parties cannot transform a loan into a sale merely by calling the transaction a sale. "Courts will not be controlled by the nomenclature the parties apply to their relationship."[11] If the transaction were recharacterized as a debt, the assets would be treated as property of the estate and the investors' rights would be impaired by the originator's bankruptcy.

Applicable state law controls whether a transaction structured as a sale would be recharacterized as a secured borrowing. In analyzing a transaction, courts usually indicate that they determine whether the transaction is a sale or a loan based on the "economic substance" of the transaction. However, case law suggests that the form of the transaction will not be disregarded unless the elements in

[11]*Major's Furniture Mart, Inc.* v. *Castle Credit Corp., Inc.*, 602 F.2d 538, 543 (3d Cir. 1979) (citations omitted).

favor of a recharacterization substantially outweigh factors that argue for respecting the form in which the transaction is cast.

In addressing the true sale issue, courts generally look at the extent to which the transferor has parted with the risks and the benefits of owning the assets. Although no single factor or even group of factors is considered dispositive of the issue, the following factors are particularly relevant to the inquiry:

- The form of the transaction and the consistency of the parties' treatment of the transaction, including how the transaction is characterized in the documents, how tax and accounting disciplines treat the transaction, and whether the originator executes a promissory note to the purchasers.

- The nature and extent of the risks transferred, including whether the investor has recourse to the seller in some form, such as a guarantee or obligation to repurchase nonperforming assets and the extent of any such recourse; who is at risk if the value of the assets declines; who has the risk of reinvesting the income from the assets; and who is at risk if there is a default on the underlying assets.
- The nature and extent of the benefits transferred including who benefits from any appreciation in the value of the assets and who receives the income from the assets.
- The irrevocability of the transfer, including whether specific and identifiable assets are sold; whether and in which circumstances the transferor can reacquire the assets or substitute assets; who exercises control over and uses the assets and, if the originator services the assets, how the originator uses and accounts for the assets and their proceeds; and whether the purchaser can resell the assets without accounting to the transferor for any gain on the sale.
- The extent and timing of the purchase price, including whether the price reflects the fair market value of the assets and whether the full price is paid at the time of sale or a portion is held back, with payment subject to performance of the assets.
- The extent to which the transferor's creditors and others are provided with notice of the sale; whether the transferor retains

documents related to the assets and, if so, the extent of the purchaser's right to inspect or require delivery of the documents; how the maturity dates of the assets compare with the maturity dates of the obligations sold to investors; and whether public policy issues are implicated by recharacterization—for example, if the sale were recharacterized as a loan, would applicable usury law be violated?

Bankruptcy-Remote Entities

A second method of insulating an obligation and the related assets and cash flows from the originator's bankruptcy is to have the obligation incurred and the assets owned by an issuer that is bankruptcy remote—usually a special-purpose corporation.

A special-purpose corporation is eligible to become a debtor and, theoretically, could become involved in a bankruptcy proceeding in two ways: First, the special-purpose corporation could itself incur debts that it could not pay, thus resulting in the filing of a bankruptcy petition by or against it. Second, the corporate separateness of the special-purpose corporation could be disregarded and its assets and liabilities, including the rated obligation and related assets, could be consolidated with those of its parent and become part of the parent's bankruptcy proceedings.

To forestall the likelihood that the special-purpose corporation would itself become the subject of bankruptcy proceedings, its business activities are severely limited by its charter. The charter limits its activities to the purchase of assets and the issuance of rated obligations. The charter also prohibits it from incurring any additional debt that would impair the rating of its rated obligations. Thus, restrictions on the special-purpose corporation virtually eliminate the possibility that it would incur debt that it could not pay and, accordingly, make it bankruptcy remote. In addition, banks and thrifts are regarded as bankruptcy remote because they are not eligible for relief under the Bankruptcy Code.

The bankruptcy remoteness of a special-purpose corporation would not protect the holders of its debt, however, if its separateness from its parent could be disregarded by a court. If this were to occur, the special-purpose corporation's assets, including those pledged for the debt, would become subject to the bankruptcy proceedings of the parent.

The general rule is that a corporation is a distinct legal entity separate from its shareholders, and, therefore, its assets are not directly available to satisfy the claims of its shareholders' creditors. However, exceptions exist to this general rule when the subsidiary corporation has failed to maintain its separate identity and when prejudice would result from giving effect to the separateness of the corporation. Exceptions are generally given effect under the doctrines of "piercing the corporate veil" or substantive consolidation.

Piercing the corporate veil is an equitable doctrine that typically arises under common law at the request of a creditor of an affiliated entity. In determining whether to pierce the corporate veil, courts have generally focused on three principal elements necessary to find a person, corporation, or other entity responsible for the obligations of a different, legally distinct entity: (1) complete domination and control of the corporation by the entity on which liability is sought to be imposed; (2) the use of such control to commit a fraud or other wrong, to violate a statutory or other duty, or to engage in unjust conduct; and (3) proximate causation of the movant's injury by such wrongdoing.

Substantive consolidation, a doctrine that arises under federal bankruptcy law, could be applicable if the parent were to become a debtor under the Bankruptcy Code. The test to determine whether two entities should be substantively consolidated is inherently factual and is made on a case-by-case basis. In determining whether to order consolidation, courts have traditionally considered certain objective factors. These factors include (1) the degree of difficulty in segregating and ascertaining individual assets and liabilities, (2) the presence or absence of consolidated financial statements, (3) the profitability of consolidation at a single physical location, (4) the commingling of assets and business functions, (5) the unity of interests and ownership between the various corporate entities, (6) the existence of parent and intercorporate guarantees on loans, and (7) the transfer of assets without formal observance of corporate formalities.

The cases suggest, however, that the elements considered by the courts to be the most significant are (1) hopeless confusion of assets and liabilities and (2) substantial integration of operations. However, more recent cases have stressed an approach that gives substantial weight to a balancing of prejudices—whether the prejudice for creditors that would result from ordering substantive consolidation would outweigh the prejudice of respecting the separate corporate existence of the subsidiary.

Although no single factor determines whether a corporation's separate identity and existence should be disregarded, observance of legal, organizational, and business factors that evidence corporate separateness, observance of corporate formalities, and avoidance of actions that could lead to confusion among creditors as to the separateness of the parent and the subsidiary should provide a basis for concluding that the special-purpose corporation would not be substantively consolidated with its parent and that its separate corporate existence would not be disregarded under the doctrine of piercing the corporate veil.

Thus, to protect the special-purpose corporation from having its corporate separateness disregarded, it must comply with certain procedures and corporate formalities. These procedures include, for example, compliance with procedural corporate requirements (such as having appropriate meetings of the board of directors), having appropriate books and records, and avoidance of any implication that the parent is responsible for the special-purpose corporation's obligations or that the special-purpose corporation's assets are available to the parent or its creditors.

Securitizable Cash Flows

Successful securitization requires that the assets securitized *and* their cash flows survive a bankruptcy of the originator. Thus, if assets or their cash flows may be impaired in a bankruptcy beyond normal credit protection, the full benefits of securitization will not be obtained.

For example, cash flows from executory contracts or leases may be interrupted or terminated by the bankruptcy of a party to the contract or lease. This is usually not an issue if a lessee becomes a debtor because credit enhancements would protect against a loss on any particular lease.

However, if the lessor enters bankruptcy proceedings, the trustee or debtor in possession could, in theory, reject *all* of the leases. Absent other protections or considerations, the holder of the leases would then be left as an unsecured creditor of the bankrupt entity. Thus, careful attention should be paid to whether the bankruptcy of an originator could have an adverse impact on the quality of the asset.

FEDERAL INCOME TAX CONSEQUENCES

From a tax viewpoint, two basic questions should be considered in structuring asset-backed security transactions: (1) How is the entity or arrangement that holds the assets taxed? Is it a flow-through vehicle that is not taxable separately or is it treated as an association that is taxable as a corporation? (2) Who is the owner of the assets for tax purposes? Have they been sold to investors or pledged by the issuer as collateral for a debt issued to investors? The answers to these questions determine the nature and timing of taxation of the sponsor or servicer, the issuing entity, and investors.

Taxation of the Issuing Entity

Arrangements in which property is beneficially owned through an entity are classified under applicable Treasury regulations as trusts, partnerships, or corporations (including associations taxable as corporations). Owners of a trust must be passive investors that are not jointly engaged in business activity, whereas investors in a partnership or corporation are viewed as so engaged. Corporations have the characteristics of continuity of life separate from their investors, centralization of management, liability limited to corporate assets, and free transferability of ownership, while partnerships lack these characteristics. However, an entity with no more than two of these factors will generally be classified as a partnership instead of a corporation.

Grantor Trusts and the Sears Regulations

In a sale of assets, the vehicle used to hold legal title to the assets is most commonly structured as a grantor trust, in which the investors' ownership interests are represented by pass-through certificates that evidence fractional undivided interests in the pool of assets. Grantor trusts are structured as passive vehicles to hold assets and are self-liquidating; the trustee cannot reinvest the proceeds of the assets beyond distribution dates and must pass them through to the investors, usually monthly. Grantor trusts are not taxed at the entity level; instead, investors report their share of gross income (interest and, if applicable, original-issue discount or market discount) and expenses (servicing or other administrative fees and, if applicable, amortization of purchase premium) with respect to the assets.

Grantor trusts are treated as "fixed investment trusts" under regulations that were amended in 1986 to forestall offerings of multiple classes of pass-through certificates made by Sears Mortgage Securities Corporation (hence the name Sears Regulations). In general, grantor trust pass-through certificates may only be issued in one class, with exceptions for certain transactions, including stripped bonds, stripped coupons, and senior/subordinated offerings (in which a senior class is sold to investors and a subordinated class, typically representing up to 10 percent of the undivided interests in the trust, functions as a support for payments to the senior class). Failure to comply with the Sears Regulations results in classification of the entity either as a partnership or, more likely for a pooled investment vehicle of this type, as an association taxable as a corporation (with a resulting entity-level tax on net income).

REMICs

The Tax Reform Act of 1986 introduced a new vehicle for issuing mortgage-backed securities that is generally not subject to tax at the entity level: the real estate mortgage investment conduit (REMIC). REMICs may issue two types of securities: regular interests (that is, one or more classes of debt or pass-through instruments) and a single class of residual interests (which may be in any form, but is taxed similarly to interests in a partnership that owns the mortgages and has issued debt secured by the mortgages). REMICs can hold any mortgages secured by real property, including commercial mortgages. The advantage of REMICs is that they offer specific tax accounting rules for treating multi-class securities that could otherwise have been addressed only by using less cost effective structures to overcome tax problems by ensuring debt classification.

Vehicles for Offering Asset-Backed Debt

As the typical corporate debt issuer is a special-purpose finance subsidiary within a corporate group, earnings are generally subject to only one level of tax. An alternative structure uses an owner trust, which is structured under state law as a trust whose equity owners beneficially own the assets and finance them by issuing secured debt. The organizational documents of an owner trust should be drafted so that the issuer will not be treated as an association taxable as a corporation but as either a grantor trust or a partnership—without an entity-level tax. The owner-trust structure was developed so that the sponsor could sell off residual interests in the assets to investors by using a vehicle that would not be subject to an entity-level tax.

Sale versus Debt Treatment

Determination of Sale Treatment

Characterization of the transaction as a sale for federal income tax purposes requires that the seller transfer the economic ownership of the assets, including the risks and benefits of ownership. The main factors are:

- *Credit risk.* This risk is frequently transferred to third parties through use of credit enhancement, such as guarantees or pool insurance, but may be borne directly by the seller in a senior/subordinated arrangement.
- *Risk of changes in value.* The investors must be at risk with respect to market fluctuations and must have the right to dispose of their beneficial interests in the assets.
- *Interest rate risk.* The investors' interest rate must be keyed to the interest rate on the assets. For example, if the assets bear a floating interest rate but the investors receive a fixed rate, the sponsor's retention of interest rate risk gives the appearance of debt.
- *Prepayment or reinvestment risk.* The investors must have the risk of reinvesting principal cash flows so that, for example, cash flows on monthly payment assets should be passed through monthly to the investors.

Other typical features of a pooled arrangement do not preclude sale treatment. Thus, the seller may continue to service the assets and may have the option to repurchase the assets when the aggregate principal balance of the assets is less than 10 percent of their original amount, termed a clean-up call.

Coupon Stripping and Excess Servicing

In the case of interest-bearing obligations, the seller may sell different percentages of interest and principal payments on the obligations, creating stripped bonds (the rights to principal) and stripped coupons (the rights to interest). The stripped interests are treated as obligations issued with original-issue discount (in the amount of the difference between the face amount and the price paid) issued on the date on which the stripping occurs. The coupon-stripping rules may also apply to excess servicing, which is the spread retained by the seller of assets between the assets' interest rate and the interest rate passed through to investors in excess of reasonable servicing compensation.

Determination of Debt Treatment

Assets may be used to secure the indebtedness of the issuer, typically in the form of pay-through debt, which matches to a greater or lesser degree the cash flows on the asset pool. The issuer will continue to be the owner of the assets for tax purposes and will receive the income generated by the assets, will bear the costs related to their servicing, and will deduct interest and original-issue discount expense to the debt holders. Likewise, investors will have interest and, if applicable, original-issue discount income on debt instruments. They may also have market discount income or amortization of premium expense, generally on secondary market purchases.

To support debt treatment, the issuer should retain credit risk on the assets (which is generally ameliorated through the use of various credit support techniques), should retain reinvestment risk (by varying the frequency of payment in the debt from that of the assets), should have the ability to call the debt when a significant portion remains outstanding (so as to benefit from increases in the market value of the collateral), should be able to withdraw or substitute collateral, and should have a residual value in the collateral cash flows, including reinvestment income, in excess of debt service. For example, a pledge of monthly pay automobile loan receivables to secure bonds with quarterly payments and a call when 15 percent to 20 percent of the receivables are expected to be outstanding, with the originator retaining a residual value between 1 percent and 2 percent of the value of the receivables pool, should support debt treatment.

Debt versus Equity of the Issuer

It is critical that the securities be treated as the issuer's indebtedness (generating deductible interest expense) instead of as an equity interest in the issuer (generating dividends that are not deductible by the issuer and, thus, resulting in taxable income at the issuer's level). Although the formal characteristics of indebtedness are important, the form alone is not determinative; thus, a multifactor analysis is applied to determine whether the purported loan has been placed at the risk of the business. The typical asset-backed bonds represent an unsubordinated obligation that is fully secured by high-quality collateral, is held by persons who were not nominal shareholders, and should not be recharacterized as equity. In general, counsel requires that the debt be supported by an equity cushion, typically between 1 percent and 2 percent, so that the debt to equity ratio is not regarded as unreasonably high.

Special Considerations Applicable to Certain Assets

The tax principles discussed earlier that govern the securitization of assets are largely derived from the mortgage-backed securities field. Assets other than mortgages raise some unique problems in the structuring of asset-backed securities.

Rule of 78 Automobile Receivables

Where permitted by state law, many consumer loans use the Rule of 78 method to allocate monthly payments of principal and interest. Accordingly, they multiply the total interest (finance charges) payable over the life of the loan by a fraction, whose numerator is the number of months remaining on the loan when the calculation is made and whose denominator is the sum of the digits represented by the number of months in the entire term of the loan. Most often, the loan document calls for application of the Rule of 78 method to a prepayment to compute unearned finance charges. The Internal Revenue Service has taken the view that, in general, the Rule of 78 method is not permissible as a tax accounting method for the reporting of monthly interest, except for that of 60-month or shorter consumer loans. Taxpayers are given the option to report such loans under an actuarial (economic) method. Thus, a pass-through certificate backed by a pool of Rule of 78 automobile loans that computes and reports interest actuarially will be consistent with the tax accounting method used by most investors, although some provision should be made for investors that choose to continue to report under the Rule of 78 method.

Lease Receivables

Although leases are obligations, they are not evidence of indebtedness. Thus, rules that relate to original-issue discounts, market discounts, and premiums do not apply to them. Accordingly, the law is somewhat unclear about how investors in pass-through certificates backed by lease receivables and how issuers of debt collateralized by such receivables compute gross income with respect to such receivables acquired at a discount. Arguably, a reasonable method that is consistently applied, such as a constant yield method or pro rata method, should be acceptable.

Credit Card Receivables

The revolving, short-term nature of credit card receivables led to the creation of securities that, while in the form of pass-through certificates, are believed by tax counsel to be, in substance, debt securities. Typically, although the receivables have high fixed coupons and may pay either minimum principal amounts or up to their entire current balances each month, the securities generally have much lower fixed rates or floating rates (subject to a cap), an interest-only nonamortization period of up to two or more years, and a seller's retained ownership percentage, which can shift in relative size as the accounts grow and pay off over time.

Under the criteria discussed earlier in the "Sale Versus Debt Treatement" section, it is strongly indicated that the issuer has created a new obligation and has not disposed of beneficial ownership of the receivables for tax purposes. Even if the seller and the investors are somehow viewed as co-owning the pool, many transactions would be treated as partnerships between the seller and the investors, rather than as associations taxable as corporations.

FEDERAL SECURITIES LAW

The Investment Company Act of 1940

In the structuring of asset-backed securities, a major focus is on whether a proposed structure results in the creation of a separate entity that could be considered an investment company for purposes of the Investment Company Act of 1940, as amended (1940 act). The 1940 Act defines "investment company" broadly to include any entity that primarily owns securities and issues securities. As assets used in securitizations are generally securities for purposes of the 1940 Act, any structure in which a newly formed entity holds assets and issues securities backed by those assets may result in the formation of an investment company.

Unless an exemption is found, such an investment company would be required to register under the 1940 Act and comply with various regulations promulgated by the Securities and Exchange Commission (SEC) regarding its management, capital structure, and investment policies. Because these regulations are generally unworkable in the context of a structured financing, an exemption from the requirements of the 1940 Act is necessary.

Statutory exemptions from the requirements of the 1940 Act exist for banks, insurance companies, savings and loan associations, and similar institutions, as well as for issuers not making a public offering of their securities and whose outstanding securities (other than short-term paper) are held by no more than 100 persons. Nevertheless, the most frequently used statutory exemption from the 1940 Act is Section 3(c)(5), which exempts issuers that are not issuing redeemable securities and that are primarily engaged in purchasing certain assets. Section 3(c)(5)(C) exempts issuers that are primarily engaged[12] in purchasing mortgages and other liens on or interests in real estate. Qualifying investments for purposes of Section 3(c)(5)(C) include (1) whole loan mortgages; (2) whole pool[13] Government National Mortgage Association (GNMA), Federal National Mortgage Association (FNMA), and Federal Home Loan Mortgage Corporation (FHLMC) mortgage pass-through certificates (GNMAs, FNMAs, and FHLMCs, respectively); and (3) whole pool private label pass-throughs, although the SEC has not taken a position. With respect to nonmortgage assets, Sections 3(c)(5)(A) and 3(c)(5)(B) of the 1940 Act exempt issuers primarily engaged in purchasing "notes, drafts, acceptances, open accounts receivable, and other obligations representing part or all of the sales price of merchandise, insurance and services" or "making loans to manufacturers, wholesalers, and retailers of, and to prospective purchasers of, specified merchandise, insurance, and services."

If the assets of the issuer consist of partial-pool pass-through certificates (that is, certificates that represent less than the entire pool of underlying assets) or if a transaction not covered by any explicit statutory exemption is contemplated, it may be necessary to seek an exemption from the SEC through an exemptive application under Section 6(c) of the 1940 Act. In the Section 6(c) application, the issuer must show that granting of the exemption is consistent with the policies of the 1940 Act and is in the public interest. The Section 6(c) application process is often slow and time consuming, and the SEC may impose conditions in the course of granting an exemption. As a result, issuers rarely use this process unless precedent indicates that exemptions are granted for the type of transaction desired.

The Securities Act of 1933

The offer and sale of securities must be registered under the

[12]With respect to the meaning of "primarily engaged," in the context of mortgage receivable transactions, the SEC has interpreted this to mean that 55 percent or more of the assets of the issuer must be in qualifying investments. This standard is often used by analogy in nonmortgage transactions.

[13]For purposes of the Section 3(c)(5)(C) exemption, the SEC has taken the position that ownership of a pass-through security that represents less than a 100 percent interest in a pool of mortgage loans (and, therefore, is not whole-pool collateral) is not equivalent to ownership of the underlying receivables.

Securities Act of 1933, as amended (1933 Act), unless an exemption from registration is available. To be exempt from registration, a security must either be an exempt security or be sold in an exempt transaction. Securities issued or guaranteed by a bank or issued by a savings and loan association are exempt securities. However, securities offered by a subsidiary of a bank or savings and loan association are not entitled to the bank or savings and loan exemption, although other exemptions may be available.

Securities offered and sold in "transactions by an issuer not involving a public offering" (private placements) are sold in exempt transactions. However, a private placement under Section 4(2) of the 1933 Act will limit the number of potential investors in an issue and will result in restrictions on the resale of securities. Although there are other types of exempt transactions, they are generally not appropriate for securitizations.

If a security is neither an exempt security nor sold in an exempt transaction, three possible forms of registration are generally used. Public offerings of mortgage securities are registered pursuant to a registration statement on Form S-11 or Form S-3. Form S-11 is prescribed for registration of securities issued by real estate investment trusts and issuers whose primary business is acquiring and holding for investment real estate or interests in real estate. Form S-3 is generally available for the issuance of both mortgage and nonmortgage asset-backed debt securities if the issuer is a majority-owned subsidiary of an established company that is obligated to file periodic reports under the Securities Exchange Act of 1934 (1934 Act). The primary advantage of Form S-3 is that it expedites SEC review of the registration statement. Public offerings of nonmortgage asset-backed securities issued in pass-through form or cases in which an S-3-qualified parent is not involved are generally registered on Form S-1, which is to be used when no other forms are available.

Rule 415 of the 1933 Act permits an issuer to register a large amount in one "shelf" filing and to make periodic offerings thereunder on a delayed or continuous basis after the effective date of the registration statement. Availability of shelf registration is limited to certain types of securities, including mortgage-related securities (which include both debt and pass-through securities registered on any registration form) and debt securities registered on Form S-3.

Accordingly, Rule 415 is generally unavailable for the issuance of nonmortgage asset-backed securities in pass-through form.

Due Diligence

Due diligence procedures in the securitization of assets focus primarily on the adequacy and creditworthiness of the collateral and structure, rather than on traditional underwriting criteria such as financial statements and corporate management data. Although due diligence procedures must be tailored to the specific transaction, such procedures will generally include reviewing the integrity of the seller's underwring standards, confirming characteristics of the receivables to be securitized (for example, delinquency and loss and payment characteristics), and working with the seller to ensure that its data processing system can handle the cash flow tracking requirements of the structure. Other aspects of due diligence include reviewing material contracts of the seller and obtaining accountants' verification of the integrity of the seller's file and record-keeping systems. In addition, a securitization must be structured with a view toward ensuring compliance with federal and state consumer protection laws, applicable usury ceilings, and, in the case of automobile receivables, state title laws. These statutes must be carefully reviewed to assess the feasibility of the structure contemplated and to tailor relevant prospectus disclosure.

The Securities Exchange Act of 1934

The 1934 Act principally regulates (1) secondary trading in securities sold on exchanges and in the over-the-counter market and (2) the operations of brokers and dealers. Although most of its provisions have little direct relevance to asset-backed securities, relevant provisions include reporting and margin requirements. The 1934 Act imposes ongoing reporting requirements on issuers of securities subject to an effective registration statement. Because much of the income statement and balance sheet information ordinarily required is not meaningful in the context of asset-backed securities, the SEC has permitted issuers to file more appropriate information, such as servicer reports supplemented by reports of materially important events and certain annual report information. Additionally, since asset-backed securities are not typically subject to abuses of inside information, the SEC has exempted pass-through certificate holders from applicable requirements of Section 16 of the 1934 Act, which imposes reporting requirements and liability for short-swing trading profits on officers, directors, and holders of 10 percent or more of an issuer's equity securities.

Section 11(d) of the 1934 Act, which relates to the extension of credit for purposes of purchasing and carrying securities, prohibits a broker-dealer that participates in a distribution from extending credit against the securities being distributed (other than exempted securities, such as FNMA-, GNMA-, and FHLMC-guaranteed securities) for 30 days after the distribution. However, bona fide delays in delivery of up to 35 days [and, in the case of a mortgage-related security) (see discussion followng in "Blue Sky Considerations"), up to 180 days] between the contract of sale and the physical delivery of a security are generally permitted.

The Trust Indenture Act of 1939

The Trust Indenture Act of 1939 (1939 Act) was enacted to prevent trustee conflicts of interest and to protect the rights of the holders of debt securities. The 1939 Act, which applies only to debt securities, requires covered securities to be issued pursuant to an indenture that meets the requirements of the 1939 Act and that has been filed and qualified with the SEC. Such filing and qualification is a part of the registration process of the 1933 Act. Securities that are exempt from registration under the 1933 Act or that are sold in exempt transactions will generally be exempt from the 1939 Act, as will asset-backed securities issued in pass-through form.

THE UNIFORM COMMERCIAL CODE AND LIEN PERFECTION

As in effect in all states except Louisiana, the Uniform Commercial Code (UCC) classifies mortgages notes as instruments, and, if a transaction is characterized as a sale, the issuer must deliver the mortgage note to the trustee to transfer valid title to the purchaser (holding through the trustee). If the transaction is characterized as a pledge, the mortgage note must be similarly delivered to the trustee or a custodian on its behalf to perfect a security interest in favor of the trustee. Additionally, rating agencies will likely require a copy of the mortgage, the mortgage and note assignment, and title policies to be delivered to the trustee and may require the assignment of the mortgage to the trustee to be recorded, when required to protect the interests of investors under state recording laws. To perfect a security interest in a book-entry FHLMC or FNMA mortgage security, the owner usually must direct the Federal Reserve Bank to make an entry on its books that indicates a change in the bank in whose name the ownership of the security is reflected on the books of the Federal Reserve Bank. In this case, perfection usually occurs when such bank registers the certificate on its books in the name of the purchaser (trustee) and sends confirmation that it is holding the certificate on the purchaser's behalf.

The UCC considers automobile receivables to be "chattel paper" becuase they represent both the monetary obligation of the vehicle purchaser and the security interest in the vehicle financed. Under the UCC, a sale of chattel paper, as well as a security interest in chattel paper, is perfected either by filing a financing statement or by taking possession of the chattel paper. It is generally not feasible to give the trustee possession of the contracts or even to stamp them to evidence the interest of the trustee because of the large number of contracts involved in a securitization, each of which has a relatively small outstanding balance. In most recent transactions involving the securitization of automobile receivables, the servicer's computer records are flagged to indicate the interest of the trustee, and a financing statement is filed in favor of the trustee. However, in certain circumstances, a secured party that obtains possession of chattel paper may have priority over a secured party that has filed a financing statement. Accordingly, an investor in automobile receivable–backed securities bears the risk that, through administrative error or fraud, the servicer will deliver the contracts to a bona fide purchaser (that is, a purchaser that buys the chattel paper in good faith without knowledge that the paper is subject to a security interest) that will have priority over the security interest in favor of the investors.

Credit card receivables are considered either accounts or general intangibles under the UCC. For purposes of the UCC, an account is defined as a right to payment for goods or services that is not evidenced by an instrument or chattel paper, and a general intangible is defined as personal property other than goods, accounts, chattel paper, documents, instruments, and money. In either case, a security interest that evidences the sale or pledge of credit card receivables is obtained through a UCC filing and through flagging of the computer records of the taxpayer.

BANK AND THRIFT REGULATORY CONSIDERATIONS

Authority to Issue Asset-Backed Securities

Most corporate entities, which are subject to the corporate or business laws of their state of incorporation, are authorized under such laws to engage in any type of business activity that is not otherwise prohibited by law or their corporate charters. By contrast, depository institutions generally have the authority to engage only in activities that are expressly or implied to be authorized by their enabling statutes or that are otherwise deemed to be incidental to authorized powers. Therefore, whenever a depository institution wishes to engage in a particular activity, the threshold question is whether it has the statutory authority to do so.

National Banks

In recent years, the Office of the Comptroller of the Currency (OCC) has consistently maintained that national banks are authorized to issue securities backed by or representing interests in mortgages and other assets.[14] Depending on the accounting, tax, and other structural aspects, securitization activities of national banks have been justified as a means of either borrowing funds or selling assets. In both cases, securitization of bank assets is perceived as a way to enhance liquidity; manage capital and other balance sheet ratios, as well as interest rate exposure; reduce asset concentrations; and diversify income sources.

[14]See the "Glass-Steagall Act Considerations Applicable to National Banks" section.

Under 12 C.F.R. Section 5.34, national banks also have the authority to establish operating subsidiaries to issue any securities that the bank could have issued directly. The authority of national banks' subsidiaries to issue securities collateralized by mortgages or securities backed by pools of mortgages was established by the OCC in a May 22, 1986, letter regarding Liberty Norstar Bank, N.A., in Buffalo, New York.[15]

Federally Chartered Thrift Institutions

Federally chartered savings and loan associations and savings banks (federal associations) are statutorily authorized to borrow, to pledge assets as security therefor, and to issue notes, bonds, and other securities under 12 U.S.C. Section 5(b)(2). This statutory provision has been interpreted to permit the issuance of securities backed by or representing interests in mortgages or other receivables.

Moreover, under 12 C.F.R. Section 545.82, federal associations may establish single-purpose finance subsidiaries to issue any securities that the parent could issue directly.

State-Chartered Thrift Institutions and Banks

State-chartered savings institutions and state-chartered banks must look to state law for authority to issue securities directly or through finance or operating subsidiaries or service corporations.

Securities Offering Registration with Federal Banking Agencies

Bank Regulatory Requirements

Although bank-issued securities are exempt from the registration and prospectus delivery requirements of the 1933 Act, pursuant to Section 3(a)(2) thereof, OCC regulations [12 C.F.R. Section 16.3(a)] require a national bank that issues securities to file an offering circular with the OCC's Securities Disclosure Division and to have that offering circular declared effective by the OCC prior to any offers or sales of securities, unless an exemption applies. The only exemp-

[15]*Ibid.*

tion from the offering requirements that is relevant in most asset-backed security offerings applies to transactions that do not involve any public offering under 12 C.F.R. Section 16.5. Pass-through securities supported by cash flows on collateral that is sold by a bank to a trust formed by the bank are deemed to be issued by the trust—not by the bank—for purposes of the offering circular requirements. Hence, they must be registered under the 1933 Act.[16]

State banks should consult their own state banking and security regulations for applicable disclosure requirements. The Federal Reserve Board (FRB), which regulates state banks that are members of the Federal Reserve System, and the FDIC, which regulates nonmember FDIC-insured state banks, do not require security offering materials to be filed with them prior to any offers and sales.

Thrift Regulatory Requirements

Under 12 C.F.R. Section 563g.2(a), federal associations and state-chartered institutions that are insured by the FSLIC are required to file an offering circular on Form OC with the Corporate and Securities Division of the Office of the General Counsel of the FHLBB and to have that offering circular declared effective by the FHLBB prior to any offers or sales of securities. Exemptions from this offering circular requirement are afforded to nonpublic offerings under 12 C.F.R. Section 563g.4 and to offerings of debt securities that are issued in denominations of $100,000 or more and that are fully collateralized by cash; by any security issued or guaranteed by the United States, the FNMA, the FHLMC, or the GNMA; or by interests in mortgage notes secured by real property under 12 C.F.R. Section 563g.3.

Reserve Requirements

The General Rule

Regulation D of the FRB requires all depository institutions to maintain non-interest-bearing reserves against certain categories of deposits. Under 12 C.F.R. Section 204.2(a)(1)(vii), the term "deposit" is defined to include any:

[16]See Bank of America National Trust and Savings Association, SEC No-Action Letter, [1977 Transfer Binder], Fed. Sec. L. Rep. (CCH), paragraph 81,193, April 19, 1977.

liability of a depository institution on any promissory note, acknowledgment of advance, banker's acceptance, or similar obligation...including mortgage-backed bonds that is issued or undertaken by a depository institution as a means of obtaining funds.

The 1986 Proposal

The FRB takes the position that a deposit is also created when a depository institution retains a conditional liability or reversionary interest in assets that it sells. Pursuant to revisions to Regulation D, proposed in May 1986 (1986 Proposal), the definition of deposit would be amended to clarify that sales of assets would constitute deposits "where the depository institution retains an interest in or is liable for the assets sold (whether the interest or liability retained is conditional, unconditional, contingent, complete, or partial)" under 51 Fed. Reg. 16855 (May 7, 1986).

Examples of sale transactions deemed to create deposits include:

- The transfer of excess assets and the depository institution's retention of the right to any remaining portion of the excess
- The use of interest rate spreads to create an insurance fund that will revert to the depository institution after losses are paid
- The depository institution's retention of a subordinated interest, which is used to protect holders of the senior interest

In addition, under the present rule [12 C.F.R. Section 204.2(a)(1)(v)], certain obligations of affiliates are reservable deposits if the proceeds are used to supply or maintain the availability of funds to the depository institution. The 1986 Proposal would extend this provision and otherwise change the treatment of affiliates' obligations.

The 10 Percent Mortgage Exclusion

To foster the secondary mortgage market, the definition of deposit under 12 C.F.R. Section 204.2(a)(1)(ix) excludes sales of one- to four-family mortgages when no more than a 10 percent interest is retained by the selling depository institution. The 10 percent exclusion permits the use of senior/subordinated structures and other forms of self-insurance in mortgage securitizations, but is not available for automobile-, credit card–, and other non-mortgage-backed asset sales.

Third Party Credit Enhancement

Under the 1986 Proposal, asset sales without direct recourse to the depository institution are not considered deposits. In particular, no deposit is created when a third party credit enhancer (such as an insurance company or a letter-of-credit issuer) provides credit support and investors cannot make claims directly against the institution, even if the depository institution retains full recourse to the third party credit enhancer. Because investors are not looking at the creditworthiness of the depository institution, the FRB takes the view that the asset sale is not a deposit in the depository institution.

Amount Reservable

"Nonpersonal time deposits" with a maturity of less than 18 months are subject to a 3 percent reserve requirement, whereas nonpersonal time deposits with a maturity of 18 months or greater have no reserve requirement. Determination of the maturity of a deposit can be problematic.

Under current FRB staff interpretations, obligations calling for amortized payments of principal [such as collateralized mortgage obligations (CMOs)] are considered multiple maturity time deposits, with each portion of the principal having its own maturity date established by the required date of payment. Thus, the staff takes the view that reserves would have to be maintained only against principal payments that are scheduled to be made within the first 18 months after an obligation is issued and, potentially, against any prepayments that are expected to occur during that period.

Questions arise as to whether acceleration clauses should be viewed as shortening the maturity of the deposit. The FRB staff takes the view that usual acceleration clauses (such as insolvency) do not shorten maturity. However, to date, it has been unwilling to include in this category amortization or payout events based on delinquencies or write-offs. Similarly, the staff deems put options to shorten the maturity of obligations to the date on which the put is exercisable.

Determination of Sale Treatment by Regulatory Accounting Practices

National banks and state-chartered commercial and savings banks that are insured by the FDIC are subject to bank regulatory accounting practices (RAP) dictated by the Federal Financial Institutions Examination Council (FFIEC), an organization comprising representatives of the OCC, the FDIC, and the FRB, among others. When adopted by the aforementioned bank regulatory agencies, FFIEC pronouncements establish guidelines that are to be used by national banks and state-chartered commercial and savings banks in the preparation of their consolidated reports of income and condition (call reports), which are filed with each bank's respective primary federal bank regulatory agency.[17]

By contrast, when filing monthly and quarterly thrift financial reports, federal associations and state-chartered, FSLIC-insured savings institutions apply generally accepted accounting principles (GAAP) to determine whether certain transfers of assets should be recorded as sales.

Sales of Assets Using Participation Certificates

Under both GAAP and RAP, the transfer of mortgage or other assets entirely without recourse to the transferor is normally treated as a sale.

The manner in which federal associations and state-chartered, FSLIC-insured institutions account for transfers with recourse is governed by Financial Accounting Standards Board (FASB) Statement of Financial Accounting Standards (SFAS) No. 77, *Reporting by Transferors for Transfers of Receivables with Recourse.* Under SFAS

[17]The FDIC is the primary federal regulator for state-chartered, FDIC-insured commercial and savings banks that are not members of the Federal Reserve System. The FRB is the primary federal regulator of state-chartered member banks. Although the OCC is the primary federal regulator of national banks, the OCC has delegated authority to the FDIC to compile and disseminate call reports for national banks.

No. 77, a transfer of receivables with recourse will be treated as a sale if:

- The transferor has surrendered control of the future economic benefits embodied in the receivables
- The transferor's obligation under any recourse provisions can be reasonably estimated
- The transferee cannot require the transferor to repurchase the receivables, other than pursuant to the recourse provisions

Thus, conceivably, transactions may be structured with significant recourse to the thrift, provided that the above conditions are met.

By contrast, under RAP, a transfer of mortgages on one- to four-family residences (including loans on cooperative apartments) will be deemed a sale only if the transferor's retained risk is not significant. (The level of recourse that is deemed significant is not well defined and appears to be the subject of divergent regulatory views.) The transfer of mortgages on multifamily property (that is, greater than four families) or other commercial real estate or the transfer of nonmortgage assets, such as automobile or credit card receivables, will be treated as a sale only if the transferor retains "no risk of loss...from any cause" on the assets.

The FFIEC has indicated that if properly structured, use of a spread or escrow account (created from the differential between the interest rate paid to security holders and the interest rate on the underlying assets) to absorb losses would permit a transfer of nonmortgage assets to be characterized as a sale. In particular, the FFIEC requires that there be no further possible charge to the bank's earnings or capital (including the allowance for loan losses) after the transaction has been recorded by the bank as a sale. Other methods may also be available to achieve a desired sale of assets.

Financing of Receivables Using Debt Obligations

Because CMOs are generally bonds secured by mortgage pass-through securities or mortgage loans, they are normally reported as borrowings. Although a CMO can theoretically be recorded as a sale if the conditions imposed by FASB Technical Bulletin No. 85-2 are met, satisfying this bulletin is normally not feasible because it requires that any residual interest be "insignificantly small or trifling." Nevertheless, other means exist for issuers to obtain sale treatment, such as the establishment of an owner trust and the sale of a majority of the residual interest therein.

FSLIC and FDIC Receivership Considerations

Bonds Issued Directly by Banks or Thrifts

When a financial institution directly issues pay-through bonds, such as CMOs, in an offering that is not required to be registered under the 1933 Act and is not subject to the 1939 Act, the indenture ordinarily provides that, in the event of insolvency, the trustee is precluded from liquidating the collateral in circumstances in which cash flows available under the indenture would be sufficient to make timely payments of principal and interest on the bonds.

In correspondence with counsel to Standard & Poor's Corporation (S&P), the general counsels to the FSLIC[18] and the FDIC[19] have independently stated that, notwithstanding such an indenture provision, the FSLIC or the FDIC, as receiver of an insolvent thrift or bank, may attempt to liquidate the collateral. The FSLIC asserted the option to accelerate the debt or to continue performing under the indenture. The FDIC stated that it would take action to liquidate immediately the collateral, which would obviously require acceleration of the outstanding debt obligations. Consequently, S&P requires indentures to contain provisions allowing the option to accelerate.

However, in the Raiden and Persinger letters, both the FSLIC and the FDIC, respectively, indicated that neither would seek acceleration of the debt and liquidation of the collateral if the market value of the collateral was insufficient to pay principal and accrued interest on the bonds. In such circumstances, acceleration and liquidation would not produce any excess collateral for the benefit of the insolvent thrift or bank or their creditors.

[18]See letter of Norman H. Raiden, General Counsel to the FSLIC, December 12, 1983.

[19]See letter of Daniel W. Persinger, Deputy General Counsel to the FDIC, September 30, 1983.

Special-Purpose Subsidiary

In correspondence with counsel to S&P, the general counsels of the FSLIC[20] and the FDIC[21] have independently opined that a court would not uphold an attempt by the FSLIC or the FDIC, as receiver of an insolvent thrift or bank, to disregard the separateness of a corporate subsidiary that is, among other things, properly established and operated as a corporate entity separate from its parent depository institution. As a result, pay-through bonds issued by a special purpose subsidiary would be insulated from the insolvency of a parent thrift or bank and would have "call protection" from a FSLIC or FDIC receiver's attempt to accelerate the bonds and liquidate the collateral.

Glass-Steagall Act Considerations Applicable to National Banks

In the case of security activities by financial institutions, the most relevant provisions of the Glass-Steagall Act are Section 16 and Section 21 [12 U.S.C. Section 24 (seventh) and 12 U.S.C. Section 378, respectively]. Section 16 prohibits national banks from engaging in the business of dealing or underwriting in securities, other than certain bank-eligible instruments. 12 U.S.C. Section 355 applied this provision to FRB member banks. Section 21 prohibits depository institutions from being "engaged in the business of issuing, underwriting, selling or distributing securities" other than bank-eligible instruments. However, Section 21 states that its restrictions will not affect any right that "any bank...may otherwise possess to sell, without recourse or agreement to repurchase, obligations evidencing loans on real estate."

June 16, 1987, Letter to Security Pacific National Bank[22]

The OCC has consistently held that the Glass-Steagall Act does not restrict a national bank's ability to issue mortgage- and other

[20]See letter of Norman H. Raiden, General Counsel to the FSLIC, March 23, 1984.

[21]See letter of John C. Murphy, Jr., General Counsel to the FDIC, April 9, 1986.

[22]OCC Interpretive Letter No. 388, reprinted in [1987–88 Transfer Binder] Fed. Banking L. Rep. (CCH), paragraph 85,612, June 16, 1987.

asset-backed securities. In addition, it takes the view that national banks may publicly distribute securities that represent sales of their own assets. The OCC's position on these issues was most clearly articulated in the Security Pacific letter, which related to the bank's issuance and distribution of pass-through certificates representing interests in conventional mortgages originated by the bank in the ordinary course of its mortgage lending activities. (Although the security issuance in question involved mortgage-related assets, the OCC made clear that the legal analysis in the Security Pacific letter was not limited to mortgage assets and suggested strongly that it could extend to other receivables.)

In the Security Pacific letter, the OCC concluded that the issuance of pass-through certificate is no more than the lawful negotiation or sale of underlying assets. The OCC also concluded that mortgage-backed pass-through certificates are not securities for purposes of the Glass-Steagall Act because certificate holders have essentially the same rights, liabilities, and risks as if they were the owners of the underlying assets.

However, the OCC went on to conclude that, even if mortgage pass-throughs are securities for Glass-Steagall Act purposes, that act is not intended to prohibit a bank's distribution of its own securities. In this regard, the OCC noted that "Section 16 is intended to control the types and amount of national bank purchase and sale activity with respect to securities issued by others, but this section does not affect a bank's activities with respect to its own securities." Similarly, the OCC noted, "we do not believe that Section 21 is intended to affect a bank's ability to raise funds for its operation through the issuance (and distribution and sale) of certificates representing interests in its own assets."[23] The OCC supported this conclusion by noting that the bank's activities did not raise the "subtle hazards" that underlie the Glass-Steagall Act.

[23]However, it should be noted that the Securities Industry Association has filed suit against the OCC, seeking a declaratory judgment and injunctive relief and alleging that the OCC acted in an arbitrary and capricious manner in issuing the Security Pacific letter and that the activity authorized in that letter violates the Glass-Steagall Act. *Securities Industry Association* v. *Clarke,* 87 Cir. 4504 (S.D.N.Y.), filed June 23, 1987.

The February 17, 1988, Letter to The Chase Manhattan Bank, National Association[24]

The analysis employed in the Security Pacific letter was subsequently applied to a proposal by The Chase Manhattan Bank to securitize and distribute certificates representing interests in commercial real estate loans selected from the bank's own portfolio.

Although those certificates would be registered with the SEC under the 1933 Act, the OCC noted that they would be marketed "in the manner of a private placement." The OCC thus concluded that because Chase's activities would "involve marketing securities only in large denominations to a limited number of institutional investors and with limited advertising," the proposal did not involve Glass-Steagall Act underwriting. The OCC also noted that the mortgage certificates would not be Glass-Steagall Act securities because of their pass-through nature and that the Glass-Steagall Act would not constrain the proposed activity because Chase would simply be selling its own mortgage loans or borrowing funds collateralized by those assets.

The February 17, 1988, Letter to The First National Bank of Boston[25]

Because the securities at issue in the Security Pacific letter and The Chase Manhattan Bank letter were, in each case, underlain by mortgages originated by the bank, the extent to which those letters can be used as precedents in the context of assets that were not originated by the bank or its affiliates has been the subject of debate.

This matter was clarified, to some extent, in The First National Bank of Boston letter, which pertained to a proposal to issue pass-through certificates representing interests in and debt obligations collateralized by mortgages originated by unrelated parties. In that letter, the bank estimated that approximately 50 percent of the mortgages employed in its offerings would be purchased from other institutions in the secondary mortgage market, but stressed that it would purchase only mortgages that complied with its own under-

[24]OCC Interpretive Letter No. 417 [Current Developments], reprinted in Fed. Banking L. Rep. (CCH), paragraph 85,641, February 17, 1988.

[25]OCC Interpretive Letter No. 418 [Current Developments], reprinted in Fed. Banking L. Rep. (CCH), paragraph 85,642, February 17, 1988.

writing criteria. In approving the proposed activity, the OCC noted that:

> This mortgage banking business includes making loans and holding them in portfolio, making loans and selling them on to other lenders, purchasing loans from other loan-originators and holding them, purchasing loans and selling them on, and servicing loans. The mix of activities in any given bank's mortgage banking business at any particular time depends on such factors as local lending opportunities, secondary market lending opportunities, local funding opportunities, second market funding opportunities, and so on.

The OCC noted that "the bank intends to use an independent investment bank and will not itself participate in the selling efforts." However, there was no suggestion that this fact was crucial to the OCC's approval.

The May 22, 1986, Letter to Liberty Norstar Bank, N.A.[26]

In an earlier letter, the OCC took the view that a subsidiary of Liberty Norstar could issue, underwrite, and deal in CMOs collateralized by GNMAs, FNMAs, FHLMCs, or non-federally insured conventional residential mortgage loans. However, the OCC subsequently made clear that the Norstar letter was not intended to authorize national banks to underwrite and deal in CMOs issued by third parties.[27] Rather, the OCC emphasized that it was merely authorizing Liberty Norstar to obtain funds through borrowings secured by or through the sale of the bank's mortgage-related assets.[28]

BLUE SKY CONSIDERATIONS

All of the 50 states, the District of Columbia, Puerto Rico, and Guam have adopted their own security laws (commonly known as

[26]OCC Interperetive Letter No. 362, reprinted in [1985–87 Transfer Binder] Fed. Banking L. Rep. (CCH), paragraph 85,532, May 22, 1986.

[27]See letter of Robert L. Clark, Comptroller of the Currency, to the Hon. Alphonse M. D'Amato, U.S. Senate, June 18, 1986.

[28]See Liberty Norstar letter, op. cit. See also OCC Interpretive Letter No. 378, reprinted in Fed. Banking L. Rep. (CCH), paragraph 85,602, which elaborates on various legal issues relating to national bank issuance of CMOs.

blue sky laws). With the exception of the District of Columbia, each of these jurisdictions, requires a registration or similar filing before securities may be offered and sold to its residents.

Most mortgage pass-through certificates and CMOs—but not typical mortgage-backed bonds—will qualify as mortgage-related securities, as defined in Section 3(a)(41) of the 1934 Act as amended by the Secondary Mortgage Market Enhancement Act (SMMEA) of 1984. Here, a mortgage-related security is a security that is rated in one of the two highest rating categories by at least one nationally recognized statistical rating organization and that either (1) represents ownership of mortgage notes or participations in mortgage notes, provided that such notes are secured by first liens on residential or mixed residential and commercial structures and were originated by a depository institution, insurance company, or the Department of Housing and Urban Development–approved mortgagee, or (2) is secured by such notes or participations and provides for payments of principal in relation to payments or for reasonable projections of payments on such notes or participations.

Pursuant to Section 106(c) of SMMEA, securities that qualify as mortgage-related securities are exempt from registration or other filings under blue sky laws to the same extent as securities issued by or guaranteed as to principal and interest by the United States or any agency or instrumentality thereof. The purpose of this provision was to preempt the states, since none of the blue sky laws at that time required filings to sell U.S. government securities. Although the states were given seven years (through October 3, 1991) to override such preemption, only Arkansas, Louisiana, Minnesota, and New Mexico have done so. By recently requiring filings to perfect an exemption for U.S. government securities, Nevada has indirectly overridden the preemption.

As regards other asset-backed securities, including those backed by second and commercial mortgages and credit cards and automobile loans, no state has adopted an automatic exemption for such securities, although most have provisions that exempt placements under varying conditions, as well as sales to various types of institutional investors. Blue sky registrations can be time consuming and expensive, and certain jurisdictions apply so-called merit standards whereby they may reject filings when they deem the offering unfair to investors. Asset-backed offerings are particularly vulnerable to challenge (notably in Minnesota and Tennessee) under guidelines that generally prohibit offerings of debt or preferred stock by newly organized entities.

Legal Investment Considerations

Securities that qualify as mortgage-related securities under SMMEA also enjoy special privileges under state legal investment laws. Sections 106(a) and 106(b) of SMMEA provide that mortgage-related securities may be purchased by various entities subject to state laws to the same extent as securities issued by or guaranteed as to principal and interest by the United States or any agency or instrumentality thereof. Again, states were given seven years to override this preemptive provision. None has done so to date, although some banking regulators have issued policy statements that prohibit or restrict investments in interest-only and principal-only strips.

Other asset-backed securities are frequently restricted investments (under "leeway" provisions) or prohibited investments, since many statutes—particularly those that govern insurance companies and state pension plans—do not allow investments in debt securities issued by newly formed entities or noncorporate issuers or, as regards pass-through securities, in participations in loans that cannot be made or purchased directly by the regulated entity. For example, as most insurance companies are not authorized to make or purchase automobile loans or offer credit cards, they cannot purchase interests in such receivables. Likewise, second and commercial mortgages may not meet loan-to-value and appraisal requirements.

On the federal level, SMMEA specifically authorized national banks, federal savings and loan associations, federal savings banks, and federal credit unions to invest in mortgage-related securities, subject to regulations adopted by their respective regulators. Although none has issued restrictive regulations, certain regulators have issued policy statements modeled on the FFIEC's *Supervisory Policy on the Selection of Securities Dealers and Unsuitable Investment Practices,* which includes guidelines for investments in stripped mortgage-backed securities and residuals.

As regards other asset-backed securities, national banks can invest in debt and pass-through securities that qualify as investment securities, federal thrifts can invest only in rated corporate debt and pass-throughs that evidence interests in loans they can make themselves (including auto loans and credit card loans), and federal credit unions are generally prohibited from making any such investments.

ERISA CONSIDERATIONS

Appropriate analysis of a sale of an asset-backed security to a pension plan depends on whether it is a debt or equity instrument. There are issues under ERISA in either event, although such issues are usually more manageable if the security is debt. Under a U.S. Department of Labor (DOL) ERISA regulation that defined plan assets [29 C.F.R. 2510.3-101, 51 F.R. 41262, November 13, 1986 (DOL Regulation)], interests in entities (for example, trusts) are equity interests for ERISA purposes, unless they are considered debt under applicable local law *and* they have no substantial equity features. The DOL has not offered much more by way of formal guidance on characterization, and many lawyers rely on the body of pre-REMIC tax considerations in this area, although its formal applicablility is not clear. Under these rules, a REMIC residual would seem to be an equity interest.

ERISA prohibits the extension of credit between a plan and a party in interest, unless an exemption applies. Such a prohibited transaction can occur if a plan buys a bond and if the issuer or an affiliate of the issuer is a party in interest. Also, such a transaction can occur if a plan buys a residual interest and a party in interest buys a bond. (An additional important non-ERISA consideration in the latter circumstance is that normally tax-exempt pension plan trusts can incur unrelated business income tax on unrelated debt-financed income.)

Prohibited extensions of credit may be covered by one or more DOL-prohibited transaction exemptions (PTEs). The three PTEs that are most commonly relevant for this purpose are:

- *PTE 84-14.* This covers certain transactions with parties in interest effected on behalf of a plan by a qualified professional asset manager.

- *PTE 80-51.* This covers certain transactions effected by bank collective investment funds for plans.
- *PTE 78-19.* This covers certain transactions effected by insurance company pooled separate accounts for plans.

If the asset-backed security acquired by a plan is equity, under the DOL regulation, the plan's assets will include such security, as well as undivided interest in each asset of the issuing entity, unless:

- The equity security is publicly offered, that is:
  —There are 100 independent investors,
  —It is freely transferable, and
  —Appropriate registration takes place under the 1934 Act, or
- Plan involvement is not significant, that is, plans of all types own less than 25 percent of equity at all times. The 25 percent test is a moving test.

If the equity security is not publicly offered and plan involvement is 25 percent or more, parties dealing with assets held in the entity (for example, the trustee or the servicer) might be viewed as plan fiduciaries, in which case their activities would be subject to ERISA fiduciary standards, including prudence, the exclusive benefit rule, and the entire statutory and administrative scheme of prohibited transactions and exemptions. In such circumstances, the PTEs referred to above and others may apply, depending, in part, on the nature of the assets in the entity, the nature of the entity, and who is buying for the plan or plans. However, the operation of some pools of assets (for example, certain monthly pay REMIC pools of government agency certificates) is so passive that it is difficult to conceive of the trustee or servicer as an ERISA fiduciary or to conceive of their activities as involving prohibited transactions.

CHAPTER 4
Accounting for Asset-Backed Transactions

Raymond T. Sloane, Jr.
Thomas A. Tranfaglia, Jr.

INTRODUCTION

The recent increase in the popularity of asset securitization, including the expansion of the concept to previously unanticipated asset types and the flexibility afforded by the creation of the real estate mortgage investment conduit (REMIC) vehicle, has resulted in wide variation in securitized asset structures. The primary accounting issues that arise in connection with such creative structures can be summarized as:

- Sale versus financing treatment of the segregated pool of assets for the sponsor or issuer
- Consolidation of the issuing entity by the sponsor
- Accounting for loan servicing
- Accounting for the investment in purchased residuals

In very significant measure, each of these issues, along with tax law and securities law issues, affects the exact structure that a particular transaction will take to achieve the result sought by the issuer and sponsor.

This chapter will address these and other financial accounting topics related to the issuance of asset-backed securities, especially mortgage-backed securities, and will include discussions of the most recent developments in the area.

BACKGROUND INFORMATION: ACCOUNTING STANDARD SETTING

To better understand how generally accepted accounting principles are developed and evolve, some background information concerning the two groups currently primarily responsible for the establishment and interpretation of accounting standards may be useful.

Financial Accounting Standards Board

The Financial Accounting Standards Board (FASB), recognized as authoritative by the American Institute of Certified Public Accountants (AICPA) and by the Securities and Exchange Commission (SEC), is the organization in the private sector that is responsible for establishing financial accounting and reporting standards.

Although the SEC has the statutory authority to establish financial accounting and reporting standards for publicly held companies, it has historically relied heavily on the private sector for this function. Provided that the private sector discharges its responsibility in the public interest, the SEC is reluctant to interfere in the process.

Among its responsibilities, the FASB prescribes rules for the financial accounting and reporting of asset-backed security transactions. Because these FASB reporting requirements have a direct impact on the ability of many entities to participate in the issuance of certain securities, they have been and remain the source of controversy.

The FASB has various means of providing guidance. The highest level of authoritative literature that the FASB can issue is a formal Statement of Financial Accounting Standards. The complexity of an issue determines how long it will take from the time that it is added to the FASB's agenda to the time that a final statement is issued; a time span of several years is not unusual for a complex topic.

The FASB also has at its disposal the option of issuing Technical Bulletins, which are intended to provide clarification and guidance on the application of accounting principles on a more timely basis than a formal statement. The following types of guidance may be provided in an FASB Technical Bulletin:

- The guidance in the bulletin may clarify, explain, or elaborate on an underlying standard.
- The guidance in the bulletin for a particular situation, usually in a specific industry, may differ from the general application required by the standard in an Accounting Research Bulleting (ARB), Accounting Principles Board (APB) Opinion, or FASB statement or interpretation. For example, a bulletin may specify that the standard does not apply to enterprises in a particular industry or may provide for a deferral of the effective date of a standard for that industry.
- The guidance in the bulletin may address areas not directly covered by existing standards.[1]

It should be noted that whether the FASB is contemplating the issuance of a formal statement or a Technical Bulletin, certain due process procedures are followed. After the FASB staff has considered an issue and reached tentative conclusions, an Exposure Draft, which contains the proposed standard, background information, and an explanation of the FASB's basis for its conclusions, is issued.

At this point, responses to the Exposure Draft (both negative and positive) are prepared by companies that expect to be affected by the proposed pronouncement. Certified public accountant (CPA) firms are also active in preparing responses. Public hearings are held on most issues. Responses are carefully considered, and suggested alternative proposals are evaluated; modifications, to the extent considered necessary or appropriate, are made prior to the issuance of the final statement or Technical Bulletin.

[1]Technical Bulletin No. 85-1(R).

Criticisms of the FASB

In recent years, the FASB has come under attack by many in the industry. Most of the criticism has been directed toward the long period of time required to issue a pronouncement. As creative investment bankers produce innovative financial instruments on what seems like a daily basis, it has become increasingly evident that a standard-setting body with the requirements of full due process, such as the FASB, is not capable of responding quickly enough to satisfy an ever-quicker Wall Street.

Emerging Issues Task Force

In response to this criticism, in 1984, the FASB established the Emerging Issues Task Force (EITF) to assist in the early identification of emerging issues that affect financial reporting and of problems in the implementation of authoritative pronouncements. The membership comprises individuals who are knowledgeable in accounting and financial reporting and are in a position to be aware of emerging problems as they develop.

The EITF membership includes the senior technical partners of major national CPA firms, as well as representatives of major associations of preparers of financial statements, such as the Financial Executives Institute, the Business Roundtable, and the National Association of Accountants. The FASB's director of research and technical activities serves as EITF chairman. The SEC's chief accountant participates in EITF meetings as an observer, with the privilege of the floor. Although a nonvoting member, his opinion is accorded a great deal of weight.

The EITF meets approximately every six weeks and discusses a variety of issues. A consensus is reached when not more than 2 of the total 16 members object to a proposed accounting treatment. In some instances, the EITF will come to a majority agreement even if no consensus can be reached. To date, issues that involve financial institutions and financial instruments have dominated EITF discussions.

The EITF has been fairly successful in resolving issues brought to its attention. Of the 178 issues discussed through June 1988, the

EITF was unable to resolve issues in one manner or another in only 22 instances.

The objective of forming the EITF was not to create a new standard-setting body. The consensus views of the EITF are supposed to reflect practice, rather than set it. However, the SEC's chief accountant has said on more than one occasion that companies filing with the SEC will be called on to justify a departure from EITF consensus views. Therefore, for all intents and purposes, the EITF has become a de facto standard-setting body without full due process. This has enabled the FASB's constituency to obtain more responsive guidance in areas that cannot wait for the issuance of formal statements.

DEVELOPMENT OF ACCOUNTING STANDARDS WITH RESPECT TO MORTGAGE-BACKED SECURITIES

It is important to note that the overriding intent of generally accepted accounting principles is to record the economic substance of a transaction, rather than merely its legal form. In most cases, economic substance and legal form are the same. However, for monetary transactions, such as securitized asset structures using mortgage securities, substance and form are often considerably different. Throughout this chapter, readers will observe the ongoing struggle to record substance over form for accounting purposes.

As the mortgage-backed security industry evolved, the accounting profession found itself with no authoritative accounting guidance that dealt with certain of the unique aspects of such instruments. The profession wrestled with the problem by attempting to apply, by analogy, accounting principles germane to similar types of transactions, while simultaneously addressing the collateralized mortgage obligation (CMO) issue directly through its due process channels.

Sale versus Financing Treatment

The proper accounting treatment of issuances of mortgage-backed securities has been anything but clear cut. In particular, the accounting for issuances of CMOs has been debated at length, and new issues continue to arise.

Prior to the issuance of Technical Bulletin No. 85-2, *Accounting for Collateralized Mortgage Obligations,* accountants struggled with existing literature to find the appropriate treatment for CMOs. The first place that some accountants turned was Statement of Financial Accounting Standards (SFAS) No. 76, *Extinguishment of Debt.*

SFAS No. 76 allows debt to be considered extinguished (that is, removed from the balance sheet) if the following conditions are met:

- The debtor pays the creditor and is relieved of all its obligations with respect to the debt.
- The debtor is legally released from being the primary obligor under the debt—either judicially or by the creditor—and it is probable that the debtor will not be required to make future payments with respect to that debt under any guarantees.
- The debtor irrevocably places cash or other assets in a trust to be used solely to satisfy scheduled payments of both interest and principal of a specific obligation, and the possibility that the debtor will be required to make future payments with respect to that debt is remote. In this circumstance, debt is extinguished even though the debtor is not legally released from being the primary obligor under the debt obligation.[2]

In addition to these requirements, SFAS No. 76 also specifies that the nature of the assets held by the trust must meet the following requirements to effect an extinguishment:

- The trust shall be restricted to owning only monetary assets that are essentially risk free as to the amount, timing, and collection of interest and principal.

- The monetary assets held by the trust shall provide cash flows (from interest and maturity of those assets) whose timing and amount approximately coincide with the scheduled interest and principal payments on the debt that is being extinguished.[3]

[2]SFAS No. 76, paragraph 3.

[3]SFAS No. 76, paragraph 4.

Although many felt that SFAS No. 76 applied to CMOs, the FASB took the position that it did not. Specifically, the requirement that the monetary asset be essentially risk free with respect to the payment of principal and interest is not met because most CMOs are backed by mortgage or mortgage-backed securities, which can be repaid at any time.

Those who felt that SFAS No. 76 did not apply to CMOs, but still wanted to apply existing literature to the transaction, did not have very far to look. By turning the page, they found SFAS No. 77, *Reporting by Transferors for Transfers of Receivables with Recourse* as guidance. Recourse is defined in Paragraph 12 of SFAS No. 77 as:

> The right of a transferee of receivables to receive payment from the transferor of those receivables for:
> (a) failure of the debtors to pay when due,
> (b) the effects of prepayments, or
> (c) adjustments resulting from defects in the eligibility of the transferred receivables.[4]

Because sales of receivables with recourse have many of the same characteristics as loans collateralized by receivables, the statement was promulgated to clarify the circumstances in which a transfer of receivables with recourse should be treated as a loan, rather than a sale.

The statement establishes standards of financial accounting and reporting by transferors for transfers of receivables, with recourse, that *purport to be sales* of receivables. It also applies to participation agreements (that is, transfers of specified interests in a particular receivable or pool of receivables) that provide for recourse. The statement specifically does not address accounting and reporting of loans collateralized by receivables, for which the receivables and the loans are reported on the borrower's balance sheet.

SFAS No. 77 also provides that a transfer of receivables with recourse shall be recognized as a sale only if all of the following conditions are met:

- The transferor surrenders control of the future economic benefits

[4]SFAS No. 77, paragraph 12.

embodied in the receivables. Control has not been surrendered if the transferor has an option to repurchase the receivables at a later date. However, a right of first refusal based on a bona fide offer by an unrelated third party is ordinarily not considered an option to repurchase.

- The transferor's obligation under the recourse provisions can be reasonably estimated. Lack of experience with receivables similar to those being transferred or other factors may impair the transferor's ability to make a reasonable estimate of the probable bad debt losses, and so on.
- The transferee cannot require the transferor to repurchase the receivables except pursuant to the recourse provisions. To keep the cost of servicing those receivables from becoming unreasonable, some transfer agreements require or permit the transferor to repurchase transferred receivables when the amount of outstanding receivables is minor. If those reversionary interests are not significant to the transferor, their existence alone does not preclude a transfer from being recognized as a sale.[5]

If a transfer meets all of the above requirements and, therefore, qualifies for recognition as a sale, the difference between the sales price and the net receivables must be recognized as a gain or loss on the sale of receivables.

One theme that recurs throughout the accounting literature in this area is that if the receivables are sold with servicing retained and the stated servicing rate differs materially from a current (normal) servicing fee rate, the sales price must be adjusted to provide for a normal servicing fee in each subsequent servicing period, which shall be not less than the estimated servicing costs. This is to prevent the transferor (seller) from reducing the amount of loss or increasing the gain recorded in the period of sale.

For transfers of receivables with recourse reported as sales, the transferor's (seller's) financial statements shall disclose (usually in the footnotes):

[5]SFAS No. 77, paragraph 5.

- The proceeds to the transferor during each period for which an income statement is presented
- The balance of the receivables transferred that remains uncollected at the date of each balance sheet presented, if such information is available

If any of the conditions of SFAS No. 77 are not met and, accordingly, the transaction does not qualify for recognition as a sale, the amount of the proceeds from the transfer of the receivables shall be reported as a liability.

Effect on Transactions

The desirability of application of SFAS No. 77 prior to the release of Technical Bulletin No. 85-2 was dictated by the composition of a given institution's portfolio. If the pledging of collateral to a trustee in the typical CMO issuance could be treated as a sale of the underlying mortgages, the entire amount of such debt could be removed from the balance sheet of the issuer, with gain or loss recognized on the sale. Thus, if an institution's portfolio consisted primarily of newly originated mortgages bearing market rates of interest, any gain or loss on the transaction would be minimal and the mortgage debt would be removed from the balance sheet. On the other hand, an entity whose portfolio consisted of older low-interest-rate mortgages would seek to avoid sales treatment under SFAS No. 77 because it would require the entity to recognize significant losses on the transaction.

In any event, it should be noted that the attempted application of SFAS No. 77 to CMOs ignores the language in the statement that limits its scope to transactions that purport to be sales of receivables. A collateralization, by definition, is not a sale and is significantly different from a sale in legal terms. Collateralization is the pledging of assets to secure an obligation; this point is repeatedly borne out in cases of bankruptcy. Accordingly, the FASB's position is that SFAS No. 77 should not apply to CMOs. This was later clarified when the FASB issued Technical Bulletin No. 85-2.

Whereas SFAS No. 77 provided some guidance for determining when sales should be accounted for as collateralized borrowings, Technical Bulletin No. 85-2 specifies when CMO debt instruments should be accounted for as sales of underlying collateral. In summary, it provides that CMOs should be presumed to be borrowings unless:

- All but a nominal portion of the future economic benefits inherent in the associated collateral have been irrevocably passed to the investor
- No affiliate of the issuer can be required to make future payments with respect to the obligation

The term "nominal," which is used in the Technical Bulletin to mean insignificantly small or trifling, implies a lower amount than that normally associated with materiality. Quantification of such nominal or trifling amounts, however, is a problem that continues to vex issuers and their accountants.

Expanding on the converse of the summary, the bulletin provides very specific details. The existence of *all* of the following conditions as of the date of issuance of the CMO would generally indicate that the borrowing presumption has been overcome, that the associated collateral should be eliminated from the issuer's balance sheet, and that gain or loss should be recognized:

- The issuer and its affiliates surrender the future economic benefits embodied in the collateral securing the obligation.
  —Neither the issuer nor its affiliates have the right or obligation to substitute collateral or obtain it by calling the obligation. Cleanup calls to keep the cost of servicing the underlying mortgage loans, relative to the remaining outstanding balances, from becoming unreasonable are permitted, provided that the amount of reacquired collateral is expected to be minor.
  —The expected residual interest, if any, in the collateral is nominal. The expected residual interest in the collateral should be computed using the present value of all amounts expected to revert to the issuer or its affiliates, including reinvestment earnings. Excess (above-normal) servicing fees should be considered part of the expected residual interest. This condition would not be met if an affiliate of the issuer retained a partial ownership interest in the mortgage-backed securities or mortgage loans that secure the obligation.

- No affiliate of the issuer can be required to make any future payments with respect to the obligation. The retention of servicing rights by an affiliate of the issuer does not, in itself, preclude the associated collateral from being eliminated from the balance sheet.
  —The investor can look only to the issuer's agents or third parties, such as insurers or guarantors, for repayment of both principal and interest on the obligation, and neither the sponsor of the issuer nor its other affiliates are secondarily liable.
  —Neither the issuer nor its affiliates can be required to redeem the obligation prior to its stated maturity, other than through the normal pay-through of collections from the collateral.[6]

Other Consequences of Sale Treatment

Other consequences of sale treatment are:

- If the associated collateral is eliminated from the balance sheet because all of the above conditions are met, any expected residual interest in the collateral—which, by definition, would have to be nominal—should not be recognized as an asset. Rather, such residual interest should be recorded as it accrues to the benefit of the issuer or its affiliates.
- Again present is the concept that if servicing rights are retained by an affiliate of the issuer and the stated servicing fee rate is less than a current (normal) servicing fee rate, the CMO proceeds should be adjusted to provide for a normal servicing fee in each subsequent servicing period. (See Technical Bulletin No. 87-3, discussed later in this chapter.)
- All transaction costs associated with the offering should be charged to expense when the associated collateral is eliminated from the balance sheet.

In addition to resolving the issue of the appropriate accounting treatment of the issuance of CMOs, Technical Bulletin No. 85-2 sets forth rules for consideration of a majority-owned issuer with its parent. These rules will be addressed later in this chapter.

[6]Technical Bulletin No. 85-2, paragraph 2.

Once Technical Bulletin No. 85-2 established ground rules for determining sale treatment versus financing treatment for CMOs issued by a minimally capitalized special-purpose subsidiary, financial institutions next raised the issue of sales treatment when an *unrelated* third party establishes the CMOs. The EITF addressed this issue in late 1986 and early 1987. The following fact situation is presented in EITF Issue No. 86-24:

> A financial institution sells mortgage loans to an unrelated third party that then uses the mortgages as collateral to issue collateralized mortgage obligations (CMOs) through an entity owned and controlled by the unrelated third party. As part of the transaction, the financial institution acquires the right to receive a defined portion of the total payments received from the mortgages in excess of the amount required to service the CMOs (hereafter referred to as the residual interest).[7]

The issues are (1) whether the transaction represents a sale of the mortgages from the viewpoint of the financial institution and, if so, (2) whether the pesent value of the expected residual cash flows to be received by the financial institution can be included in the computation of gain or loss on the sale.

The EITF reached a consensus that the sale of mortgages to an unrelated third party in the conditions described in the issue summary should be accounted for as a sale by the financial institution. Any gain or loss from the sale, including the present value of the residual interest *if it can be reliably estimated,* should be recognized in the period in which the transaction occurs. Most EITF members indicated that, because there was a legal sale, Technical Bulletin No. 85-2 did not apply and SFAS No. 77 should be consulted for guidance.

Notwithstanding the fact that a consensus was reached and, therefore, should be followed in practice, the FASB staff expressed its concern that such transactions are, in substance, financings. The EITF consensus was, therefore, brought to the FASB, which discussed the consensus and elected to address the issue as part of the recognition phase of the FASB's project on financial instruments, which is discussed later in this chapter.

[7]EITF Issue No. 86-24.

Another note of caution: The SEC observer present at the EITF meetings indicated that the SEC staff may challenge these transactions on a fact-specific basis if they are not reported in a manner consistent with their economic substance. Particular concern was expressed regarding the ability to reliably estimate the residual value.

Convertible, Adjustable-Rate Mortgages

The increasing popularity of convertible, adjustable-rate mortgages (CARMs) has added a new wrinkle to the accounting for certain asset securitizations, which was recently addressed by the EITF. In Issue No. 87-25, *Sale of Convertible, Adjustable-Rate Mortgages with Contingent Repayment Agreement,* the EITF was asked to consider the following transaction:

- A lending institution originates an adjustable rate mortgage that allows the mortgagor to convert the mortgage to a fixed-rate loan during a specified time period, provided that the mortgagor meets certain conditions and pays a conversion fee. The fixed-rate loan offered by the lending institution will have an interest rate that is *higher* than that of similar loans available to customers of the lender at the time of conversion.
- The CARM is transferred by the originator to a third party investor, and the originator continues to service the CARM in return for a normal servicing fee.
- The originator must repurchase the CARM at the remaining unpaid principal, plus accrued interest, if the mortgagor elects to convert the CARM to a fixed-rate loan.

Of course, the question presented was whether the transfer of the mortgages could be treated as a sale. The EITF did not reach a consensus; however, the majority of EITF members believed that sale treatment would be appropriate. However, the FASB staff believed that the transaction should be treated as a financing.

The SEC observer stated that if the transaction is accounted for as a sale and the CARMs are originated and sold simultaneously, the SEC staff would view the gain on the transfer as a commitment fee that should be deferred and amortized in accordance with the provisions of SFAS No. 91, *Accounting for Nonrefundable Fees and Costs Associated with Originating or Acquiring Loans and Initial Direct Costs of Leases.* He also stated that any gain on loans that is not transferred simultaneously should be teated similarly unless it is clearly evident that the gain results from changes in interest rates or credit risk.

Multiple-Class Pass-Through Certificates

In 1984, a new breed of pass-through certificates was formulated to combine the advantages to the issuer of a pass-through certificate with the marketing advantages of a CMO: the multiple-class pass-through certificate. Regulations issued by the Treasury Department in 1984 and published in final form in 1986 indicated that most forms of multiple-class pass-through trusts of this type, in which shifting of interest of the trust occurred as a result of prepayments, were to be treated as associations taxable at that level. Accordingly, tax considerations effectively killed this innovation. However, later REMIC legislation, enacted in 1986, made the issue moot.

The concept of the multiple-class pass-through certificate has some interesting accounting results. Despite being the functional equivalent of a CMO, the multiple-class pass-through certificate receives a completely different accounting treatment. As we just saw, CMOs are covered by Technical Bulletin No. 85-2 and are presumed to be collateralized borrowings. However, because a multiple-class pass-through certificate purports to be a sale, SFAS No. 77 provides that, as long as its requirements are met, sale treatment is appropriate.

In determining whether such multiple-class pass-throughs are structured as sales, an accountant should look to the disclosure document characterization. It is well recognized that attorneys are in the best position to determine whether the transaction is *legally a sale.* From the attorneys' point of view, sale characteriztaion is of paramount importance in the event of bankruptcy. However, the accountant should bear in mind that, for legal purposes, a true sale has occurred when there is *no significant recourse* to the seller. This position is to be contrasted with SFAS No. 77, which permits sale treatment, provided that the recourse provisions can be reliably estimated.

Conflicting Accounting Guidance

It is no wonder that accountants and others have struggled to determine the appropriate accounting treatment for asset-backed security transactions. Although the FASB has issued statements and Technical Bulletins that attempt to deal with the sale versus financing issue, the guidance provided has been disjointed and inconsistent. The FASB has vacillated in its approach to issues that are similar in concept—alternating between providing general, theoretical guidance and very specific, "cookbook" solutions.

- SFAS No. 77 and Technical Bulletin No. 85-2 seem to be in direct contrast to each other. As noted previously, SFAS No. 77 applies only to transfers of receivables that purport to be sales. Therefore, it does not apply to CMOs. SFAS No. 77 allows sale treatment even when there is 100 percent recourse to the transferor. This is true even if the transferor retains the risk of interest rate changes and the effect of prepayments. The transferor may also retain a substantial undivided interest in the receivables. When we contrast the liberal provisions of SFAS No. 77 with the strict criteria of Technical Bulletin No. 85-2, we see how little sense the two standards make. By structuring an asset-backed transaction as a borrowing, a transferor falls under the Technical Bulletin No. 85-2 umbrella and, therefore, must meet significantly stricter conditions to obtain sale treatment. Under Technical Bulletin No. 85-2, lack of recourse to the transferor is not sufficient to overcome the borrowing presumption; rather, the transferor must meet a lengthy list of conditions to obtain sale treatment, as previously described.
- SFAS No. 77 is also inconsistent with SFAS No. 76. Once again, SFAS No. 77 is more liberal with respect to sale treatment because such treatment is permitted even if future payments by the transferor are probable, as long as such payments are reasonably estimable. In contrast, SFAS No. 76 allows assets and debt to be considered extinguished only if the probability of future payments being made by the debtor is remote.
- SFAS No.76 is also inconsistent with Technical Bulletin No. 85-2. (This is especially troubling because Technical Bulletin No. 85-2 is effectively an interpretation of SFAS No. 76). Most CMO transac-

tions violate the provision of SFAS No. 76 that requires the timing of collection of interest and principal to be risk free, because most mortgages allow borrowers to prepay. Therefore, removal of debt from the balance sheet would be allowed in situations in which the borrower remains primarily obligated, but meets the criteria of SFAS No. 76. In contrast, a CMO transactions that relieves the borrower of all responsibility may have to be accounted for as a borrowing because of the possibility of prepayment.

The theoretical weakness in the FASB's approach has been its failure to consistently identify which criteria should govern the sale versus financing issue: Should the accounting be based on whether the entity has surrendered control over the assets in question or on whether the entity has effectively transferred the risks and rewards of ownership?

The Future

The FASB is currently working on a comprehensive long-term project on financial instruments. The first phase of the project dealt with disclosure about financial instruments and resulted in the issuance of an Exposure Draft of the same name in November 1987. The FASB is currently working on the second phase of the project, which deals with recognition and measurement.

The authors anticipate that the FASB will be forced to reconsider as part of this project all of the conclusions reached in the standards we have discussed in this chapter. Preparers of financial statements have thus far criticized these conclusions as both inconsistent and illogical.

The greatest fear that issuers of asset-backed securities have is that the FASB will reverse the position taken in SFAS No. 77. Many feel that the FASB believes that it "gave away the store" in that statement and will use this opportunity to increase the conditions that a transferor must meet to obtain sales treatment. In any case, the ultimate issuance of a statement is expected to have a very significant impact on future issuances of asset-backed securities.

Consolidation Issues

Among its accomplishments in resolving CMO accounting

issues, FASB Technical Bulletin No. 85-2 established rules for consolidation of a majority-owned issuer with its parent.

ARB No. 51, *Consolidated Financial Statements,* issued in 1959, has long provided the general guidance that there is a presumption that consolidated statements are more meaningful than separate statements and that they are usually necessary for a fair presentation when one of the companies in a group either directly or indirectly has a controlling financial interest in the companies.

FASB Technical Bulletin No. 85-2, (paragraph 3), states that because majority-owned entity that formed to issue the CMO is merely a *conduit* for the sponsor, the financial statements of that entity should be consolidated with those of its sponsor. Consistent with ARB No. 51, Technical Bulletin No. 85-2 does *not* require a parent company engaged in manufacturing operations to consolidate the accounts of an unconsolidated finance subsidiary that, in turn, consolidates the CMO issuer. This was one of several exceptions to the general rule in ARB No. 51 that required consolidation, which had become known as the nonhomogeneous operations exception. This exception had become the basis for excluding from consolidation the greatest number of majority-owned subsidiaries. Business enterprises have increasingly used nonhomogeneity as a basis for excluding from consolidation majority-owned (even wholly owned) subsidiaries considered different in character from the parent and its other affiliates. Subsidiaries most commonly not consolidated on that basis have been finance, insurance, real estate, and leasing subsidiaries of manufacturing and merchandising enterprises. This practice had been criticized because exclusion of some subsidiaries from consolidation results in the omission of significant amounts of assets, liabilities, revenues, and expenses from the consolidated statements of many enterprises. This perceived abuse, known as one aspect of off-balance-sheet financing, provided the stimulus for the issuance of SFAS No. 94, *Consolidation of All Majority-owned Subsidiaries,* in October 1987. SFAS No. 94 eliminates three of the exceptions to the general rule that majority-owned subsidiaries should be consolidated, including that for nonhomogeneous operations.

Accordingly, the exception provided in Technical Bulletin No. 85-2 has been eliminated, requiring even a parent company engaged in manufacturing operations to consolidate the finance subsidiary that, in turn, consolidates the CMO issuer. SFAS No. 94 is required to be applied for fiscal years ending after December 15, 1988, although early adoption is encouraged.

However, it is of interest to note tht SFAS No. 94 did *not* eliminate the exception to consolidation when control is likely to be temporary. The FASB has indicated, however, that consideration of this exception is deferred as part of its broader project on the reporting entity, including consolidations and the equity method.

Thus, as of this writing, another of the issues discussed by the EITF retains its applicability. In that issue, Issue No. 85-28, the EITF considered whether consolidation is required when a financial institution that forms a majority-owned subsidiary (the issuer) to issue CMOs, which are accounted for as borrowings on its balance sheet, expects to sell the issuer to an unrelated third party, but a specific sale has not been arranged. The EITF reached a consensus that consolidation would always be required if the subsidiary was formed by an institution that normally originates mortgages and then transfers those mortgages to the subsidiary.

The EITF failed to reach a consensus, however, as to whether consolidation would be required by an investment banker that does not normally originate mortgages and that establishes a special-purpose subsidiary to house the mortgages, if control is likely to be temporary.

Accounting for Loan Servicing

Servicing by Originator

As defined in paragraph 34 of SFAS No. 65, *Accounting for Certain Mortgage Banking Activities,* servicing of a loan includes collecting payments, forwarding payments and related accounting reports to investors, collecting escrow deposits, and disbursing escrow funds.

SFAS No. 65 recognizes that the right to service a loan is a function that has potential economic value. It states, "When servicing fees exceed the cost of performing servicing functions, the existing contractual right to service mortgage loans has economic value."[8]

SFAS No. 65 paragraph 11, also provides the authoritative accounting guidance with respect to servicing fees, as follows:

[8]SFAS No. 65, paragraph 2.

If a loan is sold with servicing retained by the seller and the stated servicing fee differs materially from a current (normal) servicing rate, the sales price shall be adjusted, for purposes of determining gain or loss on the sale, to provide for the recognition of a normal servicing fee in each subsequent year.[9]

Although the concept of reducing the sales price when a below-normal servicing fee is retained by a seller is very straightforward, mortgage bankers and accountants have struggled for some time with the question of what constitutes a normal service fee rate.

Federally sponsored secondary market makers for mortgage loans, such as the Government National Mortgage Association (GNMA), the Federal Home Loan Mortgage Corporation (FHLMC), and the Federal National Mortgage Association (FNMA), set minimum servicing fee rates for transactions with them. As early as 1985, the EITF considered the question of whether mortgage servicers should consider the servicing fee rate set by such organizations to be the minimum level for a normal servicing fee rate, as that term is used in SFAS No. 65. However, the EITF was unable to reach a consensus.

At the end of 1987, the FASB issued Technical Bulletin No. 87-3, *Accounting for Mortgage Servicing Fees and Rights,* which, it is hoped, will settle the issue once and for all. In the bulletin, the FASB staff concluded, "The rates set by GNMA, FHLMC and FNMA in servicing agreements *should* be considered a normal servicing fee rate for a transaction with those agencies." (Paragraph 3, emphasis added)

The FASB staff also provided guidance with respect to the servicing fee rate for loans sold directly to private sector investors:

- The seller/servicer should first select the federally sponsored secondary market maker whose servicing terms are most comparable to those specified in the servicing agreement.
- The seller/servicer should then select the rate used by that federally sponsored agency for loans similar to those sold under the servicing agreement.
- If the seller/servicer determines that the selected federally spon-

[9]SFAS No. 65, paragraph 11.

sored agency does not make a secondary market for the type of loans sold, the seller/servicer should use a similar process to select the predominant rate used by major private sector secondary market makers as the normal servicing fee rate for similar loans.[10] (Paragraph 6)

The rate determined through one of these methods is then compared with the *actual* rate specified in the sales agreement to determine whether the sales price should be adjusted as noted earlier.

A similar issue was discussed in EITF Issue No. 84-21, *Sale of a Loan with a Partial Participation Retained.* In that issue, the following scenario was presented to the EITF:

> An enterprise sells a loan to pay a yield below the face rate of the loan, thereby retaining a share in some of the interest income over the period that the loan remains outstanding.
>
> The question presented was whether the present value of the estimated future interest income stream should be recognized immediately in calculating a gain or loss on the sale or recognized over the life of the underlying loan.[11]

Although the EITF was unable to reach a consensus on the issue:

- Several members stated that immediate gain recognition is the predominant practice.
- The FASB staff representative pointed out that the *Savings and Loan Guide* specifically addresses the issue and requires gain treatment.
- The FASB staff representative said that the FASB staff believes that the amount of gain recognized on such a transaction should not exceed the gain that would be recognized if the loans were sold outright because any higher gain recognition would be evidence of unrealistically low prepayment estimates.

[10]Technical Bulletin No. 87-3, paragraph 6.

[11]EITF Issue No. 84-21.

Purchased Servicing

With respect to purchased servicing, SFAS No. 65 also states:

A. The right to service loans for other than an enterprise's own account is an intangible asset that may be acquired separately, in a purchase of loans, or in a business combination.
   1. The amount to be capitalized shall not exceed the amount by which the present value of estimated future servicing revenue exceeds the present value of expected future servicing costs. (Paragraph 18)
   2. The cost of this asset must be capitalized and amortized in proportion to, and over the period of, estimated net servicing income. (Paragraph 19)

B. Amortization of the amount capitalized must be adjusted for the effects of prepayments. (Paragraph 17)
   In an issue related to this requirement, the EITF concluded that such adjustments should be made prospectively, rather than retroactively.

C. When the loan is sold with servicing retained, the amount capitalized for servicing shall be reduced by any amount that the final sales price of the loans to the permanent investor exceeds the market value of the loans at the purchase date. (Paragraph 17)
   The intent of this provision is to require the mortgage banker to defer the income on a transaction such as this.[12]

It should be noted that the EITF has concluded that a literal reading of this clause is required. In Issue No. 86-39 *Gains from the Sale of Purchased Mortgage Loans,* The EITF considered the question of whether a gain on the sale of the loan (when servicing is retained) should be reduced and offset against the corresponding capitalized servicing rights when the gain arises solely due to a decrease in interest rates between the date on which the loan is purchased and the date on which the loan is sold. The EITF reached a consensus that the gain should be offset against the capitalized cost of servicing, irrespective of the reason for the gain.

Accounting for the Purchase of a Residual Interest

A residual interest represents the holder's right to receive cash payments over and above the amounts necessary to pay the primary

[12]SFAS No.65, paragraphs 17-19.

note holders. The purchase of a residual interest is actually the purchase of a future cash flow of uncertain amount and duration.

Purchased residuals have characteristics of both debt and equity, and the way in which the investor views the investment may have an effect on the accounting treatment. Currently, no authoritative accounting literature provides specific guidance on the accounting for an investment of this type.

The possible alternative accounting treatments will be examined from two perspectives: first, for entities that carry investments at market value or fair value and, then, for all others.

Investments Carried at Market Value or Fair Value

Entities that carry their investments at market value or fair value include investment companies (mutual funds), brokers and dealers in securities, pension plans, and banks (for their investment accounts). Fair value is defiend as the amount that a holder could reasonably expect to receive for an asset in a current sale between a willing buyer and a willing seller. Clearly, the market price of any asset is the most objective method of determining fair value. In the absence of an active market, fair value may need to be estimated using a valuation method, such as discounted cash flow.

Entities that carry their investments at market value or fair value would initially record their investment in a residual at cost and would, thereafter, adjust its value to market, with the offset recorded as a gain or loss.

Investments Not Carried at Market Value or Fair Value

Entities that do not use fair value have a more difficult time determining the proper accounting for an investment in a residual interest. Three common alternatives are:

- Lower of cost or market
- Equity method
- Constant yield method

The first two methods may be appropriate for entities that view their investment in a residual as an investment in an equity security, as opposed to a debt security, while the third would only be applicable if the investment is viewed as debt.

Lower of Cost or Market. Under this method, the investment is initially recorded at cost and is only adjusted if market value drops *below* that amount. Increases in market value are not recognized.

Equity Method. APB Opinion No. 18, *The Equity Method of Accounting for Investments in Common Stock,* applies only to investments in common stock and, therefore, does not technically apply to an investment in a residual interest. However, APB Opinion No. 18 does state that many of its provisions may be appropriate in accounting for investments in unincorporated entities, such as a trust. (For purposes of this discussion, it is assumed that the residual is in the form of a trust, as this has become a popular method.)

APB Opinion No. 18 requires the use of the equity method to account for investments in common stock, if the investor has the ability to exercise influence over operating and financial policies of the investee. This ability is assumed to exist for investments of 20 percent or more and is presumed not to exist for investments of less than 20 percent. These presumptions may be overcome by predominant evidence to the contrary. For example, most would agree that the sponsor of a trust would have significant influence over it, regardless of how small the investment may be.

Under the equity method, the investor would initially record the investment at cost. The carrying amount of the investment is subsequently adjusted for its pro rata share of the trust's income and expenses. The trust's income would include:

- Interest income
- Amortization of premium or discount on collateral
- Reinvestment earnings

Trust expenses would include:

- Interest expense
- Amortization of debt discount and issuance expenses
- Administrative expenses

Cash distribution from the trust would reduce the carrying amount of the investment. Any difference (excess) of the cost of the investment over the underlying equity in the net assets of the trust would have to be amortized over the life of the investment. The investment would be shown on the balance sheet of the investor as a single amount.

The advantage of the equity method is its simplicity. The investor does not need to make any calculations, as the trust would provide the investor with the amounts of income and cash dividends. This is in contrast to the constant yield method, discussed next, which requires numerous calculations.

Constant Yield Method. The constant yield method is clearly the most appropriate method for an entity that views its investment as a debt instrument. As its name implies, the objective of the method is to account for income earned on the residual as though it is earned based on a constant yield on the carrying amount of the investment, which would initially be cost. This is consistent with the accounting treatment for other types of interest-bearing investments.

To apply the constant yield method, the investor must first compute the internal rate of return (IRR) on the investment, which would be determined based on the investor's best estimate of the timing and of amounts of future cash flows from the residual. The IRR should be equal to a discount rate that, when applied to all expected future cash flows, would compute the price paid for the residual.

In each subsequent accounting period, the IRR would be applied to the carrying amount of the investment at the beginning of the period to calculate interest income, with an offsetting increase in the carrying value of the residual. Cash distributions received would reduce the carrying value of the residual.

Although, theoretically, the most supportable accounting method, the constant yield method is also the most difficult to apply, because it requires these calculations, as well as significant assumptions, such as those for prepayment rates, when estimating future cash flows. As differences will normally arise between estimated and actual amounts and timings of cash flows, the IRR will continually require adjustment.

SFAS No. 91 provides the current guidance for adjusting an IRR for the effect of changes in estimated cash flows. SFAS No. 91 requires that the IRR be recomputed, using the initial investment amount and the revised expected cash flows. The carrying amount of the investment is then adjusted to an amount that would have existed had the *revised* IRR been applied since acquisition of the residual.

Although SFAS No. 91 does not specifically address residual interests, the EITF recently reached a consensus that SFAS No. 91 *should* be followed for changes in cash flow estimates from interest-only certificates. As interest-only certificates and residual interests share common attributes—that is, they entitle the holder to an unspecified cash flow—the accounting for the two should be analogous. Accordingly, the provisions of SFAS No. 91 are also applicable to residual interests. Of course, regardless of which accounting treatment is employed, the ultimate return to the investor will be significantly affected by the rate of prepayments.

TAX CONSIDERATIONS

Pre-REMIC

Prior to the enactment of legislation creating the real estate mortgage investment conduit (REMIC) as part of the Tax Reform Act of 1986, accounting and tax considerations in the issuance of CMOs were in direct opposition. This conflict created significant stumbling blocks to successful offerings, which could often only be overcome through a sacrifice of profitability and efficiency, as other structures were developed to compensate for the accounting or tax restrictions.

As discussed in the section about Technical Bulletin No. 85-2, for an issuer to achieve sales treatment for accounting purposes and, thereby, remove the debt from its balance sheet, it must retain only a nominal portion of the future economic benefits inherent in the associated mortgage collateral. For tax purposes prior to REMIC, the retention by the issuer of only a nominal interest would preclude the classification of CMO securities as debt obligations of the issuer, thereby forcing sale treatment and resulting in taxable gain or loss to the issuer. However, perhaps the most serious pre-REMIC tax concern was the avoidance of double taxation, which could result if the pools of segregated assets were treated as an association taxed as a corporation.

At the issuer level, tax would be imposed if a grantor trust issued multiple-class mortgages or was actively managed. A second level of taxation would be imposed at the certificate holder level. The resultant inability to manage cash flows in the grantor trust structure left potential investors unprotected from redemptions caused by prepayments.

Post-REMIC

The REMIC device eliminated many of these tax constraints and provided the flexibility necessary for creating multi-class mortgage-backed securities, thereby permitting financial, regulatory, and securities law considerations to dominate planning and structuring.

The flexibility thereby afforded begins with the form of organization that a REMIC vehicle can adopt: A corporation, partnership, trust, or even a designated segregated set of accounts within the sponsor's accounting system can each elect REMIC treatment. Regardless of the organizational structure selected, an entity making the REMIC election must meet the following criteria to qualify as a REMIC:

- Substantially all of the segregated assets must be either (1) qualified mortgages secured by an interest in real property, including pass-through certificates, various stripped mortgage-backed securities, and senior/subordinated participations in mortgage pools, or (2) permitted investments, which include short-term interest-bearing instruments used to temporarily reinvest the cash flows from the underlying mortgages and certain long-term investments used to satisfy certain reserve fund and similar requirements.
- All interests in the entity must be either regular interests or residual interests. Like CMOs, the regular interests may be issued in multiple classes, but they need not be debt instruments. Regular interests may be in the form of common or preferred stock, partnership interests, trust interests, bonds, pass-through certificates, or participations. The regular interest must have a fixed interest rate and principal amount; however, the timing of the payment of the principal may be contingent on prepayments.

- The entity must have one—and only one—class of residual interests, and all distributions with respect to such interests must be made pro rata to its holders.

Under the REMIC provisions, no gain or loss is recognized by the transferor of property to a REMIC in exchange for regular or residual interests in the REMIC.

The flexibility that resulted from the removal of previously existing tax impediments by the REMIC legislation has sparked a new period of development in the secondary mortgage market.

OTHER SECURITIZED ASSET STRUCTURES

The majority of this chapter has focused almost exclusively on mortgage-backed securities. This is because of the predominance of CMOs and other mortgage-backed structures in the marketplace. However, significant innovations have been made in the securitization of such assets as:

- Automobile receivables
- Credit card receivables
- Cash surrender values of life insurance policies
- Home equity loans
- Equipment leases
- Taxicab medallions (hack-backed bonds)

Many of these, as well as others, are covered in detail in other chapters. However, some special considerations and distinctions of these other securitized asset structures should be mentioned here:

- REMIC legislation applies only to real estate transactions.
- Technical Bulletin No. 85-2 applies only to CMOs. Therefore, accounting rules for sales of receivables generally apply to these other asset-backed securities.

Remember that paragraph 5 of SFAS No. 77 requires, as one of the conditions for sales treatment, that the transferor's obligation under the recourse provisions can be reasonably estimated. This appears to be the most difficult provision for other asset-backed securities to meet.

Certain of the assets being pooled may not have a sufficient historical track record with respect to collectibility (including timing thereof). In some cases, the lack of homogeneity of the asset pool is another factor that complicates estimation of the transferor's obligation under the recourse provisions.

The effects of the recourse provisions prove especially difficult to estimate for credit card receivables. Because of the revolving nature of the receivables (substitution), cash flows are not identified as new receivables or old receivables. Due to the uncertainties involved, many large accounting firms have not allowed sale treatment for credit card receivables.

Before sale treatment can be condoned, each of these other securitized asset structures will have to be examined on a fact-specific basis to determine whether there is sufficient basis for estimating the transferor's obligation under the recourse provisions.

CONCLUSION

As explosive as the growth in asset securitization has been to date, the authors believe that we have seen only the beginning. The flexibility in structuring transactions that the REMIC legislation provides has unleashed the full creative talents of investment bankers and other players in the secondary mortgage market. In addition, the spread of asset-backed securitizations to previously unanticipated asset types is expected to result in a geometric increase in the volume of such issuances. The enhancements and variations that issuers use to achieve a competitive edge in the marketplace will, in all likelihood, challenge the limits of current generally accepted accounting principles.

The FASB has added to its agenda a comprehensive long-term project on financial instruments and off-balance-sheet financing arrangements. The first phase of this project has resulted in the issuance of an Exposure Draft addressing expanded disclosure of the risks inherent in such instruments and arrangements. Subsequent phases of the project are expected to deal with:

- Whether financial assets should be considered sold when there is recourse or some other continuing involvement
- The appropriate accounting for securities with both debt and equity characteristics
- The appropriate accounting for financial instruments and transactions that transfer market and credit risks

However, because the project is expected to take as many as three more years to complete, it is likely that the EITF will continue to play a leading role in providing guidance on the issues that are sure to confront the accounting profession in the interim.

CHAPTER 5

Systems Requirements for Asset-Backed Transactions

Stuart Lewtan with Lisa Fink and Lois C. Johnson

INTRODUCTION

This chapter will discuss the systems issues specific to the sale of automobile receivables. Most of the concepts apply to other types of consumer installment loans and, in some cases, securities backed by revolving debt. This chapter has two purposes: First, to highlight important systems issues, and, second, to identify and clarify some of the more difficult nuances of the concepts involved.

The systems issues addressed in an asset-backed transaction can be broken down into pretransaction functionality or ongoing servicing functionality. Pretransaction functionality includes portfolio analysis, conversions, pool selection, and structuring. Ongoing servicing functionality includes initial servicing, daily servicing, monthly servicing, and termination.

PRETRANSACTION FUNCTIONALITY

Before securitizing of assets is considered, the loan portfolio must be analyzed. Portfolio analysis is an effort to see the big picture.

This analysis provides information on trends, institutional posture, and potential value. This information is important for all parties involved in the transaction, including the rating agency, investors, and the underwriter, who performs due diligence on behalf of the investor.

Portfolio Analysis

The portfolio analysis determines several things. First, it determines what a company has to sell (demographics). It also determines the historical behavior of what it is selling (performance statistics). Finally, it determines the expected future behavior based on historical behavior (cash flow signature). Once these issues have been addressed, a company can create a structure based on the findings and subject that structure to a "stress test," with adverse scenarios based on the given projections.

Demographics

The first segment of the portfolio analysis is a demographic analysis. The objective is to categorize the type of loans in the portfolio. Analysis of the loans by state and zip code provides an excellent overview of the geographic concentration in the portfolio. A narrow and unevenly distributed concentration of loans increases the chances of event risk due to regional economic downturns or other acts of nature. On the other hand, a widely dispersed distribution of loans may signal a servicer that has spread itself too thin and, therefore, might be unable to service the portfolio effectively. (See Table 5-1.)

Another type of demographic analysis involves distributing the loans by annual percentage rate (APR). This provides insight into the credit quality of the portfolio. Statistically speaking, loans with higher APRs have been shown to have increased credit risk. (See Table 5-2.) A system can be designed to generate reports on the loans in a portfolio.

Performance Statistics

Besides studying the demographic distribution of the loans in a portfolio, the portfolio analysis also takes performance statistics into consideration.

Table 5-1. State Distribution for Issuer ABC Entire Active Portfolio Fitting Pool Selection Criteria*

State Name	*No. of Contracts*	*Percentage of Total Contracts*
Alabama	3	0.03%
Arizona	1	0.01
Arkansas	2	0.02
California	15	0.14
Colorado	2	0.02
Connecticut	5	0.05
Delaware	519	4.78
District of Columbia	380	3.50
Florida	22	0.20
Georgia	7	0.06
Illinois	2	0.02
Indiana	1	0.01
Iowa	1	0.01
Kansas	2	0.02
Maine	1	0.01
Maryland	7,434	68.47
Massachusetts	7	0.06
Michigan	2	0.02
Minnesota	2	0.02
Montana	1	0.01
Nebraska	1	0.01
Nevada	2	0.02
New Hampshire	1	0.01
New Jersey	21	0.19
New York	20	0.18
North Carolina	17	0.16
Ohio	6	0.06
Oklahoma	1	0.01
Pennsylvania	2,097	19.31
Rhode Island	3	0.03
South Carolina	3	0.03
Tennessee	4	0.04
Texas	8	0.07

Table 5-1. State Distribution for Issuer ABC
Entire Active Portfolio Fitting Pool Selection Criteria* (Continued)

State Name	*No. of Contracts*	*Percentage of Total Contracts*
Vermont	1	0.01
Virginia	245	2.26
Washington	3	0.03
West Virginia	3	0.03
Wisconsin	1	0.01
Other	12	0.11
Total	10,858	100.00%

*Pool criteria:
- Original term not greater than 60 months.
- Remaining balance not less than $1,000.
- Not currently 30 days overdue.
- Never been 90 days overdue.
- New cars only.
- APR not less than 5%.
- Remaining maturity of more than 6 months.
- No loans with balloon payments.
- Seasoned at least 90 days.

Performance statistics include figures on the number of charge-offs, delinquencies, and various weighted averages in the portfolio. These statistics not only provide extraordinary insight into the portfolio, but into the seller's skills in servicing that portfolio.

Cash Flow Signature

Each portfolio has unique cash flow idiosyncrasies. These peculiarities help to make up the cash flow signature, which is a graph of points that depicts the changes in principal as a percentage of the original principal. The objective is to identify a fingerprint for a portfolio from among the graphed points.

The cash flow signature is affected by the payments received on the portfolio. For example, consumer installment loans are usually designed to be paid in level monthly payments. In a perfect world, level monthly payments—no more, no less—arrive consistently on the same day of the month. However, the truth of the matter is that the borrower makes payments for any amount and at unpredictable

Table 5-2. APR Distribution for Issuer ABC
Entire Active Portfolio Fitting Pool Selection Criteria*

APR Range	*No. of Contracts*	*Percentage of Total Contracts*
Under 10.00%	1,297	11.95%
10.00–11.99%	5,609	51.66
12.00–13.99%	2,602	23.96
14.00–15.99%	778	7.17
16.00–17.99%	304	2.80
18.00–19.99%	140	1.29
20.00 and above	128	1.18
Total	10,858	100.00%
Lowest: 8.50%		
Highest: 23.00%		

Pool criteria:
- Original term not greater than 60 months.
- Remaining balance not less than $1,000.
- Not currently 30 days overdue.
- Never been 90 days overdue.
- New cars only.
- APR not less than 5%.
- Remaining maturity of more than 6 months.
- No loans with balloon payments.
- Seasoned at least 90 days.

times during the life of the loan. Therefore, payments can be classified by amount and time frame, such as partial payments, multiple payments, overpayments, prepayments, and nonexistent payments. These different types of payments affect the cash flow and influence the script of the cash flow signature. Furthermore, prepayment from the perspective of the originator is not the same as prepayment from the perspective of the investor. To the investor, in a typical pass-through structure, charge-offs and repurchases appear as prepayments, as do the usual insurance claims (for accidents), refinancings, and trade-ins, which represent types of prepayments.

To facilitate the cash flow signature in a simple form, analysts have developed prepayment statistics, such as the commonly used absolute prepayment rate (ABS) and conditional prepayment rate (CPR), which project cash flows. As these statistics can be generated algorithmically, they are much easier to use than a unique cash flow signature. In reality, these statistics could be considered straight-line or simple curve signatures. These statistics, which were borrowed from the mortgage markets, have three primary advantages: First, they are easily computed, compared with the sophisticated signature. Second, unlike the signature, they are easy to manipulate mathematically and are inherently extrapolated; third and most important, they are viewed in numeric instead of graphic form; thus, an investor can easily use them as benchmarks. For example, it would be easy for an investor to apply a fixture such as 1.3 percent ABS, as shown in Figure 5-1.

As convenient as ABS and CPR make cash flow projections, their simplistic nature makes them fall apart under certain scenarios. For example, ABS and CPR work well for projecting cash flows of automobile receivables. However, they do not hold water when projecting cash flows of marine loans.

Figure 5-2 shows the percentage of accounts closed due to normal amortization and prepayment across ten years in a portfolio of marine loans. Such a graph would be one component used to create an empirical cash flow signature. Although the scale of this slide is skewed by the enormous percentage of closures at the 120-month mark, spikes can be seen in most of the 12-month periods. These spikes can be attributed to the following causes:

- A very high percentage of marine loan originations are written in the same three-month period. In that same period, there is also a very high propensity for these loans to prepay. The reason for the accentuated seasonality should be intuitively obvious. In most geographic regions, boats are used primarily during only a third of the year.

- A great deal of upgrading is done each year.
- Losses on marine loans tend to be minimal, due to the affluent nature of the borrowers.
- Use of a simple signature to project future cash flows, instead of a more intricate spiked or sinusoidal signature, skews the results. What accentuates inaccuracies even more is that marine loans are generally written over a large span of original maturities. Sometimes a single portfolio contains original maturities ranging from 1

Figure 5-1. Measures of Prepayment

Mortgage Market Measures:

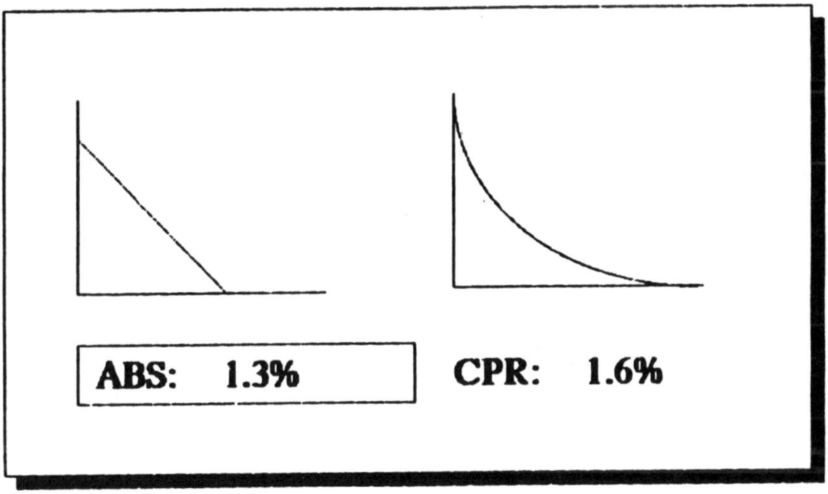

Lewtan Technologies Measures:

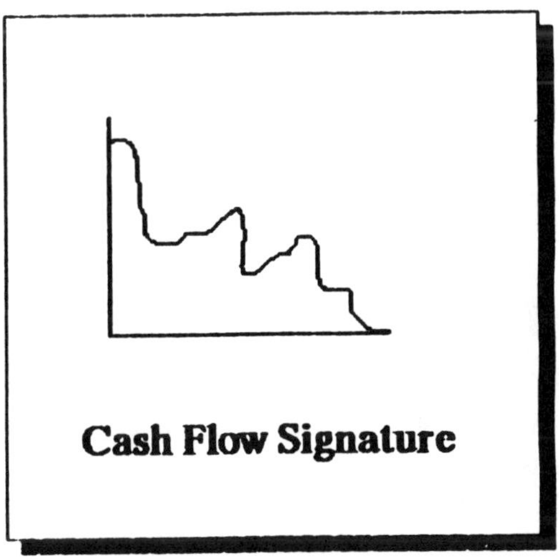

Figure 5-2. Cash Flow Signature

The Prepayment Component of the Cash Flow Signature

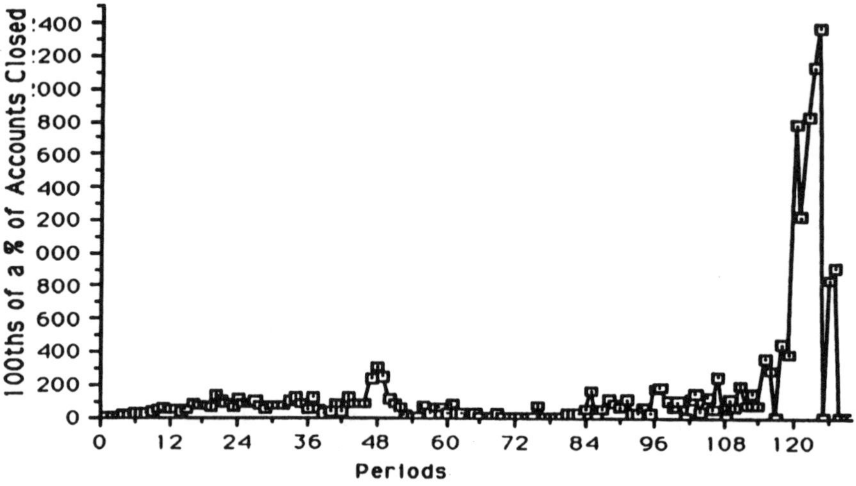

to 25 years. The danger of applying a generic formula signature across a range of maturities—and this does not apply only to boat loans—is that the natural maturities of loans appear as prepayments.

Notice the large spike in Figure 5-2 at 48 months. There happened to have been a large number of 48-month loans. If you derived an ABS or CPR for this portfolio, the normal closings on or near 48 months would appear to the statistic as a high propensity for 120-month loans to pay off at 48 months, when in reality these were only four-year loans reaching maturity. Prepayment statistics should not be applied to heterogeneous original maturities.

Conversions

Rule of 78 loans are precomputed interest loans that amortize at a slower rate than simple or actuarial accruals. The net effect is that Rule of 78 loans collect more of their interest up front. To facilitate most sales of these loans, a mathematical algorithm has to be applied to convert them into actuarial accruals. This is required because the interest rate to the investors is usually accrued on an actuarial basis.

This so-called conversion process occurs in the system and is entirely transparent to the borrower, whose payments remain the same regardless. The conversion can take place in one of two ways: Either the principal balance or the APR is modified from the perspective of the investor. It is important to remember that seasoned Rule of 78 loans have taken much of their interest up front and are not worth as much when they are converted to the actuarial basis.

Table 5-3 shows the losses in basis points when three loans are converted from the Rule of 78 basis to the actuarial basis. Each loan has an original balance of $10,000 and a 12 percent APR. The difference between each loan is in the stated maturity: The first loan is for three years, the second loan is for four years, and the third loan is for five years. The losses are quite dramatic at the two-year point for each loan, when losses approach 100 basis points.

Table 5-3: Losses Due to Conversion of Rule of 78 to Actuarial (Basis Points—Annualized)

Original balance = $10,000
12% APR

Stated Maturity (Months)		*Seasoning (Months)*			
	0	3	12	24	
36	0	13	25	48	92
48	0	13	25	49	94
60	0	13	26	50	95

One bonus to the seller is that prepayments on Rule of 78 loans are usually larger than the amount of principal required to be passed through to the investor. This happens because the borrower is making payments based on the larger outstandings of the slower Rule of 78 accruals, while the investor is being paid off based on an actuarial outstanding principal.

Figure 5-3 shows the delta between the balances of the same loan for the life of that loan amortized by the Rule of 78 method and amortized by the actuarial method. The amplitude of the hump represents the premium that the servicer retains if the obligor prepays at that point. The specific loan viewed here is a three-year loan at 12 percent APR, with an original balance of $10,000. The maximum differential appears around the one-year mark, with a delta of close to $35.

Figure 5-3. Delta Outstanding Balance Between Rule of 78 Method and Actuarial Amortization

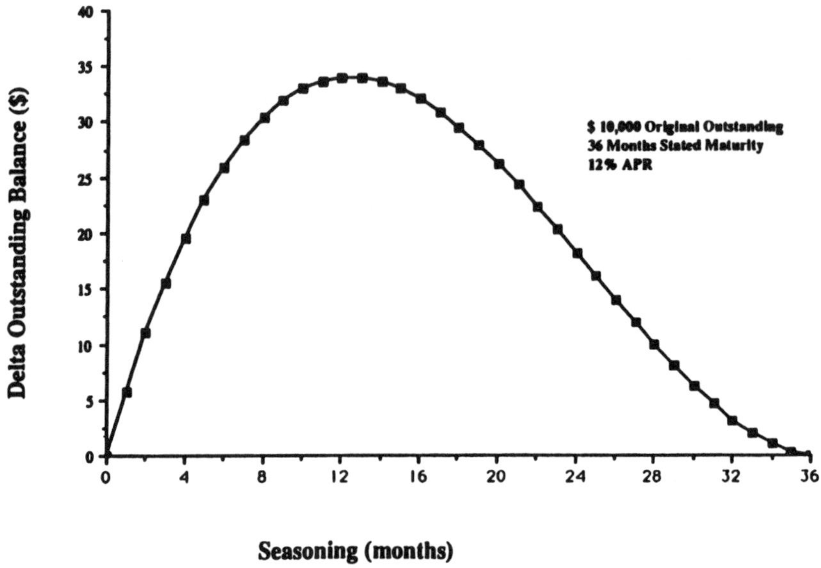

Pool Selection

Once the portfolio has been converted, the pool can be selected. This system allows you to select a pool based on three types of criteria: empirical requirements, filters, and optimization criteria. The steps in pool selection include filtering out unacceptable loans, ranking the remaining loans by the optimization criteria, and sorting through them until the empirical requirements are attained. Empirical requirements deal with the size of the pool. For example, an empirical requirement is $100 million. A Filter can be one exclusionary constraint or a series of exclusionary constraints joined together. For example, a filter can disqualify loans that are currently 30 days overdue, loans with balloon payments, loans that are not seasoned at least 90 days, or loans to employees or directors of the selling institution.

The optimization criteria used to select a pool are more esoteric than the empirical requirements and filters. During the optimization process, the filtered loans are ranked and the highest-ranked loans are selected to be in the pool. The system achieves this order by numerically ordering—from highest to lowest—the loans on a designated field. For example, an optimization criterion could be the highest weighted-average life. Depending on a number of circumstances, taking the highest ranked loans from the portfolio—a practice referred to as cherry picking—may not be acceptable.

Structuring

The next step is to structure a transaction that will stand on its own. The system structure can be broken down into special considerations, reserve account and credit enhancement vehicles, and cash flow projections.

It is in the best interest of the servicer to structure the deal with an eye toward how the structure will translate into a system. For example, once a company has determined what the special considerations are and how to account for them, it must design a system that is as firm a foundation as the structure that it supports.

Special Considerations

Actuarial and Rule of 78 loans are written so that borrowers are required to pay interest through the end of the given month, regardless of when the payment came in. On the other hand, simple interest loans accrue interest from payment to payment. Thus, a payment coming in on the twentieth of the month will only be paying 20 days' worth of interest at the balance, but the investor still has to be paid for the full month. To correctly structure an asset-backed deal for simple interest loans, provisions sometimes have to be made for the servicer to advance the missing interest components to the investor. Usually, the servicer recoups interest advances to the investors on the subsequent payment. When a loan is paid off, however, the seller will never be reimbursed the advanced interest component for the final month. Part of the monthly servicing fee is designed to compensate the servicer for the use of the funds being advanced, plus funds that will never be reimbursed. By the same token, the system designed for the deal must be able to keep track of these complicated advances, recoveries, and nonreimbursable payments and able to produce indicative reports. (See Figure 5-4.)

Figure 5-4. Interest Components

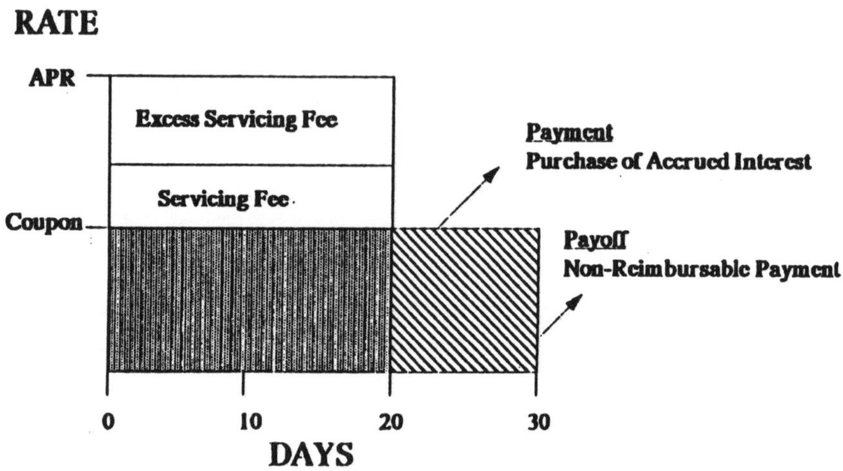

Reserve Accounts/Credit Enhancement

For most transactions, the systems must be able to accommodate the flow of funds to and from the credit enhancement vehicle. Typically, credit enhancement is buffered by a reserve account. The excess servicing fee, seen in the chart as the amount of interest above the coupon rate and servicing fee, is funnelled into the reserve account each month. Other functions associated with these credit enhancement vehicles include their being drawn on for cash shortfalls that may occur and their overflow being skimmed when the reserve account reaches certain prespecified levels. (See Figure 5-4.) This area of securitization has experienced the most creativity and the greatest number of variations in structures, as well as systems that facilitate these structures.

Cash Flow Projections (Stress Testing)

Once a pool has been selected for potential sale, cash flows are projected based on those loans by extrapolating the cash flow signature derived during the portfolio analysis. The objective of the projections is to determine the expected amount of interest and principal payments throughout the life of the security, while taking into account all of the components of the cash flow signature. Table 5-4 provides an example of cash flow projections. These projections should be run under a variety of scenarios to stress test the structure—that is, increase deliquencies, charge-offs, and so on, over multiple historical peaks. For example, if historical charge-offs have been 50 basis points, scenarios should be run at 25, 50, 75, 100, 150, and 200 basis points. The outputs of these adverse cash flow scenarios will be useful in the structuring stage to test if the structure—particularly the credit enhancement vehicle—will stand up under unusual circumstances.

Table 5-4. Extrapolated Cash Flow Signature

Prepayment: 1.3% ABS
Charge-offs: 2.0%
Delinquencies: 3.0%

Month	*Pool Balance*	*Cash Flow*	*Delinq.*	*Charge-Offs*	*Reserve Balance*	*Balance Letter of Credit*
17	$30,363,497	$1,700,318	$58,000	$15,080	$1,230,000	$1,700,980
18	28,111,376	1,680,200	57,107	15,001	1,200,980	1,689,830
19	27,435,998	1,500,170	52,363	14,898	1,280,760	1,675,570

ONGOING SERVICING FUNCTIONALITY

Once a security has been determined and sold, the asset-backed security system has to provide a way to address the ongoing servicing functionalities, which can be categorized as initial, daily, and monthly. Although existing consumer installment loan systems may handle all of the processing, monitoring, and allocating for a portfolio of loans, these systems cannot support the servicing of most asset-backed transaction. Securitization requires a much more robust type of system. Such a system must be able to isolate a pool of loans, segregate payments that apply to those loans, allocate funds to facilitate the various vehicles within the structure, and produce coherent reports for all concerned parties.

Initial

Even before ongoing servicing begins, the system must address a number of initial servicing responsibilities. First, it must flag all loans that were selected to be part of the pool. This ensures that all transactions associated with the loans in the pool can be identified as such. Conversion from the Rule of 78 method to the actuarial method is required here as well.

Daily

On any given day, the system must segregate funds that apply to a sold pool of loans from funds collected for unsold loans. These sold loan payments must then be funnelled into a collection account. This segregation insulates the investors from the risk of the servicer becoming insolvent and having the funds frozen with its other assets.

In addition to the usual segregations, the system must also take into account unusual payment allocations, which may appear at any point in the life of the security. Some of the more usual, but less commonly considered, anomalies follow.

Forced Placed Insurance

It is generally required that a borrower maintain insurance on the vehicle throughout the life of the loan. If this insurance lapses, the lending institution has the right to purchase insurance for the borrower and tag the premium of the insurance onto the note amount.

Understandably, the investor will not want to purchase the price of the premium. (It is generally accepted that any borrower who allows insurance to lapse is not one of the more creditworthy obligors in the pool.) The result is that two separate balances have to be maintained. One tracks the balance with the premium for the servicers' remittances, and the other tracks the net of the premium for the investors' remittances.

Reversals

Reversals take place when an account is credited for a payment that is later determined to be incorrect. The most common case of a reversal is a bounced check. The difficulty arises when such payments are forwarded to the investors before the reversal is discovered: The servicer cannot ask for the money back from the investors. Other methods have to be used to rectify the discrepancy.

Charge-Offs

When a borrower is delinquent for x number of days, the credit enhancement vehicle must buy the loans out of the pool.

Repurchases

When a loan has breached the servicing agreement, the servicer is obligated to repurchase that loan from the pool. A breached loan is one whose payment is received within 30 days of the cutoff date, in compliance with the servicing agreement, but then bounces, not in compliance with the servicing agreement.

Holiday Programs and Extensions

Holiday programs are designed to allow obligors to skip a payment near the holiday season. These can have a whiplash effect on the credit enhancement covering the shortfall of cash. Also, many lending institutions allow extensions, which must be accounted for.

Monthly

In addition to daily ongoing functionality, monthly ongoing servicing must be performed. Every month, on an account-by-account basis, the system calculates the principal, interest, prepaid principal, charge-off amounts, late charges, and other pertinent amounts. These are called account-level allocations. Once these account-level allocations are computed, they are rolled up to a pool level and are allocated to the various system-holding accounts as dictated by the structure of the transaction.

After the account- and pool-level allocations are processed, the reports required by all parties involved in the transaction are generated. Examples of these reports include originator reports, credit enhancement reports, rating agency reports, trustee reports, and certificate holder reports. (Table 5-5 shows one of the simpler reports generated by such a system.)

Table 5-5. Certificate Holder Report
Effective Date 00/00/00
Pool Number AAA

Remittances

Based on 90% senior tranche supported by 10% subordinated tranche, the amounts are per $1,000 original outstandings of 90% tranche.

Monthly Principal	
Regular principal payments	$
Principal prepayments	$
Delinquent principal advanced	$
Other prepayments (repurchases, breaches, etc.)	$
Total principal	$
Monthly interest	
Regular interest payments	$
Delinquent interest advanced	$
Total interest	$
Total certificate holder	$

Pool Balances and Statistics

Based on 90% senior tranche supported by 10% subordinated tranche.

90% of previous payment period's principal balance	$
−90% of principal	
90% of principal balance	$
Number of accrual periods spanned by payment period	
Earned interest factor of first accrual period in current payment period	
Pool factor	

CONCLUSION

Asset-backed securitization programs should be commenced by addressing the following questions: What do I have to sell? What do I want to sell? What will be the future behavior of what I am selling? How will I structure the deal? How will I service the transaction in the long run? How will I account for loans that do not behave as expected? As overwhelming as this may sound, once identified, solutions can be implemented. Basically, if you were to take a pooling and servicing agreement, add diagrams, insert formulas, and strip out 80 percent of the verbiage, you would have a system specification for a securitization system. Of course, before attempting this, you should consult with experts on this subject.

Inclusion of this system into a securitization program enables more lucrative deals to be completed more quickly. The system chosen should be flexible enough to account for changing structures and unlikely circumstances and should have a dedicated support staff throughout the entire life of the transaction.

Remember, this system is an integral part of any securitization program. The design of an effective asset-backed security system requires true understanding of both the financial and systems issues. By integrating this system into securitization plans and uniting financial and system forces during the embryonic stages of the program, the institution ensures its competitiveness in this evolving market.

CHAPTER 6

Credit Enhancement for Asset-Backed Transactions

Russell B. Brewer II and Linda S. Iseley

INTRODUCTION

Credit enhancement has been an essential catalyst to the phenomenal growth of the market for asset-backed securities. As the market has grown to include a broader range of issuers and investors, asset-backed transactions have become more complex and more difficult to analyze without specialized expertise. Credit enhancement addresses these concerns. It facilitates the securitization process and provides a measure of homogeneity to the market.

In fact, during the first half of 1988, nearly 100 percent of the dollar volume of new publicly issued asset-backed securities relied on some form of credit support. In 83 percent of these transactions, credit support was provided by a third party unrelated to the issuer of the securities.

This chapter begins with an overview of the role played by credit enhancement in the asset-backed security market. It goes on to describe the various forms of credit protection available in the market. Finally, it illustrates how particular forms of credit enhancement are used to meet specific issuer objectives. Although the last section takes the issuer's viewpoint with respect to certain credit enhancement objectives, investors will find it of interest as many of these objectives have critical implications for them.

One preliminary note: All references to issuers in this discussion refer to the companies or agencies that benefit from these securitizations, rather than the special-purpose entities, such as trusts and special-purpose corporations, that function as conduit vehicles.

AN OVERVIEW OF CREDIT ENHANCEMENT

Credit enhancement is not a new concept. For decades, individuals and corporations have provided various forms of credit support to lenders. These supports, which have included personal guarantees, comfort letters, and net worth maintenance agreements, have enabled borrowers to secure more attractive lending rates by simplifying complex securities and attracting the broadest possible investor market.

However, the process of securitizing assets does not represent an opportunity for issuers to transfer the true credit risk of an asset pool to an independent credit enhancer. In virtually all asset-backed securities, the issuer provides some form of "first-loss" protection. This protection may be either extended directly to investors—as overcollateralization, for example—or extended indirectly to investors through a third party credit enhancer.

In the latter case, the issuer will provide the credit enhancer with an amount of first-loss protection sufficient to cover all but the most remote risks. The credit enhancer, in turn, will "wrap" this first-loss amount with its own guarantee to investors. Often, the enhancer will provide a further guarantee for as much as the full value of the issue. The guaranteed security will trade primarily on the basis of the guarantor's credit rating—not the rating of either the issuer or the underlying assets. This pricing advantage is the value added by the third party credit enhancement.

In general, credit enhancement serves two broad purposes. First, it plays an intermediation role—bridging the gap between the limitations of the issuer and the demands of the investor. In transactions as complex as public asset-backed securities, the credit quality and cash flow characteristics of a given asset pool will rarely match exactly the investors' objectives. Issuers will have to either pay investors a premium to induce them to accept securities in this unattractive form or modify the characteristics of the securities to better match investor requirements. Credit enhancement is a tool that helps to bridge this gap—enabling issues to be structured with the cash flow timing and certainty that investors require, while retaining the flexibility that issuers need to meet accounting, regulatory, and funding goals.

For example, for commercial banks to receive sale treatment for securitizations of nonmortgage assets under regulatory accounting rules, they must limit their recourse in the transaction to the future spread income on the assets. In most cases, the amount of recourse protection offered by future spread income is insufficient for the transaction to obtain top credit ratings, irrespective of the credit-worthiness of the commercial bank issuers. As a result, issuers of these types of securities have three options: (1) pay the premium demanded by investors for securities with lower credit ratings, (2) provide recourse in excess of the available amount of spread income and forgo regulatory accounting sale treatment, or (3) use third party credit enhancement to bridge the gap between the amount of recourse provided by the future spread and the amount of recourse demanded by the market for top credit ratings. Given these three choices, it is not difficult to understand the value of third party credit enhancement.

Second, credit enhancement provides an analytical service for investors. Most securitizations are complex financings that involve a host of parties—trustees, sellers, servicers, custodians, and so on—and a myriad of underlying assumptions, opinions, representations, warranties, and the like. Each of these parties and each of these underlying provisions represents a risk, to some degree, for investors, which should be evaluated. Yet, it is a costly process for each individual investor to complete this analysis independently, assuming that he or she has access to the necessary information.

Unlike an individual investor, who will most likely invest in only a portion of an issue, the credit enhancer is putting its capital at risk against the total financing. Therefore, it can afford to do the in-depth analysis required to understand thoroughly each issue affecting the performance of the transaction.

When most investors think of structured financing risks, they think of credit quality risks. Will there be defaults? When will they occur? How high will delinquencies run? Will there be recoveries? These are the types of risks that stem from the credit quality of the underlying assets. While they do represent real exposures for investors, they are fairly easily evaluated and controlled. Historical performance data and sophisticated mathematical techniques for analyzing these data are widely available.

On the other hand, investors in an asset-backed security invest only indirectly in the underlying assets. They invest directly in the structure that repackages those assets. In short, even though the assets perform as anticipated and the credit quality risks are fully covered, the investment can still collapse if the securitization structure fails. The risks that can lead to such failure are known as securitization risks. The credit enhancer may have special qualifications to evaluate these risks, and, as a party to the transaction, is in a position to minimize many of them. Some of the more common securitization risks inherent in any asset-backed security include (1) the credit quality of the key participants to the transaction (such as the servicer), (2) the strength of the legal structure designed to protect investors from any bankruptcy risks, and (3) the possibility of fraud. Credit enhancement protects investors against not only asset quality risk, but also a variety of securitization risks. Moreover, it affords protection against securitization risks that are identified at the outset of a transaction, as well as against those that may develop during the life of the financing.

PRIMARY FORMS OF CREDIT ENHANCEMENT

The three primary forms of credit enhancement in the asset-backed securities market are: (1) issuer-provided enhancement, (2) third party partial enhancement, and (3) third party full enhancement. Each of these forms offers varying levels of protection to investors and poses different analytical challenges.

Issuer-Provided Enhancement

One of the first forms of credit enhancement used in the asset-backed security market—issuer-provided enhancement—was introduced in the public market by General Motors Acceptance Corporation (GMAC) in 1985. GMAC packaged its automobile loans into securities backed by limited recourse to General Motors for defaults on the underlying loans. Issuer-provided enhancement generally takes one of two forms: direct recourse or overcollateralization. Each of these forms of issuer protection accomplishes the same basic objective: It reduces investors' exposure to the credit risks associated with a pool of assets based on an estimate of the behavior of that pool under a variety of economic circumstances.

Direct recourse is a general, unsecured obligation of the issuer. Structurally, it is the simplest form of enhancement that an issuer can provide. However, it is the most difficult form of issuer enhancement for an investor to evaluate. First, the investor must analyze and understand the strengths and weaknesses of the issuer. Then, the investor must factor into this analysis any correlation of risks that exists between the pool of assets being securitized and the credit quality of the issuer providing the recourse. For example, if, as in many cases, the issuer's primary business is generating and servicing the type of asset that has been securitized, a deterioration in that asset type could negatively affect all of the issuer's business. The result: an erosion of the recourse protection precisely when it is likely to be called on.

On the other hand, overcollateralization is a secured form of issuer enhancement that provides excess collateral to cover a percentage of deterioration in the underlying assets. It is most often used when the issuer is unrated or rated below investment grade. Overcollateralization is somewhat easier for investors to evaluate because the credit protection provided is reasonably isolated from the general operating risks of the issuer. However, this form of enhancement is also subject to a certain correlation of risks. If asset quality in a securitized pool deteriorates to the point at which investors must rely on the overcollateralization, it is very likely that this protection will also be experiencing deterioration. Thus, in the evaluation of the amount of protection that a given amount of overcollateralization truly provides, the potential cash flow diminution of the entire pool, including the overcollateralization, must be estimated.

Third Party Partial Enhancement

Third party partial enhancement can take the form of either a first-loss letter of credit or a first-loss surety bond. Both forms are typically provided by highly rated financial institutions, which may be either fully or partially dedicated to the credit enhancement business. As the name implies, first-loss credit enhancement covers less than 100 percent of the potential credit risk. In other words, investors are protected against only the first x dollars of loss. As in issuer-provided enhancement, the objective of this type of enhancement is to reduce investors' exposure to the credit risks associated with a pool of assets, based on an estimate of the performance characteristics of that pool in a variety of economic scenarios.

Third party partial enhancement is not subject to the same correlation of risks that issuer-provided enhancement is because the credit quality of the third party is generally unrelated to the credit quality of the assets being enhanced. Yet, it is still relatively difficult for investors to evaluate because they must assess not only the strength of the third party provider, but also the adequacy of the size of the first-loss protection.

In most public asset-backed securitizations, the amount of the first-loss protection is determined in conjunction with rating agency standards for the desired rating level and is designed to absorb some multiple of historic losses. AAA ratings can be obtained with less than 100 percent coverage, based on the assumption that even under adverse conditions, losses on a pool of assets will not approach 100 percent, but will be limited to some lower statistically derived level. Although the amount of such protection is intended to cover 100 percent of estimated losses, actual losses can, of course, exceed the available protection. In such cases, the unanticipated losses are borne by the investors.

To date, no transactions in the relatively young public asset-backed securities market have experienced losses in excess of their first-loss policies. However, this precedent has been clearly established in the secured lending industry, which predates the development of the securitized market. For example, in the 1970s, a major insurance company provided asset-based financing to a well-known firm, using "high-quality" secured agricultural loans as its protection. The transaction was structured to withstand in excess of ten times historical charge-offs. However, historical performance proved to be a poor estimate of potential losses, and charge-offs exceeded ten times historical levels by a very significant amount. The insurance company in this case suffered substantial losses and ultimately withdrew from lending to this market.

Third Party Full Enhancement

Third party full enhancement in the form of 100 percent letters of credit or 100 percent surety bond guarantees assure investors of the timely payment of full principal and interest. Full enhancement differs significantly from the other forms of credit enhancement previously discussed in that its objective is not to *reduce* an investor's exposure to the credit risks in a pool of assets, but rather to *eliminate* it.

Third party full credit enhancement—the most straightforward form of credit protection—is the easiest form for investors to analyze because evaluation of the adequacy of the amount of credit protection or of the exact credit characteristics of the underlying asset pool is unnecessary. Only the creditworthiness of the party that provides the enhancement needs to be evaluated. Moreover, as with third party partial enhancement, the creditworthiness of the provider of the enhancement is generally not significantly correlated with the performance of any specific pool of assets that underlies any single transaction. Overall, third party full enhancement offers investors the greatest protection because all credit losses are covered.

THE ROLE OF CREDIT ENHANCEMENT IN MEETING USER OBJECTIVES

Credit enhancement is a multidimensional tool that enables issuers to maximize the financial benefits of a securitization, while, at the same time, accommodating the diverse nonfinancial considerations that impact any financing decision. Issuers use credit enhancement to achieve (1) rating objectives, (2) balance sheet objectives, (3) cost savings, (4) funding diversification, and (5) downgrade protection, among other things.

Rating Objectives

The public asset-backed security market is almost exclusively a highly rated market. The overwhelming majority of all new public asset-backed financings are rated in one of the top two rating categories by at least one nationally recognized rating agency. Yet, the majority of the issuers of these securities are, themselves, rated below this level. It is through credit enhancement that such lower-rated companies have been able to issue top-rated securities.

The rating of a credit-enhanced asset-backed security is somewhat unique. It is not simply a reflection of the creditworthiness of the issuer of the security, nor is it a direct function of the rating of the entity that provides the credit enhancement. It is a more complex assessment of the overall strength of the enhanced instrument, based on both the amount of credit enhancement provided and the form of credit enhancement used.

In rating asset-backed securities, rating agencies first determine the amount of credit protection necessary to achieve a specific rating. The higher the rating desired by the issuer, the greater the level of required protection. The rating agencies then analyze the form of credit enhancement employed to determine (1) the aggregate amount of protection available to investors and (2) the strength of that protection. In issuer-provided credit enhancement, the rating is influenced by how isolated the investors' credit protection is from the general creditworthiness of the issuer. In issuer-provided direct recourse, the rating on the enhanced security can be no higher than the rating of the issuer because the protection represents an unsecured obligation of the issuer. Alternatively, in the case of overcollateralization, the rating on the enhanced instrument can exceed the rating of the issuer because the protection provided represents a secured obligation isolated from the general credit quality of the issuer.

Overcollateralization, however, is not always isolated from deterioration of the issuer's credit quality. If the issuer deteriorates to the point of bankruptcy, overcollateralization levels may be reduced, replaced, or even removed at the discretion of the issuer's bankruptcy judge. This is not a frequent occurrence, but such actions have been taken in the past to the detriment of the parties that rely on this type of protection.

With third party full credit enhancement, the investors' credit protection is truly isolated from the creditworthiness of the issuer, even in the event of the issuer's bankruptcy. Therefore, securities backed by this form of credit enhancement are rated without regard to the issuer's rating. Instead, they are rated based on the rating of the third party credit enhancer.

Balance Sheet Objectives

One of the primary reasons that issuers turn to asset securitization is to improve their balance sheets. The two most common types of improvement sought are (1) greater liquidity and (2) reduced leverage. The extent to which each of these objectives can be achieved depends, in part, on the form of credit enhancement that is used in the securitization.

Of the two objectives, liquidity is less sensitive to the form of enhancement used in a transaction than is leverage. By definition, securitization is a process that liquifies future financial claims. Thus, irrespective of the form of enhancement used, all securitizations improve an issuer's liquidity to some degree. Only the extent of this improvement is influenced by the type of security issued and the form of credit enhancement used. Transactions that are structured to generate 100 cents per dollar of asset provide the maximum liquidity benefit. Structures that require the transfer of assets at an effective discount provide a reduced liquidity benefit. In general, if we assume acceptable asset quality, assets may be securitized at par using either third party credit enhancement or direct recourse. Overcollateralization creates discount liquidation rates and, therefore, offers a somewhat reduced liquidity benefit.

Although the liquidity impact of an asset securitization on an issuer's balance sheet is a matter of degree, the leverage impact on the balance sheet is more clearly defined. Either the assets are sold for accounting purposes or they are not. Accordingly, the impact of credit enhancement on the issuer's leverage can be similarly dramatic. Either the form and amount of protection are consistent with "sale treatment" or they are not. In most cases, sale treatment can be obtained with either form of third party credit enhancement, irrespective of the amount of such enhancement. However, in the case of issuer-provided enhancement, sale treatment may be possible only when the amount of protection provided and retained by the issuer falls within certain limited and estimable levels. As noted earlier, in the case of commercial banks, the ability to achieve sale treatment with issuer-provided enhancement is further reduced by strict regulatory accounting sale rules.

Cost Savings of Credit Enhancement

The third major factor that influences the choice of credit enhancement is the all-in cost savings achieved. This factor is a combination of several variables, including the cost of the enhancement, the tangible and intangible benefits offered by the form and provider of the enhancement, and the pricing of the enhanced securities.

Of these variables, the cost of the enhancement is easiest to assess, because it is both objective and easily compared. In general, credit enhancement is priced as an annual percentage of the par value exposure of the enhancer. It is payable either up front (on a present-value basis for multiple-year transactions) or in periodic installments over the life of the transaction.

The direct and indirect savings of a particular form of credit enhancement are also relatively easily assessed. In the direct category, issuers should examine the collateral and structural flexibility that a particular form and provider of credit enhancement provide. At a minimum, they should consider: (1) What forms of first-loss protection are acceptable to the enhancer? (2) What amount of fundamental credit risk must be borne by the issuer? (3) Will the issuer be able to retain the use of transaction funds until their required distribution to investors—the so-called commingling benefit?

Example: When the assets are unusual for the asset-backed market, a provider of 100 percent credit enhancement that is familiar with the nature of those assets will usually require less collateral than is standard for an uninsured bond of the same rating. The issuer gains this flexibility because the rating of a 100 percent–guaranteed security is largely independent of the issuer and the underlying pool of assets. In other words, this form of credit enhancement does not require every element of the transaction to be structured to the same rating level as the instrument itself.

In the indirect category, issuers will want to examine the services that various credit enhancers offer. For example, some credit enhancers handle the rating process independently, arranging for the delivery of all required rating letters at closing. Others require issuers to obtain any desired rating letters themselves. Also, some credit enhancers have marketing staffs available, at no additional cost, to work with the issuer (and its investment banker) to optimally market the enhanced securities.

The pricing that a security can be expected to achieve with various credit enhancement alternatives is the most difficult variable to assess because its actual trading value depends on many subjective elements, including investors' prepayment expectations. To estimate pricing, issuers must rely on existing indicators and certain general rules. The top two existing indicators that should be examined are (1) where similar securities have priced in the market, after adjusting, of course, for market movements, and (2) where securities guaranteed by that particular credit enhancer have priced in the market. Three general rules that should be applied are: (1) The higher the ratings on the enhanced instrument, the better the pricing; (2) The greater the secondary market liquidity, the better the pricing; and (3) The simpler the investment decision, the better the pricing.

Funding Diversification

Two important advantages that third party–provided credit enhancement has over issuer-provided support are that it allows issuers to raise money without relying on their traditional sources of funding and without increasing their "name in the market" exposure. Moreover, third party enhancement not only gives issuers access to new classes of investors, but it also enables them to access several different classes of investors with the same instrument. For example, credit enhancement can facilitate the construction of multiple-class securities, each class of which is structured to address the investing preferences of a different investor population. It can also improve the market pricing of the issuer's existing funding programs by decreasing market saturation in the issuer's name. As issuers continue to turn to the capital markets to meet their financial needs, funding diversification through credit enhancement is likely to become an increasingly important consideration.

Downgrade Protection

Downgrade protection refers to protection against the possibility of a security's rating being downgraded once it is in the market. When an outstanding security is downgraded, an issuer's image can be tarnished by the drop in secondary market liquidity, and its interest cost can increase to the extent that the security bears a floating rate of interest.

The amount of downgrade protection that credit enhancement provides depends on whether the securities are backed by partial credit enhancement or full credit enhancement. In the case of securities backed by partial credit enhancement (whether provided by issuers or third parties), measurable downgrade risk exists due to the possibility of inadequate coverage or the deterioration of other elements of the transaction.

In the case of securities backed by 100 percent credit enhancement, an issuer's downgrade exposure is most effectively limited. First, the amount of credit protection cannot prove inadequate. Second, any deterioration in the issuer's credit rating cannot affect the security's rating because 100 percent–guaranteed transactions are rated based on the credit of the guarantor.

Of course, even a fully guaranteed security can be downgraded if the credit enhancer is downgraded. Therefore, the ongoing strength of the enhancer should be a primary consideration—not only for investors, but for issuers as well. In the assessment of the credit enhancer's strength, the following, at a minimum, should be evaluated: (1) capital adequacy; (2) exposure to cyclical or risky nonguaranteed lines of business; (3) leverage; (4) ownership structure; (5) regulation; (6) exposure to event risks, such as leveraged buyouts or product liability suits; (7) diversification of book; and (8) underwriting standards.

Historically, downgrades of issuer-enhanced asset-backed securities have far exceeded downgrades of third party–enhanced asset-backed securities. As a case in point, consider that eight GMAC asset-backed issues, totaling approximately $4.4 billion, were downgraded in 1986. These issues alone accounted for nearly one half of the entire asset-backed securities market at the time of their downgrading.

CONCLUSION

Due to the complexities of asset-backed financing, the asset-backed market is—and perhaps always will be—a credit-enhanced market.

Investors face unique risks in each asset securitization. They worry about cash flow uncertainty, fraud, incorrect legal opinions, adverse legal interpretations, bankruptcy, and downgrading of the investment. If these risks are not reduced, they can result in increased funding rates for issuers and decreased marketability of the securitized instrument.

Issuers choose the type of credit enhancement that best comforts investors while economically and efficiently addressing their own needs. The factors in this decision customarily include the type of assets being securitized; the predictability of the cash flows; current market conditions; the economics of the transaction; and a host of tax, accounting, and regulatory concerns. Issuers that want to access foreign markets but are not well known internationally may also use credit enhancement to bridge the gap to world markets.

The asset-backed security has proven to be one of the most efficient, yet complex, instruments in the market. Credit enhancement has played a key role in its evolution and success. Credit enhancement has offered investors the ability to participate in a highly sophisticated, highly technical segment of the market with high rewards and limited risks. On the other hand, credit enhancement has offered issuers a way to optimally accommodate an ever-increasing list of financing objectives. As new types of issuers and investors continue to enter the securitization market, credit enhancement will continue to evolve to satisfy the diverse and often conflicting requirements of the parties to these transactions.

CHAPTER 7
How Banks View the Sale of Retail Assets

Townsend Walker

INTRODUCTION

Bank of America has sold over $2 trillion of its retail assets—automobile loans and credit card receivables. Its asset securitization group has worked with a number of other financial institutions that are doing the same. Since the beginning of 1986, 30 banks and savings and loan associations have sold about $18 trillion in retail assets, not counting mortgages.[1] There must be some strong reasons for this level of activity to exist. This chapter will look at the earnings impacts, capital effects, and financing advantages of a sale and the strategic reasons that banks sell assets. Half of the 30 issuers have been to market two or more times. Their activity suggests that they have found a comparative advantage in originating and servicing consumer loans without being constrained by funding or capital considerations. However, a number of banks have not sold retail assets; a portion of this chapter is devoted to their reasons for not selling.

[1]These numbers are an estimate of the assets that are packaged and sold in the form of securities offered publicly and privately. Packages of loans ranging in size from $5 million to $10 million are bought and sold quite frequently among banks and savings and loan associations. The overall size of the market is difficult to estimate.

EARNINGS IMPACT

Evaluation of the effect of a sale on the earnings of a bank is easier if the sale structure is examined.

Sale Structure

Figure 7-1 shows the flows of funds in a typical asset-backed security transaction. The numbers on the diagram are keyed to the description following.

Figure 7-1. Asset-Backed Security Flow

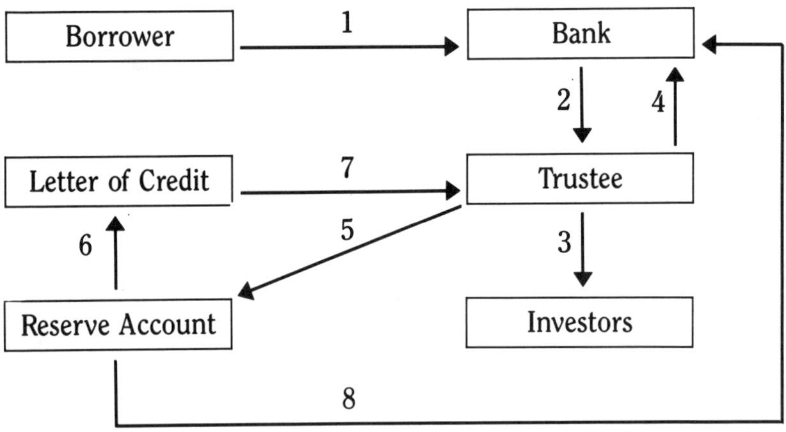

If we look only at the interest component of borrowers' payments: (1) The payments are made to the bank, as before the sale. In this example, the yield on the sold portfolio was 12 percent. (2) The bank passes the payments on to the trustee. (3) The trustee pays investors their interest, say 9 percent. (4) The trustee pays the bank a fee for servicing the loans, say 1 percent. (5) Two percent is paid to the reserve account. This is the difference between the portfolio yield of 12 percent, the investor interest of 9 percent, and the servicing fee of 1 percent. (6) The reserve account is used to reimburse the letter-of-credit bank for (7) draws occasioned by defaults by borrowers on the loans. These draws ensure that investors always receive their principal and interest payments. (8) When the reserve account reaches its

Figure 7-2. Sample Income Reporting Pattern

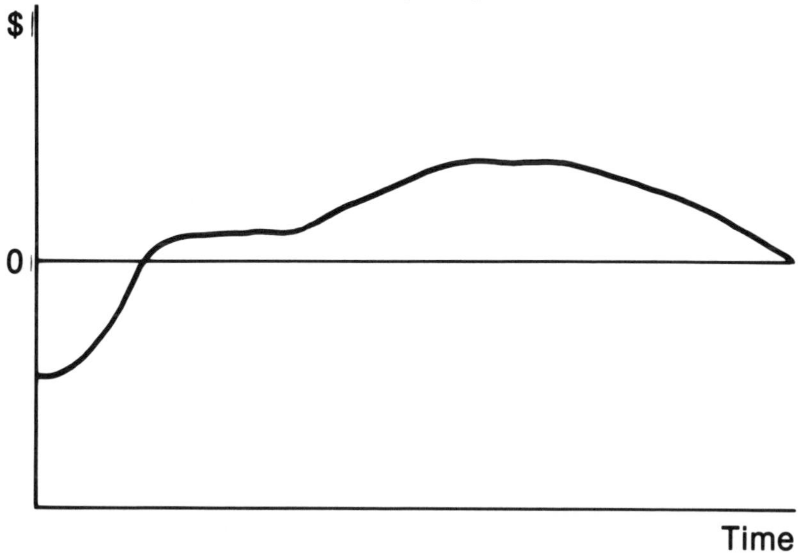

cap, negotiated between the selling bank and the issuer of the letter of credit, excess funds flow back to the selling bank. Once this flow occurs, the money cannot be brought back into the transaction for any reason.

The cash flows to the bank follow this general pattern: In the first quarter of the transaction, the expenses of the sale and the write-off of dealer origination fees, if any, cause an outflow. In the case of installment loans that are originated by dealers, the usual accounting treatment is to amortize the origination cost over the life of the loan. When the loan is sold, the portion of the dealer origination fee that has not been amortized is charged to income. For the first year or so, the only cash received is that from the servicing fee; the bank's earnings on the sold portfolio are tucked away in the reserve account. Thereafter, the reserve account limit is reached, and cash flows to the bank. By the end of the transaction, the bank receives all of the yield of the portfolio, less investor interest and portfolio losses.

Regulatory Accounting

Regulatory accounting practices require banks to record income and expenses as they occur. According to these principles, a bank's income reporting pattern over the life of a transaction is shown in Figure 7-2.

Generally Accepted Accounting

Bank holding company reporting is governed by generally accepted accounting principles. These principles allow a company to record as income the present value of the cash flows from the transaction, if they can be reasonably estimated. In sale transactions that involve installment loans, this entails the present value of the overflow of the reserve account, plus servicing fees, minus ongoing servicing expenses—the one-time transaction costs and dealer origination fees. The result is that the bank holding company can usually record a gain on sale for generally accepted accounting purposes in the quarter of the transaction.

These conflicting accounting principles allow the bank holding company to record a gain at the same time that the bank is recording a loss from the transaction. Bank management have been divided in their treatment of this issue; some have allowed the differences to coexist, while others have reported income at the holding company level in the same way that it is reported by the bank.

Credit Cards

Until recently, credit card receivable sales were treated the same as installment loan sale transactions in accounting for a gain on the sale of assets. The overflow of the reserve account for the life of the transaction was taken into the present-value calculation. This procedure has changed. The Emerging Issues Task Force of the Financial Accounting Standards Board recognized that the life of the asset being sold should be the determining factor—not the life of the sale transaction. Consequently, there is little to distinguish the earnings effect of a credit card sale on a regulatory accounting basis from that on a generally accepted accounting basis.

CAPITAL STRUCTURE EFFECTS

When retail assets are sold, the bank receives cash. The bank can use the cash to pay down liabilities, or it can reinvest the cash in other assets. If the bank uses the cash to pay down liabilities, the size of the balance sheet is reduced; the bank's capital is now supporting fewer assets and liabilities. The bank's total capital ratio increases. And there is a relative increase in the equity capital ratio. This is important because, in recent years, banks have found it more difficult to increase equity capital. The stock market has not generally been receptive to stock offerings from financial institutions, and banks and savings associations have relied principally on retained earnings for capital growth.

Interest Expense Effect

In the assessment of the overall effects of a sale transaction on bank capital, interest expense effects should be considered. They can be measured by comparing the coupon on the sale transaction with the cost of the liabilities being retired. Alternatively, a comparison can be made between the cost of the sale and the cost of new deposits that would have to be raised in the absence of the sale. If the coupon on the sale transaction is 9 percent and the liabilities being retired cost 9 percent, the bank receives the full capital effect of the sale. If the sale rate is 9 percent and the cost of the liabilities being retired is 9½ percent, the capital effect is enhanced. Net income will be greater, due to a reduction in interest expense. It follows that retained earnings will also be greater. On the other hand, if the sale rate is 9 percent and the cost of the liabilities being retired is 8½ percent, there will be an increase in interest expense, a reduction in net income, and a consequent reduction in retained earnings over the period.

As noted in the "Earnings Impacts" section, significant timing issues relate to the way in which a bank can account for the cash flow in a sale transaction. For regulatory accounting purposes, the beneficial impact of freeing up capital will be offset by the initial charge to income for transaction costs and unamortized dealer origination fees.

Reinvestment

If the cash received from the sale transaction is invested in other assets, there is no reduction in the size of the balance sheet, and the capital ratio is unchanged. With the Federal Reserve Board's risk-based capital guidelines, however, it is possible to alter the risk-based capital ratio. Consumer loans, such as credit card receivables, automobile paper, and boat loans, carry a risk rating of 100 percent. Residential mortgages are counted as 50 percent, collateralized mortgage obligations as 25 percent, and Treasuries as 0 percent to 10 percent. Investing cash in these assets will generate an increase in the risk-based equity and primary capital ratios.

Loan Loss Reserves

Because there is no recourse to the bank that sells a retails portfolio, the loan loss reserves that the bank was holding against that portfolio are no longer needed. The reserve is available to be written back into income. Alternatively, a bank can think about reserving less in the next period. This results in a shift in the primary capital structure from loan loss reserves to equity capital. The case for shifting loan loss reserves is clear in the sale of the installment loans—automobiles and mobile homes. Those assets never return to the bank's books. However, the sale of credit card receivables or of other revolving loans is less clear. At the end of the sale, balances will come back on the bank's books. Management has the choice of (1) not changing the loan loss reserve or (2) writing the reserve back into income at the beginning and building up the reserve as the balances return to the balance sheet later.

Summary

The net effect on capital is generally positive, but the initial boost is susceptible to a number of factors. Table 7-1 quantifies the previous discussion by showing the regulatory capital effects of a $100 million sale of dealer-originated automobile loans, assuming a 5 percent equity capital ratio.

Table 7-1. Regulatory Capital Effects of Dealer-Originated Automobile Loans[1]

	(in millions)
Capital freed up	$ 5.0
Transaction costs	(0.6)
Dealer origination fees	(0.9)
Funding cost differential	—
Loan loss reserves	0.5
Net capital available	$ 4.0

[1]$100 million sale with a 5% equity capital ration.

FINANCING ADVANTAGES

A retail asset sale transaction generates funds at about 70 to 90 basis points over the U.S. Treasury note corresponding to the average life of the asset being sold. The all-in cost of the transactions, including legal fees, systems costs, and investment banker fees, is on the order of 100 to 125 basis points over that of Treasuries. The average life of most transactions ranges from one and a half to four years. The all-in cost is roughly equivalent to a spread of 40 basis points over the AAA corporate spread. However, when corporate bonds are perceived to have event risk due to leveraged buyouts or other types of corporte restructuring, the spread can be somewhat narrower.

Adjustment for Capital Cost

The rate that a bank pays for balance sheet liabilities needs to be adjusted before it can be directly compared with the all-in cost of a sale transaction. The reason is that a deposit cannot be raised without considering the attendant cost of capital. We can think about a balance sheet in which every $1 in assets is supported by 95¢ in liabilities and 5¢ in capital. If the rate on a deposit is 8 percent and we ascribe a cost of 22.7 percent to capital (the pretax rate necessary to generate a 15 percent after-tax return on equity), the effective cost of the balance sheet liability is 8.74 percent. If the deposit is subject to reserves, this cost is also included. A 3 percent reserve increases the cost of the deposit to 8.96 percent. This is the number that should be compared with the all-in cost of an asset-backed security transaction.

Transaction Size

For many institutions, an asset sales transaction represents the least expensive way of raising medium-term funds. But even institutions that are able to garner funds more cheaply find it difficult to raise the same amounts at one time, which is possible in an offering of asset-backed securities. Asset-backed transactions ranging in size from $60 million to $1 billion have been effectively executed for banks. Such flexibility and size are not possible with local or national certificate-of-deposit programs or depository note programs.

Matched Funding

The sale of installment loans provides the advantage of matched funding. The transactions are structured so that when borrowers pay off their loans, the outstanding amount of the sale is reduced accordingly. As a result, the bank has no interest rate risk; the spread between the asset and the liability is locked in precisely. On the other hand, sale transactions effectively eliminate the possibility of profiting from the interest rate gap between five-year fixed-rate installment loans and short-term variable-rate deposits. The asset-backed security market makes it very explicit what the trade-offs are and also sends pricing signals to loan origination.

Diversification

A further financing advantage of an asset-backed securities transaction is that it diversifies a bank's sources of funding. The buyers of asset-backed paper have been other banks, institutional money managers, and pension funds—groups that have not been the traditional buyers of directly issued bank paper.

STRATEGIC REASONS

The strategic reason that banks sell retail loans is that they believe they have a comparative advantage in originating and servicing these loans, as compared with holding them on their balance sheet.

Banking Businesses

Some institutions have broken the banking business down into origination, servicing, holding, and distribution businesses. The origination business involves branch systems, advertising, specials on car loans, cross-selling of depositors, and establishment of banking relations with dealers. Another crucial part of the origination process is credit evaluation—screening of all the prospects brought in by the branch network, dealers, and advertising. In large operations, an automated scoring system is used. Servicing entails putting all of the loan and customer information into the computer files, sending out monthly statements, collecting payments, following those that do not pay on time, and reclaiming and selling the collateral of borrowers that do not pay at all. Originating and servicing are characerized by being people, process, and systems intensive.

Holding retail loans on the balance sheet is an investment function. In so doing, the bank considers the rate that it will earn on retail assets compared with its costs of deposits, borrowed funds, and capital. The maturity profile and prepayment characteristics of retail loans compared with those of deposits and borrowings are also considered. There are also portfolio considerations in holding retail loans: What portion of its overall portfolio does the bank wish to hold in retail assets? Also, within the retail portfolio, thought is given to the customer and collateral profiles of automobile loans, recreational vehicle loans, mobile home loans, and credit card receivables. The distribution business involves selling the bank's own liabilities and packages of its assets, as well as paper that it and others originated: commercial paper; municipal securities; Treasury bills, notes, and bonds; and federal agency securities.

In considering the various businesses in which they are engaged, many banks feel that they have a comparative advantage in the origination and servicing businesses over the investment function because there are economies of scale to the origination and servicing businesses, but none to the investment function. Economies of scale can also be seen in the current consolidation of the credit card business. In addition, capital regulations make it expensive to hold loans on the balance sheet—8 percent primary capital ratio—versus selling them—4 percent to 5 percent reserve.

Mortgage Banker Model

The model that some banks are following in the retail business is best typified by the mortgage banker. Loans are originated through a wide network of offices and contacts and then serviced centrally. Capital and funding are only used to accumulate loans into packages for sale. An institution operating in a mortgage-leasing mode will operate with far greater leverage then a portfolio lender; that is, the ratio of loans originated to capital is typically greater for mortgage bankers than for banks. The measure of return in this type of business is not the typical return on assets or return on equity, but is the return on the investment in systems, software, and offices.

Money is made in origination and servicing fees rather than in loan spreads.

WHY BANKS DO NOT SELL ASSETS

A number of banks have looked closely at selling retail assets, but have decided not to act. Among their reasons for not selling are:

- The banks are underleveraged. They are looking for assets.
- If they sold a piece of their automobile loan portfolio, they would not be able to replace it with new auto loans—or any loans.
- They have more customer deposits than they can profitably employ. Yet, banks do not turn away these deposits even if they can be matched only with low-return assets. If turned away, the depositor may not return when needed. At the level of the retail customer, deposits are more relationship sensitive than price sensitive.
- Clearly, some banks can raise money in nearly all maturities more cheaply than an asset-backed security transaction can.
- Among the practical concerns, the transactions are time consuming, they take time away from the basic businesses, the loan system must be modified, and the tax and legal issues are not simple.

THE DECISION-MAKING PROCESS

This chapter has examined a number of reasons for and against selling retail assets. The decision-making process is not always easy because some effects are positive and others are negative. Bank of America faced the same issues when it was selling retail assets. Its decision making was aided by the process shown in Figure 7-3.[2]

CONCLUSION

Many of the reasons for not selling retail assets are temporary. Although the asset securitization process is a management tool that can be used for tactical reasons, most important, it opens up a new strategic alternative for operating a bank.

[2]My colleague, David A. Coulter, was responsible for formulating this decision process.

Figure 7-3. Questions Asked in the Decision-Making Process before Selling Retail Assets

Step 1: Will the bank's portfolio limit on this type of retail asset be exceeded if the sale does not take place?

- Yes → Do the transaction
- No → Go to next decision criterion

Step 2: Will this particular transaction result in a reduction in net operating earnings?

- No → Do the transaction
- Yes → Go to next decision criterion

Step 3: Is the spread on the asset sufficient to cover the bank's cost of capital if the asset is retained? *Note:* The spread must also be adjusted to expected loan losses.

- Yes → Bank should hold on to this asset
- No → Go to next decision criterion

Step 4: Will the bank miss its minimum earnings target if the transaction is completed?

- No → Do the transaction
- Yes → Go to final step

Step 5: Sell the asset if the overall spread is not sufficient to cover the loan loss provisions appropriate for the risk involved.

CHAPTER 8

Management Challenges in the Age of Securitization

Gary J. Kopff and Jeremy Lent

INTRODUCTION

Two decades ago, the dawning of the "age of securitization" occurred when the government introduced the Government National Mortgage Association (GNMA) mortgage-backed security. This innovation was facilitated by 35 years of standardization of the underlying collateral assets—namely, Federal Housing Administration (FHA)- and Veteran's Administration (VA)-guaranteed residential home mortgages. With the "belt and suspenders" of *both* the government's FHA/VA insurance on the assets *and* the government's guarantee behind the GNMA security, credit risk for the investor was eliminated, liquidity was ensured, and the age of securitization began. Today, over $300 billion of these securities are outstanding, and their use dominates the mortgage banking industry for FHA/VA mortgages.

In the late 1970s and early 1980s, phase 2 of the age of securitization was marked by the extension of the GNMA mortgage-backed security concept first to the Federal Home Loan Mortgage Corporation (FHLMC) and then to the Federal National Mortgage Association (FNMA) mortgage-backed securities. These privately owned, government-sponsored corporations extended investor confidence to a quasigovernment guarantee for the security, in lieu of the full faith and credit of the U.S. government, with a similar substitution of *private* mortgage insurance on the collateral assets in lieu of FHA/VA guarantees. These two privately owned, government-sponsored agencies now have have over $320 billion of securities outstanding. For fixed-rate mortgages (and to a lesser extent for adjustable-rate mortgages), FHLMC and FNMA have transformed the "originate/service/hold" business employed by the nation's thrift industry since the Depression into the "originate/service/securitize" business employed by mortgage bankers.

In phase 3, asset-backed securitization has evolved over the past few years far more rapidly than have mortgage-backed securities. In fact, it has the potential over the years ahead to transform fundamentally the funding strategies of banks, finance companies, and the insurance industry—just as occurred earlier for thrifts. With over $77 billion issued since 1983, asset-backed securities have extended investor confidence to letters of credit from AAA-rated Swiss, German, and Japanese banks and to surety bonds of insurance companies from the guarantees of the government and its agencies. More recently, a type of self-insurance has enabled senior securities to achieve AAA status for the investors by seller/servicers holding a subordinated position, thereby extending investor confidence even further in the absence of guarantees from third parties.

To dimension mortgage-backed and asset-backed securitization, consider that U.S. financial assets totaled $12.3 trillion at the end of 1987 (see Figure 8-1).

Overall, $3.2 trillion of securities are guaranteed by governments (that is, debt of the U.S. government, its agencies, and state and local governments). Another $4.0 trillion is accounted for by the debt and equity securities of corporations. Nearly $1.0 trillion of assets are mortgage-backed and asset-backed securities. Finally, about $3.6 trillion of financial assets exist in nonsecuritized forms within the portfolios of banks, thrifts, finance companies, insurance companies, and other financial institutions; some significant portion of this $3.6 trillion may become securitized over the years ahead (see Figure 8-2).

In phase 3 of the age of securitization, the legal structures have evolved and the asset types have proliferated. Thus, the focus is no longer on what the "rocket scientist" financial engineers can achieve, but on what senior executives should pursue as they address the

Figure 8-1. 1987 U.S. Financial Assets

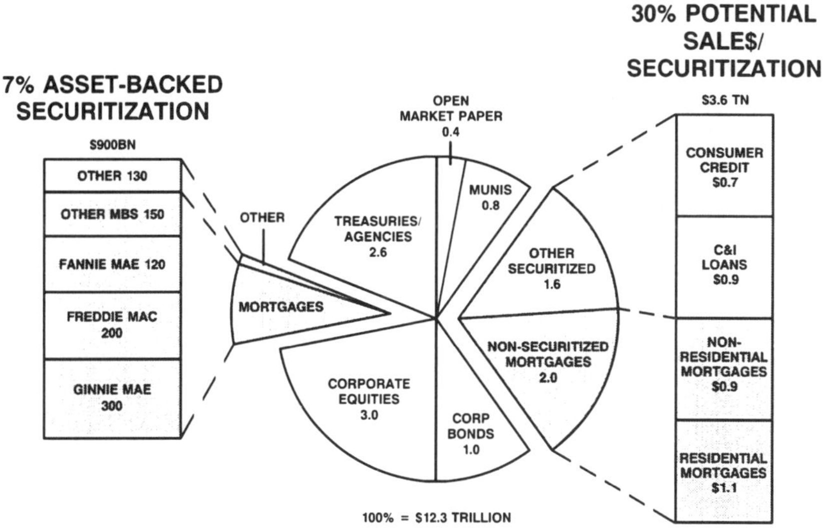

Figure 8-2. Banks Unsecuritized Assets

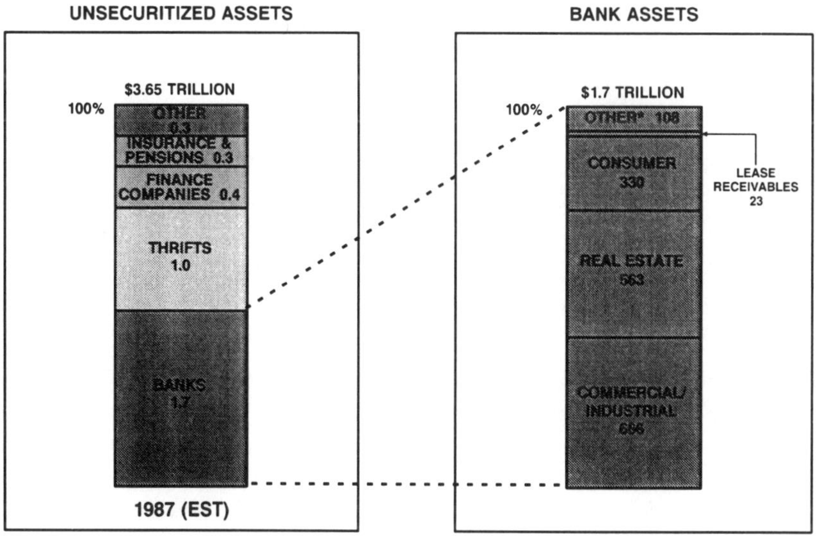

management opportunities and challenges presented by securitization. These executives must first understand what is *feasible* with financial engineering and then, more important, determine what is *desirable* to achieve the specific objectives of their financial institutions.

In this chapter, we examine three fundamental issues that senior executives face as they consider what role asset sales and securitization might play in their institution's financial management:

- What *strategic and financial objectives* can securitization enable the institution to achieve?
- Which *asset types* are appropriate for either securitization or direct sale as loans?
- How should the *profitability* of "hold" options with traditional funding and that of "sell/securitize" options be compared?

STRATEGIC AND FINANCIAL OBJECTIVES ACHIEVABLE WITH SECURITIZATION

Securitization was initially designed to funnel capital market funds into the residential mortgage market, while reducing interest rates for originators and eliminating credit risk for investors. Two added objectives now dominate asset-backed securitization:

- *Lower funding costs.* Securitization can reduce the *cash* cost of funding a portfolio if an institution is rated BBB/Baa or below by the credit rating agencies. After incurring transaction costs for a securitized transaction (for example, paying for trustee services and for a letter of credit or surety bond), a BBB-rated institution can save as much as 60 basis points in funding cost by collateralizing a security with consumer receivables, rather than funding the portfolio with corporate obligations.
- *Sale of assets to reduce cost of allocated equity.* Achieving "sale treatment" for regulatory purposes frees up expensive and scarce equity capital otherwise required by reglators under risk-weighted capitalization rules. This objective has motivated major money-center banks, reeling from the blow of the less-developed country

(LDC) debt provisioning followed by the imposition of new risk-based capital requirements, to securitize billions of dollars of assets in the past few years. As a result of the agreements reached by the Bank for International Settlements in 1987, the central bank regulators of 13 industrial nations established strict tier I and tier II capital requirements and distinguished between risk classes of assets, as well as added capital requirements for off-balance-sheet obligations. Similarly, in the United States, the thrift regulators proposed new risk-based capital rules in December 1988.

Through securitization, a bank earns fee income for servicing, with incentive profits for good results and lower fee levels for bad results (including losses)—just as it would if the assets were owned in its portfolio for regulatory accounting. However, those assets are considered sold, and the bank does *not* need to allocate equity capital against them. Many banks are finding that their toughest constraint on asset growth is the capital required to keep their institution in line with the new federal rules. Securitization provides relief fom this constraint, thereby allowing for growth opportunities that the bank has identified as attractive.

Other banks are considering turning down business and selling asset portfolios because their capital ratios are below the Office of the Comptroller of the Currency (OCC) standards. For these banks, securitization offers a way to attain the appropriate capitalization ratios without losing market share and earnings from ongoing businesses.

Most finance companies do not face capital requirements by federal government regulators, but they must satisfy the rating agencies. Moreover, recent Financial Accounting Standards Board (FASB) rules require consolidation of the debt of finance companies with that of their parents, thereby forcing a reexamination of the capitalization at the parent company level. An industrial parent company is typically significantly less leveraged than its finance subsidiary. With the new FASB rules, the parent's financial ratios are affected by its financing strategy, which encourages the use of securitization to restore the ratios to traditional expectations.

The insurance industry also has its own capital rules and rating agency controls. With the transition from whole life policies to

Single-Premium Deferred Annuities (SPDAs)—which are far more capital intensive—these capitalization requirements are under close scrutiny by top management.

In addition to lower cash costs and sale treatment, which improves capitalization, other significant benefits may be achieved through securitization:

- Reducing catastrophic and concentrated credit risk by asset type, geographic area, or industry
- Reducing prepayment risk, particularly for residential mortgages
- Achieving new sources of income from underwriting and trading, for investment banks and some of the major commercial banks
- Matchfunding a portfolio, particularly for auto finance companies
- Growing fee income in lieu of spread income, for commercial banks
- Obtaining a new funding source, which may be preferable because it is nondilutive or because it reaches investors that cannot buy loans but can buy rated asset-backed securities.

ASSET TYPES FOR SECURITIZATION OR DIRECT SALES

The $77 billion of *private*[1] mortgage-backed and asset-backed securities over the past five years are largely consumer receivables, as shown in Figure 8-3.

These types of securitized assets satisfied rating agencies, credit enhancers, and investors about their predictable behavior in terms of cash flow, including expected losses and scheduled principal repayments. This predictability of cash flow requires:

- *Actuarily predictable event risk.* Auto loans and credit cards have average borrower balances far smaller than those of home mortgages. This enables investors and the rating agencies to use past behavior to actuarily project future cash flows and credit losses.

[1] Excluding GNMA, FHLMC, and FNMA mortgage-backed securities.

Figure 8-3. Private Asset-Backed Securities Outstanding

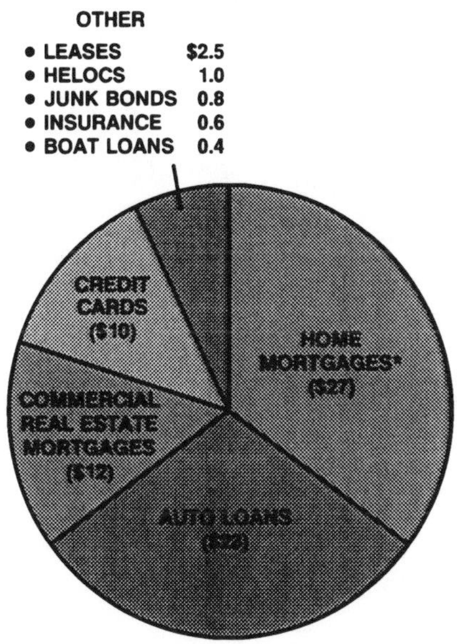

100% = $77 BILLION*

* EXCLUDING GINNIE MAE, FREDDIE MAC & FANNIE MAE GOVN/AGENCY SECURITIES

The sizable number of different creditors in a pool of assets allows for a greater degree of *geographic* diversity. On the other hand, commercial real estate and commercial and industrial loans typically have individual balances far in excess of home mortgages, and the event risk for default is an impediment to securitization.

- *Standardized, easily valued, and marketable collateral.* With this, investors can achieve a high comfort level in the reliability of the cash flows, even if defaults are unexpectedly high. In both noncomforming residential and commercial mortgage pools, rating agencies and investors focus on the loan-to-value ratios of the mortgages because it is primarily the value of the property collateralizing the mortgage that determines the credit quality.
- *Gross spread.* Credit cards carry such high gross spreads that even issuers whose portfolios have experienced relatively high losses can securitize their receivables. If loss rates are unexpectedly high, a

Figure 8-4. Asset Sales/Securitization by Major Banks

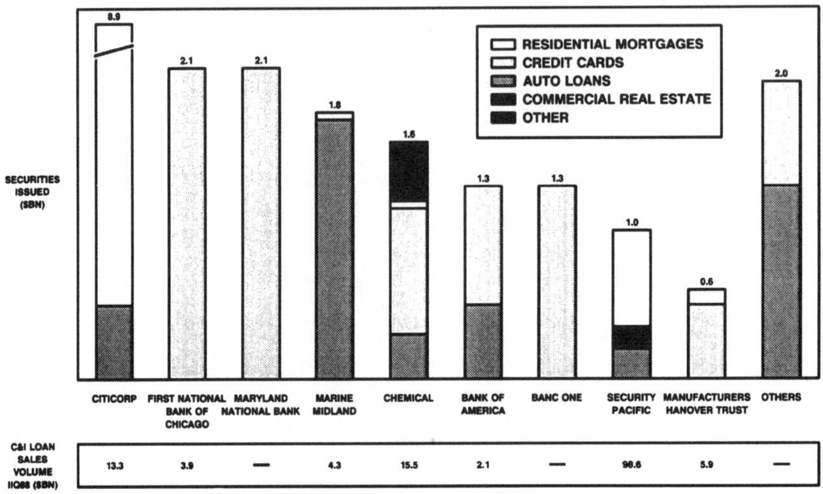

smaller residual amount of cash will flow back to the issuer at the end of the lifetime of the security. Once again, commercial real estate mortgages and commercial and industrial loans are highly competitive, with smaller spreads allowing little margin for securitization costs.

Securitized commercial bank assets are dominated by Citicorp's residential mortgage securitization (see Figure 8-4).

In future years, however, assets securitized by commercial banks are likely to be increasingly heterogeneous. In 1988, for example, Chemical Banking Corporation securitized over $2.6 billion, divided among five asset types: credit card receivables (32 percent), mortages (26 percent), auto loans (19 percent), boat loans (15 percent), and second mortgages (8 percent).

Securitization is *not* the exclusive province of thrifts and commercial banks. Finance companies have also been active from the start, led by captive auto finance firms [General Motors Acceptance Corporation (GMAC) with 17 transactions, Chrysler with 8, and, most recently, Ford Motor Credit]. The growth of securitized auto receivables was boosted by GMAC's $4 billion issue in 1986—the largest single debt transaction in U.S. history. This precedent evoked a rapid and widespread adoption of securitization to finance auto receivables. Captive finance companies have also securitized boat loans and other asset types as they prepare for the implementation of FASB Statement of Financial Accounting Standards No. 94, which forces consolidation of many finance subsidiaries with their parent corporations. Several insurance companies (for example, Prudential and The Equitable) have securitized insurance premium receivables, as well as commercial real estate and other investment assets. Retailers are also securitizing their receivables, led by Sears, J.C. Penney, Montgomery Ward, and Household.

In 1988, credit card receivables predominated in nonmortgage securitization, driven partially by the prominence of banks (rather than finance companies) in the asset-backed market and partially by advances in financial engineering. Special funding corporations date back to the GMAC/First Boston transaction, which was widely copied by other transactions. However, using such vehicles with commercial paper was a major advance, and the $1 billion Banc One transaction with Merrill Lynch and the Montgomery Ward transaction were important for their technical advances in structuring.

As issuers, underwriters, and investors become increasingly comfortable with the techniques of securitization, more diverse types of assets are being used to collateralize securities. In 1988, these included customer account receivables, boat loans, consumer term loans, home equity lines of credit, and insurance premium receivables.

COMPARING PROFITABILITY OF HOLD AND SELL/ SECURITIZE OPTIONS

Considering the wide range of sell/asset portfolios now available for securitization, management must decide which assets, if securitized, would best achieve the objectives described earlier. The decision process should be structured so that the financial and economic results of securitizing a portfolio can be compared with "funding as usual."

The most difficult part of the analytical task that confronts management is reaching agreement on the *framework* for staff to use when comparing hold and sell/securitize options. In 1987–1988,

Figure 8-5. SPA's Proprietary Modeling Software, "Securitization Projection Analytics"SM

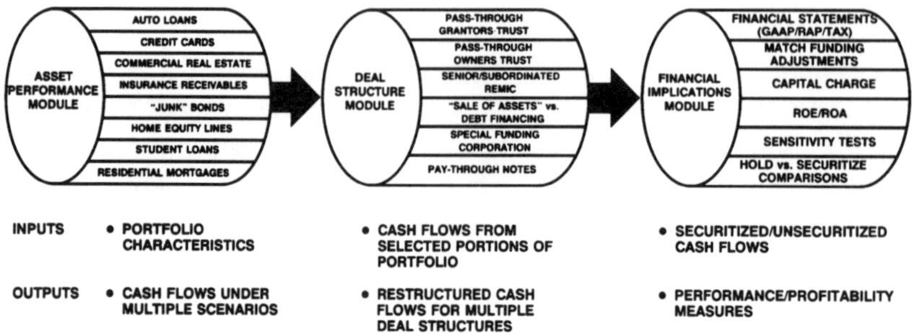

working closely with institutions in different segments of the financial services industry, we developed an analytical framework to help managers measure the value that securitization may hold for their corporations. A computer model was developed to map out the impact of securitization, following cash flows from the original assets to the final effect on the financial statements. The model was designed with three modules, as shown in Figure 8-5.

- The asset performance module is customized to evaluate the behavior of *specific* asset portfolios. The module projects the cash flow characteristics of such assets as auto loans, credit card loans, commercial real estate mortgages, home equity lines, and residential mortgages. Multiple scenarios reveal how average life, net charge-offs, and other key variables will respond to different assumptions such as interest rates in the economy, prepayment patterns, defaults, and so on.
- The deal structuring module directs the cash flow from the asset performance module through a variety of legal structures, including a grantor/owner pass-through trust, a senior/subordinated format, and a special funding corporation. The transaction costs also vary depending on whether the structure is publicly registered with the Securities and Exchange Commission or privately placed. Pricing will vary among AAA-, AA-, and A-rated securities, and the costs of achieving that rating will vary among credit enhancement techniques (for example, senior/subordinated debt, bank letters of credit, and insurance surety bonds). These factors and others that

have an impact on the economics of the securitization structure are addressed at this stage.

- The financial implications module compares the hold option for unsecuritized cash flows with the securitize option. The comparison uses various formats, including earnings with and without adjustments for the value of capital. Generally accepted accounting principles (GAAP)/regulatory accounting practices (RAP) impacts of the financing treatment or sale treatment are reflected, and sensitivity tests are made for various interest rates, prepayments, credit loss, asset growth, transaction costs, and tranche pricing.

As we refined this framework with our clients, we came across obstacles that confused the analysts—for example, the time frame for the comparison. For example, in the quarter during which the securitization occurs, the institution may record a gain or loss from sale of the assets. In the ensuing quarters, however, reported income may be lower under the securitize option because a spread account is created and funded. At the end of the life of the security, reported income under securitization may be artificially high, as the spread account flows back to the issuer. Accordingly, analysis of the transaction must extend throughout the lifetime of the security in question—*not* merely in the first year. This is especially true in credit card securitization, in which institutions have much leeway in structuring cash flows of the security in which institutions have when it wants earnings to rise and fall.

A second obstacle that confuses analysis of securitization and hold options was more difficult to correct: namely, how to value the capital that securitization frees up. As we stated earlier, freeing up capital for investment elsewhere in the institution became the major objective of most of the securitized transactions issued by banks in 1988. Yet, we discovered that, in many instances, the analysis performed to determine whether to securitize a particular portfolio completely ignored the value of the capital freed up. The reason that such analyses miss the capital factor is that most banks measure the performance of their divisions by the earnings reported each quarter. The capital used by the division is generally ignored.

A more sophisticated approach used by some bankers is return on equity (ROE) measurement when comparing the securitize and hold options. Thus, if equity is allocated at 4 percent of assets, with adjustments by asset class—in line with federal guidelines—and a significant amount of assets are securitized, the equity assigned to that division will decrease and the net interest margin may or may not decrease as it is transformed into servicing fee income. Accordingly, the analytical framework would appear to compute the divisional ROE with securitization (that is, lower equity and higher/ lower net income) and then compare it with ROE under the hold option.

Several problems arise in this approach. First, if the entire asset portfolio is securitized, the equity is zero and ROE is an indeterminate number. Second, in making this comparison for one client, we made the counterintuitive discovery that this ROE comparison could lead to *improper* decision making.

To understand the second problem, we must establish some basic precepts of the value of capital in a capital-constrained institution. If capital were free—or at least not a constraining factor—a firm would choose to grow businesses that meet or exceed its hurdle rate. For example, most banks were in this sitution before the LDC provisioning and the more stringent capital rules imposed by the Federal Reserve. Today, many large banks find that capital constraints are preventing them from growing portfolios in profitable businesses. It is axiomatic that capital freed up in one part of the bank can be redeployed to grow businesses in any other part of the bank. Therefore, the *value* to the bank of any capital that it can free up is equivalent to the hurdle rate, irrespective of the ROE of the business that frees up that capital, since at the margin the bank would continue investing in businesses until it had exhausted all above-hurdle rate opportunities. For this reason, any rule for the hold-or-securitize decision should explicitly measure the value of capital freed up—based on the corporate hurdle rate.

Now, let us look again at the ROE framework for analyzing securitization. Figure 8-6 is a simplified illustration of four divisions in a bank.

Each division is the same size, with $500 million in assets, and is, therefore, assigned equity (at 4 percent) of $20 million. However, division earnings differ, ranging from a highly profitable 50 percent to a meager 6.25 percent before tax. Suppose that each of these four divisions now securitized $100 million of their portfolio at a net cost (including underwriting fees, systems costs, and funding differen-

Figure 8-6. Bank ROE Framework for Analyzing Securitization

CORPORATE	SAME VALUE OF SECURITIZATION (EQUITY FREED UP) REGARDLESS OF BUSINESS ROE
BUSINESS	ROE IMPACT DEPENDS ON PRE-SECURITIZATION BUSINESS ROE

SIMPLIFIED ILLUSTRATION

($M)	A	B	C	D
PRE-SECURITIZATION BUSINESS LEVEL				
ASSETS	500	500	500	500
EQUITY ● 4%	20	20	20	20
EARNINGS (B/T)	10	5	2.5	1.25
ROE (B/T)	50%	25%	12.5%	6.25%
SECURITIZE $100 M ($0.5M NET COST)				
ASSETS	400	400	400	400
EQUITY @ 4%	16	16	16	16
EARNINGS (B/T)	9.5	4.5	2.0	0.75
ROE (B/T)	59.4%	28.1%	12.5%	4.7%
CHANGE IN ROE	+9.4%	+3.1%	0	1.6%

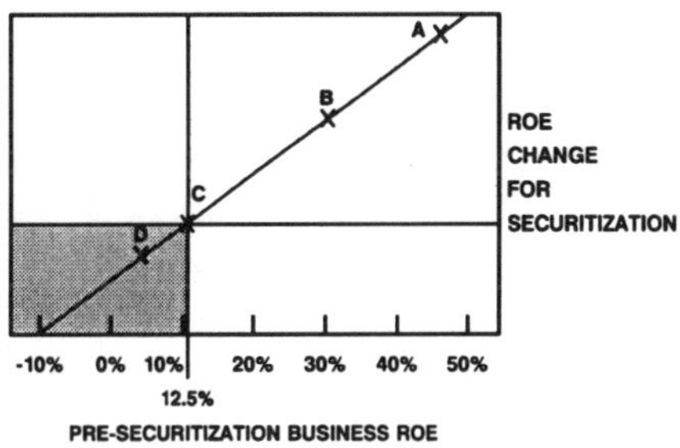

BREAK-EVEN $= \frac{\text{SECURITIZATION COST}}{\text{EQUITY FREED UP}} = \frac{\$0.5\text{ M}}{\$4.0\text{ M}} = 12.5\%$

tials) of $0.5 million—a reasonable estimate. What is the ROE for these divisions after the securitization? Their assets are all lower—$400 million—as is their assigned equity of $16 million. Earnings in each division are $0.5 million lower because of the net cost of securitizing. However, ROEs have changed dramatically and—more important—have changed in *different directions.* The ROE of the least profitable division has actually fallen to a negative 1.6 percent. The most profitable division has increased its ROE by 9.4 percent, and Division C has experienced no change whatsoever in its ROE.

Recall that the value of the equity freed up by each of these transactions is the same, since it enables the bank to invest at or above the hurdle rate in another business. Yet, using this analytical framework for comparative decision making, Division D would choose *not* to securitize and Division A would securitize as much as possible, based on the effect on divisional ROE. The reason for this strange situation is that by measuring the value of securitization based on a division's ROE, a manager is implicitly setting the value of the capital freed up as equal to the ROE of his or her division. Thus, the implied value of the capital freed up by Division D is less than that freed up by Division A. Using this approach, a manager will choose to securitize if his or her division's ROE is higher than the following ratio:

$$\frac{\text{Net cost of securitization}}{\text{Equity freed up}}$$

If this ratio is higher than his or her division's ROE, simple mathematics show that this ROE will decrease by securitization. On the other hand, securitization had no effect on Division C ROE because its ROE (12.5 percent) was exactly the same as the ratio above ($0.5 million/$4 million = 12.5 percent). However, the corporation values the capital freed up by securitization at its hurdle rate—*not* at the ROE of its least profitable division.

As we assessed this conundrum with our client, we developed a measurement methodology that would give a division manager a framework with which to make a securitization decision based on the good of the corporation, while retaining a focus on his or her own division's performance. Our framework uses the concept of charging each division's earnings for its use of the corporation's capital, based on the size of their asset portfolio and the corporate hurdle rate. The earnings that remain after this charge are called excess shareholder contribution, since they represent what the division has earned over and above the return that the bank's shareholders expect from the use of their capital. If the measure is negative, the business is not earning a return for shareholders that is at or above the corporate hurdle rate.

Let us look again at the four divisions of the bank, using excess shareholder contribution as the analytical framework (see Figure 8-7).

Once again, they all begin with $500 million in assets and $20 million in equity. Their earnings range from 50 percent to 6.25 percent, as they did before. Now, however, instead of looking at their ROEs, we charge each division for the capital that its portfolio is using. This charge is computed by multiplying the assigned equity by the corporate hurdle rate—in this case 25 percent pretax. The excess shareholder contribution demonstrates each division's profitability. A positive number indicates that the division is earning above the corporate hurdle rate; a negative number indicates the opposite. Notice that Division B, which was exactly at the hurdle rate, earned zero excess shareholder contribution.

Figure 8-7. Bank Excess Shareholder Contribution for Analyzing Securitization

CORPORATE THE VALUE OF SECURITIZATION REMAINS THE SAME REGARDLESS OF BUSINESS ROE

BUSINESS THE ROE IMPACT OF SECURITIZATION DEPENDS ON THE PRIOR BUSINESS ROE

($M)	A	B	C	D
PRE-SECURITIZATION BUSINESS LEVEL				
ASSETS	500	500	500	500
EQUITY	20	20	20	20
EARNINGS (B/T)	10	5	2.5	1.25
LESS: CAPITAL CHARGE	(5)	(5)	(5)	(5)
EXCESS SHAREHOLDER CONTRIBUTION	5	0	(2.5)	(3.75)
SECURITIZE $100 M ($0.5M NET COST)				
ASSETS	400	400	400	400
EQUITY	16	16	16	16
EARNINGS (B/T)	9.5	4.5	2.0	0.75
LESS: CAPITAL CHARGE	(4)	(4)	(4)	(4)
EXCESS SHAREHOLDER CONTRIBUTION	5.5	0.5	(2)	(3.25)
CHANGE IN "EXCESS SHAREHOLDER CONTRIBUTION"	+0.5	+0.5	+0.5	+0.5

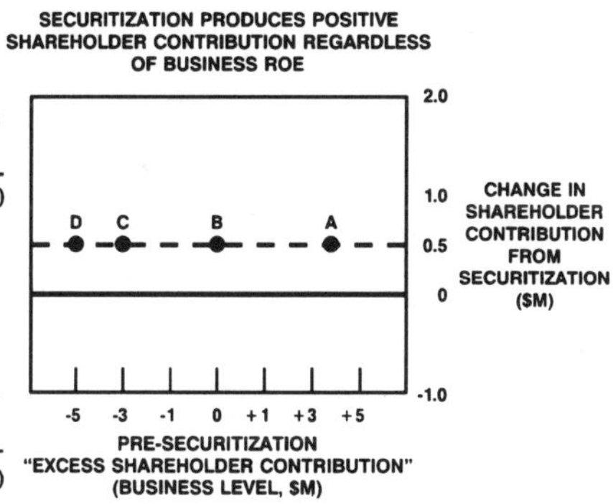

NOTE: VALUE OF SECURITIZATION = (VALUE OF EQUITY FREED UP - NET COST OF SECURITIZATION)
= ($4 MM x 25%) - $0.5 MM = $0.5 MM

Now, suppose that the four divisions securitize from their portfolios again in exactly the same transaction as before. Their capital charge is now $1 million less, as a result of the $100 million reduction in assets. The change in the excess shareholder contribution reported by each division is a $0.5 million increase, after netting out the $0.5 million securitization cost. Now, each division manager will see the same positive effect on his or her division's bottom line by securitizing, in marked contrast to the ROE method of comparison. The reason for this is that the capital freed up by securitization was already explicitly valued at the corporate hurdle rate in the capital charge. From the manager's point of view, as well as from that of the corporation, the value of securitization is as follows:

Value of securitization	=	Value of equity freed up–Net cost of securitization
	=	($4 million × 25%)–$0.5 million
	=	$0.5 million

With this framework, a bank can analyze multiple-asset port-

Figure 8-8. Securitization Economics

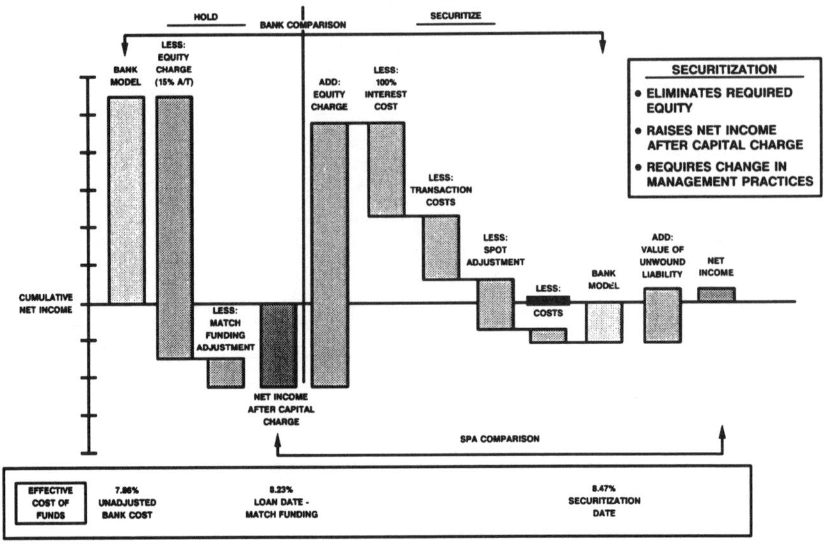

folios for potential sale/securitization. To demonstrate this approach, we examine illustrative decision-making processes for four asset types: auto loans, credit cards, C&I loans, and commercial real estate mortgages.

Auto Finance

Securitization in the auto finance industry is well advanced, with nearly $25 billion issued in over 75 transactions by the captive auto finance subsidiaries (GMAC, Chrysler, and Ford), as well as by the larger banks. Most transactions use the grantor trust format and use auto loans, rather than leases, as collateral.

Figure 8-8 compares the hold and securitize options from two analytical perspectives: first, as they might be perceived by a bank that did not value equity capital explictly or adjust for maturity differences, and, second, as recommended by the authors.

In the traditional approach, cumulative net income constitutes the hold option, and transaction and hedging costs are subtracted to create a securitize option, which is less attractive. The author's framework adds two hidden costs to the hold option: (1) the capital charge for holding assets, referred to above, and (2) a match-funding

Figure 8-9. Five-Year Projected Financials, 1989–1993

ASSETS	NO SECURITIZATION		SECURITIZATION ($ x MILLION EVERY y DAYS)	
• SERVICED	18.0% CAGR		18.0% CAGR	
• BALANCE SHEET	15.0% CAGR		9.0% CAGR	
RETURN ON EQUITY (MULTIPLE INTEREST RATE FORECASTS)				
• FORECAST	16.9%		19.4%	
• CYCLE INVERTED	14.8%		16.7%	
• FLAT	14.5%	5-YR MEAN	15.9%	5-YR MEAN
• CYCLE	14.1%		15.2%	
• INVERTED FORECAST	12.0%		12.0%	
NET INCOME (FLAT RATES)	$ 309 MILLION		$ 258 MILLION	
EXCESS SHAREHOLDER CONTRIBUTION (FLAT RATES)	($ 1.5 MILLION)		$ 22.7 MILLION	

adjustment to eliminate "gapping" profits from funding assets with shorter-term liabilities in economic environments with a positively shaped yield curve. Note that these two adjustments demonstrate that holding the assets *fails* to meet the bank's profitability target.

To compare the hold option with the securitize option in the recommended framework, the equity charge is deleted because sale treatment will be achieved under GAAP/RAP. Various transactional and timing adjustments are made, and the value is included for unwinding liabilities previously incurred. The resulting net income under the securitization option is a substantial improvement over the hold option.

Next, we build on the microeconomic comparison to illustrate a five-year comparison between an 18 percent compound annual growth rate in origination/servicing funded on the balance sheet and the same origination/servicing growth funded predominantly with securitization (see Figure 8-9).

Credit Cards

To compare the hold and securitize options for a portfolio of $500 million of credit card receivables, we again employ the capital-charging analytical framework. The methodology for this comparison is to isolate items that are different in the securitization option and in the hold option. Other items, such as loan losses and operating costs,

Figure 8-10. Credit Card Securitization ($ Millions)

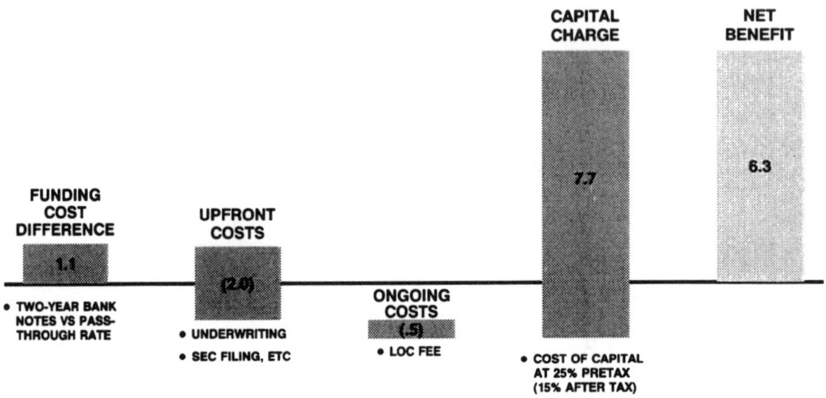

are the same under both options. Figure 8-10 shows that, for all the complexity of the modeling process, the decision to securitize is ultimately based on four key variables:

- The funding cost difference between the pass-through rate on the securities and the rate that the bank would pay to fund the credit card portfolio if held on its books. The comparison with the hold option should be on a *match-funded* basis, rather than confusing maturities. Treasuries in different banks have different opinions about what constitutes the true maturity of a credit card portfolio, and some managers have fallen into the trap of comparing, for example, an 18-month transfer price for their credit card portfolio with a 36-month pass-through rate on the security—thus finding that the security would be relatively more expensive. A credit card–backed security can be structured with a wide range of maturities, from commercial paper to four years, and this maturity should be the choice of the bank's asset liability management committee. For this reason, if the security is elected to mature in two years, the most appropriate hold comparison may be the rate that the bank would pay at the margin for an issuance of two-year notes.
- Up-front costs consist largely on the underwriting commission paid to the investment bank to structure and place the securities.

- Ongoing costs include the monthly or quarterly fee payable to the credit enhancer for guaranteeing timely payment of interest and principal to investors.
- Net capital charge shows the value of the equity that the corporation has freed up by securitizing the assts, compared with holding them on its books.

Figure 8-10 shows how important it is to handle the capital charging correctly.

On a cash basis alone, the bank would choose not to securitize. It is only when the value of the freed-up equity is factored into the comparison that it becomes clear that securitization presents a $6 million benefit to the corporation.

Commercial and Industrial Loans

Commercial and industrial loans present a different set of problems for securitization and require a different analytical framework to compare hold and sell options. Commercial and industrial loans have not yet been securitized to any significant degree; however, selling such loans is a viable strategic option today.[2] For each portfolio within a commercial and industrial business, the economics of originating and selling may be very different. As a general rule, a low-spread portfolio produces relatively more value than a high-spread portfolio by freeing up capital to be invested. Major factors that differentiate the economics for each business are:

- Spread that the loan would earn if held on the books
- Skim retained after the loan is sold
- Origination and servicing fees earned and retained by the business
- Incremental expenses incurred through increases in origination volume

Because of widely varying factors across different businesses, an originate-to-sell strategy cannot be applied across the board. Each

[2] See *Strategies for Sales and Securitization of Commercial and Industrial Loans*, an annotated version of a presentation made before the Economic Advisory Panel of the American Bankers Association on April 14, 1988, by Gary J. Koppf, with assistance provided by Jeremy Lent.

Figure 8-11. Sample $600 Million Portfolio

$ MILLIONS

	I BASE CASE	II 10% ASSET SALES	III 10% SALES AND 20% ORIGINATE-TO-SELL
LOANS ORIGINATED	$600	600	720
LOANS SOLD	0	60	180
ASSETS	600	540	540
EQUITY @4%	24	21.6	21.6
HOLD NII [1]	11.0	10.55	10.5
(+) SKIM [2]	-	0.15	0.5
FULL NII	11.0	10.7	11.0
(-) EXPENSES	(5.0)	(5.0)	(5.0)

[1] 75 BP GROSS SPREAD FOREGONE ON ASSETS SOLD
[2] 25 BP EARNED ON PARTICPATIONS

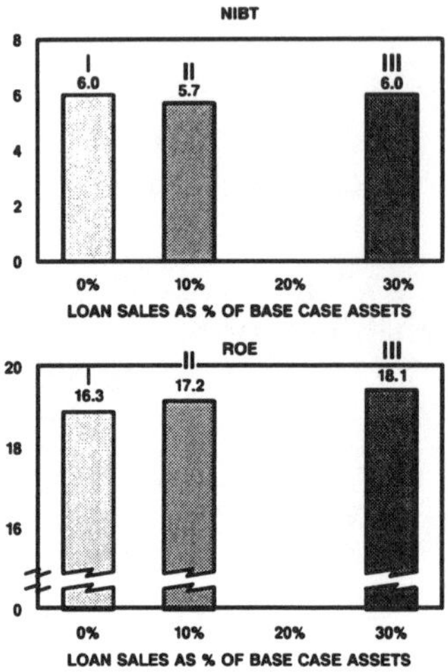

business has an optimal mix of loans to be held and sold, which can change as one of the underlying factors changes in the market. To illustrate the economics of a comparison of hold or sell options for commercial and industrial loans, consider the $600 million portfolio in Figure 8-11.

With no loan sales and a spread of 75 basis points, the net income is $11 million, or $6 million after expenses of $5 million. With a 4 percent equity allocation, the after-tax ROE is 16.3 percent. Now consider two options that involve varying amounts of loan sales:

- *With 10 percent sales,* the assets decline to that $540 million; therefore, the equity allocation declines to $21.6 million. Assuming that 25 basis points are earned on the participated portion of the loan and that expenses remain at $5 million, the Net Income Before Tax drops to $5.7 million, but after-tax ROE rises to 17.2 percent.
- *With 10 percent sales and an added 20 percent originated for sales,* the assets on the books are again $540 million, but the Net Income Before Tax rises to $6.0 million, thereby increasing the after-tax ROE to 18.1 percent.

Loan sales represent a way to increase earnings without adding to the balance sheet. However, to succeed in this, origination volume must increase at an even greater rate. The necessary increase in volume can only be accomplished through significant changes in the normal procedures of doing business, as currently conducted in most banks. This leads to a series of management challenges in loan officer culture, credit approval process, and information systems architecture that must be dealt with to achieve the value that increased loan sales can bring.

Commercial Real Estate

As the fourth illustration of a comparison of hold and securitize options, consider portfolios of fixed-rate and floating-rate commercial real estate mortgages. One approach to securitization would be to sell the assets into a grantor trust and purchase a sufficiently large letter of credit or surety bond to enhance the pass-through securities to an AAA rating. For a portfolio of loans—as opposed to a single property or a small number of properties—the costs of credit enhancement may prove prohibitive, due to the need to assess each property individually. Credit card receivables and auto loans do not encounter this problem because the number of loans in their portfolios is far greater and actuarial approaches are used to project their loss potential.

Another structure that avoids the need for costly or unavailable third party credit enhancements is the senior/subordinated structure. The subordinated securities bear the risk, thereby enabling the senior securities to achieve an AAA rating without payment of a sizable fee to a third party bank or insurance company. However, the bank regulatory framework denies sale treatment if the subordinated securities are retained by the originating bank. If we assume sale of the subordinated securities and compare the results with the hold option, as shown in Figure 8-12, the securitize option—even including the value of the freed-up capital—is not as attractive as continuing to hold the assets on the books.

CONCLUSION

In this chapter, we have identified (1) strategic and financial

Figure 8-12. Securitization of Portfolios of Commercial Real Estate Mortgages

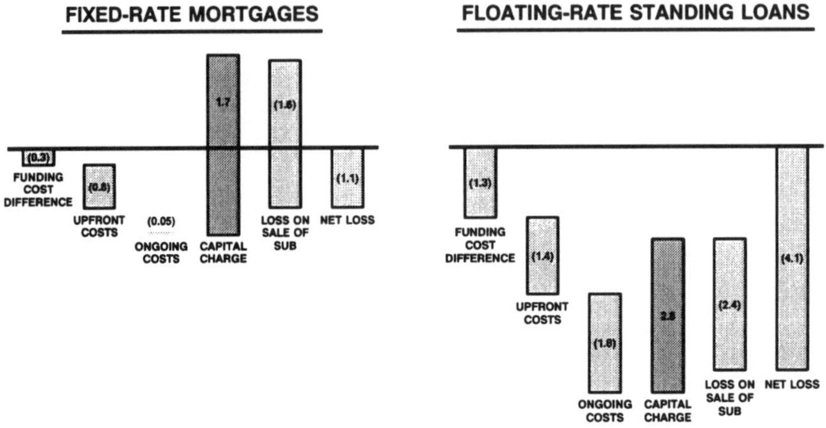

objectives that can be pursued with asset sales and securitization, (2) asset types currently appropriate to consider for securitization or for sale without securitization, and (3) an analytical framework for comparing profitability of the hold and sell/securitize options, based on assigning a capital charge to a business and then comparing the excess shareholder contribution after securitization.

When these three management challenges are addressed, what obstacles may still block effective action in many major financial institutions? In our experience, one of the last management challenges to be overcome is performance measurement systems still based on achieving an earnings—or even an ROE—level, rather than excess shareholder contribution. In such circumstances, managers may be in the uncomfortable position of being asked to act for the sake of the corporation, which may have significant deleterious effects on their own performance as traditionally measured. Often, managers' sense of importance in a bank is partially based on the dollar amount of assets they control, and if they are asked to voluntarily reduce that amount, *even* in the best interests of the corporation, they may become highly anxious. Managers and staff will tend to drag their heels over resolving problems that arise in the securitization when they consider the process hostile to their interests.

Figure 8-13. Comparison of Three Divisions in a Bank's Business Performance

ILLUSTRATIVE

CURRENT ECONOMICS

- SPREADS ON DRAWN-DOWN COMMITMENTS OFTEN BELOW HURDLE RATE
- FEES ON UNDRAWN PORTIONS INCREASE ROE TO ABOVE HURDLE RATE

RISK-BASED CAPITAL ENVIRONMENT

- EQUITY ALLOCATED TO UNDRAWN COMMITTED AMOUNT (AT 50%)
- INCREASED FEES OR SPREADS MUST COVER NEW EQUITY ALLOCATION
- "ORIGINATE TO SELL" STRATEGY BECOMES INCREASINGLY ATTRACTIVE

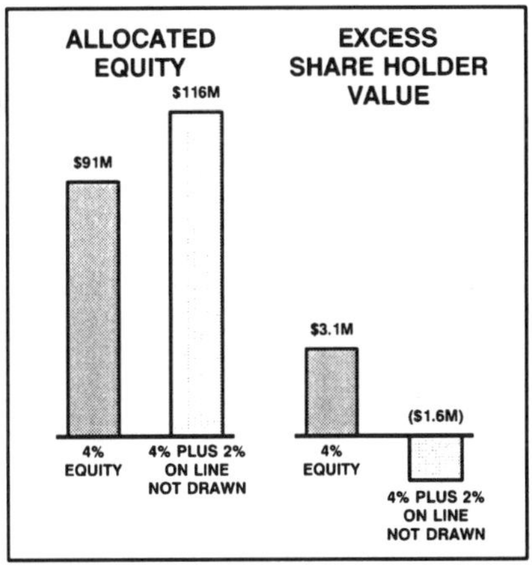

In a capital-constrained financial institution, the solution to this discrepancy between the best interests of the managers and those of the corporation is to extend capital charging as an integral part of the performance measurement system. By doing so, the incentive problem takes care of itself, and managers will make decisions regarding securitization—and any other topic relating to capitalization—with their own interests and corporate interests fully aligned.

Consider an illustrative bank with three divisions, Business 1 (Successful), which is highly *successful* by our proposed measure; Business 2 (Big), which is *very large* by traditional measures, such as the after-tax margin; and Business 3 (Small) which is *small* and generates a large ROE, as shown in Figure 8-13.

Comparing the divisions' performance using the after-tax margin alone, Business 1 (Successful) appears to be as successful as Business 2 (Big) because such a measurement fails to differentiate between differing *efficiencies* in equity. Switching to an ROE measurement, Business 3 (Small) beats Business 1 (Successful) by 1 percent because ROE fails to differentiate between *levels* of absolute earnings contribution. Finally, by using excess shareholder contribu-

Figure 8-14. Earnings Growth Through Asset Sales/Securitization

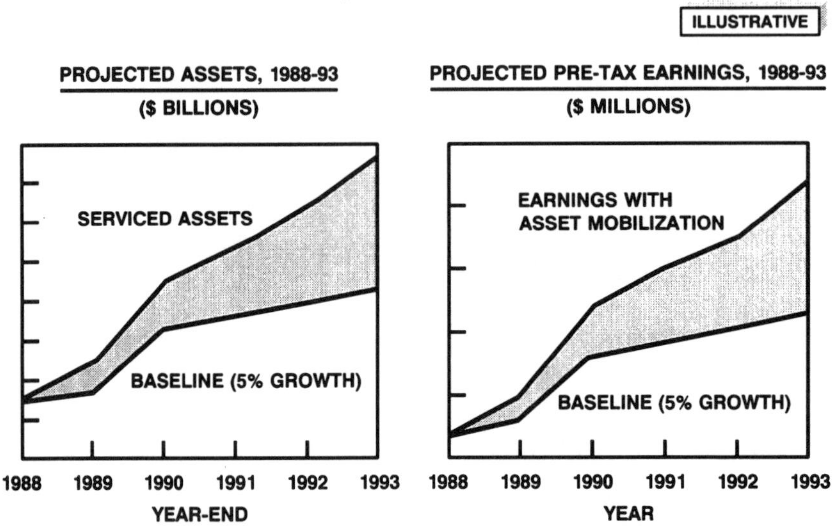

tion, Business 1 (Successful) comes out as the clear winner, which is where it deserves to be, because this measure takes into account both absolute earnings and the use of equity. Business 2 (Big) is penalized because it is *not* making hurdle rate, and Business 3 (Small) is seen to be of far less importance to the corporation's shareholders.

To illustrate the impact of successfully overcoming these management challenges in the age of securitization, consider the contrast in Figure 8-14.

A firm with 5 percent growth in serviced assets, leading to 5 percent growth in pretax projected earnings, is contrasted with a strategic shift to accelerate asset sale securitization to increase serviced assets *without* violating capital constraints. The improvement can be highly significant, as the increased level of serviced assets, with added efficiencies from economies of scale, translates into major earnings improvement. This result should inspire excellent managers to overcome their challenges in the age of securitization.

CHAPTER 9

Asset Securitization and Corporate Financial Health

Harold H. Goldberg, Robert W. Burke, Samuel Gordon, Kenneth J.H. Pinkes, and M. Douglas Watson, Jr.

INTRODUCTION

The opportunities that result from securitization, particularly its potential as a more efficient form of financing, are placing strong pressures on financial intermediaries to use securitized lending as a competitive tool. The possibilities are particularly attractive for (1) national lenders that desire to capture major shares in a nationwide loan origination market without having to raise a proportionate amount of capital and (2) security houses that wish to underwrite, distribute, and trade the growing portion of U.S. capital raised in security form.

However, this new technology is significantly altering the industry's scale of competition, raising the relative importance of technology and cost efficiency as critical variables to success, and shifting the underlying predictability of future earnings. In addition, the specific structures employed by some institutions to securitize assets do not, at times, significantly reduce overall credit risk. In fact, some structures may be increasing it by retaining significant off-balance-sheet residual risks that relate to the assets securitized and by shifting the originator's asset mix to assets of lower credit quality.

The purpose of this chapter is to outline Moody's Investors Service's approach to assessing the impact of asset securitization on the general credit quality of the commercial banks, investment banks, thrifts, mortgage banks, home builders, manufacturers, retailers, insurance companies, and finance companies that it rates.

ASSET SECURITIZATION AND ITS ECONOMIC BENEFITS

Definition of Securitization

In its broadest sense, securitization is simply the process whereby credit demand shifts away from commercial banks, finance companies, and other traditional lenders toward publicly traded, open market debt underwritten by securities firms. In effect, securitization is a process of disintermediation, whereby high-cost producers of credit are displaced at a lower cost by institutional investors and the public capital market. The cost savings are shared by the issuers, security houses, investors, and consumers that are involved in the process.

Clearly, the best examples of securitization are the secular loss of the commercial banking industry's high-quality corporate customers to the commercial paper market and its loss of middle market customers to the speculative-grade bond sector. Growing from a base of $50 billion in the mid-1970s, the commercial paper market has exploded to over $350 billion in outstandings. Similarly, the speculative-grade bond market has increased from $15 billion to over $125 billion in only ten years. Borrowings in the Euromarket under note-issuance facilities are a third example of this broad trend toward securitization.

Asset securitization is that subset of securitization that involves the public market financing of pools of assets. The securities issued thus far have been either debt or equity instruments and have generally used cash flow from the pool of assets to make payments to security holders. Credit enhancement, usually in the form of a guaranty, letter of credit, surety bond, or additional assets, has been provided as protection against losses on the pool.

Although the pool of assets that backs the securtity may be virtually any type, residential mortgages that enjoy the full guaranty of a federally sponsored agency have been the most popular securitized product to date. In the 1970s, approximately $100 billion in mortgage-backed securities of this type were issued. Most of these were Government National Mortgage Association guaranties and Federal Home Loan Mortgage Corporation participation certificates.

As of 1987, mortgage-backed securities outstanding exceed $600 billion, while trading volume in mortgage-backed securities was an estimated $2.5 trillion last year. At the same time that mortgage-backed security issuance and trading activity are at unprecedented highs, the variety of instruments is increasing—particularly synthetic or derivative securities, such as collateralized mortgage obligations, private label strip pass-throughs, and other securities that are bondlike.

Benefits of Securitization

The benefits of securitized lending, which are many, are the major motivating factors that drive financial intermediaries to use this financial tool.

For issuers, the securitization of financial assets improves returns on capital by converting a spread banking business into off-balance-sheet, less-capital-intensive sources of income. Depending on the type of structure used, securitization may also offer the originator lower borrowing costs, reduced leverage, capital immediately available for expansion or reinvestment, diversification of funding sources, and improved asset/liability management.

For investors, securitized issues offer high and stable credit ratings at a time when traditional corporate bonds are declining in credit quality and are increasingly susceptible to event risk. High credit ratings, along with the existence of worldwide computerized secondary markets, enhance the liquidity of securitized issues. They also offer added flexibility in portfolio management because their repayment streams may be structured to meet investors' particular portfolio requirements. A final important benefit to investors is the attractive yields that they offer compared with other high-quality instruments.

For consumers, competition is forcing loan originators and

underwriters to share their cost savings with consumers. Over time, Moody's anticipates that the attractiveness of securitization and competition will force spreads to narrow and will ultimately save consumers one percentage point or more in rates for many types of credit. A second important benefit to consumers is the increase in credit offered.

Potential of Asset Securitization

Although mortgage-backed securities either issued directly or guaranteed by government-related agencies currently provide the bulk of securitized credit outstanding, the issuance of securitized issues by private (that is, non-government-related) issuers has grown in importance. Publicly rated securities of this type now aggregate in excess of $200 billion outstanding. In 1986, the volume of new asset-backed issues underwritten totaled $75 billion and represented one third of all publicly rated, taxable domestic debt issues. This volume results from the securitization of such diverse asset types as agency-backed mortgage pass-throughs, whole loan residential mortgages, credit card receivables, automobile loans, trade receivables, lease receivables, and commercial mortgages. In addition, the private placement market for privately guaranteed asset-backed securities has also grown; bank-to-bank loan sales and the ongoing sale of trade receivables by industrial corporations to financial institutions are examples of this trend.

Moody's expects that the scope of asset securitization, particularly that involving non-government-supported securities, will continue to grow throughout the next decade. The potential opportunities that securitization offers to issuers, intermediaries, and investors will drive asset securitization in four directions: a greater number and variety of originators securitizing assets; more players underwriting, distributing, and trading the securities issued; continued growth in acceptability among investors; and more markets active in the entire process.

We anticipate that consumer receivables other than U.S. government–supported mortgages, such as conventional first and second mortgages, vehicle-related debt, and credit card receivables; commercial mortgages; and traditional corporate bonds will play a much greater role in securitization. The potential for asset securitization from these sources is extremely high. Commercial and industrial loans at commercial banks exceed $550 billion, consumer installment debt is in excess of $500 billion, residential and commercial mortgage debt aggregates more than $2.5 trillion, and more than $1 trillion of speculative-grade corporate and sovereign debt could be credit enhanced and reissued in the public market in securitized form.

Additional forces that fuel the asset securitization movement include the increasing ability of commercial banks to take a more active role in the underwriting, distribution, and trading of collateralized securities, as well as the accelerating role that we anticipate the European and Asia/Pacific financial markets to assume in both investing and issuing publicly traded asset-backed securities.

ASSESSING THE IMPACT OF ASSET SECURITIZATION ON CORPORATE FINANCIAL HEALTH

Much public discussion by the accounting, regulatory, and tax professions has been devoted to the impact of asset securitization on the balance sheets of those who originate, service, and trade the assets. However, little comment has been forthcoming from rating agencies about the ongoing credit health of the asset originator.

Moody's analysis of the impact of securitization on a corporation's credit quality focuses on two key issues: First, how does a specific securitized transaction affect the originator's credit quality? Second, how does the general trend of securitization affect the credit quality of the financial sector as a whole?

In dealing with the first issue, the credit analyst should begin with the practices developed by the accounting and regulatory world. However, these guidelines often do not fully capture the true economic risks of a securitized asset sale to the originator's credit quality. Moody's focus is not on whether a sale of assets is arbitrarily put on or kept off the balance sheet, but instead on assessing the fundamental residual credit risks left with the originator from the asset sale and the amount of the firm's equity base tht should be allocated to support the transaction. Resolving this issue involves a joint analysis by Moody's Structured Transactions Group and the industry specialist responsible for the originator's credit rating. This group analyzes structured transactions in detail, including structural protections, legal issues, collateral quality, and support agreements, so as to rate specific structured transactions, as well as to evaluate the residual risks left with the originator. This group is staffed by individuals with direct experience in the mortgage banking, consumer and commercial lending, and commercial real estate businesses, as well as in the legal and structural analysis of mortgage-backed and asset-backed securities. Once the group completes its analysis, the industry specialist is then responsible for examining the rating of the originator and factoring the residual risks of securitized asset sales into the appraisal of the originator's credit quality.

The second issue on which Moody's focuses—how the general trend toward securitization affects the credit quality of the financial sector as a whole—is much more global in scope. This extremely complex and challenging issue is addressed within the rating process. Moody's approach is (1) to form its opinion of the impact of securitization on the financial sector as a whole, based on its own analysis, as well as the insights gained from meetings with major issuers, intermediaries, and public policymakers, and (2) to then factor this outlook into specific rating conclusions.

The Credit Impact of Asset Securitization on the Financial Intermediation Industry

Although it is difficult to generalize about all sectors of financial intermediation, several forces that are either direct or indirect consequences of the trend toward asset securitization appear to be reshaping the way in which financial intermediaries conduct their business. The primary attractions of asset securitization, particularly its use as a more efficient financing tool, are placing enormous pressures on financial intermediaries to securitize—due to competitive necessity—at least a portion of their loan origination volume. These pressures will likely increase, as more intermediaries make use of this financing alternative and as competition forces much of the cost savings to flow back to the consumer in terms of lower borrowing costs.

A second important impact that asset securitization is having on financial intermediation is an increase in the scale of competition from a local or regional basis to one of national and international scope. This trend is most evident within the residential mortgage origination and servicing industry, in which several major originators now directly set mortgage rates at an increment above the pass-through rate and limited documentation underwriting standards are aggressively being used as competitive weapons to differentiate products. The consolidation under way within this highly fragmented industry is a direct result of these forces.

The new competitive environment has also enhanced the importance of servicing efficiency to financial intermediaries. In particular, economies of scale from large volume and the use of technological advances to cut servicing costs are variables critical to the success of servicers in the 1990s. Consolidation within the mortgage banking industry, referred to earlier, is a logical reaction to these pressures. In addition, several major mortgage servicers are well down the path to using computer-scanning techniques and other technological advances to trim costs within the document-intensive mortgage servicing business. Based on these trends, we expect a shakeout within the mortgage origination and servicing business of marginal, less-efficient operators by the early 1990s.

A final important effect that asset securitization is having on financial intermediation is a change in the factors affecting the industry's earnings. As pure brokering and servicing of assets assume a larger role, earnings will be subject to differing stresses. First, up-front transaction fees will become a more important component of total earnings, and profitability will depend more heavily on a continuous flow of new transactions. This differs significantly from the traditional loan origination business, in which profits are heavily influenced by spreads on a book of business generated in the past that still has a remaining life of several years. Second, income from servicing will become a more important part of the originator's profitability. This may dampen earnings volatility to the extent that funding risk and credit risk are eliminated; however, earnings will be more affected by the speed at which loans prepay, which is largely influenced by interest rate movements.

Overall, competitive necessity is driving financial intermediaries to use securitized lending as a competitive tool and is simultaneously altering the risk dynamics of the business. How intermediaries handle the challenges that this changing environment presents is a critical issue that Moody's considers when it assesses the credit strength of the industry and its participants.

The Credit Impact of Asset Securitization on the Originator

Moody's views securitized asset sales as hybrid financing vehicles that fall somewhere between a pure sale encountered in the normal course of business and a secured financing. Exactly where a securitized asset sale would fall in this spectrum is a qualitative decision based on thorough analysis of the residual risks that may or may not remain with the originator following the sale.

Transfer of Default Risk

A critical issue in any securitized asset sale is the extent to which the default risk on the assets sold has been transferred from the originator/seller to the purchaser. This question involves three separate issues: (1) Has default risk been legally transferred? (2) To what degree has it been transferred? (3) Even if it has been legally transferred, is there any unwritten obligation or understanding to cover defaults?

The first hurdle is the most critical—that is, legally, has a "true sale" of assets taken place? Although originators may recognize a transfer of assets as a sale for accounting or tax purposes, our standards for treating transactions as sales are more conservative because we look for assurance that the assets would not be part of the originator/seller's estate in the event of its involvency. This involves analysis of the facts concerning the transaction and may also involve analysis of legal opinions rendered by nationally recognized bankruptcy counsel. Upon reviewing the facts of the transaction and the substance of any legal opinions, Moody's may not be satisfied that a true sale of assets has occurred. In that case, the assets and related liabilities would be recapitalized on the originator's books, and the transaction would be viewed as a secured financing involving an uncertain transfer of risk.

If the transaction is judged to be a true sale for rating agency purposes, our second task is to quantify (1) the residual default risk remaining with the originator and (2) the extent to which a portion of the originator's equity base should be allocated to support this activity. Quantification of the residual default risk or contingent liability of the originator in a securitized asset sale requires an in-depth review of the structure of the transaction, third party support agreements, if any, and the originator's policies to establish loss reserves. In many securitized asset sales, the originator provides a limited guaranty—either directly or indirectly—for losses on the assets. This contingent liability may entail significant credit risk to the originator because it absorbs the first-loss or equity risk in the assets transferred.

The final step in analyzing the transfer of default risk in a securitized asset sale involves an assessment of whether the originator may be morally obligated to cover defaults above and beyond its legal obligations. In addressing this issue, Moody's assesses the originator's incentives to cover defaults. This assessment is influenced by the importance of securitization to its core business and by the investment community's perception of these securities. Moody's recapitalizes assets when these incentives are judged to be extremely high.

Improved Asset/Liability Management

A second issue that Moody's focuses on is the extent to which securitized asset sales affect the originator's ability to manage its asset/liability mismatch. In many instances, securitization affords originators the ability to significantly reduce this risk through improved interest rate and maturity matching. In short, asset-liability concerns may be eliminated for the asset sold. This is an important point, because the asset/liability risk in financing assets may be greater than the default risk. For example, the thrift industry has availed itself of an interest rate decline and the ability to securitize fixed-rate mortgages so as to conduct a wholesale restructuring of thrift balance sheets to a much better asset/liability-matched position. Improved asset/liability management, fee generation, and meeting of regulatory capital requirements were the motivating forces behind these restructurings, rather than a desire to reduce default risk.

Shift in Asset Quality

Securitization readily lends itself to high-quality assets that enjoy a steady cash flow. Therefore, an issue important to Moody's is the degree to which the originator's asset quality deteriorates as a result of securitized asset sales and concurrent reinvestment of proceeds in new assets. To analyze this issue, Moody's focuses on the specific quality of the assets being sold in relation to that of the entire portfolio, the availability of suitable reinvestment opportunities, and management's plans for the use of securitized asset sales as a continuing financing alternative.

In addition to a possible shift downward in asset quality, Moody's also assesses the degree to which diversification may be affected. Many financial originators have distinct regional biases to their business. Securitization gives these institutions the ability to diversity their aggregate credit risk by packaging assets into securities, selling them off as regionally concentrated pools, and then repurchasing pools that represent other geographic regions.

Diversification of Funding Alternatives

Diversification of funding alternatives is a major issue in the evaluation of the credit quality of any business. Traditionally, selling assets as whole loans was always a cumbersome and expensive process. It took substantial resources to transfer thousands of individual loans, and because documention and products were not standardized, whole loan packages were relatively illiquid. Although a secondary market for whole loans has existed for some time, these factors limited its development.

However, securitized asset sales opened up a new, large source of potential investors, by skirting many of the physical problems associated with whole loan sales while offering investors a product that promised safety, liquidity, and attractive yields. Indeed, most securitized issues are rated higher than the debt obligations of the originator and are structured to achieve a stability in credit rating that few corporates have historically enjoyed. An additional factor that supports the expansion in the investor base that results from this new funding alternative is that securitized transactions generally fall outside the single-obligor lending limits of commercial banks and institutional investors.

Securitized asset sales have, in general, signifiantly broadened the investor base available to originators. However, two caveats must be expressed: First, as with any funding alternative, too great a reliance on a single funding vehicle may result in increased risk to the originator. A second concern involves the value of securitized asset sales as a long-term, ongoing funding tool. At issue is the certainty that the market for publicly rated asset-backed securities will continue to provide the same degree of depth as it has in the past. In this regard, Moody's focuses on two questions: First, what is the refinancing risk to the originator in terms of its access to the asset-backed securities market being impaired by company-related factors? Second, what is the refinancing risk to the originator in terms of its access being restricted by exogenous factors?

Assessment of the refinancing risk that stems from company-related factors is of particular importance when financing of the assets being sold is critical to the fundamental business activity of the originator/seller. For example, if a financial institution were precluded from using securitized asset sales when its credit rating fell into the speculative-grade range, Moody's would consider the refinancing risk in using asset-backed securities to be relatively high.

However, asset-backed securities may be structured so that the credit quality of the originator has little, if any, bearing on the rating of the security. Although some securitized asset sales rely on the originator to furnish a limited guaranty for losses on the securitized assets, the originator's guaranty is usually incorporated into a transaction only if the originator is highly rated and would not normally play a role in new transactions if it were under financial stress. Thus, an originator's credit quality would be a hindrance to ensuring its ability to refinance using asset-backed securities only to the extent that the originator's credit quality was ultimately used to entice a third party to enhance the pool of assets. A second factor that mitigates the refinancing risk stemming from company-related factors is that, although most securitized asset sales rely on the originator to service the portfolio of assets, well-structured transactions provide for a substitute servicer if the originator encounters serious financial problems.

For these reasons, the company-related refinancing risk for well-structured securitized asset sales may be quite low. In fact, during the last recession, investors preferred highly rated asset-backed securities over straight debentures or secured debt for the financing of several thrifts, commercial banks, and finance companies that were under financial duress.

Several points are worth noting with regard to the refinancing risk stemming from exogenous or non-company-related factors. The publicly rated asset-backed security market is still a relatively young market that lacks the full development and maturity that only time and several market cycles can bring about. Nevertheless, the market today is over $200 billion in size and encompasses a wide variety of new structures, asset types, and market participants. An extremely strong secondary market exists in the rated agency-backed mortgage sector, and one is actively being supported by major intermediaries in the privately guaranteed area. Second, the asset-backed securities market has demonstrated a resilience to credit-related stresses; the 1985 default of a large, unrated mortgage-backed security collateralized by investor properties is the most prominent example of this.

A third, and final, point supporting the ability of the asset-backed security market to remain a long-term, ongoing source of capital to originators involves the fundamental growth of the asset-backed security market in relation to the traditional issuance of unsecured corporate debt. In the past three years, the asset-backed share of total new publicly rated corporate debt increased from 21 percent to 33 percent, while the total new-issue volume of corporate securities more than tripled.

Servicing Efficiency

Most securitized asset sales occur with the originator retaining responsibility for servicing the assets. Since the administrative expense incurred by an originator in fulfilling its ongoing obligation to service the portfolio is usually reimbursed by the purchaser on a fixed-rate fee basis, the risk of inefficiency from an operational point of view is retained by the originator.

The originator's retention of servicing risk is clearly a residual risk that involves an ongoing use of financial flexibility. Moody's focuses on four key issues when assessing servicing risk: the servicing fees generated by the portfolio, the originator's administrative efficiencies, the ease with which servicing rights may be sold to third parties, and the credit quality of the serviced book of business.

Servicing efficiency is a critical variable that is assuming greater importance within the analysis of a loan originator. As discussed earlier, securitization is changing the scale of competition from a regional basis to one that is national and international in scope, with resulting pressures on pricing, underwriting standards, and profitability. This new environment has thereby significantly raised the importance of servicing—particularly the use of economies of scale and technological advances to gain competitive efficiency. The credit quality of the serviced portfolio is also an important issue in regard to servicing efficiency, as Moody's has found that servicing costs correlate with loan quality.

Several factors may partially mitigate the amount of equity that needs to be dedicated to support the servicing function. First, servicing is a business activity that may provide significant benefits to the originator in terms of ongoing profits and cash flow to support its debt obligations. The unrecognized profit potential of a servicing portfolio has aptly been demonstrated by the recent sale of several large servicing portfolios at premium prices. A second mitigating factor is that, at least within the residential mortgage industry, a ready market exists to purchase servicing rights and to provide these vital functions.

Funding Costs

The lower borrowing costs that result from securitized asset sales have been a factor in the growth of this financing technique, particularly with certain originator types. For instance, home builders have frequently financed home sales through builder bonds, because of the favorable installment sales treatment that they are permitted on the gains. In addition, several low-rated originators have tapped the securitized asset sale market to significantly reduce their funding costs.

Financial Constraints to Market Share Growth

A final issue that Moody's assesses when analyzing the impact of securitization on an originator's financial health is the degree to which the use of securitized asset sales mitigates the financial constraints that, heretofore, may have limited market share growth. In some instances, markets have grown at a faster pace than the retained earnings of the originator. Corporations that maintained good, solid balance sheets were, thus, forced to make the difficult decision of whether to potentially deplete their credit quality, raise additional equity, or limit their market participation.

The option to effect well-structured securitized asset sales grants originators the ability to preserve or even to increase their market share by funding only part of their originations internally against their balance sheet—to the extent that retained earnings can carry them—and selling off the balance in a securitized form. The potential of securitization is substantial for large national lenders because it allows them to capture major shares in the national loan origination market without having to raise a proportionate amount of capital. Evidence of this potential has already surfaced in the mortgage banking industry, in which a consolidation among the largest 10 to 20 players is clearly under way.

In assessing the importance of securitized asset sales to an originator's potential for market share improvement, Moody's evaluates many aspects of the originator, including the competitive environment, regulatory support, and credit quality of the new business that the originator is seeking.

CONCLUSION

In general, the evolution of financial intermediation is compelling participants, out of competitive necessity, to add securitized lending to their financial alternatives. It is also reshaping the nature of the financial intermediation business. Asset securitization often entails potential pitfalls and additional risks to the originator; however, Moody's is also keenly aware of the accompanying benefits—in particular, that capital funds are being recycled to finance originators' future market activities at economically attractive rates.

In analyzing the impact of asset securitization on a corporation's credit quality, Moody's considers how securitization is changing the credit dynamics of both the industry and the company's competitive position within that industry, as well as the specific attributes of a corporation's asset securitization program. Because of the structural complexity of securitized asset sales, our analysis is conducted on a joint basis by Moody's Structured Transactions Group and the Corporate Research Group responsible for the originator's credit rating. How financial intermediaries face the challenges presented by securitized lending is a critical issue that Moody's focuses on in assessing the effect of securitized asset sales on the general credit quality of the commercial banks, investment banks, thrifts, mortgage banks, home builders, manufacturers, retailers, insurance companies, and finance companies that it rates.

PART II
ASSET-BACKED SECURITIES

CHAPTER 10

Asset-Backed Securities: An Attractive Addition to the Low-Duration Sector of the Fixed Income Market

William J. Curtin and Stephen H. Deckoff

INTRODUCTION

While the growth of the mortgage-backed pass-through security market has slowed considerably over the past year, a cousin of this market, the asset-backed security market, is experiencing rapid growth. The asset-backed security market essentially evolved from the mortgage-backed security market. Asset-backed securities are similar in many respects to mortgage-backed securities. As opposed to real estate loans, however, asset-backed securities are backed by loans, installment contracts, or leases on personal property, such as credit cards, automobiles, boats, or computers. These individual receivables are packaged into securities in a manner similar to the pooling process for mortgage-backed securities.

The first asset-backed security was launched in 1985. This market has flourished since then, as currently about $20 billion is outstanding.[1] At this level, however, it has only touched the tip of the iceberg of supply. A tremendous amount of consumer installment

[1]This includes only the publicly issued non-mortgage-related securities with initial terms greater than one year. It does not include privately placed deals or asset-backed commercial paper programs.

debt remains outstanding, which provides plenty of room for the market to grow further, as well as diversity in the types of receivables. In addition, the proposed new bank capital guidelines provide a greater incentive for banks to securitize such assets. At present, the automobile receivable–backed security and the credit card receivable–backed security have emerged as the backbone of the asset-backed security market. The structures found in the asset-backed security market are similar to those found in the mortgage-backed security market, as asset-backed deals have generally been structured on pass-through participation certificates or pay-through bonds.

Although asset-backed securities are similar to mortgage-backed securities, there are some important differences. One major difference is that asset-backed securities lack a U.S. government guarantee. Unlike mortgage-backed securities, in which governmental agencies guarantee the payment of principal and interest, credit enhancements, such as letters of credit, private insurance, and senior/subordinated structures, are necessary to obtain AA and AAA ratings. To achieve these high ratings, an asset-backed security deal must be structured so that it could cover many times the historical loss rate on the underlying assets.

There is also an important difference in the cash flows of asset-backed securities and mortgage-backed securities. Although, as with mortgages, borrowers have the ability to prepay their loans at any point in time, automobile loans and credit card receivables do not show wide payment variations in response to interest rate shifts, which have been thoroughly documented with mortgages. Instead, the repayment of principal for asset-backed securities tends to be fairly consistent, regardless of the interest rate or economic environment. The cash flow patterns of asset-backed securities often more clearly resemble those of short-term corporate bonds, rather than mortgage-backed instruments.

For the originator of the loans, securitization provides a way to remove assets from the balance sheet and sell them to provide capital to the firm, which may be less expensive than more traditional forms of debt or equity financing. Capital raised in this manner is ideal in that the maturity of the assets matches the subsequent liabilities. Additionally, by securitizing assets, the issuing firm is also able to take advantage of available capital gains. Other benefits include a

Figure 10-1. Asset-Backed Security Issuance, 1985–1988

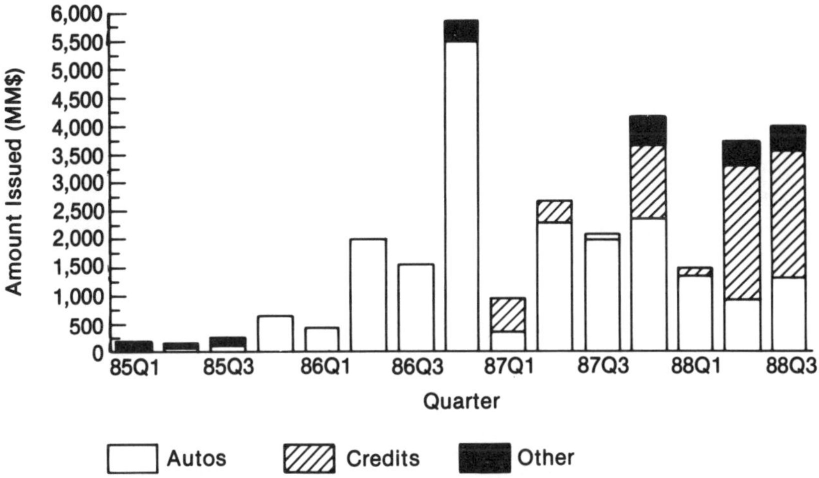

reduction in interest rate risk and an improvement in the capitalization ratio. For the investor, asset-backed securities are a relatively high-yielding addition to the low-duration sector of the fixed income product line. The asset-backed security market continues to trade at high yields compared with corporates and provides favorable return profiles compared with mortgage-related products. Investors who seek short- to intermediate-term high-quality paper should find asset-backed securities an attractive option.

GROWTH OF THE ASSET-BACKED SECURITY MARKET

Despite its recent beginnings, over $30 billion of asset-backed securities have been issued to date. The public issuance of asset-backed securities from 1985 through the third quarter of 1988 is shown in Figure 10-1. The first public asset-backed security deal, which was issued by Sperry Lease Finance Corporation in March 1985, was collateralized by computer equipment leases. In May of that year, Marine Midland introduced the first public security backed by automobile receivables. The deal amounted to just over $60 million and was followed later in the year by three more automobile receivable–backed securities, which totaled $525 million. Issuance of asset-backed securities increased sharply in 1986, as a number of major automobile lenders used this new structure. General Motors Acceptance Corporation (GMAC), for example, issued some very large deals. One issue, GMAC Series 86-B, was collateralized with 98,150 car and truck loans and amounted to over $1 billion. Another deal, which used GMAC loans, had a total face value of $4 billion. These large deals were prompted, in part, by the heavily promoted low-financing campaigns in vogue at the time. Lenders desired to get these below-market-rate loans off of their books to raise cash for new loans.

In January 1987, credit card installment debt was securitized for the first time, as RepublicBank of Delaware issued the first credit card receivable–backed security. The use of credit card installment debt rose rapidly during 1987; by 1988, the issuance level of credit card receivable–backed securities approached that of automobile receivable–backed securities.

The amount of outstanding publicly issued asset-backed securities totals about $20 billion; because of the product's short term and high prepayments, it tends to pay down rapidly. Although this is small compared with the over $600 billion mortgage-backed pass-through market, it is similar to more comparable sectors, such as the $23 billion AA and AAA short-term noncallable corporate sector, the $34 billion collateralized mortgage obligation (CMO) floater market, or the $35 billion mortgage-backed security Adjustable Rate Mortgage (ARM) pass-through market. The composition of the asset-backed security market is illustrated in Figure 10-2. Automobile and credit card receivable–backed securities, the cornerstones of the market, account for approximately 51 percent and 40 percent of the amount outstanding, respectively. These two security types are the focus of this chapter. The remaining 9 percent comprises securities backed with other types of receivables, such as airplane leases, computer equipment leases, boat loans, and consumer credit loans.

Whereas the cyclical pattern of mortgage-backed security issuance has continually plagued the mortgage market, the pattern will most likely not be similar for asset-backed securities. The supply of mortgage-backed securities typically rises sharply when interest rates fall and declines dramatically during periods of rising interest rates. This variation in issuance tends to cause a similar fluctuation in the relative value of mortgage-backed securities. As originations rise,

Figure 10-2. Composition of the ABS Market (Percent of Dollars Outstanding)

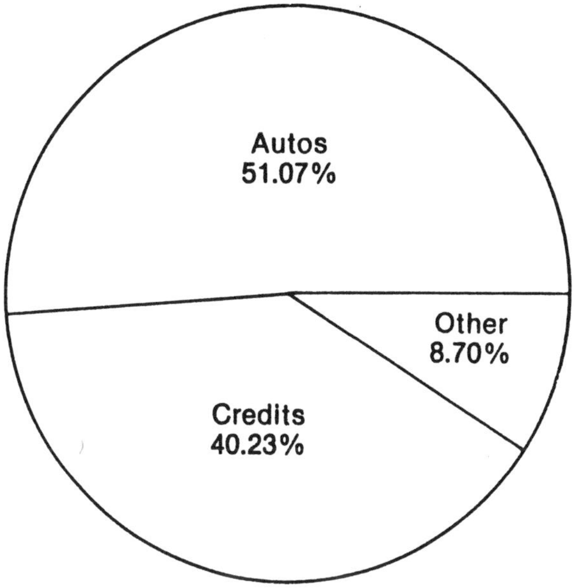

yield spreads of mortgages to Treasuries tend to widen; generally, they tighten when issuance declines. Asset-backed securities should exhibit supply characteristics drastically different from those that have been observed in the mortgage-backed security market. Because consumers must frequently borrow to replace retiring debt, there should be a more steady creation of new asset-backed securities. This can considerably reduce the level of fluctuation of relative value for asset-backed securities as compared with that of mortgage-backed securities.

With the tremendous amounts of unsecuritized debt outstanding, this market could continue to expand. Even proposed bank capital guidelines encourage the issuance of asset-backed securities. Currently, it appears that assets such as credit card and automobile loans will be assigned a 100 percent risk weighting; thus, there will be an 8 percent capital requirement for loans of this type. These rules provide a great incentive for banks to securitize these assets, sell them, and reinvest the proceeds in products that require lower levels of capital. These rules are a major reason for the expectation that the asset-backed security market will become a very important component of the fixed income universe.

ASSET-BACKED SECURITY STRUCTURES: FROM COLLATERAL TO SECURITY

In this section, the structures of automobile and credit receivable-backed securities are discussed. The specific cash flows of the respective securities are described in more detail in a later section.

Automobile Receivable-Backed Securities

Similar to a mortgage-backed security, which is created by pooling individual mortgages, the creation of an automobile-backed security starts with the pooling of individual automobile installment sales contracts. These contracts can be for new, as well as used, cars and trucks. Compared with a Government National Mortgage Association (GNMA) mortgage pool, which might contain 20 or 30 loans, a typical automobile-backed security pool contains tens of thousands of loans. While this diversity is usually attractive to an investor, the work required to service the security can be substantial for the issuer.

Like a mortgage, an automobile loan is an amortizing asset. Car owners make monthly payments that consist of both principal and interest. These payments support subsequent payments to the bond holders, which occur either monthly or quarterly. Many investors prefer the quarterly paying structure because of lower reinvestment risk, as well as reduced administrative costs.

Auto deals have been structured as both pass-through certificates, which constitute a sale of assets for the issuer, as well as pay-through bonds. These structures are basically the same as those that have been used successfully in the mortgage-backed security market. In both cases, all of the principal is passed on to the security holder, and, therefore, the cash flow depends on how quickly the installment contracts in the pool prepay. Many investors have been attracted to deals that contain provisions reducing this cash flow uncertainty. Features such as guaranteed minimum prepayment rates and final maturities earlier than those of the underlying contracts have been enthusiastically received in the market.

Besides pass-throughs and pay-throughs, there have also been issues whose principal payments are fixed. This eliminates the prepayment risk associated with pass-throughs and pay-throughs and resembles the cash flows of a corporate bond. Some of these fixed payment deals have final bullet maturities, while others return principal according to a fixed schedule in the deal's indenture. Using techniques that have been successful for CMOs, these deals typically contain multiple classes.

Credit Card Receivable-Backed Securities

In a credit card receivable-backed security deal, individual credit card accounts are pooled together. The credit cards can be either bank cards, such as MasterCard and Visa; travel and entertainment cards, such as American Express; or retailers' cards, such as Sears. As opposed to mortgages and automobile loans, which have a specific loan size, the balances of credit card accounts fluctuate as card holders continually borrow and repay their debts. To accommodate this revolving nature, credit card receivable-backed securities are nonamortizing for a period, usually 18 to 36 months, over which interest only is paid, followed by an amortization period over which the principal is returned. Investors are sold certificates whose initial face value represents a specific interest in the pooled receivables. The remaining balance of the debt is retained by the issuer. Over the nonamortization period, the investors' principal balance remains constant, while the issuer's balance may vary, as it must absorb the fluctuations in the pooled accounts. If, for example, the balance of pooled accounts is initially $200 million and the investors are sold a $90 million security, the issuer has retained $110 million of the pooled accounts balance. If card holders borrow an additional $10 million during the nonamortization period, raising the balance of the pooled accounts to $210 million, the investors' principal balance is still $90 million, while the issuer's principal balance rises to $120 million. If, on the other hand, the card holders' repayment of debt is greater than their new borrowings, the issuers' principal balance declines, while the security holder's principal balance again remains unchanged.

Although the nonamortization period of a credit card receivable-backed security has a stated length, provisions usually exist that allow amortization to occur prematurely should specific extreme events occur that jeopardize the ability of the cash flows to support the structure. Such "amortization events" include abnormally high defaults or a sharp drop in the average finance (or interest) rate on the underlying accounts.

Once the amortization period starts, principal payments are no longer absorbed solely by the issuer, but are also passed through to the bond holders. Two methods are used to determine how principal collections are allocated between the bond holders and the issuer. One method provides investors with a pro rata share of the principal payments on all the underlying accounts. If, for example, at the start of the amortization period, the total amount of the pool receivables is $200 million and the investors' share is $90 million, the investors' portion of any principal received is 45 percent. If $20 million is repaid, the investors receive 45 percent, or $9 million.

With the other method, all principal payments are funnelled from the pooled accounts to the investors until the bonds are retired. With this method, the investors receive principal at a faster rate. Using the example above, if a total amount of $20 million in principal is paid by card holders, the investors receive the entire $20 million. It is important to note that, with either method, when new debt is taken on by the credit card holders during the amortization period, it does not offset or affect the principal paydowns in any way.

To eliminate the possibility of principal remaining outstanding for an excessive period of time (a long "tail"), credit card receivable–backed securities have stated maturities that occur shortly after the beginning of the amortization period. In addition, other clean-up provisions often exist. Such provisions require the issuer to retire the bonds when the outstanding principal balance falls to less than a given percentage of the original face amount, usually 2 percent to 5 percent. In either case, if principal collections are insufficient to make the final payment, the issuer is obligated to repurchase any bonds that are still ouststanding. If the issuer is unable to comply with this obligation, any additional credit support used in the deal is used to cover the principal payment.

CREDIT QUALITY

The success of the asset-backed security market has, in large part, been the result of its ability to create securities that can obtain credit ratings of AAA and AA. These high ratings make asset-backed securities a possibility for investors who require investment-grade securities.

Before an agency assigns a rating, the asset-backed security is put through a comprehensive, methodical evaluation. Historical loss rates for the loan portfolio, the issuer's underwriting practices, and the ability of the issuer to service an asset-backed deal are all primary concerns that are investigated extensively. The rating agencies painstakingly examine past default rates, one of the best indicators of credit quality, and search for any patterns that may exist. Recovery rates for defaulted contracts are assessed and help to measure the ability of the issuer to collect. Additionally, an examination is made of delinquencies, which are one of the best indicators of future losses. The greater the number of past-due contracts, the greater the perceived credit risk.

The issuer's underwriting practices are also thoroughly reviewed. For example, mass-marketing mail campaigns that offer preapproved credit cards, which are frequently used to increase an issuer's business, can add to the credit risk of the portfolio. A portfolio developed in this manner requires a greater degree of credit enhancement. Also, the rating agencies closely check the operations of the issuer, such as record keeping and bookkeeping, to ensure that payments to the bond holders can be made on a timely basis.

In addition, various other features of the loans may influence the amount of credit enhancement that the rating agencies require for the deal to achieve an AA or AAA rating. For example, the demographic and geographic diversity of the portfolio is examined. Geographic regions with high industrial diversification are considered preferable to those dominated by just a few industries. In addition, the rating agencies may require a greater degree of credit enhancement if the loans are geographically concentrated. The seasoning of the loans is another characteristic that is possibly important. Older contracts that have built up substantial equity and have demonstrated a track record of timely payment are often considered preferable to newly originated loans.

After carefully studying these criteria, the agencies test the integrity of a structure—the ability of the collateral to support the bonds—by exposing it to extreme economic stresses and monitoring the resulting cash flows. As the desired rating category increases, the severity of the stresses with which the portfolio is tested is further increased. The agencies must determine if the loss protection that the credit enhancement provides is sufficient to achieve the rating for which the issuer is applying.

Typically, issuers establish reserve funds to be used if, for some reason, the cash flows from the collateral are insufficient to meet the payments on the securities. These reserve funds are built in a number of different ways. With one method, the excess cash flow caused by the difference between the interest rate on the collateral and that of the coupon on the security accumulates to form the reserve.[2] For credit card receivable-backed securities, the paydowns during the nonamortization period are sometimes used to build the reserve fund. Regardless of the method employed to build the fund, these reserves typically form the first line of defense when ensuring the soundness of the structure.

Methods that issuers use to provide additional credit enhancement are usually letters of credit, private insurance, and senior/subordinated structures. Letters of credit have been a popular method to protect against shortfalls in available cash. Some letters of credit provide coverage for a fixed percentage of the original face value in the deal. Others are based on the current amount outstanding and decrease as the security amortizes. Another form of widely used credit support is private insurance. For example, Western Financial Savings Bank in Orange, California, uses a surety bond that guarantees timely payment of 100 percent of the interest and ultimate payment of 100 percent of the principal at the stated maturity. One drawback of the letter of credit and the private insurance methods, however, is the rating agencies' "weak link" approach, which makes clear that a deal is not rated higher than the credit rating of the third party that is either insuring or providing the letter of credit.

To avoid the high costs associated with third party enhancements, some issuers have made use of senior/subordinated structures. In this approach, a senior note and a subordinated note, which absorbs the credit risk of the portfolio, are created. Payments are not made to the subordinated note until the senior note has received its total scheduled payment. Although instances exist in which both classes have been sold, the senior notes are usually sold and the subordinated notes are usually retained by the issuer.

[2]A reserve built in this manner is sometimes referred to as a spread account.

Figure 10-3. Auto Receivable-Backed Security Cash Flows

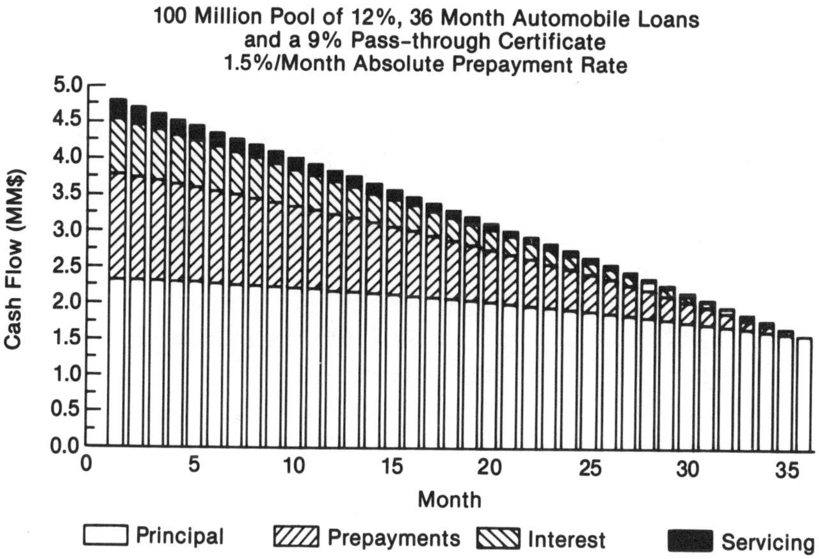

CASH FLOW CHARACTERISTICS OF ASSET-BACKED SECURITIES

Automobile Receivable-Backed Securities

Like any other investment, to evaluate asset-backed securities, one must understand the nature of their cash flows. The cash flow characteristics of an automobile-backed security vary from that of a credit card receivable-backed security. The cash flows of an automobile-backed security are typically similar to those of a mortgage-backed pass-through, although there are a few important differences. One major difference is that most mortgages usually have 15- to 30-year maturities, while the typical car loan usually matures in 3 to 5 years. Another is that prepayments for car loans are more consistent than those of mortgages.

If the cash flow diagram for a mortgage-backed security is compressed, it looks similar to the cash flow for an automobile-backed security. The cash flows from a pool of auto loans with an original term of 36 months are displayed in Figure 10-3. The cash flow generated by a pool of auto loans consists of both interest, a percentage of which is retained by the issuer as a servicing charge, and principal, which can be both scheduled and unscheduled. Like a mortgage-backed security, it is this unscheduled amount, known as the prepayment, that leads to uncertainty in the cash flows of the security. Thus, to be comfortable with the nature of automobile-backed security cash flows, one must understand the prepayment characteristics of these loans.

The asset-backed security market actually uses two methods to measure the prepayment speed of automobile-backed securities: conditional prepayment rate (CPR) and absolute prepayment rate (ABS). The CPR, which is the standard measurement of prepayments for mortgage-backed securities, measures the amount of prepayments conditional on the amount outstanding in the previous month. It also can be viewed as the percentage of outstanding loans that prepay. On the other hand, the ABS calculates prepayments as a percentage of the *original* number of loans in a pool. For example, 1 percent ABS means that, every month, 1 percent of the original number of loans prepay. ABS was adopted because studies showed that the prepayment pattern of automobile-backed securities varied from that of mortgage-backed securities and that this method may better reflect automobile-backed security prepayment trends. Both ABS and CPR can be stated as either a monthly rate or an annual rate.

A comparison of the survival factors for a pool prepaying at 1 percent CPR per month and 1 percent ABS per month is presented in Table 10-1. In the first month, ABS and CPR produce the same results. The difference between the two keeps widening, however, as the pool ages. After the first month, the ABS rate always produces a higher paydown than the same CPR (since it is calculated using the original number of loans). A change in ABS rate can affect yield and average life numbers significantly more than the same change in CPR can. At lower factor levels, the differences produced by the same CPR and ABS can be substantial.

Table 10-1. Loan Survival Factors: ABS Versus CPR at 1 Percent/Month

Month	*0*	*1*	*2*	*3*	*4*	*5*	*6*
ABS	1.0000	0.9900	0.9800	0.9700	0.9600	0.9500	0.9400
CPR	1.0000	0.9900	0.9801	0.9702	0.9606	0.9510	0.9415

Contrary to the payments for mortgages, the shorter term of automobile loans results in a large portion of each monthly payment being principal. Therefore, the principal balance of an automobile-backed security deal decreases rapidly and, as a result, changes in a prepayment assumption do not have as great an effect on the cash flows as they do on a mortgage-backed security. This reduced sensitivity is illustrated by the average life changes when prepayments are varied for GMAC Series 87-D, which is shown in Table 10-2. If the prepayment rate is zero, the average life of the bond is 1.79 years. If prepayments are 0.5 percent CPR per month, the average life decreases by only 0.11 to 1.68 years, while at 3.0 percent CPR, the average life is 1.24 years. Although this change is small, it is not unimportant, as discussed later.

Table 10-2. Sensitivity of an Automobile-Backed Security to Prepayment Rates

Issue:	GMAC Series 87-D
Coupon:	8.15%
Delay:	14 days
Stated final maturity:	June 15, 1992
Settlement date:	November 21, 1988
Price:	98:20

Prepayment Rate (CPR)	*Bond Equivalent Yield*	*Average Life (Years)*	*Modified Duration (Years)*
0.0%	8.95%	1.79	1.62
0.5	9.00	1.68	1.52
1.0	9.04	1.57	1.43
1.5	9.09	1.48	1.35
2.0	9.13	1.39	1.27
2.5	9.18	1.31	1.20
3.0	9.23	1.24	1.14

Most automobile-backed security deals typically trade near par because of their short terms. As a result, prepayment variations do not have a significant impact on the yields of these deals. Owing to this effect, some investors pay little attention to prepayment assumptions when purchasing automobile-backed securities. However, there is a serious flaw in this logic, as it overlooks the process by which asset-backed securities are priced. Like many other fixed income securities, automobile-backed securities are quoted at a spread to some point on the Treasury yield curve. The exact point on the curve that is typically used is determined by the average life of the security. The average life of an asset-backed security usually falls in the steepest section of the yield curve. Thus, a slight change in prepayments, causing a corresponding change in average life, can have a significant impact on the price of the security. Due to this, the pricing of an asset-backed security is typically more sensitive to changes in average life than is that of a mortgage-backed security. Before purchasing an asset-backed security, investors should evaluate whether the prepayment assumptions are reasonable.

Since prepayment rates do, in fact, significantly influence the pricing of automobile-backed securities, it is important to gain some insight into them with respect to automobile-backed securities. Great efforts have been made in the mortgage market to understand the external factors that influence prepayments and to develop models that use these factors as inputs to project prepayment rates. While there is nowhere near the amount of data on auto loans that exists for mortgages, the data that are available suggest that prepayments for auto loans differ fundamentally from those observed for mortgages. A prepayment of an auto loan can occur for a number of different reasons, including the transfer of title from a sale or trade-in, the loss of a vehicle from accident or theft, default on a loan, voluntary prepayment by the vehicle owner, and, on occasion, an individual loan that is found not to meet the requirements of the indenture, at which time the issuer is required to buy back the contract from the pool. An example of the last type of prepayment is a car owner allowing his or her insurance policy to lapse, in which case the loan is no longer permissible and has to be removed from the pool. This occurs most frequently in the initial months subsequent to pool formation.

The most important difference between prepayments on automobile-backed securities and those on mortgage-backed securities is the former's lack of sensitivity to interest rate shifts. The tendency for mortgage prepayments to increase as interest rates fall and decrease as rates rise is clearly evident from historic data. Due to the large payment and long term of mortgages, a reduction in the interest rate can result in a significant drop in the home owner's monthly payments. As a result, when mortgage rates fall below the rate on the mortgage, prepayment activity rises.

Figure 10-4. Historical Prepayment Experience

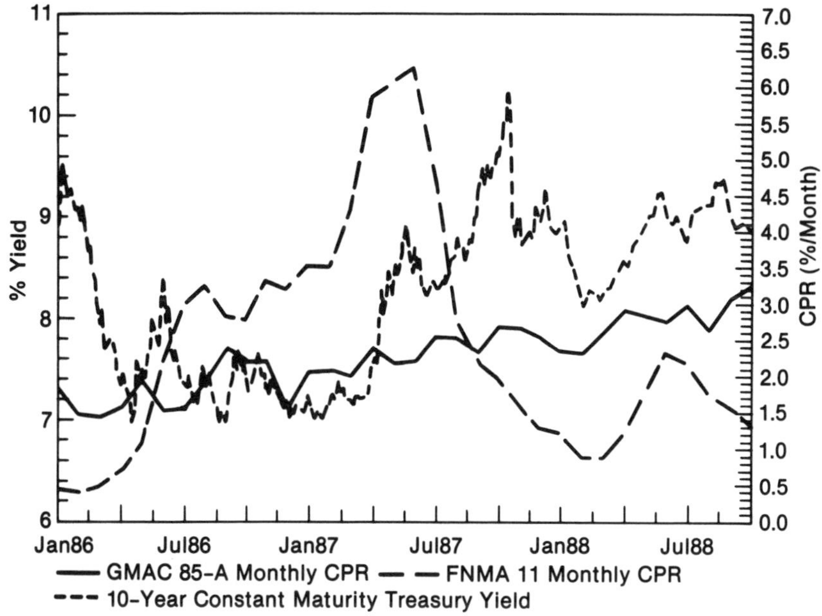

The greater the difference, the higher the prepayments. These prepayments are due to refinancings and an increased level of housing turnover. Conversely, when mortgage rates rise above the rate on the mortgage, prepayments slow as refinancings are not economically feasible and housing turnover is retarded.

While this relationship is fundamental to mortgage-backed securities, the relationship does not seem to hold for asset-backed securities. In short, prepayments for automobile-backed securities are not particularly sensitive to changes in interest rates. The historical prepayment experience of GMAC Series 85-A, which is plotted against those of the generic (Federal National Mortgage Association) mortgage pass-through certificate (FNMA) 11s in Figure 10-4, shows the relative lack of interest rate sensitivity. From January 1986 to April 1987, the rate on the ten-year Treasury fell over 250 basis points, causing prepayments on FNMA 11s to increase by over 1,000 percent, from 0.5 percent to over 6.0 percent CPR. On the other hand, the lower rates had little impact on prepayments on the selected GMAC deal, which fluctuated closely around 1.75 percent CPR. Also revealing is the prepayment pattern of asset-backed securities during the second half of 1987, when the rate on the ten-year Treasury climbed over 300 basis points. Although the rise in interest rates did not cause prepayments for the asset-backed securities to slow, prepayments for FNMA 11s plummeted to around the 1 percent CPR level.

A number of reasons account for the asset-backed securities' lack of prepayment sensitivity to a change in interest rates. First, many banks refuse to finance used cars, and those that do usually charge rates considerably higher than those for new cars. Second, because of the rapid pace at which automobiles usually depreciate in value, the car owner typically cannot obtain a new loan for the amount that is outstanding on the original loan. Third, compared with a house, the sharply lower outstanding balance on an automobile makes the savings from a new loan negligible and not worth the hassle involved. Monthly payments for typical 36- and 48-month automobile loans at different interest rate levels are shown in Table 10-3. If we neglect any fixed charges, which are common in car financing, refinancing a $10,000 loan from a rate of 16 percent to 8 percent saves just $39 a month. The above factors add up to provide very little economic incentive to refinance an automobile loan.

Table 10-3. Monthly Payments for a $10,000 Automobile Loan

Interest	*Monthly Payment*	
Rate	*36-Month Loan*	*48-Month Loan*
8%	$313	$244
10	323	254
12	332	263
14	342	273
16	352	283

Although automobile-backed securities accrue interest at the stated coupon, a number of deals contain car loans that accrue interest on a Rule of 78 basis. Unlike actuarial loans, which accrue interest at a constant rate over the life of a loan, Rule of 78 loans have a front-loaded interest rate structure. In other words, higher rates are paid in the early months, and lower rates are paid in the later stages of the loan. This unlevel structure serves, in effect, to further reduce the incentive to prepay. A pool with Rule of 78 loans should be expected to prepay more slowly than a similar pool with all actuarial loans.

Figure 10-5. Historical Prepayments versus Age (GMAC 85-A)

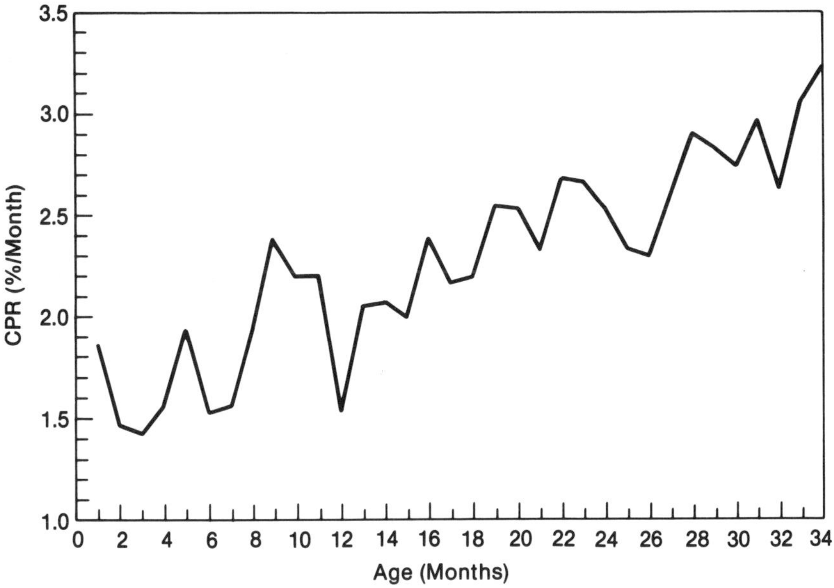

One prepayment feature of automobile loans that is similar to mortgages is that prepayments on automobile loans tend to rise as they season. In the early months, just after the purchase of the automobile, there is a low probability that the car owner will terminate the loan. As the car ages, however, the likelihood of the loan being paid off steadily increases. Data indicate that a large percentage of new car buyers trade in their cars every two to three years. The tendency for prepayments to increase as the auto seasons can be seen in Figure 10-5. In addition, Figure 10-5 illustrates the tremendous consistency on a month-to-month basis of prepayments on automobile–backed securities. This consistency is due to the large number of loans, which can total in the tens of thousands.

Credit Card Receivable-Backed Securities

The typical credit card receivable-backed security deal displays a cash flow pattern that is significantly different from that of an automobile-backed security. Cash flows of credit card receivable-backed securities consist of an interest-only period, which usually

Figure 10-6. Credit Card Receivable-Backed Security Cash Flows

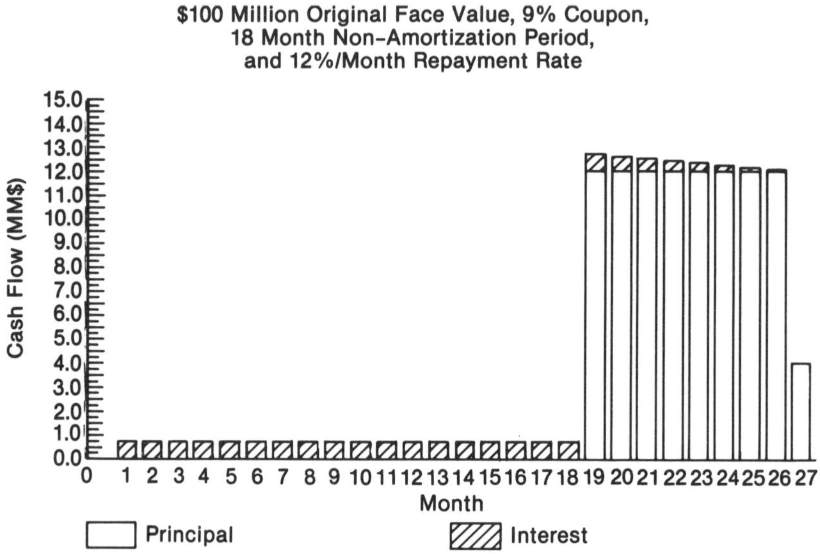

varies from 18 to 36 months, followed by a repayment period in which the outstanding principal is returned to the investor. Because credit card holders pay off their debt quickly, the principal payments are usually made within a 6- to 12-month period. The projected cash flows for a credit card receivable-backed security deal are shown in Figure 10-6. As opposed to automobile-backed securities, which have a more evenly distributed cash flow, cash flows of credit card receivable-backed securities are highly concentrated in the later months (when the security amortizes). With interest-only payments for most of the life of the credit card receivable-backed security and the principal payments highly concentrated, the cash flows of a credit card receivable-backed security resemble those of a corporate bond more closely than those of a mortgage-backed security.

As with most other securities that are backed by loans, there is some cash flow uncertainty for credit card receivable-backed security deals. The length of the repayment period for a credit card receivable-backed security depends on how quickly credit card holders are paying off their debt. Historically, these repayment rates have been very fast, ranging from 10 percent to 20 percent per month. This speed is attributable to so-called convenience users—people who pay their balance in full each month—as well as to the minimum monthly payments that are required. Interest rates and general economic conditions appear to have little effect on the speed at which credit card debt is repaid. The most prominent pattern has been that payments decrease in the fourth quarter of the year, as people become more dependent on their cards during the holiday season.

The effect of different repayment speeds on a credit card receivable-backed security, in this case the Great American Credit Card Trust A, is shown in Table 10-4. This structure is not very sensitive to repayment variations, as the average life changes little when repayment rates vary significantly. For example, doubling the speed from 10 percent monthly to 20 percent monthly only lowers the average life by approximately two and a half months—from 1.28 years to 1.07 years. With automobile-backed securities, however, this difference is important due to the typical steepness of the short end of the yield curve.

Table 10-4. Sensitivity of Credit Card Receivable-Backed Securities to Repayment Rates

Issue:	Great American Credit Card Trust A
Coupon:	9.05%
Delay:	14 days
Stated final maturity:	August 31, 1992
Nonamortization period:	24 months
Settlement date:	November 21, 1988
Price:	99:24

Repayment Rate	*Bond Equivalent Yield*	*Average Life (Years)*	*Modified Duration (Years)*
10.0%	9.11%	1.28	1.20
12.0	9.11	1.21	1.14
14.0	9.10	1.16	1.09
16.0	9.10	1.12	1.08
18.0	9.09	1.09	1.04
20.0	9.09	1.07	1.01

As mentioned previously, credit card receivable-backed securities are structured so that they mature shortly after the beginning of the amortization period. In addition, there are clean-up provisions that require the securities to be retired if less than an original percentage of the face amount—usually 2 percent to 5 percent—exists. Reserve funds and credit enhancements are used, if necessary, to ensure that these provisions are met.

RELATIVE VALUE OF ASSET-BACKED SECURITIES

Performance Characteristics of Automobile and Credit Card Receivable-Backed Securities

It is important to highlight one important performance difference between asset-backed securities and mortgage-backed securities. Because of their more consistent prepayment and repayment pattern, automobile-backed securities and credit card receivable-backed securities do not have the negative convexity problems that plague mortgage-related products.

The price changes in different interest rate scenarios for an automobile-backed security, credit card receivable-backed security, and the first tranche of a CMO are compared in Figure 10-7. As with most mortgage-related securities, the short-term CMO tranche is negatively convex. Therefore, as interest rates fall, the price of the tranche does not increase at a linear rate, but, instead, increases at a slower rate. The reason for this is that the mortgages underlying the CMO are extremely sensitive to interest rate changes. When interest rates rise, declining prepayments cause the security's average life to lengthen; conversely, when interest rates fall, prepayment rates increase and average life shortens. The automobile-backed securities and the credit card receivable-backed securities are slightly convex, however. The prices of the automobile-backed security and the credit card receivable-backed security are slightly convex, however. The prices of the automobile-backed security and the credit card receivable-backed security move by almost the same amount when interest rates fall as when rates rise. In contrast to mortgages, the payments on the underlying loans do not vary materially when interest rates change. Thus, the duration and average life of the bonds should not vary significantly as interest rates change. If the market values convexity correctly, automobile-backed securities and credit card

Figure 10-7. Price Sensitivity to Yield Shifts

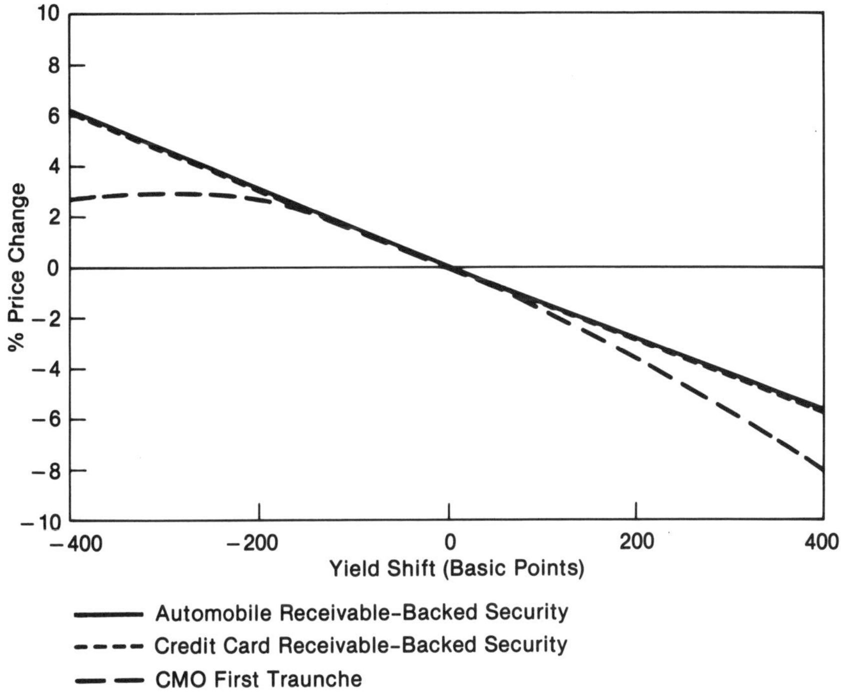

receivable-backed securities should be priced with a lower yield than comparable short-term CMO tranches.

Basic differences in cash flow patterns cause the automobile-backed security to be slightly more convex than the credit card receivable-backed security. Unlike the credit card receivable-backed security, whose cash flows are similar to a short-term bullet bond, automobile-backed security payments are more evenly dispersed. The result of this is that, as interest rates decline, the present value of the automobile-backed security's more distant payments increases. Therefore, the duration and average life of the security increase. On the other hand, should rates rise, the present value of later payments decreases, causing a drop in the duration and average life.

Total Rate of Return of Automobile and Credit Card Receivable-Backed Securities

Before comparing automobile-backed securities and credit card receivable-backed securities with other low-duration fixed income

Table 10-5. Total Rate of Return over a 12-Month Horizon

	Credit Card First Chicago Master Trust B	Automobile CFC-2 Grantor Trust
Coupon	8.50%	8.55%
Settlement date	November 21, 1988	November 21, 1988
Repayment Speed	12.0%	
Prepayment speed		1.5% ABS
Average life	1.46 years	1.46 years
Interpolated Treasury yield	8.47%	8.47%
Spread	+65 basis points	+65 basis points
Bond Equivalent Yield	9.12%	9.12%
Price	99:02+[1]	99:03+

End of Horizon Price Gain (Loss)

Shift	–200	–100	0	+100	+200
Credit Card	1:14	1:00+	0:17	0:03	(0:11)
Automobile	2:06+	1:06	0:06	(0:25+)	(1:24)
Difference	–0:24+	–0:05+	+0:11	+0:28+	+1:13

Total Return

Shift	–200	–100	0	+100	+200
Credit card	10.27%	9.88%	9.43%	9.01%	8.60%
Automobile	10.15	9.68	9.23	8.80	8.37
Difference (basis points)	12	20	20	21	23

[1]For purposes of abbreviation: denotes thirty-seconds.

securities, it is useful to compare their specific risk/return profiles with each other. The total rate of returns over a 12-month horizon for a credit card receivable-backed security over different interest rate scenarios is compared with that of an automobile-backed security in Table 10-5. The automobile-backed security and the credit card receivable-backed security both have an initial average life of 1.46 years and are priced 65 basis points above the Treasury yield curve. In the flat interest rate scenario, the prices of the credit card receivable-backed security and the automobile-backed security increase by $^{17}/_{32}$ and $^{6}/_{32}$, respectively. These price increases result from the securities "riding down the yield curve." As a security's average life and duration fall, it is benchmarked off a lower point on the Treasury yield curve. If the yield curve is sloping upward, which is its

Figure 10-8. Projected Principal Cash Flows and Average Life: Auto versus Credit (November 1988)

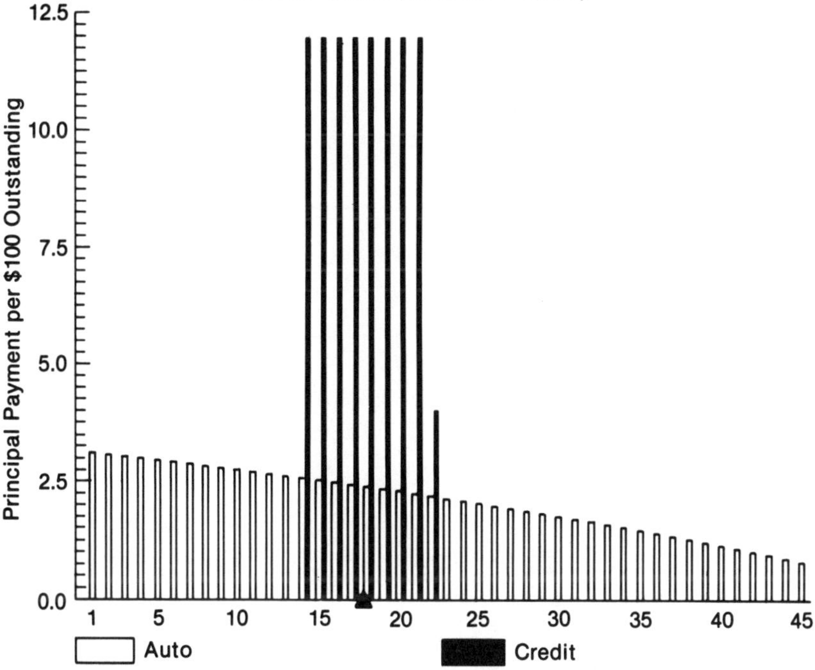

usual shape, and the required spread is unchanged, the required yield on the automobile-backed security or credit card receivable-backed security declines, causing its price to appreciate. The reason that the credit card receivable-backed security appreciates more than the automobile-backed security is that its average life decays quicker; therefore, at the horizon, it is priced off an even lower point on the yield curve than the automobile-backed security. The more concentrated cash flow of the credit card receivable-backed security causes the quicker decay of its average life.

The quicker decay in the average life of the credit card receivable-backed security is examined in Figures 10-8 and 10-9. The cash flows and average lives of a credit card receivable-backed security and an automobile-backed security are graphed in Figure 10-8, where the current average lives of both are shown. Despite the significantly different cash flow patterns, the average lives of the bonds are the same. The cash flows and average lives of the same deals 12 months from the settlement date are displayed in Figure 10-9. In this case, notice that the average life of the credit card

Figure 10-9. Projected Principal Cash Flows and Average Life: Auto versus Credit (November 1989)

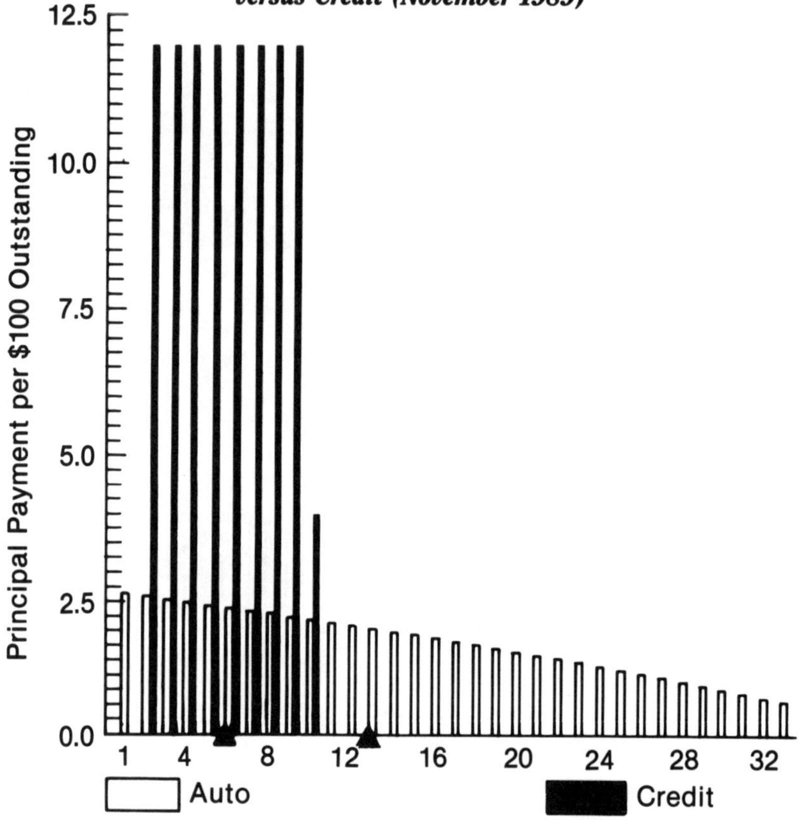

receivable-backed security is significantly shorter than that of the automobile-backed security. The later maturity of the automobile-backed security results in a slower decay in its average life. After 12 months, the credit card receivable-backed security's average life is 0.47 years, compared with 1.10 years for the automobile-backed security. As a result, the credit card receivable-backed security is priced off a lower point on the yield curve at the end of the horizon period, which causes a greater price appreciation. Thus, over the 12-month period, the credit card receivable-backed security outperforms the automobile-backed security in a stable interest rate environment by approximately 20 basis points. The above examination is yet

[3]The automobile-backed security used in this example had a generic pass-through structure. An automobile-backed security structured with an early final maturity that provides for a large final payment would have a total return closer to that of the credit card receivable-backed security.

another illustration of the misleading results that can be obtained when an investor uses a "rule of thumb" analysis—in this case, uses average life to price a security.[3]

In this particular case, over the various interest rate scenarios, the difference in total return between the credit card receivable-backed security and the automobile-backed security remains within the range of 12 to 23 basis points. As with the average life (and for the same reasons), the duration at the end of the horizon is greater for the automobile-backed security than for the credit card receivable-backed security. At the end of the horizon, in the flat interest rate scenario, the duration for the automobile-backed security is 1.04 years, as compared with 0.46 years for the credit card receivable-backed security. As a result of the higher duration, the price of the automobile-backed security is more sensitive to a shift in interest rates than is that of the credit card receivable-backed security. For example, if interest rates fall 200 basis points, the price of the automobile-backed security increases by 2.22 percent, while that of the credit card receivable-backed security increases by only 1.45 percent. On the other hand, if rates rise 200 basis points, the price of the automobile-backed security falls 1.77 percent, and that of the credit card receivable-backed security drops only 0.35 percent. Based on the price peformance of the securities, one would expect the automobile-backed security to provide superior results in the falling interest rate environment, but to significantly underperform in the rising rate scenario. However, as shown in Table 10-5, the credit card receivable-backed security outperforms the automobile-backed security in all interest rate environments.

The other important component that is influencing the total rate of return is the reinvestment income.[4] Since the cash flows of the credit card receivable-backed security are heavily concentrated toward maturity, its holder is less exposed to reinvestment risk than is the holder of the automobile-backed security, who is burdened with reinvesting the large monthly principal payments. In the falling interest rate scenario, the holder is less exposed to reinvestment risk than is the holder of the automobile-backed security, who is burdened with reinvesting the large monthly principal payments. In the falling interest rate scenario, the holder of the automobile-backed security is negatively affected by having to reinvest the cash flows at

[4]The analysis assumes that cash flows are reinvested at the 30-day repossession rate, which is initially 8.47%.

the lower interest rates. In this particular case, this effect overwhelms the superior price performance of the automobile-backed security. Conversely, in the rising interest rate scenario, the automobile-backed security investor is positively affected by the higher reinvestment rates. This offsets the poorer price performance of the automobile-backed security, but not enough to provide a return superior to that of the credit card receivable-backed security.

If the yield curve steepens, the performance of the credit card receivable-backed security is enhanced, as it benefits even more from being priced off a shorter-maturity Treasury at the horizon. In this case, the required yield declines further, causing the credit card receivable-backed security's price to rise. Conversely, if the Treasury yield curve flattens, being priced lower down the curve becomes less of an advantage for the credit card receivable-backed security, and the difference in returns decreases. Should the yield curve invert, short-term rates become higher than long-term rates, and the credit card receivable-backed security's rapid decay in average life is actually a disadvantage. In this scenario, assuming that they are sold at equal yield levels, the automobile-backed security should outperform the credit card receivable-backed security.

Asset-Backed Securities versus Comparable Securities

Asset-backed securities compare favorably against other low-duration fixed income securities on a total rate-of-return basis. Typically, they are priced at a wider yield spread than AA or AAA corporates but tighter than mortgage-backed securities. The asset-backed securities are priced in this way because the market tends to analyze the products in this sector of the curve on a yield or yield spread basis. What this approach fails to incorporate, however, is the superior rate-of-return performance of this product compared with many of the other comparable securities. Due to a lack of negative convexity and the likelihood that asset-backed securities will roll down the yield curve quickly, they display relatively favorable rates of return.

Return profiles of an automobile-backed security and credit card receivable-backed security are compared with those of selected low-duration fixed income securities in Figure 10-10 and Table 10-6. The securities examined are a noncallable AA corporate, a short-term

Figure 10-10. Realized Rate of Return Profiles (Over 12 Month Horizon)

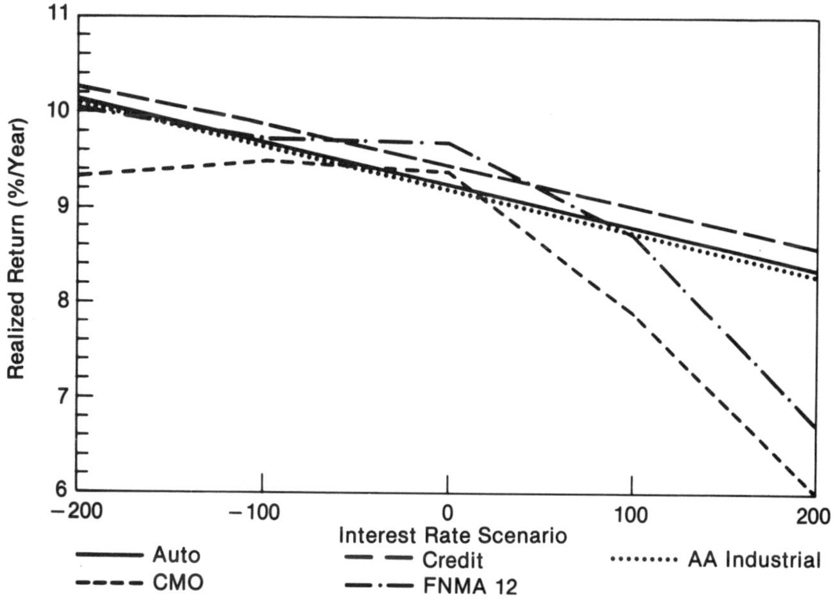

tranche CMO, and a premium mortgage-backed security, specifically a FNMA 12. Detailed information about each of the securities is given in Table 10-6. As before, the analysis is performed over a 12-month horizon. The rate-of-return profiles for the automobile-backed security, credit card receivable-backed security, and corporate are basically linear and run almost parallel to one another. The reason for this is that the cash flows of these securities are virtually independent of the path that interest rates take and, therefore, are not plagued by negative convexity. As a result of rolling further down the Treasury yield curve over the 12-month holding period, the credit card receivable-backed security outperforms the automobile-backed security by approximately 20 basis points over the entire range of interest rate scenarios. Similarly, because the corporate has a bullet payment at maturity, it also rolls down the yield curve faster than the automobile-backed security. The greater price appreciation relative to the automobile-backed security, as a result of rolling down the yield curve faster, helps to compensate for the fact that it is initially priced at a tighter yield spread than the automobile-backed security (currently, 35 basis points versus 65 basis points). The automobile-backed security still outperforms the corporate in all interest rate scenarios, however.

Table 10-6. Rate-of-Return Comparison of Selected Low-Duration Fixed Income Securities

Security	*Coupon*	*Maturity*	*Rating*	*Average Life (Years)*	*Initial Bond Yield*	*Price*
Credit card						
First Chicago Master Trust B	8.50%	12/15/91	AAA	1.46 (1.36)	9.12%	99:01
Automobile						
CFC-2 Grantor Trust	8.55	10/15/92	AAA	1.46 (1.33)	9.12	99:03+
Corporate						
GMAC	8.375	6/01/90	AA−	1.53 (1.30)	8.90	99:08+
CMO						
Drexel Burnham Trust B, Class 2	8.50	12/01/14	AAA	1.44 (1.32)	9.32	98:31
Mortgage-Backed Security						
Generic FNMA 12	12.00	4/25/14[1]	NA	4.33 (1.31)	9.79	106:04

Realized Rates of Return over 12-Month Horizon

Shift	*−200*	*−100*	*0*	*+100*	*+200*
Credit card	10.27%	9.88%	9.43%	9.01%	8.60%
Automobile	10.15	9.68	9.23	8.80	8.37
AA corporate	10.10	9.64	9.18	8.73	8.29
CMO	9.32	9.48	9.37	7.90	6.00
FNMA 12	10.04	9.72	9.68	8.72	6.71

[1]For FNMA 12, the weighted-average maturity of the mortgages composing the generic class is shown.

Unlike the relatively static cash flows of the asset-backed security and the corporate bond, the cash flows for the low-duration CMO and the premium mortgage-backed security can be affected tremendously by changes in interest rates. This fundamental difference is the driving force behind the nonlinear shapes of their return patterns. The CMO and the FNMA were priced at a level that results in the highest yields among the securities analyzed: 9.32 percent and 9.79 percent, respectively. If interest rates remain stable, the FNMA outperforms the other securities. Similarly, the CMO outperforms the corporate and the automobile-backed security, but slightly underperforms the credit card receivable-backed security.

Due to the negative convexity inherent in mortgages and the fact that the average life of mortgage-related products does not decay as quickly, the mortgage product begins to underperform as interest rates change. It takes only a slight movement in interest rates in either direction to cause the return of the CMO to fall below that of the corporate and the automobile-backed security. Owing to the higher yield of the FNMA, a greater interest rate shift is required to make the FNMA underperform the credit card receivable-backed security, automobile-backed security, and corporate. The premium mortgage-backed security has the highest return—even outperforming the credit card receivable-backed security—if interest rates remain within a 50-basis-point range of the current level. It outperforms the automobile-backed security and corporate if interest rates remain within an 100-basis-point range.

It should be noted that the return patterns of the corporates and the mortgages are not necessarily consistent with their patterns for higher-duration securities. Specifically, the premiums of discount mortgage-backed securities do not have nearly as much negative convexity.

This analysis shows that, at current pricing levels, credit card receivable-backed securities and automobile-backed securities are cheap relative to low-duration corporates and mortgage-related products. It is useful to examine the recent pricing trends of asset-backed securities relative to these other securities. Asset-backed security yield spreads compared with those of noncallable three-year industrial notes since July 1987 are shown in Figure 10-11. Over this interval, asset-backed securities maintained an attractive spread of 30 or more basis points over three-year bullet AAA industrials. In 1987, the credit card receivable-backed security was generally priced five to ten basis points above the automobile-backed security. As investors have become more comfortable with the product and have developed an appreciation for some of its advantages, the credit card receivable-backed security is now usually trading even with and sometimes slightly tighter than the automobile-backed security.

Figure 10-11. Treasury Yield Spreads: ABSs versus Corporate Notes

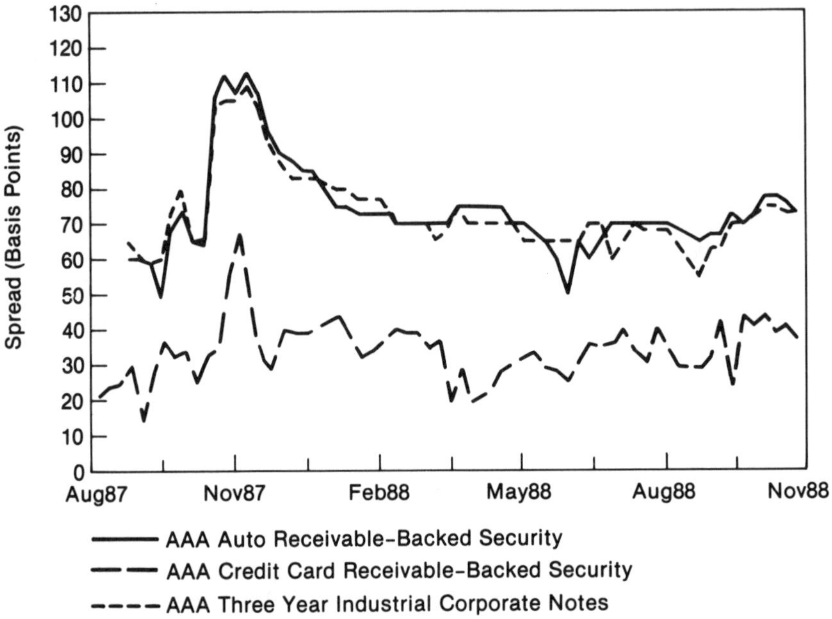

CONCLUSION

Although the asset-backed security market has grown considerably over the past few years, the large amount of unsecuritized consumer debt in the United States provides enough potential collateral for asset-backed securities to expand substantially. In fact, the new bank capital guidelines implicitly promote the active securitization of consumer debt, which should lead to a much greater supply of these securities.

Automobile receivable-backed and credit card receivable-backed securities, presently the cornerstones of the market, have cash flows different from those of mortgage-backed securities. Asset-backed securities are typically shorter-term securities. In addition, unlike mortgage-related securities, the payment patterns of automobile-backed securities and credit card receivable-backed securities are, for the most part, insensitive to movements in interest rates and, therefore, should be more predictable. Also, automobile-backed securities tend to have a nonamortization period, in which no principal is paid; then, the principal payments are concentrated during an amortization period. This consistency of cash flows results in securities that perform much more like corporate bonds than mortgage-related securities. As a result of their consistent cash flows, asset-backed securities are characterized by a low probability of extending should interest rates rise and a low probability of shortening should rates drop. Mortgage-related products are typically priced at a wider spread to the Treasury curve than are asset-backed securities, but the positive convexities of asset-backed securities produce a relatively attractive rate-of-return profile. Asset-backed securities, especially credit card receivable-backed securities, also benefit from the fact that their average life decays more quickly, causing them to roll down the yield curve faster than mortgage-related products.

Asset-backed securities are an attractive alternative to AA- and AAA-rated noncallable corporates. They are typically priced much cheaper and tend to outperform the corporates over all interest rate scenarios. In addition, asset-backed securities are not subject to the event risk problem that has plagued the corporate bond market.

Asset-backed securities are an attractive and growing sector of the low-duration fixed income market. Although they have tightened relative to Treasuries since originally issued, they still appear cheap. Investors should seriously consider this rapidly growing sector when adding to the low-duration part of their fixed income portfolio.

CHAPTER 11

Automobile Loan Securitization

Joan Barmat

INTRODUCTION

In several key respects the securitization of automobile loans is similar to the securitization of short-term mortgages. This similarity helps explain why automobile loans were among the first non-mortgage assets to be used in securitization transactions. The aspects of automobile loans most familiar to mortgage-backed security underwriters and investors are:

- Scheduled loan life with a beginning and an end
- Retail loan collateralized with property, presumably mitigating credit loss
- Usually fixed coupon with fixed monthly payments
- Yield subject to prepayment risk
- Pool description semantics:
  —Weighted-average coupon
  —Weighted-average remaining maturity
  —Weighted-average life
  —Prepayment speed (monthly or annual)

Despite these similarities, several critical differences require separate analysis of automobile loan-backed securities. These include:

- Lack of U.S. government insurance to cover credit loss, thereby requiring alternative modes of credit enhancement to reduce credit risk
- Lack of standardization in loan origination, processing, and servicing
- Prepayment patterns less related to interest rates and more related to other (sometimes unpredictable) factors

AUTOMOBILE LOAN CHARACTERISTICS AND RISK FACTORS

Sources of Automobile Loans

Automobile loans are made by U.S. financial institutions and finance companies (primarily automobile manufacturer related). A recent Federal Reserve breakdown of holders of auto loans, as shown in Table 11-1, indicates that as of June, 1988, commercial banks and thrifts held proportionately more auto loans than did finance companies (48 percent versus 35 percent) and that their relative share has been increasing.

Table 11-1. Auto Loans Outstanding by Type of Lender

	1987		*1988*	
Automobile Loans	*Total Outstanding (in mil.)*	*% of Total*	*June*	*% of Total*
Commercial banks	$100,907	41.00%	$117,640	41.74%
Credit unions	38,413	15.61	46,438	16.48
Finance companies	92,350	37.52	99,900	35.45
Savings institutions	14,439	5.87	17,856	6.34
Total	$246,109	100%	$281,834	100%

Auto loans are either made directly between the lender and the retail borrower (called direct loans) or are purchased by the lender from automobile dealers (called indirect loans). It is important to note that in both types of loan origination, the lender is making a case-by-case, independent credit judgment. Thus, purchased, indirect auto loans should not be assumed to be of any lower credit quality than direct loans. However, it is not unusual for a lender with both direct and indirect auto loan portfolios to experience different payment patterns (prepayment, loss, and delinquency) on each portfolio. This generally reflects demographic differences between consumer groups likely to be contracted directly given the method of direct contact (for example, from branch bank, by telephone) as compared with consumers who obtain loans through auto dealers. In some cases, the nature of a certain group of dealers selling loans (for example, those selling relatively expensive foreign cars) creates a demographic bias toward certain payment behavior.

Indirect auto loan applications are usually faxed by dealers to one or more potential lenders for approval. Lenders generally compete with each other to have dealers direct loan applications to them. Dealers are inclined toward certain lenders for various reasons, which can include:

- Lender finances dealer directly ("floor planning")
- Lender provides response (turnaround) quickly
- Lender finances more of auto retail value (require less downpayment)
- Lender pays dealer a larger share of the gross loan coupon
- Lender does not require dealer recourse

Dealers generally receive a portion of the gross annual percentage rate (APR) paid by consumers for auto loans. Lenders may pay a dealer the present value of their share of total interest earnings on a loan up front or may employ many types of slower release (that is, reserve) mechanisms.

A traditional form of indirect auto lending called for lenders to have recourse during a certain period to dealers who sold them loans if the loans defaulted (recourse lending). Thus, if a borrower defaulted, the lender could require the dealer to repurchase the automobile at its then-outstanding loan value. Depending on the credit quality of dealers from whom loans were purchased, recourse can have a significant effect on auto loan net loss experience. However, use of recourse lending has been declining in recent years, primarily due to competition among lenders for dealer paper.

Underwriting Standards

Lenders apply an array of credit criteria when reviewing auto loan applications. Consistency in applying credit standards is important in assessing potential future loss. Credit criteria may be applied in a formalized credit scoring model or on a more informal basis. However, most criteria include the following factors relative to a potential borrower:

- Length of time at residence
- Employment and length of time at employer/job function
- Overall sources of income
- Credit history (from credit reporting agencies)
- Income to debt ratio
- Type of automobile purchased
- Down payment amount

Payment Practices and Collections

Once a lender accepts a loan, a monthly coupon book is generally sent to borrowers. In some cases, lenders send monthly invoices in place of coupons. Monthly consumer payments are divided into interest and principal based on simple interest or Rule of 78 amortization. For securitization purposes, auto loans are purchased at their simple interest or actuarial balance at the time of sale, even when The Rule of 78 amortization method is used by the seller.

Thus, a sale of loans amortized originally using the Rule of 78 will usually cause a loss on sale to the seller, due to effective overaccrual of interest in prior periods. Once a loan has begun, three payment possibilities exist:

- The loan will be paid monthly to maturity, according to its scheduled life
- The loan will be prepaid, usually in full and usually due to automobile trade-in rather than due to refinancing (as can be the case with mortgage loans)
- The loan will default and the automobile will be repossessed and resold, causing an effective prepayment and possible loss

It should be noted that, in the context of securitization, any loss between the resale proceeds and the loan value at the time of default is usually covered by credit enhancement. Thus, to a lender, default represents an uncertain prepayment value in that the sale proceeds may be greater or less than the loan value. However, investors in higher rated auto loan–backed securities will generally experience full prepayment from a loan default when any shortfall is covered by credit enhancement.

If an auto loan becomes delinquent most servicers apply standardized collection procedures. These generally include a series of dunning notices, followed by telephone (and, in some cases, personal) contact. At a given number of days delinquent, typically 45 to 60 days, lenders will initiate vehicle repossession proceedings. Once repossessed, lenders attempt to sell the vehicles, usually through auctions, dealers, or their own used-car sale operations. The proceeds of a resale are the recoveries on a defaulted loan. Resale proceeds vary, but generally range from 50 percent of the loan value to 100 percent or more if near the end of the life of a loan or if for certain types of vehicles that retain high resale value.

The credit underwriting, payment tracking, and collection procedures of a given auto loan seller/servicer determine much of the credit quality of a loan pool. Other factors, such as the porportion of new versus used automobiles financed and the types of vehicles financed, can also affect the quality of a loan pool.

Auto loans should be covered by property and casualty insurance, usually according to state law. This is either insurance obtained by borrowers; forced placed insurance added by lenders, whose premium is payable by borrowers; or vendor single-interest insurance, which is purchased by lenders to cover loan value (as opposed to vehicle value). In a securitization transaction, the proceeds of this type of issuance are pledged indirectly to investors.

It is important to note that considerable variations exist among the ways in which automobile lenders conduct business. For example, the proportion of direct versus indirect loans held, dealer networks for originating loans, credit underwriting criteria, and collection practices can all vary significantly from lender to lender. In rated securitization transactions, the relative impact of these factors on potential credit loss is generally considered by the rating agencies, which allows investors to make simpler investment decisions.

SECURITY STRUCTURES

Automobile loans have been used to back both debt and preferred stock issues. In debt markets, the structures used to securitize automobile loans are similar to those used in the mortgage-backed and other asset-backed security markets. These are pass-through or pay-through structures.

Pass-Through versus Pay-Through

Pass-Through

In the pass-through format, selected automobile loans are either sold directly as a pool or transferred into a grantor trust as an intermediate step pursuant, in either case, to the terms of a pooling and servicing agreement. Pass-through certificates, which represent fractional undivided interests in the pool of loan receivables or in the trust that owns the receivables, are sold to investors. The proceeds of such a sale are simultaneously returned to the seller as payment for the assets sold. All collections of principal and interest during each payment period are deposited into a segregated account maintained with a trustee, unless the seller is as highly rated as the securitization transaction or extra credit enhancement to cover commingling of funds risk has been obtained. The trustee pays interest payments to investors at the pass-through rate, together with scheduled principal repayments and prepayments, on predetermined payment dates.

The transfer of assets into a grantor trust or the direct sale of a

Figure 11-1. Pass-Through Structure

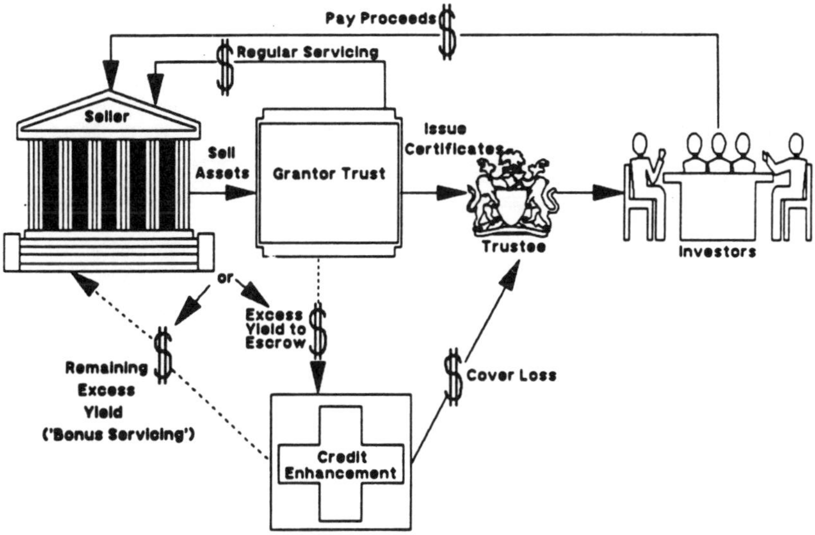

pool will be treated as a sale for tax purposes and financial reporting purposes. For bankruptcy reasons, instruments relating to the receivables, such as legal title documents, must be physically held by the trustee or its custodian, which, in many instances, is the seller/servicer. The seller remains liable only for any branches of representations and warranties (related primarily to the receivables that have been sold) set forth in the pooling and servicing agreement. *Very limited modification of cash flow (that is, no recharacterization of interest and principal) is permitted to allow the issuing entity to remain free of tax liability, and no asset substitution is allowed.*

Figure 11-1 illustrates the basic pass-through structure.

Pay-Through

In a pay-through format, the seller transfer assets to a third party–owned or "orphan" special-purpose corporation, which then issues notes collateralized by such assets. The notes issued by the special-purpose corporation are its debt obligations, which bear interest at a specified rate. The transference of assets to the special-purpose corporation is treated as a sale to the seller for bankruptcy and financial reporting purposes. By using a pay-through structure, *a*

Figure 11-2. Pay-Through Structure

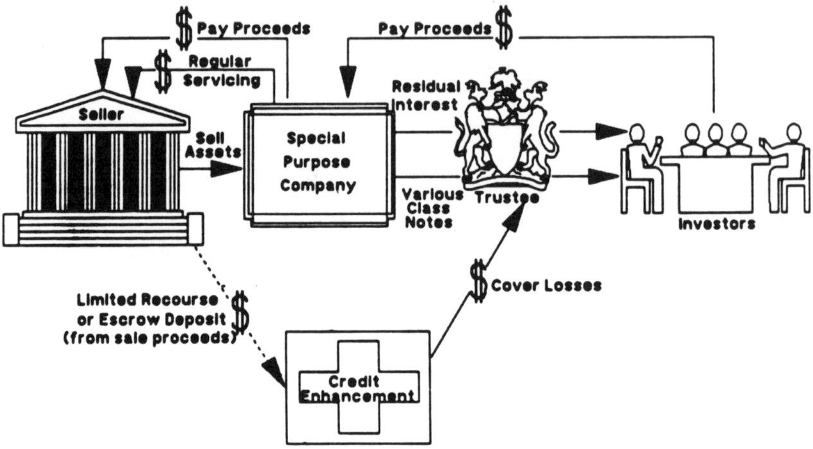

seller can substantially modify the cash flow of the underlying collateral to produce any note payment structure, as long as the cash flow from the collateral amortizes substantially all of the debt by its stated maturity. This is particularly useful for deeply discounted incentive-rate auto loan paper or for market environments in which cost can be minimized through the issuance of multi-class bonds. This latter structure is similar to a collateralized mortgage obligation (CMO), which takes advantage of a positive yield curve or of investor preference for shorter maturities and variable rates. A pay-through structure can also be used to minimize the effects of prepayment uncertainty.

Since a special-purpose corporation is used in a pay-through, this entity must have some equity capital to ensure that the securities issued are considered debt—not equity—for tax purposes. This equity can be provided by the third party, typically an investor in the residual cash flows from the assets, as in a traditional CMO structure, or by the asset seller as an equity contribution or subordinated interest.

A pay-through structure is diagrammed in Figure 11-2.

Yield Considerations

A pool of fixed-rate automobile loan assets that provides sufficient gross yield to cover a current market pass-through rate to investors, arm's-length servicing fees, and credit enhancement expense is considered premium collateral. In this case, using a pass-through (as opposed to pay-through) structure, the assets are generally sold at a slight discount to par, and any excess yield from the assets, less expected loss experience, is recognized by the seller for generally accepted accounting principles accounting as an up-front gain on the sale. In some cases, a premium purchase price is paid; however, this happens infrequently due to prepayment uncertainty.

A pool of fixed-rate assets with a yield that does not cover the sum of the investors' yield, arm's-length servicing fees, and credit enhancement expense is considered discount collateral because the cash flows of the underlying assets should be discounted to the extent that they provide sufficient coverage for the resulting transaction's cash flow requirements. This discounting process will result in a loss on sale of the assets, that is, sale proceeds less than face value.

To minimize the portion of asset yield passed on to investors, several optional rate structures are available to asset sellers. These include:

- Selling fixed-rate assets with a floating-rate yield to investors in a positive yield curve environment. The yield to the investor may be capped sufficiently below the asset yield to allow for servicing and other costs, or the seller may purchase an interest rate cap and assign the benefits to investors, allowing the floating-rate yield to investors to exceed that of the underlying assets.
- Dividing various groups of asset yield within a total pool into pass-through pools that correspond with one or more shorter and lower-cost maturities, which allow for a lower weighted-average pass-through cost than if the pool were sold as a whole.
- Using a multi-class pay-through structure, in which the repayment and prepayment flows from the underlying assets are reconfigured to provide amortization of principal of shorter-term classes first, similar to a CMO structure. The average fixed rate for the resulting various maturity bonds can be less than the yield of a single class of somewhat longer maturity bonds, which leads to an overall lower cost of issuance to the seller. "True sale" considerations may limit use of this option.

The lowest-cost option for a given seller at a given point in time should be assessed based on the characteristics of a pool and the market situation at that time.

Finally, floating-rate auto loans may be securitized in pass-through form, yielding to investors a variable rate that allows for sufficient excess margin to cover asset servicing and other securitization expenses.

Maturity Considerations

The maturity profile of a given car loan portfolio will be based on the characteristics of a specific seller's market base (demographics) and lending/credit policies. While industry practice and market competition dictate many common auto loan characteristics, types of contracts, final maturity limitations, loss experience, and, particularly, prepayment rates must be analyzed for each seller's portfolio and portfolio subset.

The prepayment rate on a particular pool of receivables is significant in establishing the life span of an asset-backed transaction and, hence, the yield that investors will realize on their investment. This is of considerable importance to investors that are paid a fixed pass-through rate, although variable pass-through rate investors would have a similar, but less, degree of concern. Most loan sellers keep prepayment data, albeit on a periodic accounting basis—for example, prepayments this month are compared with total outstanding auto loans this month. As such, most prepayment data for specific pools are estimated. Ideally, sellers should track historical prepayments according to loan origination month, which provides prepayment information that is more accurate with respect to a given pool sold.

Given historical principal repayment and prepayment patterns, most 36- to 60-month maturity car loans have weighted-average lives of 12 to 24 months. Securitized auto loans with a fixed pass-through rate are priced on the present value of monthly cash flows to yield investors a return based on the estimated average life of the assets sold (for example, 0.7 percent) above the two-year Treasury bond yield for assets with a 60-month final maturity, a 45-month weighted-averaged maturity, and a two-year average life.

When outstanding amounts become relatively small compared

with the original amount of loans sold (for example, 5 percent), the seller may repurchase ("nuisance call") any remaining outstanding loans without violating true sale accounting guidelines, which generally prohibit seller repurchase.

Ratings

For a large issuance of securitized assets (for example, over $50 million) or when the credit quality of the seller/servicer is not generally known (unrated) or is significantly different from that of the asset-backed security, a credit rating from a nationally recognized rating agency such as Standard & Poor's Corporation, Duff and Phelps, or Moody's Investors Service should be obtained. This is true for both publicly registered and privately placed asset-backed security issues.

Sellers should expect the rating agencies to review their underwriting and servicing procedures, as well as general portfolio characteristics, and to request considerable data about delinquency, loss, and prepayment. A visit to loan origination and servicing areas and to a seller's corporate headquarters for a strategic review may also be required.

Loss Protection

To provide investors with a level of protection against loss, various forms of credit enhancement are arranged in automobile loan securitization transactions. The level of credit enhancement is a function of many factors relating to transaction structure, the seller/servicer, and particular asset pool characteristics. The most important of these include:

- The desired rating of the securitized pool (for example, AA or AAA)
- Loan underwriting standards
- Historic payment behavior
- Historic loss and delinquency experience
- Seller/servicer capabilities

Somewhat separate from the determination of the level of credit enhancement, the methods for providing credit enhancement should be analyzed. These vary and should be assessed based on many considerations, including cost, accounting impact, deal structure, and anticipated market reception. The main types of credit enhancement include:

- Seller guaranty of a portion of risk.
- Overcollateralization (separate from yield/discount concept), in which excess yield on assets is used to create a reserve against credit losses.
- Subordinated interest in the pool, which would absorb the first x percent of loss. To date, sellers have retained this interest, which creates, in effect, a form of seller guaranty or overcollateralization.
- Third party guaranty from as little as 5 percent to as much as 100 percent of the face value of the collateral in the form of a bank letter of credit or insurance company surety bond. Generally, the third party guarantor is repaid by the seller or another credit enhancement source up to an agreed-on percentage and to the extent that such other sources exist.
- Reserve account to cover a percentage of loss, which would be created from excess asset yield in premium collateral cases, from overcollateralization as mentioned earlier, or from a seller's up-front deposit. Any amount remaining in such a reserve generally reverts to the portfolio servicer as bonus servicing income.

These methods may be used alone or in combination, based on the parameters of a given asset portfolio and transaction structure.

In addition to explicit loss protection, pool eligibility criteria, which are used to screen the assets sold, provide an additional method of controlling the credit quality of a securitized pool of assets. For example, choosing assets with significant seasoning and little or no delinquency history would tend to provide a higher-quality credit pool

Auto Loan-Backed Security Yields

As in many types of asset-backed securities, unexpected payment patterns—usually prepayments—will affect investors' expected

Figure 11-3. Prepayment Sensitivity: Sample Auto Pass-Through Yields at Different Constant Prepayment Rates

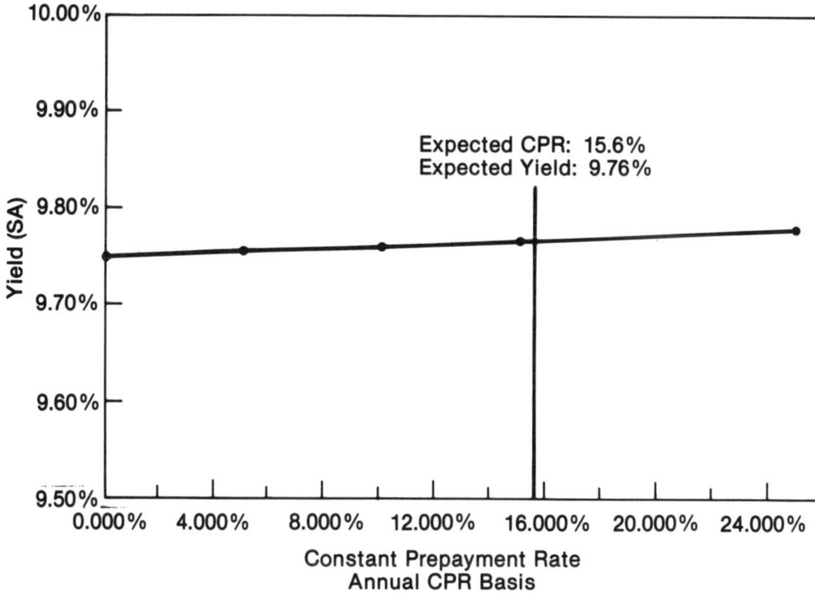

yield. In the case of auto loan-backed securities, given the relatively short maturity and average life of the underlying loan, the impact on yields of relatively wide variations in prepayment is limited. This is illustrated in Figure 11-3, in which the yield on an auto loan-backed security, intended to be 9.76 percent at a prepayment speed of 15.6 percent annual conditional prepayment rate (CPR), is affected only slightly by a variation in prepayment speed from 0 percent to 25 percent.

Historically, prepayment rates on auto loans are less sensitive than prepayment rates on mortgage-backed securities to changes in interest rates, due to the lower frequency of auto loan refinancing. This is largely due to the minimal impact on monthly consumer payments of loan rate changes on a short-maturity loan. Auto loans are seldom refinanced; instead, they are usually replaced due to trade-ins for new models, low auto prices and subvention financing.

It is widely known that prepayments on mortgage loans create negative convexity—that is, when prevailing rates rise and a normal fixed coupon security would depreciate in value according to its duration, the expected duration of the prepaying asset is increasing

Figure 11-4. Prepayment Sensitivity: Sample Auto versus MBS Yields at Different Constant Prepayment Rates

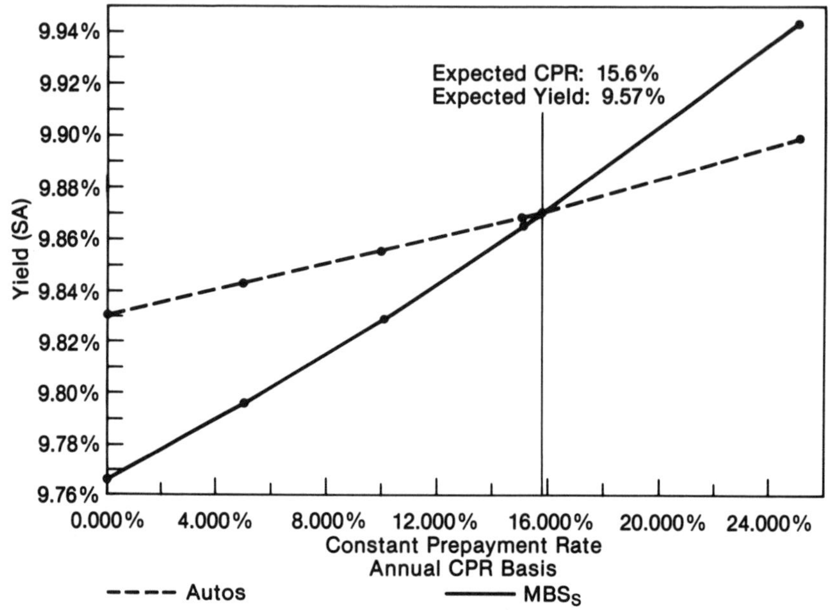

(compounding losses). When prevailing rates fall and a normal fixed coupon security would appreciate in value according to its duration, prepayments increase, weighted-average life and duration decrease, and the gain on the prepaying asset is highly limited. Figure 11-4 shows the impact of prepayment on effective yields of auto loan–and mortgage-backed securities. This figure gives a dramatic view of the high sensitivity of mortgage-backed securities compared with auto loans—even for equal changes in constant prepayment rates.

Auto Loan-Backed Security Issuance Trends

Once the largest dollar volume of asset-backed issues in the market, auto loan-backed issues have declined both in absolute volume and in the number of issues per year between 1985 and November 1988. Table 11-2 lists the volume of auto loan-backed issues during this time.

As shown on the chart above, the presence in 1986 and 1987 of GMAC, which contributed 86 percent and 36 percent of all auto loan-backed security volume, respectively, somewhat distorted the impression of growth in this market. However, a clear slowdown is evident

Table 11-2. Auto Loan Securitization

	No. of Deals	$ Volume (in mil.)	Multiple Issuers	% of Total	Repeat Issuers	New Issuers
1985	5	$898.60	None	N/A	None	GMAC
						Home Federal S&L
						Marine Midland Bank
						Valley National Bank
						Western Financial
1986	15	9,646.30	GMAC (9)	86%	GMAC	Banco Central
					Western Financial	Bank of America
						Chrysler Financial
						Empire Savings Bank
						Nissan Motors
1987	22	6,584.07	GMAC (6)	36	GMAC	BMW Credit Corp.
			Chrysler Financial (2)	23	Chrysler Financial	Empire of America
			Marine Midland Bank (2)	16	Marine Midland Bank	First NB Boston
			Western Financial (2)	4	Western Financial	GECC
			UST Corp. (2)	3		Mack Financial Corp.
			GECC (2)	3		RepublicBank Dallas
						Security Pacific
						UST Corp.
1988	22	4,473.03	Western Financial (4)	12	Western Financial	Chemical Bank
			Empire of America (2)	16	BMW Credit	Citicorp
			UST Corp. (2)	5	Chrysler Financial	Connecticut National Bank
					Empire of America	Signet Bank—VA
					UST Corp.	VW Credit
					Mack Financial Corp.	West American Bank
					Marine Midland Bank	Rochester Community Savings Bank
						Huntington National Bank
						Union Federal Savings Bank
	64	$21,602.25				

in 1988. This is due, in part, to slower auto loan volume growth during that year. However, recent (late 1988) transaction registrations indicate that the volume of auto loan-backed securities may increase in the near term.

CONCLUSION

Structurally, given their relatively short life and similarity to mortgages, auto loans offer significant advantages in credit quality, investor acceptance, and flexibility in the creation of asset-backed securities. However, lack of standardization may hamper the development of market efficiency for all but the largest volume lenders and most frequent issuers. Nonetheless, the greatest total issuance volume to date and the deepest market liquidity for any asset-backed security still belongs to auto loan-backed securities, and this should allow for a strong basis for growth into the 1990s.

CHAPTER 12

Rating Agency Criteria For Auto-Backed Securities

Thomas P. Hourican

INTRODUCTION

Standard and Poor's Corporation (S&P) now rates $16.3 billion in securities collateralized by auto loans, plus $600 million of auto lease paper. These ratings are based on actuarial analysis of the auto finance industry and individual company portfolios. S&P analyzed the repossession, loss, and delinquency performance of banks and finance companies, in addition to First Boston Corporation's 1985 static pool analysis of General Motors Acceptance Corp. (GMAC) assets. Although industry net losses to average outstandings have been under 0.5 percent for the last five years, several factors could cause significantly greater losses in a securitized pool of auto assets.

- Actual losses may be understated, as many portfolios have grown rapidly in the last few years. The average outstandings would, therefore, be higher than appropriate.
- Recent economic performance has been relatively good, but S&P expects a significantly greater frequency of default if a recession should occur in the next few years.
- Incentive financing programs of captive finance companies and

manufacturers' rebates to sell new cars have caused used-car prices to decline. This trend may continue and will affect the resale value of vehicles whose owners default on loans or leases.

- Rapid growth may test the resources and controls of many servicers and result in less effective collection efforts and increased losses.
- As the industry has become very competitive, underwriters of auto loans and leases may be pressured to accept marginal credits so as to maintain or increase market share.

To safeguard against this potentially adverse environment, an issue's equity coverage is usually three to five times the cumulative pool losses that are expected, based on historical portfolio data. The actual equity level in a particular issue is derived from a benchmark equity level, which S&P uses as a starting point for its analysis as shown in Table 12-1.

Table 12-1. Auto Loan Loss Coverage

Rating	*Repossession Frequency*	*Severity of Loss*	*Equity Coverage*
AAA	16%	50%	8%
AA	13	45	6
A	10	40	4

The benchmarks above apply to a prime pool of auto loans, characterized by conservative underwriting and an absence of significant risk concentrations. Losses and delinquencies should also be stable and consistent with the industry average.

Actual equity coverage ratios on these issues have ranged from 6 percent to 17 percent for AAA issues, reflecting differences in underwriting standards, portfolio and performance characteristics, pool selection criteria, and servicing capability. Pool risks may also depend on whether the vehicles are directly or indirectly originated and whether recourse to the dealer exists. Seasoning of the assets may decrease risk in the pool, while a significant proportion of used cars in a pool may add risk. Finally, a particular issue's liquidity requirements may also affect the necessary floor coverage and overall equity level. Each of these areas of analysis will be discussed in this chapter.

Table 12-2. GMAC Static Pool Analysis, 1985

Receivables Type	*Cumulative Net Loss to Original Principal Balance*
48 month (all types)	0.53%
36 month (all types)	0.45
48 month new	0.49
48 month recourse	0.19
48 month nonrecourse	0.74
36 month new	0.06
36 month used	1.17

NEW VERSUS USED

Captive finance organizations, most notably GMAC and Chrysler Financial Corp., have securitized auto loan pools, including installment sale contracts on ordinarily new vehicles. In contrast, many commercial banks include used-car loans in receivable pools because these loans are a larger portion of their overall portfolios. S&P requests a breakdown of loss and delinquency data by new and used vehicles. S&P then evaluates each transaction to determine whether used cars add incremental risk to the pool of receivables. The servicer's past performance as a loan underwriter and the criteria used to select pool assets are important to this assessment.

According to industry data, used-car loans suffer more frequent and more severe losses than do loans for new vehicles. This is supported by GMAC's 1985 static pool analysis. For example, the GMAC study shows that the repossession rate for new cars is 0.73 percent, well below the 6 percent rate for used cars (for 36-month loans, by number of contracts outstanding). The difference on a net basis, following recoveries, is also significant. New cars exhibit net losses of approximately 60 basis points—half the used-car rate of 120 basis points.

The relatively weak performance of used-car loans is attributed to several factors. Generally, the obligator base is of lower credit quality because most people will purchase a new car if they can afford one. This has been especially true in the last few years as 1.9 percent financing rates and longer repayment periods (60–72 months) have made new cars more affordable. Severity of loss may also increase due to the depreciating nature of the vehicle and the valuation method (for example, using the *Kelly Blue Book Leasing Guide,* a used-car guide), which may add some risk for used cars.

Table 12-3. Net Losses/Average Gross Receivables

	1987[1]	*1986*	*1985*	*1984*	*1983*
Marine Midland Bank	0.53%	0.59%	0.62%	0.55%	0.55%
Home Federal Savings & Loan Assn.	N.A.[5]	0.75	0.36	0.14	N.A.[5]
General Motors Acceptance Corp.	0.46	0.38	0.26	0.17	0.22
Nissan Motors Acceptance Corp.[2]	0.21[4]	0.68	0.32	0.07	N.A.[5]
Chrysler Corp.	0.38	0.28	0.12	0.04	0.07
Ponce Federal Bank	0.88	1.88	0.41	0.01	N.A.[5]
Western Financial Savings Bank	0.91	0.87	0.56	0.41	0.34
American Bankers Assn. Survey					
Direct	N.A.[5]	0.56	0.39	0.27	0.42
Indirect	N.A.[5]	0.40	0.29	0.21	0.32
U.S. Trust/Norfolk	0.12	0.17	0.13	0.07	N.A.[5]
Peoples Bank & Trust Co.	0.08	0.07	0.02	0.11	0.27
RepublicBank Dallas N.A.[3]	0.67	0.45	0.23	0.12	0.42

[1]Annualized.

[2]As a percentage of average net receivables outstanding. Began operation in 1984.

[3]Weighted average of 16 RepublicBank units and 20 Interfirst Bank units.

[4]Annualized pool data.

[5]N.A.—Not available.

The inclusion of used cars within a pool does not necessarily increase required coverage. The greater risk of used-car lending may be offset by conservative loan-to-value determination and underwriting. Many lenders offset the expected additional risk by requiring a higher annual percentage rate (APR) on used vehicles. This excess cash may not be retained within the issue.

DIRECT VERSUS INDIRECT LENDING

Auto loans are underwritten on a direct or indirect basis. With a direct loan, the lender is present during the application proceedings and directly determines the customer's creditworthiness. For exam-

Figure 12-1. Net Installment Credit Dollar Losses as a Percentage of Outstandings (by Type of Loan, 1967–1986)

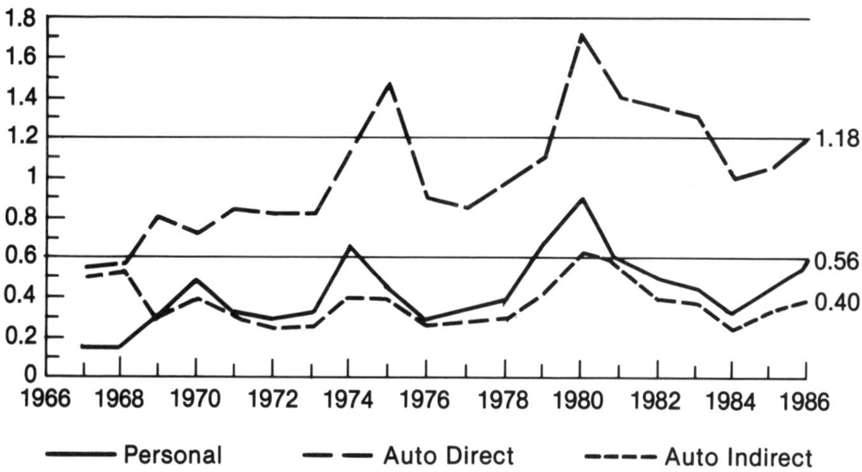

ple, a loan made by a commercial bank branch to its local customer would be a direct loan. Indirect loans, which account for much of the recent growth in auto portfolios, are originated by car dealers and then purchased by banks, thrifts, finance companies, and credit unions.

Unlike direct loans, the indirect lender may never meet face to face with its customer. With an indirect loan, the financial institution makes a credit judgment based on information provided to the dealer and on an investigation of the applicant's credit and employment history.

This failure to meet directly with customers may explain, in part, why commercial banks reported higher net losses on direct loans from 1970 to 1980 (see Figure 12-1). It is interesting that losses from 1981 to 1986 were lower for indirect loans. In both periods, the differences were not material. The more recent data may be distorted by both the large growth in such loan portfolios and the presence of recourse agreements with dealers. Lenders are also becoming more sophisticated in their approach to granting indirect credit; to curb loan losses, they are following the lead of captive finance companies in such areas as credit scoring and automated systems.

To determine if a particular indirect loan program adds risk to an asset-backed transaction, S&P performs a detailed due diligence investigation with emphasis on:

- Dealer relationships (for example, risk concentration and fraud)
- Management experience in this type of lending
- Underwriting policies and controls

RECOURSE VERSUS NONRECOURSE

Under certain circumstances, recourse loans can entail fewer risks than do nonrecourse loans. Recourse loan payments are supported, in part, by recourse to some third party. Recourse should strengthen the loan if the third party is creditworthy and if the same underwriting standards apply as those that apply to nonrecourse loans.

Many auto lenders retain recourse to the dealer. In these loans, the dealer remains responsible to the originating bank (the originator) for payment of the contract's unpaid balance, as long as the originator repossesses the car and returns it to the dealer within 90 days. Recourse financing was used heavily during the early 1980s, as increased loss rates and competition for funds offered loan terms favorable to lenders. Currently, the trend is away from recourse loans. Incentive rate financing generally reduces the dealer's retention percentage; thus dealers are less willing to cover additional recourse costs.

With recourse loans, S&P evalutes the originating bank's reliance on recourse to the auto dealer. If the same underwriting standards apply to both recourse and nonrecourse loans, their delinquency and repossession rates should not be materially different. However, recourse loans are susceptible to less conservative underwriting standards if the originator derives comfort from the dealer's obligation to take back defaulted loans. S&P evaluates the originator's program for reviewing and monitoring the dealers from which it purchases loans. An expansion-minded originator might need to purchase loans from less creditworthy dealers to gain market share.

Table 12-4. Delinquencies (31 Days +)/Gross Dollar Receivables Outstanding

	1987	*1986*	*1985*	*1984*	*1983*
Marine Midland Bank	2.38%[5]	2.46%	3.39%	3.25%	2.87%
Home Federal Savings & Loan Assn.	N.A.[11]	0.85[1]	0.86	0.67	0.45
General Motors Acceptance Corp.	1.88[7]	1.84	1.82	1.54	1.65
Nissan Motors Acceptance Corp.[2,3]	1.37[1]	1.68	1.47	0.95	N.A.[11]
Chrysler Corp.	0.75[5]	0.88	0.66	0.53	0.23
Ponce Federal Bank[2,4]	3.05[7]	2.82	3.77	0.72	N.A.[11]
Western Financial Savings Bank	1.05[6]	1.39	2.84	1.05	0.89
American Bankers Assn. Survey[3]					
Direct	1.63[7]	1.99	1.85	1.70	1.70
Indirect	1.92[7]	2.43	2.40	2.00	1.65
U.S. Trust/Norfolk	2.94	2.64	3.70	N.A.[11]	N.A.[11]
Peoples Bank & Trust Co.[10]	0.13	0.12	0.21	0.17	0.24
RepublicBank Dallas N.A.[9]	1.87[8]	2.37	1.65	1.63	1.41

[1]Pool statistics.

[2]Began operations in 1984.

[3]Number of contracts 30 or more days past due as a percentage of the total number of contracts outstanding.

[4]Delinquency 31–60 days.

[5]At September 30.

[6]At April 30.

[7]At June 30.

[8]At February 28.

[9]Weighted average of 16 RepublicBank units and 2 Interfirst Bank units.

[10]Principal payments as a percentage of the aggregate principal balance of loans outstanding.

[11]N.A.—Not available.

Nonrecourse loans generally have a higher net loss experience than loans with recourse do. The percentage of recourse loans in Chrysler's portfolio fell to 37 percent from 74 percent between July 1986 and November 1987. Although Chrysler's rate of possessions increased only two basis points during 1986 (to 1.69 from 1.67), their net losses increased 16 basis points (to 28 from 12). GMAC's portfolio has declined to approximately 7 percent currently from over 40 percent recourse in 1985. Their net losses have increased 12 basis points (to 38 from 26), while repossessions have increased 16 basis points (to 1.53 from 1.37). Interfirst Bank Dallas, which is now part of First Republic, had a portfolio that was almost entirely recourse loans. While their repossessions were very high due to the weak Texas economy, their net losses remained phenomenally low. Repossessions at the lead bank in Dallas were almost 6 percent in 1986; net losses were seven basis points. In 1987, net losses have trended upward at a somewhat greater rate than repossessions. This trend may indicate failure by some dealers under their recourse obligations.

AMORTIZATION METHODS

Three methods are used to amortize automobile receivable contracts:

- Actuarial
- Rule of 78
- Simple interest contracts

The Rule of 78 method and the simple interest contract method have certain credit implications when the amortized loans are pooled and sold in an asset-backed transaction.

Rule of 78 Method

The Rule of 78 method, otherwise known as the sum-of-the-years digits method, determines how much interest the obligor has paid at any one time. Interest earned at maturity and monthly payments are the same under both the Rule of 78 method and the actuarial method. (Figure 12-2 compares a $10,000 three-year car loan under both methods.) However, the interest component under the Rule of 78 method is higher at the beginning of the contract and declines over time. Therefore, the yield is higher than that of the actuarial method in the earlier months and lower in the later months (see Figure 12-3). As a result, the actuarial principal balance amortizes more rapidly during the early months (see Figure 12-4).

Interest payments on the receivable contracts and the pass-through certificates in an asset-backed transaction do not match. The receivables are amortized under the Rule of 78, and interest on the certificates is calculated by the actuarial method. As a result, a shortfall in cash flows is possible. For example, in month 5 in Figure

Figure 12-2. Comparison of the Actuarial Method and Rule of 78 Method

Schedule 1

Assumptions:			
	Original principal balance	$10,000.00	Standard & Poor's Creditweek
	Asset rate	10.00%	
	Original maturity (years)	3	
	Scheduled monthly payment	$322.67	

	Actuarial method				Rule of 78's method				
Beginning month	*Scheduled pymt ($)*	*Scheduled prin ($)*	*Scheduled int ($)*	*Ending bal ($)*	*Scheduled prin ($)*	*Scheduled int ($)*	*Effective yield (%)*	*Ending bal ($)*	*Prin diff (%)*
0	N/A	N/A	N/A	10,000.00	N/A	N/A	N/A	10,000.00	0.00
1	322.67	239.34	83.33	9,760.66	235.31	87.36	10.48	9,764.69	4.03
2	322.67	241.33	81.34	9,519.33	237.74	84.93	10.44	9,526.95	7.62
3	322.67	243.34	79.33	9,275.98	240.16	82.51	10.39	9,286.79	10.80
4	322.67	245.37	77.30	9,030.61	242.59	80.08	10.35	9,044.20	13.59
5	322.67	247.42	75.26	8,783.20	245.02	77.65	10.30	8,799.18	15.99
6	322.67	249.48	73.19	8,533.72	247.44	75.23	10.26	8,551.74	18.02
7	322.67	251.56	71.11	8,282.16	249.87	72.80	10.22	8,301.87	19.71
8	322.67	253.65	69.02	8,028.51	252.30	70.37	10.17	8,049.57	21.06
9	322.67	255.77	66.90	7,772.74	254.72	67.95	10.13	7,794.84	22.11
10	322.67	257.90	64.77	7,514.84	257.15	65.52	10.09	7,537.69	22.86
11	322.67	260.05	62.62	7,254.79	259.58	63.09	10.04	7,278.12	23.33
12	322.67	262.22	60.46	6,992.58	262.00	60.67	10.00	7,016.11	23.54
13	322.67	264.40	58.27	6,728.17	264.43	58.24	9.96	6,751.68	23.51
14	322.67	266.60	56.07	6,461.57	266.86	55.81	9.92	6,484.82	23.25
15	322.67	268.83	53.85	6,192.75	269.28	53.39	9.88	6,215.54	22.79

Figure 12-2. (Continued)

Beginning month	Actuarial method: Scheduled pymt ($)	Scheduled prin ($)	Scheduled int ($)	Ending bal ($)	Rule of 78's method: Scheduled prin ($)	Scheduled int ($)	Effective yield (%)	Ending bal ($)	Prin diff (%)
16	322.67	271.07	51.61	5,921.68	271.71	50.96	9.84	5,943.83	22.15
17	322.67	273.32	49.35	5,648.36	274.14	48.53	9.80	5,669.69	20.37
18	322.67	275.60	47.07	5,372.75	276.56	46.11	9.76	5,393.13	20.37
19	322.67	277.90	44.77	5,094.85	278.99	43.68	9.72	5,144.14	19.28
20	322.67	280.21	42.46	4,814.64	281.42	41.25	9.68	4,832.72	18.08
21	322.67	282.55	40.12	4,532.09	283.84	38.83	9.64	4,548.87	16.78
22	322.67	284.90	37.77	4,247.19	286.27	36.40	9.60	4,262.60	15.42
23	322.67	287.28	35.39	3,959.91	288.70	33.97	9.56	3,973.90	14.00
24	322.67	289.67	33.00	3,670.23	291.12	31.55	9.53	3,682.78	12.55
25	322.67	292.09	30.59	3.378.15	293.55	29.12	9.49	3,389.23	11.08
26	322.67	294.52	28.15	3,083.63	295.98	26.69	9.45	3,093.25	9.62
27	322.67	296.97	25.70	2,786.65	298.40	24.27	9.41	2,794.84	8.19
28	322.67	299.45	23.22	2,487.20	300.83	21.84	9.38	2,494.01	6.81
29	322.67	301.95	20.73	2,185.26	303.26	19.41	9.34	2,190.76	5.50
30	322.67	304.46	18.21	1,880.80	305.68	16.99	9.30	1,885.07	4.28
31	322.67	307.00	15.67	1,573.80	308.11	14.56	9.27	1,576.96	3.16
32	322.67	309.56	13.11	1,264.24	310.54	12.13	9.23	1,266.42	2.18
33	322.67	312.14	10.54	952.10	312.97	9.71	9.20	953.46	1.35
34	322.67	314.74	7.93	637.37	315.39	7.28	9.16	638.06	0.70
35	322.67	317.36	5.31	320.01	317.82	4.85	9.13	320.25	0.24
36	322.67	320.01	2.67	0.00	320.25	2.43	0.09	0.00	0.00

Rule of 78's calculation. Add up all the digits for the number of payments to be made. For a 36-month loan, add the numbers one through 36 which equals 666 in the first month, the obligor would pay 36 ÷ 666 of the total interest charge, in the second month, he would pay 35 ÷ 666 and so on down to the final installment of 1 – 666.

NA — Not available.

Figure 12-3. Yield of the Actuarial Method and Rule of 78 Method

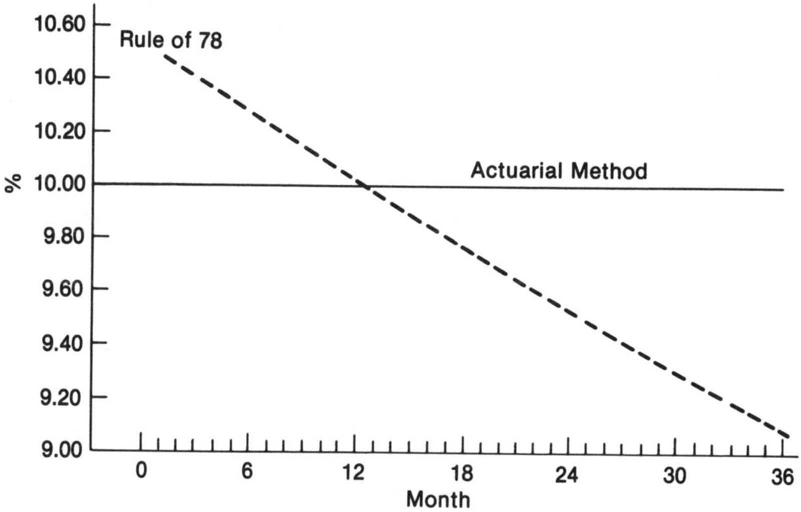

Figure 12-4. Differences in Outstanding Balances of Rule of 78 Method—Actuarial Method

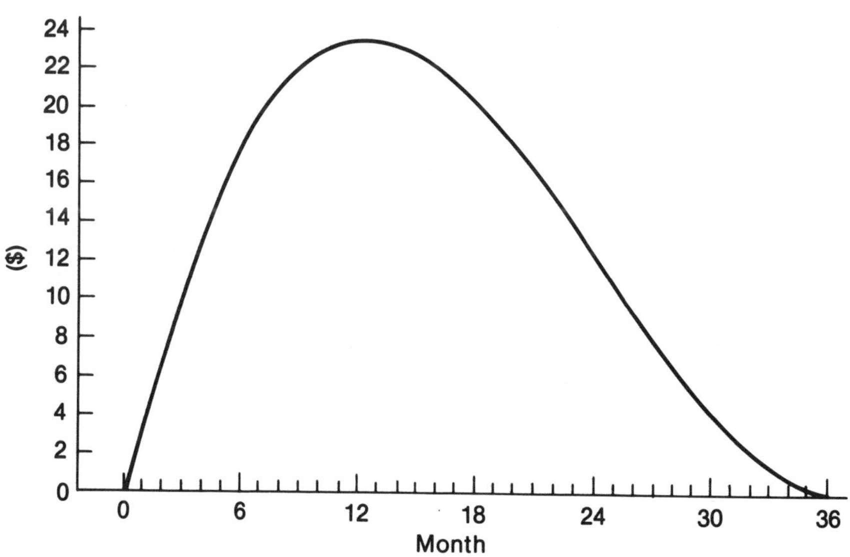

12-2, the obligor must pay \$245.02 in principal and \$77.65 in interest (a yield of 10.3 percent). If the investor is paid \$75.26 in interest (a 10.0 percent yield) and \$245.02 in principal (the principal amount received from the obligor), the extra interest of $2.39 ($77.65–$75.26) will be kept by the servicer and will be available later in the transaction. This amount is needed in later months, when the loans' yield is lower than the certificates' yield. For example, in month 30, the loans yield only 9.3 percent ($16.99), while investors must receive a 10.0 percent yield ($18.21).

To correct this mismatch, an accounting system can convert the Rule of 78 method to the actuarial method. As the total monthly payments are the same under both methods and the allocation between principal and interest can be precomputed, this is not difficult. The remaining cash flows are discounted at the contracts' APR. As shown on Figure 12-2, if the contracts were pooled and sold in month 6, the cash flows would be discounted at 10 percent and the certificates would have an original principal balance of $8,533.72. The transaction should be structured so that the lowest contract's APR is greater than the certificate rate, plus the servicing fee.

Prepayment of the automobile loans does not cause shortfalls under the Rule of 78. A full prepayment by the obligor would entitle him or her to a refund under the rule. However, no shortfall would occur because the rebate is only the portion of unearned interest. As illustration, if the obligor decides to prepay the loan in month 34, he or she would have to pay the final two payments, totaling $645.34. The lender would rebate the unearned interest of $7.28 ($4.85 + $2.43), leaving $638.07 for the investors. As the notes have an outstanding balance of $637.37, cash flow is sufficient to pay out the investors.

Prepayment can cause shortfalls under the simple interest contact method. If simple interest loan payments are made on their due dates, the yield equals the actuarial yield. However, interest on simple interest loans is calculated daily; thus, any prepayment would reduce the interest earned. Therefore, when simple interest loans are pooled in an asset-backed transaction, any prepayments can cause a shortfall. If such a possibility of shortfall exists, the credit support amount will be adjusted to reflect it.

To determine the amount of support needed, S&P assumes a worst-case scenario, in which the entire transaction prepays on day 1. In a $100 million deal with an 8 percent certificate rate and a 10 percent loan rate, S&P assumes that the full $100 million is prepaid. Therefore, the additional credit support should equal the sum of $100 million at 8 percent for 30 days, or $666,666.67 (67 basis points).

GEOGRAPHIC CONCENTRATION

An asset pool's risks can increase if the loans are concentrated in one geographic area. Issuers that underwrite a large number of loans in any one state or region should provide loss data by state, in addition to data on geographic concentrations. Regional economic problems can affect the entire pool if geographic concentration is substantial. S&P's analysis highlights concentrations of over 5 percent in a state. As a result, stricter selection criteria or greater credit enhancement may be needed for a given rating category. For example, Republic Bank Dallas N.A.'s $230 million in Series 1987A pass-through certificates indicates a concentration in Texas. S&P was particularly concerned about contracts that originated in regions suffering most from the downturn in the Texas economy, such as Houston and Midland. However, those regions provided fewer contracts to the pool, and those that were provided from those regions had greater than average seasoning. In a similar manner, Ponce Federal Bank 1987-A Grantor Trust included automobile loans originated in Puerto Rico. Accordingly, when sizing the necessary credit support, S&P considered the impact and likelihood of an economic downturn in Puerto Rico. On the other hand, all of GMAC's and Chrysler's issues comprise retail installment sale contracts drawn from a national loan portfolio. As these pools are well diversified geographically, they present no additional concentration risk.

S&P also evaluates any system for avoiding unfavorable regional concentrations that the underwriters incorporate into their credit-scoring systems. Underwriters normally examine state and regional payment patterns and economic factors at both the macro and micro levels.

The importance that S&P attaches to geographic concentration depends on the region in question. S&P recognizes that some states and regions are more stable and diversified than others. Economic stability and its impact on future pool charge-offs correlate closely with the local economy's diversity. As a result, heavy geographic concentration adds incremental risk only when the state or locality experiences unstable growth or depends on only a few industries for its revenue base. For example, Marine Midland's $600 million 1987-1 CARS Trust was selected from a portfolio whose sale contracts were originated by New York State automobile dealers. The risks associated with this geographic concentration were mitigated by New York's

Table 12-5. Repossessions as a Percentage of Average number of Contracts Outstanding

	1987	*1986*	*1985*	*1984*	*1983*
Marine Midland Bank	N.A.[6]	N.A.[6]	N.A.[6]	1.01%	1.31%
Home Federal Savings & Loan Assn.	N.A.[6]	N.A.[6]	0.19%	0.30	N.A.[6]
General Motors Acceptance Corp.	1.63[1]	1.53%	1.37	1.24	1.56
Nissan Motors Acceptance Corp.[2]	N.A.[6]	N.A.[6]	0.56	0.47	N.A.[6]
Chrysler Corp.	1.75[1]	1.69	1.67	1.64	1.96
Ponce Federal Bank	3.14[1]	3.95	3.06	0.18	N.A.[6]
Western Financial Savings Bank	N.A.[6]	1.61	1.38	1.05	N.A.[6]
American Bankers Assn. Survey[4]					
Direct	0.99[5]	1.13	1.77	1.64	1.67
Indirect	1.86[5]	2.03	2.45	2.00	1.70
RepublicBank Dallas N.A.[3]	4.72[1]	3.70	2.80	2.06	2.31

[1]Annualized.

[2]Began operations in 1984.

[3]Weighted average of 16 RepublicBank units and 2 Interfirst Bank units.

[4]Number of repossessions per 1,000 loans outstanding unadjusted.

[5]At June 30.

[6]N.A.—Not available.

relatively diverse economic base. In a similar manner, Western Financial Savings Bank's three asset-backed issues to date were collateralized by automobile loans that all originated in California, which is also an economically diverse state.

Geographic region is indicated by the automobile loan's state of origination. Most retail installment sale contracts that are included in a receivable pool are purchased by the issuer, pursuant to agreements with certain dealers. The remainder are originated directly by the bank or by the company sponsoring the issue. The contracts are classified by state, depending on where the loan was originated. In most cases, the loan's origination corresponds to the obligor's billing address, which is indicated on the sale contract.

SEASONING

Seasoning reduces the risks associated with automobile contract receivables because most losses tend to occur between 6 and 18

Figure 12-5. GMAC Net Losses* (as a Percentage of Original Outstandings—36-Month Contracts)

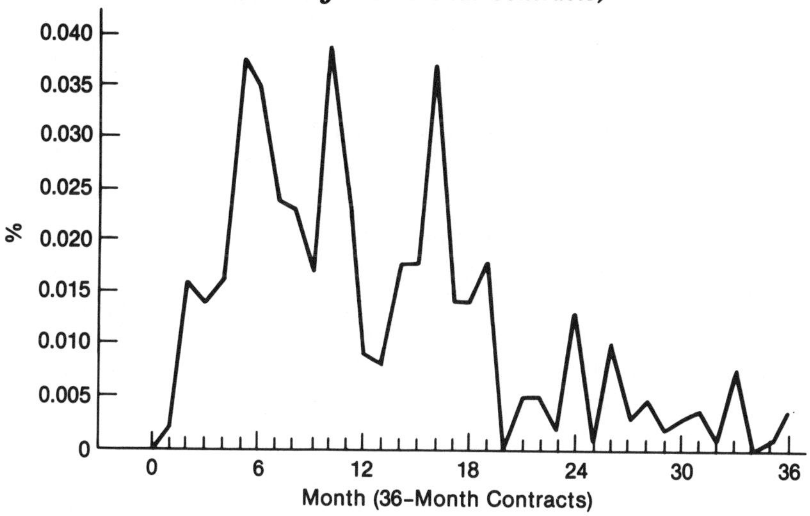

*1985 Static Pool Analysis.

Figure 12-6. GMAC Net Losses* (as a Percentage of Original Outstandings—48-Month Contracts)

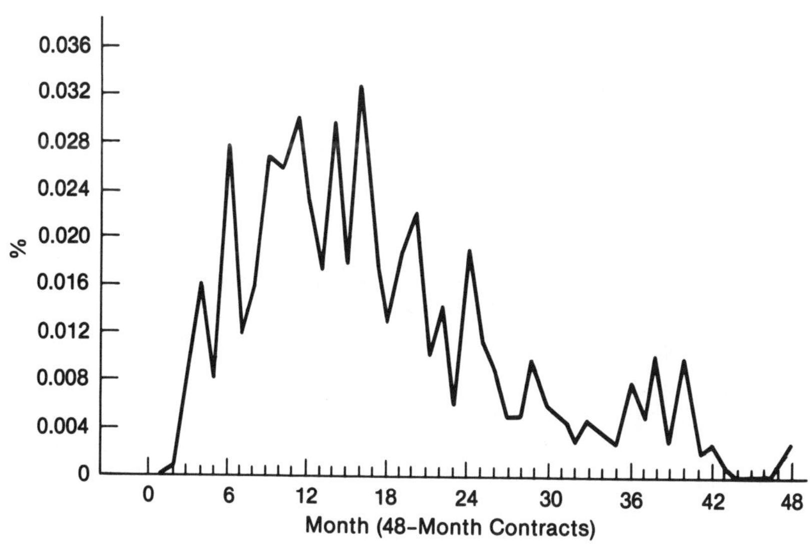

*1985 Static Pool Analysis.

months following contract origination. This loss pattern is clearly demonstrated in Figures 12-5 and 12-6, which summarize First Boston's 1985 static pool analysis of 100,000 GMAC receivable contracts. S&P's own analysis of various issuers' monthly loss statistics confirms these results.

Most losses occur at 6–18 months for several reasons. Conservative underwriting standards by the originator should allow accurate prediction of losses in the short term. In addition, most defaulters experience a delinquency cycle (usually 90–120 days) before incurring any losses. The obligor's establishment of a payment record should reduce the frequency of losses after the eighteenth month. During this 18-month period, an equity buildup should increase the severity of losses. Weaker payers are also eliminated through conservative selection criteria. For example, customarily, no contracts over 30 days delinquent are selected for the pool.

By itself, a pool with six months of seasoning would not warrant a reduction in credit support because the losses incurred in the first six months are not material. However, if this seasoning is combined with strong selection criteria, S&P believes that a lower credit support is warranted. Strong selection criteria would eliminate delinquent payers, who are the obligors most likely to default during the 6- to 12-month period. Similarly, a pool with 18 months of seasoning, as well as strong selection criteria, would receive a greater credit support reduction. Delinquent payers are eliminated, and approximately 50 percent of the pool's losses have been incurred.

S&P believes that the credit support necessary for a seasoned portfolio may be reduced as follows:

- 25 percent for 18 months of seasoning
- 12.5 percent for 12 months of seasoning
- 6.25 percent for six months of seasoning

For example, a transaction that would normally need an 8 percent credit support level is dropped to 6 percent if the portfolio is 18 months seasoned—a 25 percent reduction. Similarly, the same transaction would be reduced to 7 percent for 12-month seasoning, and to 7.5 percent for 6-month seasoning.

LIQUIDITY RISK ANALYSIS

S&P evaluates asset-backed transactions to ensure that cash flow is sufficient to meet bond holder payments, as promised. S&P's analytical approach to these offerings consists of two separate, yet related, analyses. To project potential loan losses on the underlying assets, S&P reviews the originator/seller's historical portfolio performance and data related to the specific collateral pool. This analysis enables S&P to predict cash flow, which is unavailable due to consumer defaults, but not temporary shortfalls caused by timing differences (such as delinquencies, installment contract extensions/revisions, and timeliness of repossession). Thus, S&P must perform a second test, commonly known as liquidity risk analysis, to ascertain appropriate liquidity coverage.

- *Step 1.* S&P first determines exactly what bond holders are promised. Frequently, transactions collateralized by nonmortgage products have used pass-through or pay-through vehicles, which effectively promise timely interest and principal as received. In such cases, timing differences—most often due to delinquencies—may cause an interest shortfall on the next payment date, but no principal shortfall. Although similar in most respects, other cash flow structures promise bond holders both timely interest and scheduled principal (that is, the obligor's monthly payments) on each payment date. Moreover, these structures may require bond holders to receive full repayment by a specified stated maturity. Thus, delinquent scheduled payments by obligors may create a shortfall not only of interest, but also of principal.
- *Step 2.* With these structures in mind, S&P then determines the maximum amount of cash flow that could be unavailable due to delinquent payments. S&P requests delinquency data from the originator/seller for the five prior fiscal periods, as well as written confirmation of the institution's receivable charge-off policy. The delinquency data should be prepared on a quarterly basis. Information should include the percentage of payments past due (as a ratio of average dollars outstanding) for each 30-day period, including those delinquent in the 1- to 30-day category. S&P analyzes these data to estimate the percentage of cash flow that is typically

missing from the originator's portfolio, plus amounts recovered from obligors ("cures"), during each month.

- *Step 3.* Using these data and the pool's scheduled monthly principal and interest payments (that is, no prepayments), S&P creates a transaction model to determine the required level of delinquency coverage. Varying degrees of stress are imposed on the model, depending on the underlying assets' characteristics and S&P's assessment of the servicer and the economic environment.

These three steps are illustrated as follows. Assume that Auto Lender Inc., a quality underwriter and servicer, wishes to securitize a $100 million pool of auto installment sales contracts. Furthermore, assume that this hypothetical company pools a large number of randomly selected loans with a weighted-average coupon of 10 percent, which amortize equally over 36-, 48-, or 60-month terms. Auto Lender adheres to a 120-day charge-off policy and has average delinquencies under 30 days of 4 percent. To isolate liquidity stress created by delinquencies, the model ignores defaults, assuming that all past-due loans are completely recovered by the charge-off date. Thus, cure rates in the following three months will approximate 50 percent, 25 percent, and 25 percent, respectively.

S&P's worst-case analysis assumes a recessionary environment for a portion of the transaction's five-year scheduled life. It also assumes that investors are promised timely interest and scheduled principal payments. The model imposes the following conditions:

- *Month 1.* Three times the average delinquencies under 30 days (that is, 12 percent of the total scheduled payments) are considered missing each month.
- *Month 2.* Fifty percent of the payments missing in month 1 are received (cure), but a new series of payments equal to the month 1 amount becomes delinquent.
- *Month 3.* Twenty-five percent of the month 1 payments cure, 50 percent of the month 2 payments cure, and a new series of obligor payments equal to the month 1 amount becomes delinquent.
- *Month 4.* The final 25 percent of the original month 1 payments cure, 25 percent of the month 2 payments cure, 50 percent of the month 3 payments cure, and a final series of obligor payments equal to the amount in month 1 becomes delinquent.

Table 12-6. Delinquencies by Number of Days

Month	1–30 1	31–60 2	61–90 3	91–120 4	Total
1	12	—	—	—	12
2	12	6	—	—	18
3	12	6	3	—	21
4	12	6	3	0	21
5	12	6	3	0	21
6	12	6	3	0	21
7	12	6	3	0	21
8	12	6	3	0	21
9	12	6	3	0	21
10	12	6	3	0	21
11	12	6	3	0	21
12	12	6	3	0	21
48	12	6	3	0	21
49	12	6	3	0	21
50	12	6	3	0	21
51	12	6	3	0	21
52	12	6	3	0	21
53	12	6	3	0	21
54	12	6	3	0	21
55	12	6	3	0	21
56	12	6	3	0	21
57	12	6	3	0	21
58	12	6	3	0	21
59	12	6	3	0	21
60	12	6	3	0	21

Table 12-6 shows the percentage of cash flow delinquent each month, given the above assumptions. In curing past-due accounts just prior to charge-off, the percentage increases to a maximum of 21 percent and then levels off as each new group of delinquent payments is offset by the full recovery of earlier loans. Figure 12-7, which is also derived from the $100 million hypothetical pool, reflects in dollar terms the amount of cash flow missing in each month of the transaction's life. Here too, net delinquencies (column E) increase to a maximum level ($552,138), then hold constant until the 36-month contracts are retired and scheduled monthly payments decline. A similar pattern is repeated until the 48-month contracts amortize in

Figure 12-7. Monthly Missing Cash Flows

Exhibit B

Standard & Poor's Creditweek

Assumptions:	
Original principal balance	$100,000,000.00
WAC	10.00%
Stated maturity (months)	60
Prepayments	0%

Month	*Outstanding bal ($)* *A*	*Total scheduled pmts ($)* *B*	*New monthly delinq ($)* *C*	*Recoveries ($)* *D*	*Net delinq ($)* *E*	*Net delinq as a % of outstandings* *F*	*LOC cov ($)* *G*	*LOC as a % of outstandings** *H*
1	100,000,000	2,629,227	315,507	0	315,507	0.32	8,000,000	8.00
2	98,204,106	2,629,227	315,507	157,754	473,261	0.48	7,856,328	8.00
3	96,393,246	2,629,227	315,507	236,630	552,138	0.57	7,711,460	8.00
4	94,567,296	2,629,227	315,507	315,507	552,138	0.58	7,565,384	8.00
5	92,726,130	2,629,227	315,507	315,507	552,138	0.60	7,418,090	8.00
6	90,869,620	2,629,227	315,507	315,507	552,138	0.61	7,269,570	8.00
7	88,997,640	2,629,227	315,507	315,507	552,138	0.62	7,119,811	8.00
8	87,110,060	2,629,227	315,507	315,507	552,138	0.63	6,968,805	8.00
9	85,206,750	2,629,227	315,507	315,507	552,138	0.65	6,816,540	8.00
10	83,287,579	2,629,227	315,507	315,507	552,138	0.66	6,663,006	8.00
11	81,352,415	2,629,227	315,507	315,507	552,138	0.68	6,508,193	8.00
12	79,401,124	2,629,227	315,507	315,507	552,138	0.70	6,352,090	8.00
13	77,433,573	2,629,227	315,507	315,507	552,138	0.71	6,194,686	8.00
14	75,449,626	2,629,227	315,507	315,507	552,138	0.73	6,035,970	8.00
15	73,449,145	2,629,227	315,507	315,507	552,138	0.75	5,875,932	8.00
16	71,431,994	2,629,227	315,507	315,507	552,138	0.77	5,714,560	8.00

Figure 12-7. (Continued)

Month	*Outstanding bal ($)* *A*	*Total scheduled pmts ($)* *B*	*New monthly delinq ($)* *C*	*Recoveries ($)* *D*	*Net delinq ($)* *E*	*Net delinq as a % of outstandings* *F*	*LOC cov ($)* *G*	*LOC as a % of outstandings** *H*
17	69,398,034	2,629,227	315,507	315,507	552,138	0.80	5,551,843	8.00
18	67,347,124	2,629,227	315,507	315,507	552,138	0.82	5,387,770	8.00
19	65,279,123	2,629,227	315,507	315,507	552,138	0.85	5,222,330	8.00
20	63,193,888	2,629,227	315,507	315,507	552,138	0.87	5,055,511	8.00
21	61,091,277	2,629,227	315,507	315,507	552,138	0.90	4,887,302	8.00
22	58,971,143	2,629,227	315,507	315,507	552,138	0.94	4,717,692	8.00
23	56,833,342	2,629,227	315,507	315,507	552,138	0.97	4,546,667	8.00
24	54,677,726	2,629,227	315,507	315,507	552,138	1.01	4,374,218	8.00
25	52,504,147	2,629,227	315,507	315,507	552,138	1.05	4,200,332	8.00
26	50,312,454	2,629,227	315,507	315,507	552,138	1.10	4,024,996	8.00
27	48,102,498	2,629,227	315,507	315,507	552,138	1.15	3,848,200	8.00
28	45,874,125	2,629,227	315,507	315,507	552,138	1.20	3,669,930	8.00
29	43,627,182	2,629,227	315,507	315,507	552,138	1.27	3,490,175	8.00
30	41,361,515	2,629,227	315,507	315,507	552,138	1.33	3,308,921	8.00
31	39,076,967	2,629,227	315,507	315,507	552,138	1.41	3,126,157	8.00
32	36,773,381	2,629,227	315,507	315,507	552,138	1.51	2,941,871	8.00
33	34,450,598	2,629,227	315,507	315,507	552,138	1.60	2,756,048	8.00
34	32,108,460	2,629,227	315,507	315,507	552,138	1.72	2,568,677	8.00
35	29,746,803	2,629,227	315,507	315,507	552,138	1.86	2,379,744	8.00
36	27,365,466	2,629,227	315,507	315,507	552,138	2.02	2,189,237	8.00
37	24,964,284	1,553,654	186,439	315,507	423,069	1.69	1,997,143	8.00

Figure 12-7. (Continued)

Month	Outstanding bal ($) A	Total scheduled pmts ($) B	New monthly delinq ($) C	Recoveries ($) D	Net delinq ($) E	Net delinq as a % of outstandings F	LOC cov ($) G	LOC as a % of outstandings* H
38	23,618,666	1,553,654	186,439	250,973	358,535	1.52	1,889,493	8.00
39	22,261,834	1,553,654	186,439	218,706	326,267	1.47	1,780,947	8.00
40	20,893,695	1,553,654	186,439	186,439	326,267	1.56	1,671,496	8.00
41	19,514,154	1,553,654	186,439	186,439	326,267	1.67	1,561,132	8.00
42	18,123,118	1,553,654	186,439	186,439	326,267	1.80	1,449,849	8.00
43	16,720,490	1,553,654	186,439	186,439	326,267	1.95	1,337,639	8.00
44	15,306,173	1,553,654	186,439	186,439	326,267	2.13	1,224,494	8.00
45	13,880,070	1,553,654	186,439	186,439	326,267	2.35	1,110,406	8.00
46	12,442,083	1,553,654	186,439	186,439	326,267	2.62	995,367	8.00
47	10,992,113	1,553,654	186,439	186,439	326,267	2.97	879,369	8.00
48	9,530,060	1,553,654	186,439	186,439	326,267	3.42	800,000	839
49	8,055,822	708,234	84,988	186,439	224,817	2.79	800,000	9.93
50	7,414,720	708,234	84,988	135,713	174,092	2.35	800,000	10.79
51	6,768,274	708,234	84,988	110,351	148,729	2.20	800,000	11.82
52	6,116,441	708,234	84,988	84,988	148,729	2.43	800,000	13.08
53	5,459,177	708,234	84,988	84,988	148,729	2.72	800,000	14.65
54	4,796,435	708,234	84,988	84,988	148,729	3.10	800,000	16.68
55	4,128,171	708,234	84,988	84,988	148,729	3.60	800,000	19.38
56	3,454,337	708,234	84,988	84,988	148,729	4.31	800,000	23.16
57	2,774,889	708,234	84,988	84,988	148,729	5.36	800,000	28.83
58	2,089,778	708,234	84,988	84,988	148,729	7.12	800,000	38.28
59	1,398,958	708,234	84,988	84,988	148,729	10.63	800,000	57.19
60	702,381	708,234	84,988	84,988	148,729	21.17	702,382	100.00

*Assume draws for defaults always less than amortized amount

full. Net delinquencies as a percentage of the outstanding pool balance are then calculated (column F) to determine the liquidity enhancement required in each month of the transaction.

S&P assumes that rewritten consumer contracts (with significant changes in terms or conditions) are purchased from the pool by the servicer, as occurs in most actual transactions. S&P also examines historical data and the servicer's policies regarding loan extensions to determine whether additonal liquidity coverage is required, in addition to the enhancement required for delinquency stress. For simplicity, it is assumed in this example that extension risk is minimal. As a result, total liquidity coverage remains constant at the level established for maximum delinquencies.

Asset-backed transactions often require the servicer to cover any liquidity shortfalls. S&P believes that the servicer will have the capacity to make such payments, as long as the servicer is not currently rated more than one category below the transaction's rating. If the servicer's rating does not meet this standard, an appropriately rated third party guarantee (letter-of-credit surety bond) or monies in the form of cash collateral or a reserve fund must support the servicer's advance obligation. In our example, Auto Lender is unrated, although it is a quality servicer and underwriter. Thus, it will obtain a letter of credit to back up its advances.

Column G of Figure 12-7 reflects the total letter-of-credit coverage provided for this "prime" pool's credit and liquidity risks. As the pool balance declines faster than actual losses, the letter of credit remains at a constant 8 percent with an $800,000 floor (see the "Floor Coverage" section following.

Figure 12-8 compares the relationship of delinquency stress to letter-of-credit coverage. Although minimal in the earlier years, delinquency risk increases as scheduled amortization reduces the pool's balance. However, adequate protection is provided through the floor to cover a greater percentage of liquidity stress as the transaction winds down.

FLOOR COVERAGE

Third party credit enhancement is the standard technique used to cover loss and liquidity stress in an asset-backed transaction.

Figure 12-8. Delinquencies versus LOC Coverage (as a Percentage of Outstanding Receivables)

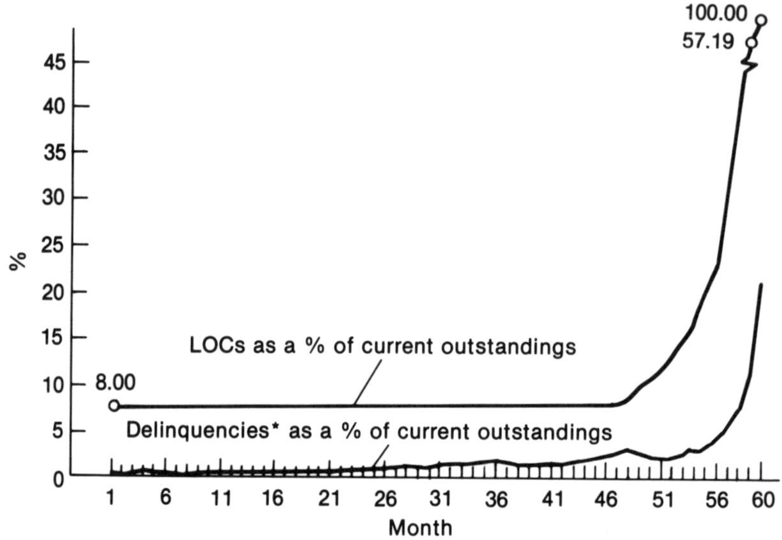

*Aggregate "payments" not received as scheduled.

S&P's "weak link" approach requires the institution that provides such support to be rated as high as the rating desired for the pooled loans. The credit enhancement, which must be irrevocable and fully transferable to a substitute trustee, is issued for a stated dollar amount, which represents a percentage of the original pool balance. The credit enhancement will decline as funds are drawn for losses or delinquencies. However, most asset-backed issues allow coverage to decline as a function of the pool's amortization should this amount exceed actual draws. Consequently, the credit enhancement may decline rapidly in absolute dollars, although it may remain a constant percentage of the outstanding receivables.

To determine if declining credit support poses additional risk, S&P examines the loss curve and historical payment pattern of the transaction's underlying assets. Specifically, S&P reviews the timing of loan defaults and consumer payment habits to judge their effect on pool quality or liquidity stress.

For example, an auto transaction's risk profile is not heightened should the credit support decline with the pool's receivable balance. To evaluate auto-backed transactions, S&P analyzed industry data, including GMAC's static pool analysis, and concluded that peak defaults occur early in a pool's life—between the sixth and eighteenth months. Two factors—the buildup of the obligor's equity in the vehicle over time and the fact that seasoned loans typically default less—explain this incidence of loss and the conclusion that pools gain in quality as they mature. Furthermore, auto loan prepayments occur among all borrower classes for a variety of reasons—the most prevalent being sale or trade-in of the vehicle—but are not due to a change in market interest rates. Thus, prepayments will probably not reduce the pool's quality.

However, as a transaction enters its final stage, additional credit and liquidity risk may arise. For example, losses may increase proportionately as the pool's obligor base becomes less diversified. Additonally, servicer policies relating to delinquencies, loan rewrites/extensions, partial prepayments, and the time required to repossess vehicles and recover funds will increase liquidity stress during the deal's latter stages.

To provide for any remaining credit and liquidity risks, transactions have required the dollar amount of the credit enhancement to remain constant when the pool balance reaches a specified floor amount. This structural adjustment ensures that, on a percentage basis, the available loss coverage will increase toward the tail end of the transaction.

Liquidity risk may be minimized if a servicer, rated not more than one category below the transaction's rating, agrees to advance funds prior to each payment date. For instance, in addition to its 5 percent guaranty of credit losses, GMAC as servicer has agreed to make reimbursable advances for delinquencies and other scheduled payment shortfalls. Since GMAC's rating equals the transaction's rating, liquidity stress is significantly reduced.

Each transaction must be evaluated independently, but a floor equal to 10 percent of the original credit support is generally sufficient for auto-backed issues that seek an AAA rating. Thus, a \$200 million pool that requires initial credit support of \$16 million (8 percent) would typically provide floor coverage of \$1.6 million. As auto pools vary in size, floor coverage of not more than \$5 million or less than \$1 million is usually sufficient to ensure AAA-quality transactions.

Appendix: Case Study

BMWCC GRANTOR TRUSTS

(BMW Credit Corp. receivables)
Rated AAA

Table 12A-1. Transaction Summary

Sale date	March 4
Securities offered	$106.3 million auto receivable asset-backed certificates: $39.8 million 7.5% Series 1988-A due 1993 and $60.5 million 6.9% Series 1988 A-2 due 1993
Structure type	Grantor trust pass-through
Collateral	Automobile retail installment sales contracts
Seller	BMW Credit Corp.
Servicer	General Electric Capital Corp.
Trustee	First National Bank of Chicago
Lead underwriter	Kidder Peabody & Co., Inc.
Credit enhancement	For each trust, a 5% limited guaranty by BMW Credit Corp. to cover losses with a floor of $1 million General Electric Capital Corp. (AAA senior debt) will guarantee BMW Credit Corp.'s obligations
Legal structure	Sale of assets from BMW Credit Corp. to the trusts
Pool data (for Series A-1)	Weighted-average annual contract rate: 10.11% New autos: 9.1% Geographic distribution: California (23.68%), New York (7.07%), New Jersey (6.97%), Florida (6.30%), and Texas (6.10%) Weighted-average remaining maturity: 54 months
Loss and deliquency experience	See Table 12-2

Figure 12A-1. Transaction Summary Chart

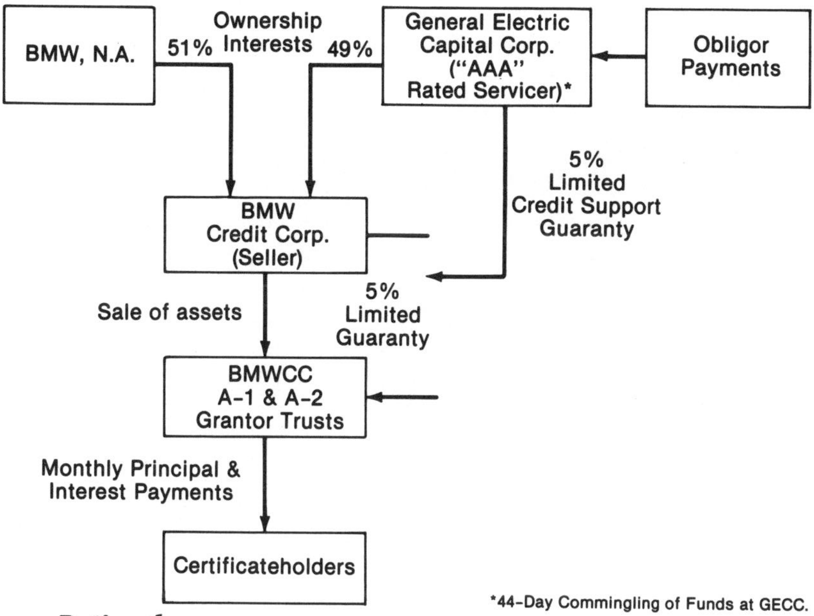

Rationale

An AAA rating is assigned to BMWCC Grantor Trusts' $106.3 million auto receivable asset-backed certificates. The offering consists of $39.8 million 7.5 percent Series 1988 A-1 and $66.5 million 6.9 percent Series A-2, both due 1993. The certificates are collateralized by pools of retail installment sales contracts after the March 1, 1988, cutoff date. All contracts have been originated by BMW Credit Corp., a joint venture formed in 1984 by BMW N.A. and General Electric Capital Corp. (AAA senior debt). The contracts will be serviced by General Electric Capital pursuant to supplemental agreements between it, BMW Credit, and the trustee. The two transactions have identical structures, but the Series A-2 pool contains all receivables with APRs equal to the 6.9 percent pass-through rate. Each series of certificates is secured by a 5 percent limited guaranty, which are themselves supported by a limited credit support guaranty from General Electric Capital. The rating is based on the underlying receivables' quality, General Electric Capital's strong servicing capabilities, and the support provided by the BMW Credit and General Electric Capital guaranties.

Legal Risks

BMW Credit sold the receivables to the trusts and assigned interests in the financed vehicles to the trustee. True sale opinions have been provided by counsel to BMW Credit. Recourse to BMW Credit under its 5 percent guaranty is high relative to 1987 net losses of 0.06 percent. The credit strength of General Electric Capital and BMW Credit (51 percent owned by BMW N.A. and 49 percent by General Electric Capital) mitigates any risk to the sale inherent in this recourse level. The servicer is obligated to repurchase any receivables that evidence a breach of representation or warranty.

Table 12A-2. BMW Credit Corp.

	Year Ended December 31		
	1985	*1986*	*1987*
Average portfolio outstanding (in millions)	$230.7	$196.0	$144.6
Average contracts outstanding (in thousands)	11.2	9.8	4.7
Total delinquencies (as % of average portfolio)	1.18%	1.11%	0.63%
Repossessions (as % of average contracts)	0.36	0.25	0.04
Net loss (as % of average portfolio outstanding)	0.06	0.05	0

Collections will be commingled at General Electric Capital for a maximum of 44 days. The risk of commingling is that in the unlikely event of General Capital's insolvency, funds would not be available to pay certificate holders in accordance with the terms of the transaction documents. Collections will be remitted in the trustee within two business days of receipt, in the event that General Electric Capital's ownership interest in BMW Credit drops below 49 percent.

Credit Risks

BMW Credit's general business includes purchasing retail installment sale contracts on new and used BMW automobiles from a network of about 600 franchised BMW automobile and motorcycle dealers. Its indirect automobile loan portfolio has performed exceptionally well relative to industry norms, as evidenced by very low delinquencies, repossessions, and net losses below 0.1 percent per year (see Table 12A-2). This excellent performance is attributable to General Electric Capital's excellent servicing capabilities and high-quality obligor base. Portfolio growth has been steady, but not overly aggressive. High concentrations of new vehicles allow S&P to assume lower loan loss severity, due to higher resale values. A short operating history and 100 percent nonrecourse lending have not adversely affected performance. Significant loan concentrations in California pose minimal risk to the portfolio at this time, given California's diverse economic base.

Receivables selected to be securitized for the two pools were originated in the United States and were not more than 30 days past due at the cutoff date. Strong pool selection criteria should help to minimize losses during the first several months of the transaction, since charge-offs generally occur when the contract is between 45 days and 90 days deliquent. Although the A-2 pool contains insufficient interest to pay servicing fees, S&P sees the risk as insignificant, given the servicer. The trustee must succeed to all servicing functions should a substitute be necessary. In addition to the servicer's maintenance of vehicle single-interest physical damage insurance coverage, all obligors are required to maintain their own insurance coverage.

Based on historical net loss experience well below that of the industry leaders GMAC (0.45 percent on an annualized basis in June 1987) and Chrysler (0.49 percent at year-end 1987), S&P feels confident that investors are well protected at the AAA level with the 5 percent guaranty.

Payment Structure

The Series A-1 and A-2 certificates pay monthly interest at the 7.5 percent and 6.9 percent pass-through rates, respectively, beginning April 15 (the distribution date). Scheduled principal and prepayments in full are passed through to certificate holders on each distribution date. Partial prepayments are held in a non-interest-bearing trust account and are passed through when scheduled. The final scheduled payment date for both classes is March 15, 1993. The servicer may employ an optional redemption when the aggregate principal balance of the receivables declines to 10 percent or less of the certificates' original face amount.

The servicer will advance for any recoverable deficiencies on each distribution date. If a shortfall is deemed nonrecoverable, a claim to the limited guaranty will be made. If BMW Credit fails to honor its guaranty by the business day preceding the distribution date, a claim to General Electric Capital's limited credit support guaranty will be made and honored on or before the distribution date. The limited guaranties will be replenished to the extent of recoveries on defaulted contracts that have been subject to repurchase. The guaranties expire only with termination of the trust.

CHAPTER 13
Credit Card Receivable-Backed Securities

Joan Barmat

INTRODUCTION

The securitization of revolving credit receivables once posed several unique difficulties. For example: What is actually pledged or sold—a revolving account or an account balance? How should principal repayments be allocated, assuming a varying monthly balance? How should the expansion and contraction of monthly balances be handled to allow for securitization of a fixed amount of receivables with a predictable repayment pattern? These and other structural, legal, tax, accounting, and technical issues have been overcome in various credit card receivable-backed security issues totaling over $8 billion to date since the first public issue in early 1987. Due in part to the inherent flexibility of the underlying credit card receivable asset, as well as the large volume of such assets among U.S. companies, a large volume of credit card receivable-backed issues can be expected to continue for years to come.

CREDIT CARD RECEIVABLES

Credit card receivables arise from unsecured, revolving installment debt obligations of consumers. The collateral underlying the receivables is a contractual agreement between the card holder and the card issuer that states the terms and conditions for repayment. The receivables consist of loans made to finance purchases of goods and services, as well as cash advances (principal receivables) and the monthly periodic finance charges, annual membership fees, and other fees (finance charge receivables) related to credit card usage.

CASH FLOW CHARACTERISTICS OF A POOL OF CREDIT CARD RECEIVABLES

For each month in which new purchases or cash advances are made or a payment is remitted on prior balances, a new minimum monthly payment is computed pursuant to the card holder's contractual agreement with the card issuer. Depending on the terms of this agreement, a card holder may choose to pay each month's new charges in full prior to the payment due date, thereby avoiding any finance charge on new purchases and taking advantage of the grace period (although cash advances are generally subject to finance charges from the date of the advance), or may choose to pay a lesser amount (a percentage of the outstanding balance) down to the computed minimum monthly payment (the minimum monthly payment is typically less than 5 percent of the outstanding balance). Any balance not paid in full is said to revolve and is subject to the application of the monthly periodic finance charge from the day on which the balances were posted to the account. Failure to make a payment greater than or equal to the minimum payment by the payment due date results in delinquency.

Unlike mortgages and auto loans, which are scheduled installment loans, credit card portfolios do not experience prepayments, but, rather, repayments. The overall payment behavior of a pool of credit card receivables is measured by the payment rate. For example, if the average outstanding balance is $1,000 (including principal and finance charge receivables) and the average monthly payment remitted by card holders is $100, the average payment rate is 10 percent.

It is important to note that included in an average payment rate for a given portfolio are card holders that generally pay off their entire balance each month prior to the payment due date. Under most agreements, these card holders never incur any finance charge. Called convenience users, they generally account for 5–20 percent of a given portfolio of receivables. Thus, 80–95 percent of the balances actually revolve each month and will be subject to finance charges. The presence of convenience usage reduces the expected yield on a credit card portfolio. For example, a credit card portfolio with an 18 percent annual percentage rate (APR) and 10 percent cconvenience usage will yield about 16.2 percent in gross interest income (that is, 90 percent of the receivables are subject to an 18 percent finance charge). Generally speaking, any economic factors that cause (1) an increase in the payment rate without a corresponding generation of new balances or (2) an increase in convenience usage will lower the yield on a portfolio of credit card receivables for a given earnings period. In this light, card issuers that offer a relatively low APR typically do not offer an interest-free grace period on either purchases or advances.

It should be mentioned that when annual membership fees are included in finance charge receivables, they boost the effective portfolio yield often by as much as 3–6 percent. Typical annual membership fees range from $15 to $50, depending on issuer marketing considerations and the additional services offered with the card.

CREDIT CARD RECEIVABLE-BACKED SECURITIES

Due to the revolving nature of the underlying credit card receivable, the nature of the securities created can vary extensively. To date, these structures have included:

- Medium-term trust certificates of participation with an amoritzing tail
- Medium-term trust certificates with a bullet maturity
- Receivable-backed collateralized debt (asset not sold to a trust)
- Receivable-backed commercial paper

The first, which is still the most prevalent structure, is described in greatest detail here. Other structures are summarized thereafter.

Medium-Term Amortizing Trust Certificates

Credit card receivable-backed trust certificates represent undivided interests in a credit card trust. Ownership of the trust is divided into a seller interest and an investor interest (see the "Seller Interest and Investor Interest" section). The property of the trust includes a portfolio of credit card receivables and the underlying card holder accounts pledged by the seller, as well as the benefits of any credit enhancement (such as a letter of credit) to cover losses. The basic idea behind a medium-term credit card securitization is to take advantage of the regeneration property of a revolving line of credit. The speeds at which payments on existing balances are made and new balances are generated, as well as the yield and charge-off experience, are key parameters in determining the ability of a pool of credit card receivables to support certificate payments of principal and interest to investors.

Using the basic trust structure for a medium-term securitization of credit card receivables, a repeat issuer may choose to use a master trust to attain greater ease of issuance. In this case, a receivable seller/servicer transfers a pool of assets to a master trust that could support the issuance of several tranches of asset-backed securities. Each time that a new group of receivables is chosen for sale, the seller interest in the master trust would be reduced.

In most cases in which credit card receivable assets are sold to a trust, the seller/servicer continues to service the receivables and accounts. The trustee pays the proceeds from the sale of the certificates to the seller and is responsible for protecting the interest of the certificate holders by providing fiduciary and agency services that assure investors that all parties to the transaction have contractually fulfilled their obligations. The amount of receivables pledged to the trust is typically larger than the aggregate value of the certificates sold. As mentioned earlier, it is divided into two pro rata portions: The aggregate value of the investor's certificate principal represents the investor interest in the trust, while the excess amount pledged to the trust represents the seller interest.

This basic credit card receivable–backed deal structure is diagramed in Figure 13-1.

Figure 13-1. Credit Card Receivables Deal Structure

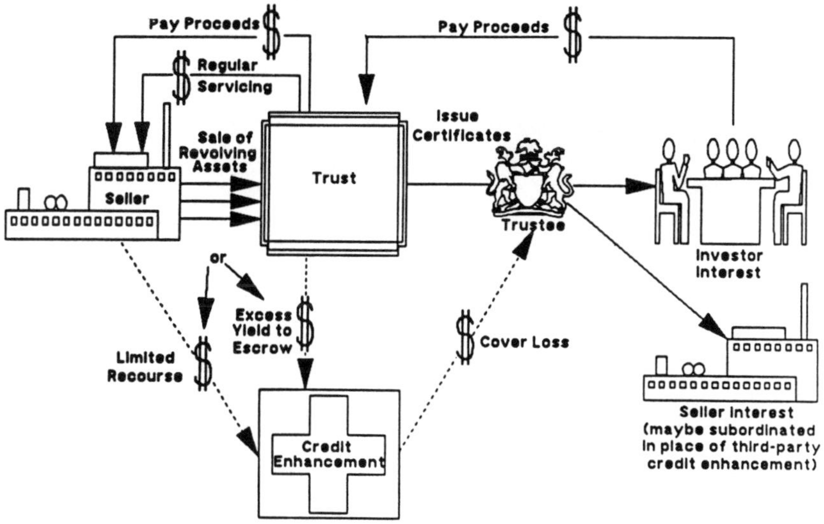

Economic Profile—Reinvestment and Amortization Periods

The structure of a medium-term amortizing credit card receivable–backed bond issue calls for two distinct periods:

- The interest-only/nonamortization period
- The amortization period

Unlike mortgage or auto loan–backed securities, which assume payments of principal and interest each month that commence in the month following the issuance, medium-term asset-backed certificates using credit card receivables usually pay interest only for some initial period, usually 18–36 months. During this period, the certificate principal is reinvested in newly generated receivables. This period is known as the interest-only/nonamortization period, or the revolving period.

While paying down old balances, card holders continue to generate new receivables. Each month during the interest-only/nonamortization period, card holder principal payments are remitted to the trustee's collection account and are then reinvested in the newly generated receivables. This process of reinvesting cardholder

Figure 13-2. Reinvestment Structure

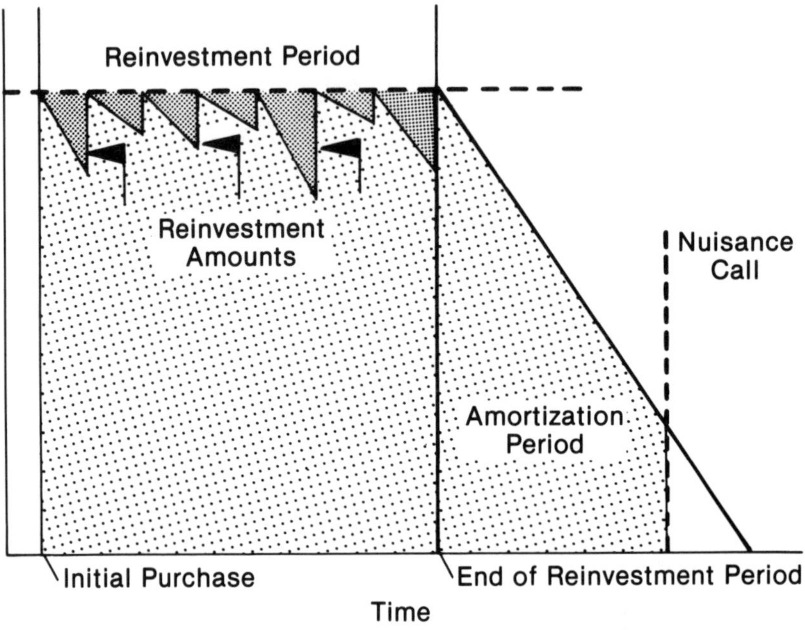

principal payments in newly generated receivables rather than passing them through to investors each month is the key to structuring the maturity profile of the medium-term credit card loan–backed security—in particular, the duration of the interest-only/nonamortization period. At the end of the interest-only/nonamortization period, the trustee passes through the investors' allocation of the principal receivables instead of reinvesting them in new receivables, until all the investor interest is amortized.

There is no guarantee that, from month to month, new receivables will be generated. However, by properly managing card holder attrition, card use, credit line increases, and balance stimulation, credit card portfolio managers attempt to maintain a nondeclining average card holder receivable that revolves to provide a constant, stable source of yield capable of supporting a securitization transaction.

The basic reinvestment process is diagrammed in Figure 13-2.

Immediately following the revolving period is the amortization period, during which investors receive payments of principal and interest until their certificate principal is fully amortized. The method for making principal payments to investors varies and determines the expected duration of the amortization period. To the extent that the duration is longer or shorter than anticipated, investors can expect their effective yield to increase or decrease. However, given the relatively short maturity of these securities and the typically limited variation in repayment patterns, the impact on expected yield should be minimal.

Principal payments to investors are generally made in accordance with one or more of the following methods:

- *Controlled amortization*. The controlled amount, usually one twelfth of the investors' certificate principal, is paid to investors each month for 12 months.
- *Monthly percentage allocation (rapid amortization)*. The investor percentage is frozen on the last day of the interest-only/nonamortization period (or at the time of a payout event). Investors receive the investor percentage of all subsequent card holder principal payments until the certificate principal is fully amortized. For portfolios with average monthly payment rates over 8.33 percent, this amortization method will result in full investor repayment in under one year.
- *Accelerated amortization*. Investors receive monthly principal payments made by obligors of all accounts pledged to the trust, which may be greater than their monthly percentage allocation (pro rata share). Instead they may receive up to 100 percent of card holder principal payments, until their certificate principal is fully amortized. This method, which essentially applies some or all of the principal payments from the seller interest in the trust to investors, will result in a faster amortization than does a monthly percentage allocation and effectively subordinates the seller interest in the trust. (It should be noted that accountants may not allow tranactions using this amortization method to be considered "true sales" of assets.)

In certain instances, it may be stipulated that, for each month during the amortization period, investors will receive the lesser of the controlled amount and the monthly percentage allocation of card holder principal payments. In any month in which the monthly percentage allocation is less than the controlled amount, a deficit is created that can be made up with any extra card holder principal payments that are available to the investor interest above the controlled amount in subsequent months.

The method or methods used to amortize the investors' certificate principal will vary from deal to deal and may result in an amortization period ranging from 6 to 18 months on bank-issued cards (as opposed to retail cards, which may have a higher payment speed). To illustrate the relative insensitivity of yield to card holder payment speed and the resulting duration of the amortization period, Table 13-1 shows the semiannual bond equivalent yields on 6-, 12-, and 18-month controlled amortization periods at various prices, each with a ten-day payment delay and an 8 percent monthly coupon.

Table 13-1. Semiannual Bond Equivalent Yields

	Amortization Period		
Price	*6 Month*	*12 Month*	*18 Month*
99.62500	8.189%	8.186%	8.183%
99.78125 (parity)	8.134	8.134	8.134
99.93850	8.078	8.082	8.084
Weighted-average life (in years)	3.33	3.58	3.83
Payment speed	16.67%	8.33%	5.56%

During the Amortization period, when the investors' certificate principal is no longer reinvested in the new loan balances generated by card holders, these new balances become receivables owned by the card issuer.

To further illustrate the importance of the reinvestment process, imagine that investors' certificate principal was used to purchase receivables at a point in time and was never reinvested—that is, it was never used to purchase new receivables. Then, commencing in the first month, card holder payments would be passed through to investors. For back-issued cards, the tenor of the security would last approximately 6–12 months. This is essentially what happens during the amortization period. It is only through the incorporation of the interest-only/nonamortization period, during which the investors' principal revolves and is reinvested in new receivables, that the relatively short-term payoff of credit card receivables is converted into a medium-term security (with an average life of one to three and a half years).

Historical data on the payment behavior of the card issuer's portfolio are typically provided in an issue's prospectus. These payment rates provide investors with a means of estimating:

- The ability of card holder payments to support monthly payments of the controlled amount during the amortization period
- The chances that the controlled amount will be higher or lower than the monthly precentage allocation of the card holder principal payments made during the amortization period
- The expected duration of a rapid or accelerated amortization period

In general, there is considerable flexibility in the choice of a method of amortization. However, for selling institutions that are U.S. financial institutions and that wish to have their transaction qualify as a true sale of assets, the seller interest must participate, at least to a minimal degree, in principal amortization.

There are several circumstances (payout events) in which an early, unscheduled accelerated amortization period could begin during either the interest-only/nonamortization period or the amortization period. These include cases in which:

- The level of loan losses exceeds x percent for y consecutive months
- The base yield on the portfolio of receivables falls below z percent
- Insufficient new receivables are available to the trust to maintain a constant investor interest, given a minimum level of seller interest, as determined by the seller's tax counsel
- The seller/servicer defaults on its ability to properly service the receivables, and an adequate backup servicer is not available
- The receivables are found to contain serious breaches of warranties and representations
- The seller/servicer fails to make certain payments or transfers of funds for the benefit of the certificate holders within appropriate time periods
- Other events to be specified

The possibility of a payout event occurring early in a medium-term transaction—such as during the revolving period—represents the chief risk to investors yield with respect to repayment patterns.

Seller Interest and Investor Interest

The outstanding receivable balance that is associated with an isolated pool of credit card accounts will run off over time, primarily due to a 5–10 percent rate of card holder attrition (the rate at which card holders close their accounts and either pay off or default on their balances). This is usually offset by a rate of new borrowing, which is greater than the payment rate. However, if no new accounts are added to a seasoned portfolio, the portfolio balance will generally decline over time. To ensure that the level of receivables pledged to the trust is never reduced below the value of the investor interest and the minimum seller interest throughout the interest-only/nonamortization period, the seller actually pledges to the trust a pool of receivables that is larger than the aggregate certificate balance. The excess amount of the pool pledged to the trust that is not represented by the investors' certificate principal (the investor interest) is the seller interest in the trust.

Based on the historical cash flow behavior of the seller's portfolio, the seller interest will be set at a level estimated to be able to absorb any anticipated changes in the total outstanding receivables pledged to the trust that can be expected to occur daily during the interest-only/nonamortization period as a result of varying rates of repaying and of new receivables generated by the original group of card holder accounts. The seller interest in the trust typically starts out at 20–30 percent of the total pool pledged (the seller percentage). Should the seller percentage fall below a minimum level, currently 5–10 percent, the seller may have the option or be required to pledge additional eligible accounts to the trust to avoid any possibility of a payout event resulting in rapid amortization. The minimum seller interest level is determined by tax counsel to the seller/issuer.

In the case of a master trust, the seller pledges a pool of receivables capable of supporting two or more tranches of certificates over time. For example, in First Chicago's master trust, First Chicago originally pledged $1.684 billion in receivables, which represented approximately half of its total credit card operations. The first tranche issued was $300 million, indicating approximately 82 percent seller interest remaining in the master trust. Upon completion of this transaction, assuming no new generation of receivables, the master trust assets will be reduced to approximately $1.384 billion. If the next tranche were $300 million, the corresponding seller interest would be approximately 78 percent, and so on, until the master trust is fully used at the minimum seller interest level.

Because the usage and payment patterns of a credit card portfolio are subject to daily fluctuations, the level of receivables is also. As a result, the seller percentage in the trust will also fluctuate, given an investor interest that is fixed at the aggregate certificate amount throughout the interest-only/nonamortization period.

Bullet Maturity Medium-Term Structures

To some, the uncertainties related to the timing of repayment of principal of amortizing receivable-backed issues in the amortization period are undesirable. Thus, structural adaptations have created one final, bullet repayment in place of monthly amortization. Given the reduced uncertainty of the bullet repayment structure, sellers should realize an issuance cost savings. However, it is difficult to assess savings given different sellers, different guaranty structures, and varying transaction maturities. To date, two structures have emerged:

- *Lender takeout.* A highly rated company lends the full outstanding amount to a trust, which then repurchases outstanding certificates from investors. The loan is repaid through the issuance of credit card receivable commercial paper or another medium-term issue.
- *Reserve buildup.* Monthly principal payments due in what would be an amortization period are, instead, reserved and reinvested such that the amount held will aggregate, by a given date, the full face amount of the notes issued. Investors are then fully repaid with these funds at the stated final maturity date.

In either structure, the possibility exists that payout events could occur that would trigger early amortization repayment, as in the standard amortizing structure described earlier.

Collateralized Debt

Owners of credit card receivables may want to achieve lower funding costs through pledging their receivables as collateral for borrowing, but they either cannot or do not want to achieve a true sale of assets in the transaction. One advantage of a collateralized debt issue is that it can be "shelf" registered and is, therefore, easier and quicker to execute than transactions using trusts as issuers, which must be registered each time with Securities and Exchange Commission.

Although most credit enhancement mechanisms can be used in collateralized debt issues, overcollateralization is usually chosen. When credit card receivables are used to back debt, cash flows to investors are often used similarly to those in trust certificates—for example, using a reinvestment-with-amortization pattern. However, it should be noted that collateralization allows for more flexible use of asset cash flows.

Commercial Paper

Credit card receivable–backed commercial paper offers card issuers a short-term funding option and, possibly, true sale treatment. (True sale treatment of this structure is currently under review.) Simplistically, receivable assets are sold to a special-purpose company, which issues commercial paper to fund the purchase. The maturities of the commercial paper issue are estimated to reflect repayment patterns of a given receivable pool or account type (for example; bank card versus private label account payment patterns). Standard asset-backed credit enhancement, as well as commercial paper liquidity support, must be added. In addition, for fixed-rate credit card receivables, an interest rate swap or other rate protection mechanism must be included in the transaction (benefits pledged) to provide additional yield if gross rates on the receivables were to fall below those required to be paid on the commercial paper.

CREDIT ENHANCEMENT AND CREDIT RISK

Credit enhancement to cover the timely payment of security principal and interest to investors (and, in some cases, the servicer's periodic fee) is often provided by a third party bank letter of credit or insurance company surety bond. Draws on the letter of credit or surety bond are typically made by either the servicer or the trustee to cover any deficiencies in monthly collections of finance charge receivables or principal receivables. In most credit card loan–backed transactions, an escrow/reserve account funded by the excess yield (any yield remaining after certificate interest, servicing fees, and credit enhancement fees are paid) on the pool of receivables is established to reimburse any draws made on the letter of credit or surety bond up to an agreed-on amount. In nonbank transactions, investors or a third party credit enhancer can have direct recourse to the asset seller—for example, limited guaranty or subordinated seller interest. However, it is important to note that the source of reimbursement for a credit enhancer (when applicable) is generally not added to the credit enhancement coverage to benefit investors. Rather, the reimbursement source generally supports the credit enhancement. Investors should usually expect their level-of-loss coverage to be only the third party credit enhancement when this method is used.

During the revolving period of an amortizing credit card receivable-backed issue, the credit enhancement level remains fixed at the predetermined percentage of the investor interest. During the amortization period, the letter of credit surety bond level is typically reduced as the investor interest is reduced—remaining a fixed percentage of outstanding investor interest certificates until it reaches an absolute dollar floor, at which it would be fixed until the certificates are fully amortized.

It should be emphasized that, although an escrow/reserve account (when applicable) generally supports a third party credit enhancement and does not add incremental credit protection for investors, its existence should be significant to investors in that it demonstrates the servicer's motivation to achieve the lowest-possible loss experience on a sold portfolio. This is because any excess amounts not required for the escrow/reserve account are returned to the servicer as bonus servicing during and at the end of a securitization transaction (or to pay investors in a seller-supported transaction). As a result of proper portfolio maintenance and servicing, low losses should result, leaving a significant amount of excess cash flow/escrow/reserve funds that would not be needed to reimburse the credit enhancer for loss coverage and would, instead, be paid by the trustee to the servicer. This potential for the servicer to achieve additional bonus income is a key motivating force behind maintaining servicing standards for a securitized portfolio at the highest-possible level.

The underlying credit quality of the pooled card holder base is essentially a function of the underwriting standards of the card issuer. The resulting financial performance of a credit card portfolio, however, depends on the underwriting standards and the servicing capabilities of the seller/servicer.

Unlike government-backed mortgage securities, such as those backed by the Federal National Mortgage Association and the Federal Home Loan Mortgage Corporation, credit card loan originators do not adhere to consistent underwriting or servicing standards. This has led to a wide variety of methods to acquire new card holder accounts and a wide diversity in underwriting and servicing standards across issuers. Competition for market share among card issuers often leads to a relaxation of underwriting standards and an increase in loss experience.

Within most pools of credit card receivables are segments of card holders that are typically originated over time, using various methods. The resulting loan losses on a pool of credit card receivables is, therefore, a blend of these various segments. The lack of standardized underwriting and servicing, combined with the diverse methodology used to originate accounts, has led to significant differences in the loan loss experience across card issuers.

The unsecured nature of credit card lending means that recoveries on defaulted receivables are typically low (about 30 percent). As a result, the net loss rate on a portfolio of credit card receivables is typically in the 3–5 percent range, as compared with secured mortgage or auto lending, which typically has loan losses under 1 percent. For year-end 1987, the net loss rate for the nation's top 220 commercial bank credit card operations was 3.41 percent.[1]

The year-end 1987 loss experience for major originators of revolving debt is shown in Table 13-2.

In the assessment of the loss experience of a credit card portfolio and the estimation of expected future losses, the following factors are of considerable importance:

[1]VERIBANC, Inc.

Table 13-2. 1987 Year-End Loss Experience

Originators	*Total Portfolio Size (billions)*	*Annual Loss Rate*
Citicorp (consolidated)	$17.4	4.37%
Chase Manhattan (consolidated)	$ 6.3	4.09
Bank of America (including Seattle First)	$ 5.1	3.00
First Chicago (consolidated)	$ 4.0	4.03
Maryland National Bank	$ 3.5	1.94
Manufacturers Hanover	$ 2.6	3.71
Wells Fargo Bank N.A.	$ 2.6	4.12
Bank of New York	$ 2.0	2.80
Chemical Bank (consolidated)	$ 1.6	2.45[1]

Source: VERIBANC, Inc.

[1]Annualized using 4Q 1987 data.

- Underwriting standards, including the minimum criteria used to extend credit and the methods used to acquire accounts (see below).
- The extent to which a portfolio of card holders is seasoned (a portfolio with an average card holder months on books of 18–36 months is considered seasoned). A seasoned portfolio will tend to have stable loss experience; this says nothing about the level.
- The servicing/collection capabilities of the card issuer—that is, the ability to maintain the customer relationship, bill, and effectively collect on delinquencies and contractual write-offs. Collections are generally performed by a combination of in-house and third party collection agents that use a variety of dunning notices and, in some instances, electronic voice link equipment to dial delinquent card holders.
- Geographic concentrations of the card holder base. A local concentration in an economically depressed region presents a more serious risk than does a geographically dispersed portfolio.

Originators of credit card portfolios frequently use sophisticated, automated credit-scoring techniques to screen out high-risk and low-response households, based on a combination of credit bureau information and demographic characteristics. As mentioned earlier, the method used to originate a new card holder account is also important in the assessment of the credit quality of a portfolio.

Various methods for acquiring accounts include:

- Direct mail solicitation, which may be a preapproved offer or a full application, using a particular mailing list that may be derived from the credit bureau or another source, such as magazine subscribers
- "Take-one" application from a bank branch or merchant that accepts the card
- Portfolio acquisition from another originator of credit card accounts
- Affinity group marketing to target groups, such as the American Automobile Association, the Vietnam Veterans of America, frequent flyers of a particular airline, or, more recently, supporters of the National Football League

Direct mail solicitations have traditionally been the most widely used, cost-effective method for acquiring large numbers of new card holder accounts. However, as market saturation increases, household response rates to direct mail solicitations fall. As an alternative strategy for growth, portfolio acquisitions often provide acquirers with a higher degree of account seasoning and lower loan losses than that associated with the first one to three years of a newly solicited, direct mail portfolio. Furthermore, portfolio acquisitions serve to consolidate the industry among high-efficiency portfolio servicers, which leads to economies of scale and a lower operating expense per account.

There are currently about 180 affinity groups in the United States. The identification formation of an affinity group is simply a marketing technique targeted to large groups of households that share a common interest, such as a hobby (boating) or affiliation (AFL-CIO). The profitability of affinity group cards is often reduced, due to the group's ability to lobby for reduced rates or special amenities.

In the selection of card holder accounts for a securitization transaction, selection criteria are often imposed to include only eligible accounts—accounts that are not currently, in a derogatory status (bankruptcy, delinquency, over limit, and so on), have an outstanding balance, have made at least one payment, have a minimum seasoning, have a maximum credit limit, are currently active, and so on. The imposition of pool seletion criteria can eliminate high-risk card holder accounts and can mitigate credit concerns.

RATING

All public market offerings of medium-term credit card-backed securities to date have carried an AAA rating from Moody's Investors Service or Standard & Poor's corporation. These ratings are a function of a number of factors, including the level of credit enhancement in relation to the historical loan loss experience (the coverage multiple) and the underwriting standards and loan servicing capabilities of the seller/servicer, as well as geograhpic concentration, portfolio yield, historic payment rates, delinquencies, and pool selection criteria. The rating on an asset-backed security is consistent with the "weakest link" approach—that is, the transaction cannot be rated higher than any rating applicable to a cash payment source of the transaction, such as a credit enhancer or reinvestment security.

In theory, the risk to those investing in different credit card-backed issues with the same ratings should be equal, regardless of differences in the underlying portfolio characteristics, as these are considered in determining the level of credit enhancement. Thus, for example, since one portfolio with significantly higher loss experience would require a higher level of loss coverage/credit enhancement to achieve the same rating as that of another portfolio with lower loss experience and a lower level of coverage credit enhancement, an investor's risk in either resulting security would be similar. The investor should have as much confidence in repayment of the higher loss/higher coverage issue as in repayment of the lower loss/lower coverage issue.

LEGISLATIVE ACTIVITY

At both the federal and state levels of government, usage laws that provide for ceilings on credit card APRs have been imposed. For example, the state usury laws that govern banks with credit card operations in Texas call for a 14 percent maximum APR and no annual fees, late fees, over-limit fees, and so on. On the other hand, Delaware and South Dakota allow out-of-state-based companies, such as Citibank, Chase Manhattan, First Chicago, and Lomas Bankers Corporation, to issue credit cards nationally with APRs as high as 21 percent and annual membership fees as high as $65. A rate ceiling could reduce an issuer's APR and, thereby, have an immediate effect on portfolio yield and ability to absorb loan losses. To date, no proposed rate ceiling has affected the cash flow related to any credit card–backed issue.

Recent changes in the federal tax law phase out, over a three-year period, the ability to deduct credit card finance charges. This effectively increases the cost of borrowing for those who itemize their deductions. This could potentially alter the payment behavior of a credit card portfolio—reducing the rate of new purchases and increasing convenience usage. In this light, the demographic profile of a given portfolio—for example, a high proportion of upper-income itemizers versus a high proportion of middle-income nonitemizers—could have a significant impact on expected borrowing and payment patterns.

INDUSTRY COMPETITION

The credit card industry is extremely competitive. In response to competitive pressure, the card issuer may choose to reduce its rates to avoid losing market share. Banks have aggressively expanded the highly profitable credit card market and, for the most part, have resisted competing directly on price. Instead, they compete on the frills offered with the card or on fee-waiver incentives. However, the industry is approaching saturation; the extent to which consumers are aware of the rates that they pay is increasing; cheaper sources of credit, such as home equity lines (which still qualify for tax deductibility), are more readily available. The average American household receives 10–20 solicitations in the mail each year and is less likely to respond positively to a credit card offer, as the number of established credit lines increases. As market saturation increases, so does competition. In fact, Manufacturers Hanover Trust Co., The Chase Manhattan Bank, and the New York Banking Division of

Citicorp (as well as others) have recently offered lower rates on their Visa and MasterCard products in an effort to stimulate card holder usage and gain market share.

Within the context of a credit card securitization, the seller/servicer of the securitized portfolio is responsible for servicing and maintaining the card holder relationship and is able to alter the terms of the contractual agreement to a limited extent, as necessary, to avoid losing the card holder to the competition.

Although the seller/servicer will do its best to maintain the portfolio yield as high as possible, any changes in the pricing of the card that result in a lowering of the portfolio yield below the base yield necessary to support the securitization transaction will ultimately lead to an unscheduled payout event and a reduction in the expected yield to investors.

CONCLUSION

Although initially considered one of the most complex assets to securitize, use of credit card receivables to back securities has become increasingly routine and less difficult and expensive to initiate. In addition, investor understanding of these securities has signficantly increased recently, along with a greater appreciation of the greater stability of underlying cash flows. This has allowed the required relative market yield to fall below that of most other types of asset-backed securities (including, from time to time, automobile loan–backed issues). Thus, in the near term, the market should expect to see increased volume, the entrance of new sellers/issuers, and a continuing refinement and evolution in structure.

CHAPTER 14

Rating Agency Criteria for Credit Card-Backed Securities

Thomas P. Hourican

INTRODUCTION

Two forms of credit card-backed securities were introduced to the public markets during 1987. In January, RepublicBank Delaware issued the first credit card-backed pay-through notes. These notes represent a general obligation of the bank, secured by a pool of receivables arising from selected credit card accounts. Bank of America established California Credit Card Trust 1987-A and issued the first certificates of ownership in a pool of credit card receivables in March. The transfer of credit card receivables from the bank to the trust was structured as a sale for regulatory and financial reporting purposes. Standard and Poor's Corporation (S&P) rated each of these transactions AAA. During 1987, S&P rated five credit card transactions, representing $2 billion in asset-backed securities. S&P's analysis focuses primarily on the quality of the seller, servicer, and underlying portfolio and the legal and structural characteristics of the transaction. The portfolio performance factors and structural characteristics discussed in this chapter largely determine the rating of credit card-backed securities.

Figures 14-1 through 14-4 represent industry performance based on quarterly statistics reported to VISA U.S.A. by its member

Figure 14-1. Average Annualized Yield

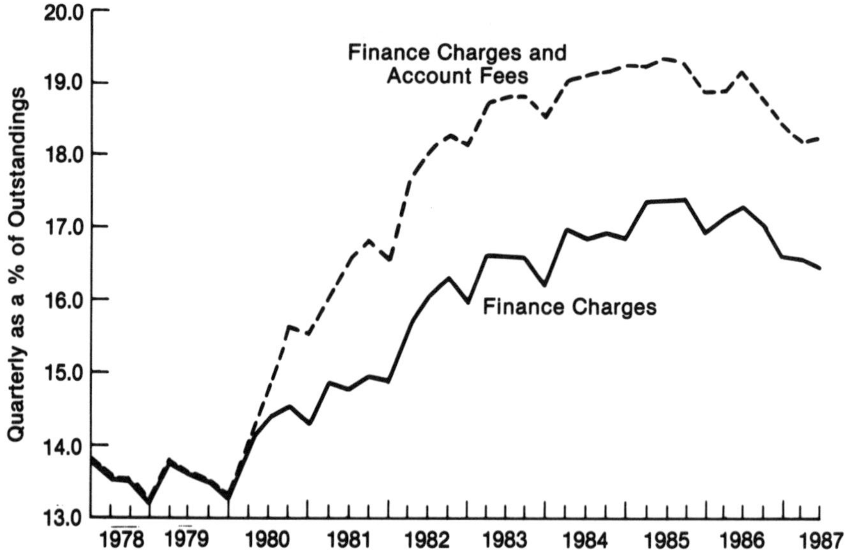

banks. Seasonal trends may have been masked by the method of reporting. Statistics presented are not based on a static pool of accounts and may be distorted by growth in accounts and outstandings.

PORTFOLIO PERFORMANCE

S&P's first step in evaluating portfolio performance is to meet with the issuing bank's senior management and tour the bank's credit card operations. S&P's on-site visit focuses on past performance, as well as strategic outlook. Topics discussed include account acquisition methods, underwriting criteria, operational controls, collection policies and procedures, and portfolio demographic characteristics.

The following portfolio performance factors directly affect investor cash flows:

- Portfolio yield
- Charge-off rate
- Payment rate
- Portfolio growth

These factors are interrelated and subject to outside influences. The most important outside influences are bank competition, government regulation, and general economic and social conditions.

Cash flow models are developed to simulate the potential adverse effects of a deterioration in portfolio performance. S&P's sensitivity analysis reflects actual and expected portfolio performance, as well as the transaction's structural characteristics.

Portfolio Yield

At current levels, portfolio yield provides significant excess cash flow. After payment of certificate interest and servicing, letter-of-credit fees, and other fees, excess yield can be used to protect investors against loan losses. However, the future levels of portfolio yield and resulting loan loss protection are uncertain.

Future yield is uncertain for several reasons. Issuing banks have retained the ability to alter account terms. This includes, under limited conditions, the ability to reduce the periodic finance charge on the pooled receivables. As the industry approaches saturation, competitive pressure could cause the issuing bank to reduce rates.

A regulatory cap on credit card rates could also cause yield to decline. A number of bills that call for regulatory ceilings have been introduced recently, at both the federal and state levels. The U.S. House of Representatives recently rejected a proposal to cap credit card rates at 8 percent above the one-year U.S. Treasury bill rate; this reduces the likelihood of a federal cap in the near future. A number of state resolutions remain outstanding. To avoid state-imposed ceilings, a number of institutions, such as RepublicBank, have relocated their credit card operations.

A third factor that affects portfolio yield is convenience use. Convenience use is the card holder's avoidance of interest charges by making a full payment during a specified grace period, typically 25 to 30 days. Most banks offer a grace period, and approximately one third of all card holders do not roll over balances each month. Convenience use, which varies by issuer, is reflected in the portfolio's yield. If the selling bank offers a grace period and convenience use increases, portfolio yield will decline.

The selling bank's flexibility to alter terms could also protect yield. To counter a decline in yield that is caused by an increase in convenience use of a regulatory cap, banks could increase fees or trim grace periods.

S&P's worst-case cash flow analysis for an AAA rating assumes a deterioration in yield as follows. The current yield level is assumed to continue for six months. During the next six months to a year, yield declines to the lowest level permitted by the transaction's structure without causing a payout event. S&P also assumes that no excess yield is available to support principal cash flows during the liquidation period.

Table 14-1 illustrates the relatively high historical yields of the securitized portfolios.

Table 14-1. Annual portfolio yield

	1984	1985	1986	1987
RepublicBank Delaware[4]	(ranged from 13.8% to 18.2%)			N.A[6]
California Card Trust 1987-A	18.8%	18.7%	18.5%	N.A.[6]
Imperial Cards Trust 1987-1[5]	12.9	15.6	17.2	17.6%
First Chicago Trust 1987-1	19.3	19.7	19.7	19.8[1]
MBNA Cards Trust 1987-A	N.A.[6]	19.5	18.4	16.7[3]

[1]Until June 30.

[2]Until March 31.

[3]Until September 30.

[4]Began operations in August 1986 upon acquisition of credit card portfolio from RepublicBank Dallas. Prior to August 1986 represents RepublicBank Dallas data.

[5]Began operations in 1983.

[6]N.A.—Not available.

Charge-Offs

Portfolio charge-off experience is a primary indicator of credit quality. The industry's lack of standardized acquisition methods and underwriting criteria is reflected in the diversity of portfolio loan experience, as illustrated in Table 14-2.

Figure 14-2. Quarterly Delinquencies and Charge-Offs

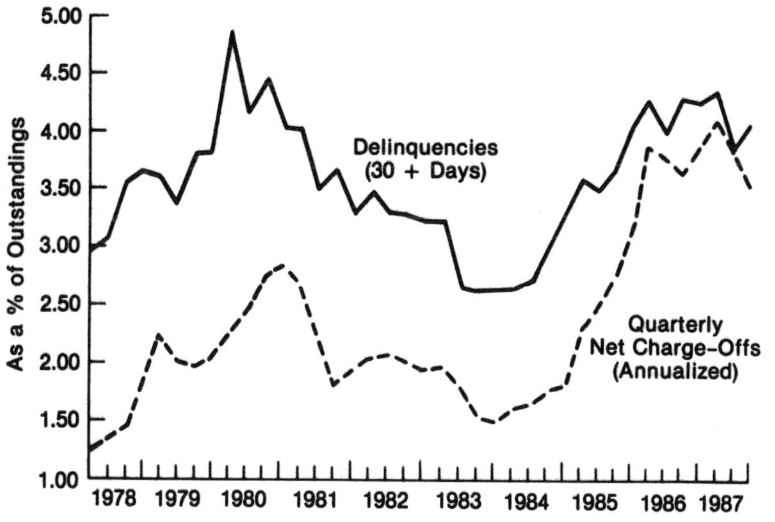

Table 14-2. Annual Gross Charge-Off Rate

	1984	*1985*	*1986*	*1987*
RepublicBank Delaware[4]	1.7%	1.8%	2.4%	N.A.[6]
California Card Trust 1987-A	2.2	2.3	2.5	N.A.[6]
Imperial Savings[5] Crds Trust 1987-1	1.9	2.8	5.6	4.4[2]
First Chicago Trust 1987-1	2.1	3.4	4.0	4.3[1]
MBNA Cards Trust 1987-A	N.A.[6]	1.3	1.9	2.0[3]

[1]Until June 30.

[2]Until March 31.

[3]Until September 30.

[4]Began operations in August 1986 upon acquisition of credit card portfolio from RepublicBank Dallas. Prior to August 1986 represents RepublicBank Dallas data.

[5]Began operations in 1983.

[6]N.A.—Not available.

Net charge-offs for the industry have risen to an annualized rate of approximately 4 percent for the first nine months of 1987 (see Figure 14-2). The growth in loan losses has been attributed to relaxed underwriting standards, growth in new accounts, and an increase in consumer bankruptcies. The rise in loan losses occurred during a period of prolonged economic expansion.

S&P's cash flow analysis assumes a recessionary economic environment and a deterioration in loan loss performance.

Table 14-3. Delinquencies (Beyond 30 Days)

	1984	*1985*	*1986*	*1987*
RepublicBank Delaware[4]	7.2%	7.0%	4.1%	N.A.[6]
California Card Trust 1987-A	3.7	3.9	3.9	N.A.[6]
Imperial Savings Cards Trust 1987-1[5]	2.7	3.7	4.4	4.0%
First Chicago Trust 1987-1	2.2	3.0	3.2	3.2[1]
MBNA Cards Trust 1987-A	N.A.[6]	N.A.[6]	2.9	2.8[3]

[1]Until June 30.

[2]Until March 31.

[3]Until September 30.

[4]Began operations in August 1986 upon acquisition of credit card portfolio from RepublicBank Dallas. Prior to August 1986 represents RepublicBank Dallas data.

[5]Began operations in 1983.

[6]N.A.—Not available.

Most credit card issuers charge off receivables at 180 days delinquent, and recoveries are not typically available to the trust. Gross charge-off assumptions at the AAA level for purposes of cash flow analysis are as follows. During the first six months to a year, charge-off rates will remain at this level for the duration of the interest-only period. It is also assumed that charge-offs will increase to three to five times historic levels during the first 6–18 months of the liquidation period. Charge-off assumptions will be adjusted downward to reflect conservative account selection criteria.

Payment Rate

The speed at which investor principal outstandings are liquidated is directly related to monthly card holder payment rates. Portfolio payment rates have varied significantly. (see Table 14-4).

Differences in portfolio payment rate behavior have been attributed to demographic concentrations, maturity of accounts, solicitation methods, and payment terms. Individual portfolios have experienced stable payment rates that are well above their respective

Figure 14-3. Estimated Average Monthly Payment Rate

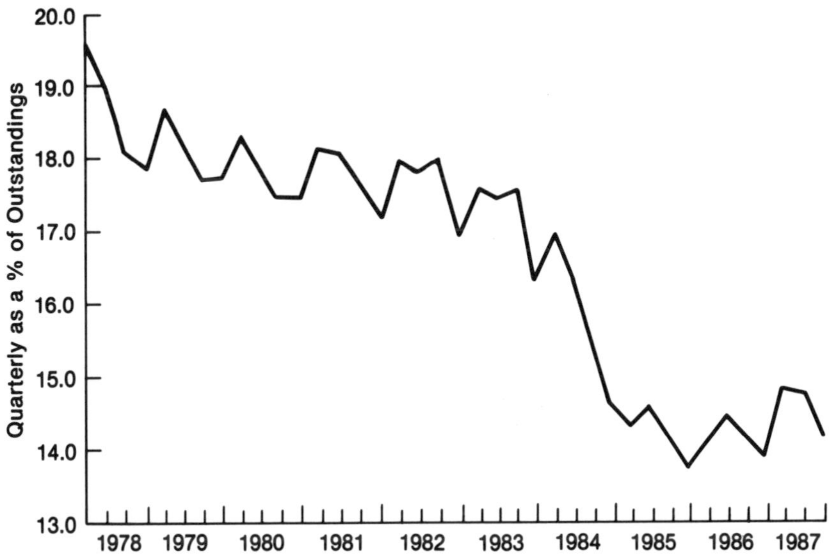

minimums. For purposes of cash flow analysis, the required minimum payment rate (below 2 percent in some instances) is not assumed. Historic payment rates are conservatively discounted by approximately 50 percent and are generally assumed to be in the range of 5–10 percent.

Table 14-4. Average Monthly Payment Rate

	1984	*1985*	*1986*	*1987*
RepublicBank Delaware[4]	17.7%	16.6%	15.0%	N.A.[6]
California Card Trust 1987-A	22.2	21.0	21.8	N.A.[6]
Imperial Savings[5] Crds Trust 1987-1	19.3	15.6	17.0	18.3%
First Chicago Trust 1987-1	13.6	12.5	12.5	13.1[1]
MBNA Cards Trust 1987-A	N.A.[6]	15.0	15.0	15.7[3]

[1]Until June 30.

[2]Until March 31.

[3] Until September 30.

[4]Began operations in August 1986 upon acquisition of credit card portfolio from RepublicBank Dallas. Prior to August 1986 represents RepublicBank Dallas data.

[5]Began operations in 1983.

[6]N.A.—Not available.

Figure 14-4. Quarterly Average Oustanding Balance

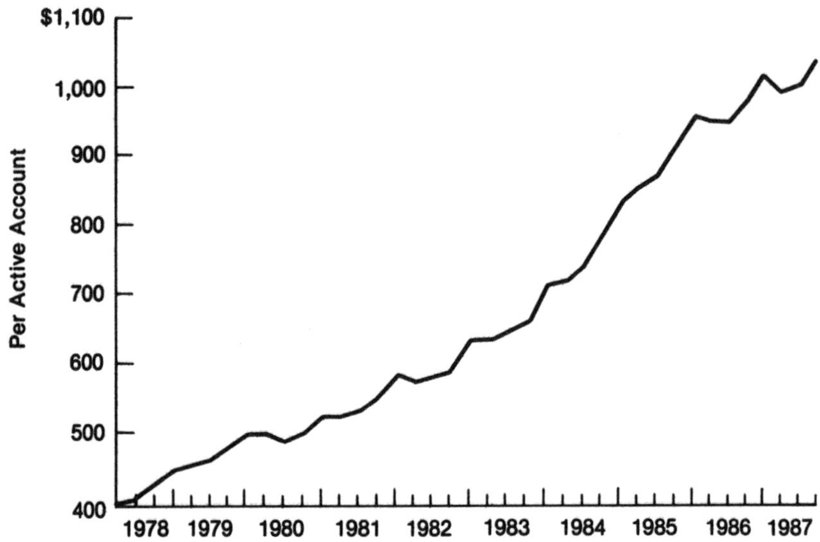

Portfolio Growth

The pass-through of principal to investors may be accelerated by growth in the portfolio. Portfolio growth occurs when card holders' reborrowings exceed principal payments, plus charge-offs. A number of issuers have attempted to accelerate distributions of collections to investors by allocating principal payments to the investor class of certificates based on a fixed percentage. This fixed percentage is equal to the investor's proportionate share of receivables at the end of the interest-only period. Any subsequent growth should cause the amount of monthly principal collections to increase, and a fixed percentage of such payments would be passed through to investors. As a result, the investor's principal outstanding amount would liquidate at a more rapid rate.

Although average balances have risen, it is uncertain how much additional debt consumers are willing to accept (see Figure 14-4). Portfolio growth is uncertain for several reasons. The availability of static pool data to support positive growth assumptions is limited. The recent change in Internal Revenue Service regulations that phases out the deductibility of credit card interest expense increases the cost of borrowing to those who itemize. Alternative sources of credit, such as home equity loans, may also have an impact on the level of future credit card borrowings. In addition, insolvency of the issuing bank may have an impact on portfolio growth. If the trust is not liquidated as a result of the bank's insolvency, new receivables may not be conveyed to the trust. As a result, the effects of new reborrowings could be diminished.

Given the uncertainty of future reborrowing rates and the possibility of the issuing bank's insolvency, S&P's worst-case analysis for an AAA rating assumes negative portfolio growth rates. As a result, S&P assumes minimal reborrowing rates in potential cash flow scenarios.

TRANSACTION STRUCTURE

The basis of each credit card-backed issue is similar, although certain characteristics vary. As of this writing, four of the five rated credit card-backed issues have been in the form of pass-through certificates. This section will focus on the characteristics of the pass-through structure. To accommodate the fluctuating nature of credit card account balances, two classes of certificates are issued: an investor class and a seller class. Both the seller and the investor have an ownership interest in the trust. Current balances, plus future receivables generated by a selected pool of accounts, are conveyed to the trust. However, in most cases, the trust does not have an ownership interest in the account relationship. The seller certificate is unrated and is designed to absorb fluctuations in the amount of receivables owned by the trust.

The investor certificates and seller certificates represent a proportionate interest in the receivables. The investors also have the benefit of some form of credit enhancement to support cash flows. The investors' interest equals the aggregate investor certificates outstanding, divided by the aggregate receivables held by the trust. The seller owns the residual interest.

A credit card portfolio typically liquidates at a rapid rate (8–20 percent per month). Therefore, assuming a constant portfolio size, the receivables would have an expected life of under one year. To extend the credit card–backed security's life, investors are paid interest only during the transaction's initial stages. During the initial interest-only period, principal payments allocated to the investors' interest are paid to the seller and are used to purchase additional receivables that arise from the pooled accounts. The term of the interest-only period has ranged from 18 to 36 months. Each transaction has incorporated early payout events to protect investors against certain adverse conditions. Payout events are designed to discontinue the purchase of additional receivables if the portfolio's credit quality deteriorates significantly. The interest-only period is followed by a liquidation period, in which investors receive monthly distributions of principal. The following is a review of certain structural characteristics that influence investor cash flows and credit quality.

Pool Selection

Issuers can reduce credit risks by applying stringent account selection standards. On one hand, some issuers take a less conservative approach to reduce administrative burdens or maximize the size of the available pool. Bank of America used conservative selection criteria in the California Credit Card Trust 1987-A transaction. The accounts were selected from Bank of America's northern California portfolio. When compared with the bank's total portfolio, the northern California segment was of superior credit quality, based on the accounts' average age and loan loss experience. In addition, the pool selection criteria eliminated accounts that were over 30 days past due or under 24 months old.

Interest-Only Period

To extend the life of the certificate holder's investment, card holder principal payments allocated to the investors' interest are reinvested in other receivables, during an initial interest-only period. As Figure 14-5 illustates, the investor certificate amount remains constant during this period. The seller certificate, which represents the residual interest in the trust, fluctuates to absorb variations in

Figure 14-5. Credit Card-Backed Securities: Cash Flow Structure

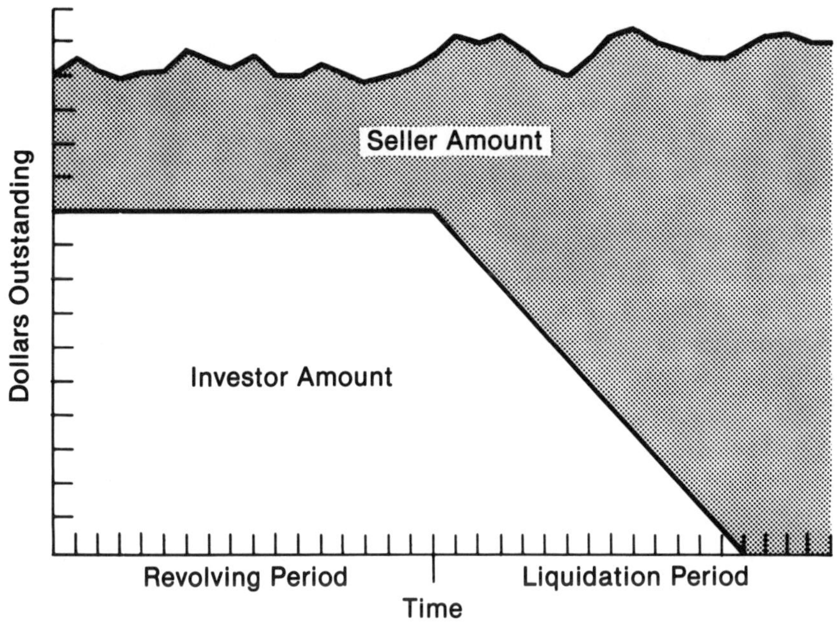

pool balances. Rated issues are scheduled to pay interest only for periods ranging from 18 to 36 months. However, the interest-only period could be prematurely discontinued by the occurrence of a payout event.

Payout Event

Payout events are designed to enhance the transaction's credit quality by discontinuing the interest-only period if the reinvestment of investor principal payments becomes significantly less desirable. Payout events that could cause the early distribution of principal to investors may include:

- Insolvency of the seller
- Servicer default
- Excessive charge-offs or delinquencies
- Significant declines in portfolio yield, growth, or payment rates

In effect, payout events, set limits on S&P's worst-case scenarios. S&P will assume that conditions deteriorate to near–payout event levels during the interest-only period. Although payout events enhance a transaction's credit quality, they also make possible the early unexpected pass-through of principal.

Distribution of Collections

Monthly collections must be allocated between the investor and seller interest. The method of allocation, which has varied, will have an impact on investor cash flows and credit quality. The two components of card holder collections are finance charges and principal payments. The finance charge component generally includes other fees.

The percentage of finance charge collections that is allocable to the investor's interest is based on the proportionate share that the investor principal amount is of the total amount of card holder principal receivables owned by the trust. This same method is used to allocate card holder principal payments during a transaction's interest-only period. The method of allocating principal payments during the liquidation period, which has varied, will have an impact on credit quality. By accelerating the pass-through of principal to investors, loan loss exposure is reduced and credit quality is enhanced. Alternative methods of accelerating investor principal pass-throughs have been applied. For example, issuers have fixed the percentage used to allocate principal to investors during the liquidation period. The investor's fixed percentage of monthly principal collections is equal to their proportionate share of principal outstandings at the end of the interest-only period. Once the liquidation period commences, the investors' proportionate share of principal outstanding can no longer increase and is expected to decline. Therefore, this fixed percentage allocation method should accelerate the pass-through of principal to investors.

The principal allocation method may also be designed to minimize draws on the letter of credit or limit the speed at which principal is passed through to investors. The First Chicago Cards Trust 1987-1 transaction applied a method designed to limit monthly letter-of-credit draws, and the MBNA Credit Card Trust 1987-A incorporated a controlled amortization period.

S&P develops a cash flow model to measure each structure's ability to protect investors against loan losses. S&P's rating reflects the likelihood of principal and interest payments as promised—not uncertainty about the timing of cash flows.

Allocation of Gross Charge-Offs

The amount of a charged-off account's balance that is allocated to the investor's interest must be funded by an internal or external cash flow support. Credit quality is enhanced by minimizing the allocation of charged-off balances to the investor's interest. Allocation methods vary by transaction, and the impact is significant. With all other characteristics of the structure constant, the most favorable method of allocating charge-offs is the method applied to the allocation of finance charges.

Fee Coverage

The current level of portfolio yield available in each of the rated transactions exceeds the level required to pay certificate interest, servicing, and other fees, as well as cover present rates of receivable charge-offs. However, if yields declined substantially or charge-offs increased, shortfalls could occur. A letter of credit or other form of credit enhancement must be available to provide the investor with a level of loss protection that is consistent with the desired rating. A number of issuers have attempted to shift some of the risk of a shortfall away from the credit enhancer by subordinating the servicing fee. The quality of servicing is extremely important, and it could be adversely affected by a failure to compensate the servicer. The following structural characteristics enhance the issuer's ability to limit risks associated with the servicer: The servicer is restricted from resigning. The trustee is obligated to obtain a substitute servicer if a servicer default occurs. If a substitute cannot be obtained, the trustee must act as servicer of last resort. The subordination of servicing fees may limit the trustee's ability to obtain a qualified substitute, if required. This additional risk may be mitigated by the quality of the servicer. If the servicer has strong servicing capabilities and is an investment-grade entity, the subordination of fees should not add significant risk to the transaction.

Credit Enhancement

Three forms of investor cash flow supports are being used to enhance credit quality: a letter of credit, subordination, and a reserve fund. Investors benefit from a letter of credit in all of the rated transactions. A portion of the seller's cash flow was subordinated to the investors' interest in the Imperial Cards Trust 1987-1 transaction. In the RepublicBank transaction, investor cash flows were supported by a reserve fund.

Terms of letters of credit may limit or enhance the level of protection provided. The available letter-of-credit amount may only decline due to draws or, in limited conditions, may decline with the investor's outstanding amount. In addition, excess yield may reinstate the available letter-of-credit amount.

Non-letter-of-credit enhancements, such as a subordinated amount or reserve fund, are internal credit supports. Their level of protection is influenced by portfolio performance.

Combined credit enhancement levels for AAA-rated transactions range from 10 percent to 22 percent, reflecting differences in portfolio credit quality, form of cash flow support, and structural characteristics. Table 14-5 indicates some of these differences.

Table 14-5. Combined Credit Enhancement Level Differences

	Cash Flow Support	*Letter-of-credit[1] Bank*
RepublicBank Delaware	5% letter of credit, 5–7% reserve fund	UBS
California Credit Card Trust 1987-A	15% letter of credit	UBS
Imperial Cards Trust 1987-1	15% letter of credit, 7% subordination	FHLB
First Chicago Credit Card Trust 1987-1	17% letter of credit	UBS
MBNA Credit Card Trust 1987-A	10% letter of credit	UBS

[1]UBS—Union Bank of Switzerland.

FHLB—Federal Home Loan Bank of San Francisco.

CREDIT CARD POOL PERFORMANCE

Credit card pool performance for issues rated by S&P to date appear in Table 14-6. All are still in the interest-only period, as they

Table 14-6. Credit Card Pool Performance, 1987

	March	April	May	June	July	Aug.	Sept.	Oct.	Nov.
Yield (annualized)									
First Chicago Cards Trust 1987-1	—	—	—	—	—	—	21.00%	20.49%	18.80%
Imperial Cards Trust 1987-1	—	—	—	21.51%	20.31%	18.83%	19.98	20.08	19.64
California Credit Card Trust 1987-A	20.66%	18.32%	19.18%	18.02	19.19	17.22	18.00	18.97	17.10
Charge-offs									
First Chicago Cards Trust 1987-1	—	—	—	—	—	—	3.96	3.87	4.43
Imperial Cards Trust 1987-1	—	—	—	5.83	5.57	4.43	6.56	6.87	6.40
California Credit Card Trust 1987-A	0.06	0.30	1.30	0.66	1.08	1.73	1.54	1.74	1.48
RepublicBank Delaware	0.25	0.42	1.22	2.75	2.91	4.02	3.84	3.68	4.00
Monthly payment rate									
First Chicago Cards Trust 1987-1	—	—	—	—	—	—	12.18	12.29	12.57
Imperial Cards Trust 1987-1	—	—	—	20.77	19.09	17.65	18.19	18.03	16.90
California Credit Card Trust 1987-A	22.82	21.97	23.18	23.20	24.33	21.40	22.15	23.09	19.24
Monthly purchase rate									
First Chicago Cards Trust 1987-1	—	—	—	—	—	—	13.52	12.29	12.51
Imperial Cards Trust 1987-1	—	—	—	26.48	24.36	22.13	23.62	22.58	19.32
California Credit Card Trust 1987-A	21.15	23.97	24.73	24.96	26.53	24.35	24.53	25.06	21.98
Delinquencies									
First Chicago Cards Trust 1987-1[1]	—	—	—	—	—	—	5.44	5.84	5.66
Imperial Cards Trust 1987-1[1]	—	—	—	4.04	4.02	4.35	4.53	4.31	4.34
California Credit Card Trust 1987-A[1]	0.98	1.15	1.24	1.32	1.33	1.41	1.47	1.49	1.66
RepublicBank Delaware[2]	0.69	0.98	1.22	1.40	1.44	1.49	1.53	1.52	1.55

[1]Balances over 30 days as % of ending receivable balance.

[2]Balances over 65 days as % of ending receivable balance.

all came to market during 1987. To date, these issues have not experienced an early payout event.

Of particular note are the extremely high annualized yields on the pools, which are highly positively correlated with the related portfolio performance. As a result, excess yield (available yield after investor interest and fees) has been available to investors to cover loan losses or to fund a reserve account (as in the RepublicBank Delaware issue).

Although pool yields are all relatively high when compared with the rates on the security, pool charge-offs and delinquencies vary significantly across issuers, due to different underwriting standards, account solicitation methods, and pool selection criteria. The relatively high charge-off and delinquency performance of Imperial Cards Trust 1987-1 reflects the fact that the portfolio consists mostly of accounts originated from a series of mass mailings of preapproved applications. Such mailings typically yield higher-risk accounts because accounts are selected based on relatively limited information.

The asset pool's performance may not always mirror the portfolio from which it was drawn. The pool can be affected by pool selection criteria and other factors. The loss and delinquency performance of California Credit Card Trust 1987-1 and RepublicBank Delaware reflect the conservative selection criteria used. As such, both statistics show a slow buildup in loss deliquency measures. This reflects the lack of conservative selection criteria. On the other hand, Imperial Cards Trust indicates a stable loss and deliquency performance, which is in line with historical portfolio behavior.

Monthly purchase rates on asset pools indicate growth comparable with that of the portfolios. Such increases in the average balances of the pools will increase the amount of cash available to make payments to the investors.

Similar to portfolio rates, individual pool payment rates have been relatively stable. For the most part, pool payment rates exceed the payment rates on the portfolio from which the pool was selected.

Appendix: Case Study

CHEMICAL BANK CREDIT CARD TRUST 1988-A (CHEMICAL BANK/CHEMICAL BANK N.A. RECEIVABLES) RATED AAA

Table 14A-1. Transaction Summary

Sale date	August 16
Securities offered	$350 million 9.3% credit card receivables-backed certificates
Structure type	Credit card receivable-backed certificates with a 20-month interest-only period and a 5-year stated maturity
Collateral	VISA and MasterCard consumer revolving credit card receivables
Sellers	Chemical Bank and Chemical Bank N.A.
Servicer	Chemical Bank.
Trustee	Bankers Trust Co.
Lead underwriters	Chemical Bank Investment Banking Goldman Sachs & Co.
Credit enhancement	11% letter of credit issued by Union Bank of Switzerland (AAA senior debt)
Legal structure	The transfer of receivables to the trust, at minimum, creates a first-perfected security interest in favor of the trustee
Pool data	Account selection was random across all of the sellers' 18 billing cycles, subject to certain eligibility criteria
Portfolio performance data	See Table 14A-2

Rationale

An AAA rating is assigned to $350 million 9.3 percent credit card receivable certificates of Chemical Bank Credit Card Trust 1988-

Figure 14A-1. Chemical Bank Credit Card Receivables-Backed Summary

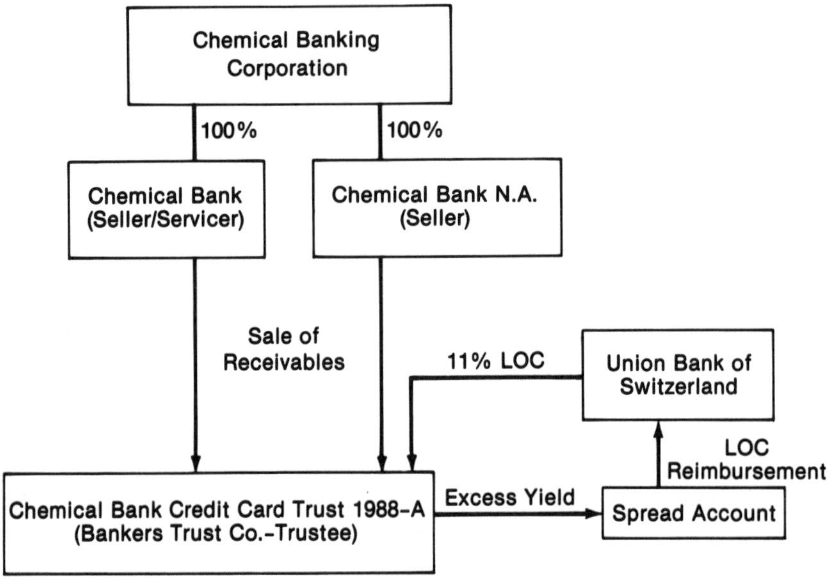

A. The certificates represent fractional undivided interests in the trust, whose property includes VISA and MasterCard receivables generated by Chemical Bank and Chemical Bank N.A. The rating reflects the sellers' consistently good historical portfolio performance, Chemical Bank's servicing capabilities, and the credit support provided by an 11 percent letter of credit issued by Union Bank of Switzerland (AAA senior debt). It also reflects the structure's protective liquidation events, which would accelerate investor principal amortization in certain adverse conditions.

Legal Risks

The transfer of receivables from the sellers to the trust is a sale for financial and regulatory accounting purposes. Counsel has opined that if the sale were to be recharacterized as a pledge, the trustee would, nonetheless, retain a first-perfected security interest in the receivables for the benefit of the certificate holders, notwithstanding the sellers' insolvency. The servicer is permitted to hold for its own use all collections received from obligors until the business day prior to each monthly payment date. The risk of the trustee becoming unperfected in these commingled collections in the event of the servicer's insolvency is mitigated by a servicer's agreement. The servicer agrees to transfer collections to the trust within one business day if Chemical Bank's short-term debt rating (currently A-1) deteriorates to A-2 or below.

Credit Risks

Chemical first offered the bank card product in 1969 and is currently ranked eleventh nationally in terms of total receivables outstanding. Between 1980 and the present, its portfolio grew to over $1.5 billion through the acquisition of Continental Illinois Bank & Trust Co.'s credit card portfolio in 1984 ($808 million outstanding at the time) and through various marketing programs. A substantial increase in card holder credit limits, which was implemented in August 1987, led to further growth. However, portfolio growth since 1984 has been moderate by industry standards; this trend is not expected to change significantly, given Chemical's conservative underwriting standards and pricing strategy. The Continental Illinois accounts now compose about 50 percent of Chemical's total outstanding balances. As many of these accounts were acquired through aggressive, preapproved mass-mail solicitations, any additional credit risk that results from such programs must be weighed against the accounts' high average seasoning of ten years. Overall, Chemical's portfolio is highly seasoned, with 81 percent of accounts opened prior to 1987 and 53 percent opened prior to 1953. Both the Continental Illinois and Chemical portfolios are now managed as an integrated and centralized business operation. Chemical's historical portfolio performance, as measured by gross charge-offs and delinquencies, has been consistently good. Gross charge-offs as a percentage of average receivables outstanding fell to 3.29 percent in 1987, well below the 4–5 percent industry average. Similarly, Chemical's 3.77 percent delinquency rate is also better than industry standards. The recent increase in credit limits has led to increased borrowings, a slower card holder payment rate, and, thus, a greater exposure to credit losses. However, portfolio performance is not expected to significantly worsen, given Chemical's conservative underwriting, moderate growth expectations, and the existing portfolio's highly seasoned accounts. Selection of accounts for the pool was random across all 18 of Chemical's billing cycles, subject to certain eligibility criteria. For example, accounts with charge-off receivables and bankrupt or deceased 1988 cutoff dates were excluded from the pool. While the selection criteria did not exclude delinquent accounts, only 2.79 percent of total pooled receivables were over 30 days delinquent at the cutoff dates—well below Chemical's portfolio average. In general, the pooled receivables are representative of the overall portfolio.

S&P's analysis of securitized credit card transactions focuses on four key variables that have an impact on the timing and certainty of investor cash flows, gross charge-offs, effective yield, card holder payment rate, and new purchase rate. In a worst-case liquidation scenario, S&P assumed that the annual gross charge-off rate rose to 14 percent, which is more than four times Chemical's current rate. Simultaneously, effective yield on the receivables drops to 12 percent, and monthly payment and purchase rates fall to 7.5 percent and 2 percent, respectively. S&P determined that even with such a severe deterioration in Chemical's credit card business, the 11 percent letter of credit provides sufficient credit protection to investors at the AAA level.

Payment Structure

The trust's initial amount totals $386.9 million in principal receivables. All new receivables that arise in the accounts will automatically be transferred to the trust. Accordingly, the sellers' percentage of the trust (initially 9.5 percent) will fluctuate daily, as new receivables are generated and existing receivables are collected or charged off. The sellers must convey additional receivables to the trust if the sellers' percentage falls below 5 percent. The investor certificates pay interest only during the first 20 months, followed by a maximum 40-month principal amortization (liquidation) period. The structure incorporates protective liquidation events that would end the interest-only period and cause early paydown of the certificates in certain adverse conditions. For example, a liquidation event would occur if, for any three consecutive months, the aggregate collection of investor finance charges, minus aggregate defaults, is less than the aggregate interest due to investors. The floating allocations of finance charges and charge-offs between sellers and investors are based on their respective participation percentages on each distribution date. This limits the amount of losses allocated to investors, particularly during the liquidation period, as the investor certificates pay down. However, in fixed allocation, investor principal payments are allocated based on the investor percentage at the last day of the interest-only period. This method accelerates the investors' principal repayment by using principal collections otherwise allocable to the sellers to pay down investor certificates—thus reducing the investors' exposure to losses and ensuring that the certificates are retired before the final maturity.

Table 14A-2. Portfolio Performance

	Year ended December 31			
	1988[1]	*1987*	*1986*	*1985*
Average receivables outstanding (in millions)	$1,499	$1,238	$1,275	$1,318
30+ day delinquencies (as % of average receivables outstanding)	3.59%	3.77%	4.29%	3.72%
Gross charge-offs (as % of average receivables outstanding)	3.44	3.29	3.86	3.26
Gross annual yield	19.00	19.06	19.79	19.72
Average monthly payment rate	17.65	19.69	18.46	16.17

[1]For six months ended June 30, 1988.

The trustee will draw on the 11 percent letter of credit for any investor cash flow deficiencies not covered by excess finance charges. The letter of credit initially equals $38.5 million and declines only for unreimbursed draws.

CHAPTER 15

Receivable-Backed Commercial Paper

Thomas P. Hourican

INTRODUCTION

Standard and Poor's Corporation (S&P) now rates over $4.5 billion in receivable-backed commercial paper and expects this number to grow substantially. This type of commercial paper offers an additional financing outlet and increased liquidity. In most cases, the program's rating is higher than that of the company that originates the receivables, which thereby reduces financing costs. The receivables in the programs rated to date include credit cards, auto leases, trade receivables, and utility leases.

Receivable-backed commercial paper is typically issued through a special-purpose corporation (issuer) organized by an investment banker, whose sole business is to finance the company's receivables. Repayment of the commercial paper is supported by payments on the receivables. Shortfalls due to losses and delinquencies are eliminated by credit support, typically in the form of an irrevocable letter of credit. Liquidity lines are also provided, as receivable payments are not usually matched with commercial paper maturities.

LEGAL RISKS

Each issuer is structured as a bankruptcy-remote entity legally unaffiliated with the company that originates the receivables. The issuer's business is limited to:

- Borrowing from the bank(s) under the credit agreement
- Issuing commercial paper
- Using the commercial paper proceeds to make loans to the company (a pledge transaction)
- Engaging in certain incidental activities

The issuer is prohibited from incurring any additional debt. All parties to the transaction other than commercial paper holders must agree not to file the issuer into bankruptcy for one year and one day after all commercial paper has been paid. The overall intent of these provisions is to insulate the issuer from proceedings under Chapter 11 of the U.S. Bankruptcy Code.

Commercial paper holders must be protected against "clawback" of payment on their maturing notes as preferential transfers in the event of bankruptcy of the issuer or of the company. The issuer's legal structure makes this event sufficiently remote. As the issuer makes payment on maturing commercial paper, bankruptcy of the company would not present a preferential transfer problem for commercial paper holders.

A "true sale" of the receivables is not necessary in most of these transactions. When the receivables are pledged to secure the commercial paper—rather than sold—company bankruptcy may delay receipt of receivable payments by the issuer. This is a result of the automatic stay provision under the code. However, unlike asset-backed bond transactions, in which bond payment is directly tied to receivables' cash flow, the liquidity banks assume this timing risk. The liquidity banks thereby assure the timeliness of payments on maturing commercial paper, notwithstanding company bankruptcy. Counsel should provide legal opinions regarding the enforceability of each bank's obligations under the liquidity facility and credit facility. An opinion regarding the applicable exemption from U.S. security registration under the Securities Act of 1933 is also required.

STRUCTURE

Receivable-backed commercial programs are legally structured to avoid a "credit link" with the receivables' originator. A pool of accounts receivable is transferred to an independent third party that issues the commercial paper. The issuer is a special-purpose corporation that is not legally affiliated with the company originating the receivables. The issuing special-purpose corporation would not be drawn into bankruptcy if the originating company filed for bankruptcy. The program's rating is, thus, based on the program's structure and the receivable credit quality—not the creditworthiness of the originating company.

The issuer raises funds by commercial paper or by obtaining loans from the banks under the credit agreement. In a pledge transaction, the issuer then loans such funds to the company that originated the accounts receivable. As security, the company pledges its interest in the receivables to the issuer. In a sale transaction, the issuer uses its funds to purchase accounts receivable from the company. In both types of transactions, the issuer grants a perfected security interest in the receivables to the banks and to the commercial paper holders equally and ratably.

Receivable payments may not be available on any particular day to pay maturing commercial paper. "Match funding" the receivables' cash flow with commercial paper maturities is generally difficult. Cash flow in a pledge transaction may also be subject to an automatic stay in a company bankruptcy. For these reasons, irrevocable bank lines must be available to ensure timely payment of maturing commercial paper. These lines must equal 100 percent of the receivables' value and must be provided by banks with ratings as high as the program's rating. Exceptions to the 100 percent bank line requirement are limited to companies whose own ratings are at least equal to the issuer's rating and that have adequate liquidity.

Losses and delinquencies reduce the value of the receivables and, therefore, the liquidity lines. For example, a $100,000 commercial paper program backed by receivables valued at $100,000 on day 1 would also be backed by a $100,000 bank line on day 1. Bank line coverage would drop to $90,000 if the receivables' value declined to $90,000 during the program's term. To protect against a potential repayment shortfall as a result of such bank line reevaluation, each program provides for credit support. The size of this support is determined primarily by the receivables' inherent credit risks (see the "Credit Risks" section following).

Each program must provide credit support through either overcollateralization, third party credit support, or a combination of both. Overcollateralization is a pledge of receivables in an amount greater than a dollar-for-dollar pledge against outstanding paper. For example, $100,000 in notes might be overcollateralized with $130,000 in receivables. Bank line support would still equal $100,000, unless the receivable value dropped below $100,000. In this example, note holders are protected by 30 percent overcollateralization, in addition to liquidity support. Third party credit support is usually provided by an irrevocable bank letter of credit. However, this support could also be provided by a secondary market repurchase agreement, a surety bond, or some other type of facility. Any third party credit support must be provided by an institution rated at least as highly as the program.

Liquidity and credit support facilities ensure coverage of any shortfall on maturing commercial paper, whether as a result of losses, delinquencies, or mismatches between payments on the receivables and commercial paper maturities. Although third party credit support is generally irrevocable, bankruptcy of the issuer may permit termination of the liquidity lines. This risk is remote due to the special-purpose nature of the issuer.

CREDIT RISKS

The criteria for evaluating the credit quality of receivable-backed commercial paper are the same as those for evaluating long-term asset-backed financings. The analysis focuses on the receivables' credit characteristics. Five years of pool data are generally required, including delinquency numbers (broken down in an aging schedule) and aggregate write-offs (broken down on at least an annual basis). These requirements are sometimes modified, based on the industry, particular pool, and availability of data. In some transactions, 100 percent credit support has been needed, due to the inability to fully analyze receivables' credit quality.

The necessary credit enhancement level is a function of the

performance of the receivables. For example, expected arrangements that allow a bank to consider receivables 30 or more days past due to be nonperforming generally require a higher credit support level than those that consider only receivables 180 days past due to be nonperforming. The short exposure of commercial paper (with a general maximum maturity of 270 days) and the potential wind-down of issuance arrangements in the event that receivables' credit quality declines may reduce support requirements.

No program can be rated higher than the rating of the banks and other institutions that provide the liquidity and credit support facilities. All but certain match-funding programs must count on liquidity facilities to provide funds for the timely payment of maturing commercial paper. All programs must also rely on credit support to cover commercial paper backed by nonperforming receivables. Credit support and liquidity support ensure payment of such commercial paper. The program's rating is based not only on the credit quality of the receivables, but also on the credit quality of this support.

Appendix : Case Studies

GELCO COMMERCIAL PAPER CORP.
(GELCO CORP. COMMERCIAL PAPER PROGRAM)
RATED A-1
MERRILL LYNCH CAPITAL MARKETS/PIPER, JAFFRAY & HOPWOOD

Rationale

GELCO Commercial Paper Corp.'s (GCPC's) $90 million receivable-secured commercial paper program is rated A-1. GCPC's receivables are automobile fleet leases originated and pledged by GELCO Corp. to GCPC. The receivables are pledged as security for loans made to GELCO by GCPC. The A-1 rating is supported by the excellent quality of the receivables. GELCO has experienced stable net losses of less than 0.1 percent on its automobile fleet lease portfolio. Liquidity is assured through committed lines of credit, provided by a group of banks whose bank holding companies' debt is rated A-1 or higher, equal to 100 percent of nondefaulted receivables. Credit support, in the form of an irrevocable letter of credit issued by Norwest Bank, equals 12 percent of outstanding commercial paper, or $6 million, whichever is greater. The letter of credit provides protection well in excess of historical and expected defaults.

Structure

GCPC is a single-purpose corporation formed solely to make loans to GELCO. GCPC will fund these loans by issuing commercial paper (notes) or borrowing from banks. GELCO will secure its repayment obligation to GCPC with a pledge of its auto fleet leases. GCPC will, in turn, pledge ratably these receivables to the banks and the note holders.

On any maturity date, the depositary (Manufacturers Hanover Trust Co.) will first repay maturing notes with proceeds from newly issued commercial paper. If these funds are insufficient, the depositary will access the auto fleet payments in the cash collateral account. Bank lines of credit will be drawn on if these payment sources are insufficient to meet note obligations. The letter of credit issued by Norwest Bank will cover insufficiencies that result from defaults on the receivables.

Credit Risks

The historical performance of GELCO's fleet leasing portfolio has been outstanding. Net losses have been less than 0.1 percent annually over the past seven years, and delinquencies of 60 days and over have been less than 2 percent. This performance is a direct result of GELCO's stringent credit standards. The company leases nationwide, and its portfolio is well diversified both geographically and by company. The lease portfolio also has no undue industry exposures. GCPC's lease pool is representative of GELCO's auto fleet lease portfolio. The pool generally consists of investment-grade lessees. Anticoncentration provisions reduce the possibility of adverse selection; no one lessee can exceed 5 percent of the pool. Credit support adequately protects note holders from lease defaults and delinquencies. Defaults are classified as lease payments that are over 180 days past due. Defaults have historically been well under the letter-of-credit coverage and are anticipated to remain so. Bank lines cover any delinquencies under 180 days.

Legal Risks

GCPC's legal structure allows the program to be rated on its own merits. The company is structured to prevent consolidation with GELCO in the unlikely event of GELCO's bankruptcy. GCPC is a single-purpose corporation that is legally unaffiliated with GELCO. This ownership prevents consolidation and, thus, any credit link with GELCO. Note holders would be paid even if GELCO's insolvency blocked the cash flow from lease payments. Auto leases are pledged to GCPC as security for GELCO's loan obligations. Any insolvency proceedings that involve GELCO could block cash flow from these leases. However, the banks take this timing risk under their committed lines of credit. The risk, itself, is also mitigated by cash collection procedures. All lease payments are made into a lockbox that is "swept daily" into an account of GCPC. All parties to the GCPC transaction, except note holders, have also agreed not to file the company into bankruptcy for at least one year and one day after all commercial paper has been paid.

PREFERRED RECEIVABLES FUNDING CORP. RATED A-1

Table 15A-1. Transaction Summary

Initial sale date	July 25, 1988
Securities offered	Commercial paper maturing within 270 days and on a continuous basis
Structure type	Asset-backed commercial paper
Collateral	Interests in pools of receivables originated by various U.S. corporations, plus pool purchase agreement with First National Bank of Chicago (rated A-1)
Issuing and paying agent	First National Bank of Chicago.
Legal structure	Preferred Receivables Funding Corp. is a special-purpose, bankruptcy-remote corporation
Credit enhancement	Overcollateralization in the receivable pool, plus the pool purchase agreement, which equals 100% of outstanding commercial paper
Liquidity protection	The pool purchase agreement equals 100% of outstanding commercial paper The agreement is revocable only in the event of Preferred Receivables Funding Corp.'s bankruptcy
Dealer	Goldman Sachs Money Markets Inc.

Rationale

An A-1 rating is assigned to Preferred Receivables Funding Corp.'s (Prefco's) section 3(a)3 commercial paper program. Prefco is a single-purpose corporation that was established to purchase interests in pools of receivables from various U.S. corporations. The sale of such interests allows the sellers an additional funding source, which may be off-balance-sheet or balance-sheet funding. The commercial paper is secured by Prefco's fractional ownership interest in the pools of receivables, plus a pool purchase agreement with the First National Bank of Chicago (rated A-1). First National Bank of Chicago is obligated to purchase all or part of Prefco's interests in the receivables whenever Prefco has insufficient funds to pay maturing commercial paper. The purchase price payable by First National Bank of Chicago will be equivalent to the amount of such insufficiency. The program's rating is based on the pool's purchase agreement and reflects Prefco's bankrutpcy-remote nature.

Structure

Prefco will purchase interest in pools of receivables on an ongoing basis from various U.S. corporations. Prefco will only purchase pools of receivables that meet its eligibility criteria. Prefco has retained First National Bank of Chicago as its administrative agent to originate, monitor, and administer its receivable pools. Collections on the receivables will be handled by the pool's sellers, subject to Prefco's right to replace the seller with another servicer.

If Prefco's share of the receivable collections is insufficient to pay the commercial paper when due or if a shortfall occurs for any other reason, Prefco will exercise its right to sell a portion of such ownership interest to First National Bank of Chicago. The bank must fund such puts subject to absence of bankruptcy proceedings related to Prefco. Prefco is a bankruptcy-remote corporation.

Legal Risks

Prefco's activities are limited to purchasing interests in pools of receivables. The company may not incur any material debt other than the rated commercial paper and liquidity lines from First National Bank of Chicago. In addition, Prefco may not sell its assets or transfer its liabilities, except through the sale of such assets of First National Bank of Chicago under the pool purchase agreement. Finally, Prefco is the beneficiary of a contract clause, whereby First National Bank of Chicago agrees not to file it into bankruptcy until a year and a day have passed following the payment of all outstanding commercial paper. These characteristics render Prefco bankruptcy remote.

CHAPTER 16
Rating Agency Criteria for Lease-Backed Securities

Thomas P. Hourican

INTRODUCTION

Both public and private markets for lease-backed securities are expanding. Standard & Poor's Corporation (S&P) already rates over $950 million in publicly sold lease receivable-backed bonds and commercial paper. S&P also rates over $600 million in privately placed issues (see Table 16-1). As the $26 billion market for all nonmortgage asset-backed securities grows, the share represented by lease receivable–backed debt is expected to increase.

S&P rates debt secured by various types of leases, including retail automobile fleet, computer equipment, hospital equipment, and utility equipment. S&P's analysis of lease portfolios is similar to that of other asset pools, but lease structures introduce additional rating concerns. These concerns include (1) the credit and cash flow implications of lease terms and residuals and (2) uncertainties regarding the legal transfer of rights to residuals. Rating concerns, which vary with the type of lease being securitized, include:

- Credit risks
- Residual risks

- Residual insurance policies
- Credit support structure
- Collateral valuation
- Legal risks

Accordingly, S&P's criteria for lease-backed securities take into account the type of lease being securitized.

Table 16-1. Publicly Sold Lease-Backed Securities

Long-Term Ratings	*Rating*	*Offering Date*	*Assets*	*Amount (millions)*	*Credit Support*
Sperry Lease Finance Corp. Series A.	AAA	3/85	Computer leases	$192.5	20%
Sperry Lease Finance Corp. Series B.	AAA	9/85	Computer leases	145.8	21
Sperry Lease Finance Corp. Series C	AAA	12/86	Computer leases	174.5	16
Goldome 1986-A Grantor Trust (FSA)	AAA	12/86	Computer leases	205.7	10
Volkswagen Lease Finance Corp.	AAA	10/87	Retail auto leases	150.0	18
Gelco Commercial Paper Corp.	A-1	12/86	Auto fleet leases	90.0+	12

CREDIT RISKS

Lease receivables are subject to two types of credit risks: (1) the risk of defaults on rent payments and (2) losses on residuals. The lease's residual value is realized at lease termination, when the asset is sold. Losses occur when the actual value realized is below residual estimates.

Residual losses are unique to lease receivables. Unlike the nonlease receivables securitized to date, which are all level pay and fully amortizing, leases may not fully amortize. The lessee's rent payments do not account for the lease's total cash flow. The remaining cash flow is the residual. Typically, residuals can account for up to 50 percent of an automobile lease's total expected cash flow.

By comparison, most equipment lease contracts securitized to date do not include a significant residual component.

The amount of residual value actually realized depends on the lease structure, the original residual assumptions, the lessor's remarketing capability, and prevailing resale prices. With certain equipment under any contractual performance, obligations would also affect the residual value.

Residual risks differ under open-end and closed-end leases. Under an open-end automobile lease, the lessee must purchase the vehicle at a price determined at the lease's outset. Thus, the lessee bears all residual risks if the car's value declines. However, under the more common closed-end lease, the lessor bears the residual risk at lease termination. The lessee simply turns in the vehicle at the end of the lease or is given the option—but not the obligation—to purchase the vehicle. The purchase option may create additional residual risk for the lessor if the exercise price is based on prevailing market prices rather than the predetermined residual amount. Lessors tyically cover all or some of their residual risk by purchasing residual insurance policies.

When evaluating the credit risks associated with securitized lease pools, S&P distinguishes between retail and wholesale lease pools. S&P applies an actuarial approach to retail pools. Wholesale pools require both an actuarial and a lessee-specific approach.

- *Retail lease pools.* S&P's credit risk analysis of retail lease pools is similar to the actuarial approach applied to pools of standard automobile installment sale contracts. The likelihood of credit losses is determined by the historical performance of the portfolio from which pooled receivables are drawn. The receivables' performance and characteristics are evaluated relative to industry norms, underwriting standards and servicing capabilities, the transaction's structural aspects, and any legal risks.

- *Wholesale lease pools.* S&P applies both an actuarial and a lessee-specific approach to pools of wholesale automobile fleet leases or equipment leases. A lessee-specific approach is needed when the pool involves a small number of lessees or significant lessee concentrations. Lessee concentrations are a credit concern if:
  —Individual lessees or groups of lessees from one industry or

geographic region compose over 5 percent of the lease pool
—Specific credit problems are associated with the individual lessee, industry, or geographic region

Where concentrations exist, S&P reviews the lessees' creditworthiness. Any additional risk that results from lessee concentrations would be covered by the credit support.

S&P applies this approach to the three Sperry Lease Finance Corp. transactions. The Sperry pools exhibit strong credit quality on an aggregate basis, as evidenced by historically low average losses on lease contracts. Furthermore, the weighted-average lessee debt ratings are in the A and AA categories. However, each pool is heavily concentrated in federal government and other municipal government leases. Accordingly, estimates of the pools' potential losses reflect certain contractual risks unique to government leases. These risks include nonappropriation, termination for convenience, and setoff.

RESIDUAL RISKS

Losses on automobile lease residuals occur when the net proceeds from the vehicle's sale (net of residual insurance proceeds and disposition expenses) are less than the booked residual value. The losses may occur prior to or at the lease maturity date. Losses realized prior to or at the lease maturity date are usually the result of vehicle repossessions following lessee defaults. Prepayments resulting from early terminations that are not related to defaults may result in a cash shortfall, depending on prevailing resale prices and the lease's payoff provisions. Losses at lease maturity may result from the exercise of purchase options at a market price below the lease residual value. If the lease contains no termination purchase option, the lessor might also resell the vehicle at a price below the lease residual value.

The credit support level needed to cover residual risk is indicated by the historical and prospective relationship between net resale proceeds and booked residual values. Given the price volatility inherent in the used-car market for some types of vehicles, S&P assumes a worst-case scenario, under which residual losses equal a multiple of (at least three times) the maximum historical negative variance between the original booked value and net resale proceeds. The residual stress test applied to any given transaction depends on factors that may affect residual risk. For example, S&P evaluates how aggressively the lease residuals are valued, relative to the residual values assigned by other lessors or by one of the independent residual forecasting services, most notably the *Automotive Lease Guide* (ALG), the *National Auto Research Black Book* (black book), or the *Kelly Blue Book Leasing Guide* (blue book). Other factors include the accounting methods employed by the lessor to account for losses on vehicle sales; the manufacturer's reputation; past and present cases involving product defects, recalls, and product liability; the lessor's remarketing capability; and supply and demand for the vehicles involved.

RESIDUAL INSURANCE POLICIES

Residual insurance policies may reduce the credit support required to cover residual risk in a securitized lease transaction. In general, a residual insurance policy covers 100 percent of a transaction's residual risk only if the following conditions are met:

- The policy must be issued by an insurer whose claim-paying ability is at least as high as that of the structured transaction. The issuer's credit standing is measured by a rating, and S&P may assign a confidential "shadow" rating to the insurer, subject to the availability of information.
- The coverage must be complete and comprehensive to prevent cash shortfalls. For example, any deductibles would reduce the amount of available coverage.
- Any limitations on claim payments should not undermine residual risk coverage. For example, some policies will pay if the lease reaches final maturity, but do not cover residual risk in the event of an early termination.

S&P evaluates these factors to determine how much credit support the policy provides. The policy could provide partial support if it did not meet these conditions, but such policies are evaluated on a case-by-case basis.

CREDIT SUPPORT STRUCTURE

The credit support structure in an asset-backed transaction should be consistent with the shape of the loss curve for those assets. For example, static pool analysis of automobile installment sale contracts demonstrates that losses tend to peak during months 6 to 18 after contract origination. Thereafter, losses decline as the obligors establish a payment history and build equity in the vehicle. Accordingly, credit support should decline with pool amortization for this type of asset. The loss curve for retail automobile lease/rent payments is similar to that of automobile installment sale contracts.

However, the shape of the loss curve for leases may not follow a definite pattern, depending on the type of lease. For example, wholesale leases exhibit a flatter loss curve, with a lower correlation to seasoning, than do retail automobile leases. Furthermore, substantial residuals in any type of lease increase the probability of additional losses at the end of the transactions. Therefore, S&P recommends that credit support allocated to cover residual or any other tail-end risk should be incorporated into a credit support "floor," which would decline only for drawdowns to cover losses.

COLLATERAL VALUATION

S&P applies the same collateral valuation criteria to a pool of lease receivables as applied to other securitized assets. In general, the note value for each piece of collateral must equal the lesser of:

- The principal amount of the notes that the collateral piece could support if were to prepay
- The present value of the future scheduled cash flows (assuming no prepayments) discounted at the highest-note interest rate

In applying this test to different types of leases, S&P examines a lease's payoff provisions to determine whether 100 percent prepayment or 0 percent prepayment results in the most conservative note valuation. This collateral valuation method ensures that the collateral pool will support the amount of bonds issued.

The presence of discount collateral or assets with nonlevel payments such as balloon mortgages and leases, can cause liquidity shortfalls in structured transactions. Shortfalls can occur even if the collateral valuation criteria mentioned earlier are satisfied. Collateral cash flows from lease pools with large residuals are concentrated at the end of the lease. As a result, cash flow from monthly lease payments may not cover any immediate debt servicing requirements. To overcome this problem, the bond payment structure can be modified to match more closely the timing of collateral cash flows. Credit support or a servicer advance mechanism should also be available to cover liquidity shortfalls.

LEGAL RISKS

A lessor's bankruptcy or insolvency presents two separate legal risks to a lease-backed transaction, which arise if legal title to the underlying assets is not registered in the name of the issuer. The first risk is that bond holders may not hold a first-priority security interest in the asset; thus, they could lose any lease residual proceeds that fall outside the lease contract (that is, proceeds received by the lessor from the sale of the asset upon repossession, due to a lessee default or nonexercise of the lessee's option to purchase the asset). This problem applies primarily to retail automobile lease pools because of the cost and administrative burden of transferring title to thousands of vehicles in various states. The magnitude of the potential risk varies with the size of the lease's residual component and the amount of residual proceeds outside the lease contract. S&P sizes the risk based on the lessor's historical repossession, prepayment, and lease termination experience. S&P also examines the credit standing of the lessor in light of a transaction's time horizon to evaluate the probability of a lessor insolvency. If the lessor's credit standing is determined to be integral to the structured transaction's rating, S&P may still assign the transaction a rating higher than that of the lessor, but only with the understanding that such rating may change if the lessor's credit standing changes.

The second legal risk applies to lessors subject to the Bankruptcy Code. In a bankruptcy proceeding of such a lessor, an unexpired lease may be rejected pursuant to or under Section 365 of the code. In this scenario, the entire amount of the unamortized lease proceeds, including residuals, is at risk. S&P examines the probability of rejection in light of any relevant business considerations. For example, if leasing is highly profitable and is central to a company's overall business strategy, rejection and the subsequent liquidation of the leased assets may be a less likely alternative. In conjunction with this analysis, S&P also evaluates the lessor's credit standing to determine the probability of a lessor bankruptcy. Again, S&P may assign ratings to lease-backed transactions that are contingent on the lessor's credit standing.

The legal risks previously cited present difficult problems for issuers of lower credit quality that seek high credit ratings on securitized lease transactions. If transferring title to the assets is not feasible and the legal risks cannot be discounted, the transaction must provide adequate credit support to protect bond holders from all legal and credit-related risks. Legal research in these areas continues, and alternative securitization structures are being developed to address some of these risks. Accordingly, S&P will continue to update its rating critieria for lease-backed securities.

CHAPTER 17
Junk Bond Securitization

Thomas P. Hourican

INTRODUCTION

Junk bond securitization was initiated in 1987, when Imperial Savings Association offered three bond-backed issues, using a traditional mortgage-backed bond structure. Two of Imperial's issues, which are overcollateralized by as much as 220 percent, were rated AAA. Subsequently, issues by Far West Savings and the New American High Income Fund were rated AAA, using similar Standard & Poor's Corporation (S&P) methodology.

The market value structure, which all of these issues used, called for frequent valuation, substantial overcollateralization, and diversification of collateral. These four transactions called for the junk bond collateral to be marked to market every two weeks. In the event that the value of the collateral is less than predetermined levels, the issuer has two weeks in which to regain sufficient collateral. Failing that, the trustee could be directed to liquidate collateral to repay note holders. Therefore, investors in these notes are assuming junk bond market risk for one month (valuation and cure)—not ten years!

DIVERSIFICATION AND LIQUIDITY

Collateral diversification by issuer and industry was a key area of strength in these transactions. For example, bonds rated B by S&P are subject to a 3 percent issuer and 8 percent industry limitation and are overcollateralized 180 percent. Therefore, the bonds of 34 different issuers (3 percent issuer limit) in 13 different industries (8 percent limit) could fall in value from 100 percent to 56 percent of par in one month, and investors would still be protected.

Collateral liquidity was also important because the liquidation of speculative-grade bonds would be the source of repayment if the issuer could not meet its obligations. Bonds used as collateral come from liquid, well-known issues. At least 80 percent of speculative-grade collateral comes from original issues in excess of $100 million. Bonds must pay interest in cash. The more volatile pay-in-kind, zero coupon, and convertible bonds are excluded. Furthermore, if two bids are not obtained on any bond, it would not be eligible as collateral.

Quantitative portfolio analysis, as well as discussions with market participants, revealed that while individual junk bond prices tend to be more volatile than those of investment-grade bonds, pools of junk bonds exhibit greater stability. The benefits of diversification can be seen in the following sample portfolio in Table 17-1. In the two-year period ended July 24, 1987, the worst price change in a 50-day period for the entire portfolio was 7.93 percent, while the worst performance for any individual bond was 61.8 percent. The stability that diversification creates is quite apparent.

Table 17-1. Sample Junk Bond Portfolio From July 24, 1985, to July 24, 1987

Portfolio	*20-Day Period*	*50-day Period*
Average change	(0.13)%	(0.25)%
Maximum gain	4.05	6.41
Maximum loss	5.82	7.93
Individual bond		
Maximum loss	55.1	61.8

ADVANTAGES FOR ISSUERS

The advantages for thrift and nonthrift issuers are clear. The ability to gain liquidity and to lock in low-cost funding is a benefit to the asset/liability management process. S&P expects market value–based securitization to grow rapidly during the next several years.

From an issuer's perspective, the major drawback to market value transactions is the substantial overcollateralization required. With overcollateralization ranging from 170 percent to 220 percent, issuers are seeking more efficient uses of their collateral. The next frontier for junk bond securitization will be cash flow–based transactions, in which credit and cash flow characteristics, as opposed to market value, will be the basis for repayment. This type of transaction will call for a fixed pool of bonds, combined with some form of credit enhancement to be packaged in a pass-through or pay-through structure.

To rate these transactions, S&P is developing an actuarial model to assess the likelihood of default based on history, as well as S&P's expectations for the future. The successful development of this financing vehicle would have a major impact on the junk bond market. As investment-grade conduit for channeling funds from investors to borrowers would certainly increase the funds available to speculative-grade companies. This, in turn, would increase investor participation.

HIGH-YIELD CASH FLOW CRITEIRA

Effective immediately, S&P will rate cash flow transactions backed by high-yield corporate bonds. These transactions rely on cash generated by underlying collateral for repayment. S&P assigns investment-grade ratings to these transactions, based on credit enhancement added to a fixed pool of assets, which is similar to pass-through/pay-through transactions. Analysis for cash flow transactions focuses on credit and default statistics.

Previously, S&P developed criteria for rating market value transactions backed by high-yield paper. Similar in concept to a margin account, the market value transaction relies on collateral liquidation—not cash flow—to repay note holders. Therefore, in contrast to cash flow transactions, market value analysis looks at liquidity and price volatility.

BASE CASE

S&P modeled its criteria around a base case pool. The following are the pool characteristics:

- Five percent industry concentration
- Two percent issuer concentration
- Implied senior debt ratings split 60 percent rated BB, 40 percent rated B; securities with an implied senior B–rating are not included
- Fixed-rate, nonconvertible, cash-paying bonds

Based on these pool characteristics, S&P developed default scenarios for various ratings of collateralized debt, as well as a stress test for the cash flows. Table 17-2 shows default frequencies for each rating category.

Table 17-2. Collateral Default Frequency

Collateralized Bond Rating	*Default Frequency of Collateral*
AAA	67%
AA	50
A	38
BBB	32

Recoveries on the underlying collateral are assumed to be 25 percent for senior debt and 10 percent for subordinated debt and are assumed to be received six months after default.

In stressing cash flows, losses would occur as shown in Table 17-3.

Table 17-3. Stress Test Default Timing

Year	*Loss*
1	5%
2	30
3	30
4	30
5	5

For example, in an A-rated transaction, cash flows would show 5 percent × 38 percent losses in year 1, 30 percent × 38 percent in year 2, and so on.

Consequently, for a base pool, an issuer should submit cash flow runs showing that an instrument expected to be rated A could withstand 30 percent of the pool defaulting over five years, with recoveries between 10 percent and 25 percent. The actual level of overcollateralization depends on the structure. Deviations from these characteristics result in either greater or less credit enhancement levels. For example, an overweighting of BB-rated bonds compared with B bonds will lower overcollateralization requirements, while excessive industry concentrations will require increased overcollateralization. Furthermore, triggers could be incorporated into the transaction to provide some increased flexibility for the manager if the pool's performance substantially exceeded original expectations.

Potential issuers have indicated to S&P that the static pool concept—that is, no trading of bonds unless a default occurs—is too restrictive, given the changing fortunes of individual high-yield bonds. Issuers intend to sell bonds before they default and reinvest the proceeds in higher-quality bonds. S&P expects issuers to provide strict guidelines stating when bonds with increasing credit risk may be sold. Furthermore, after any sale or purchase of bonds, the transaction would still have to satisfy diversification requirements and cash flow stress tests. However, a bond is assumed to be sold within six months of its default, while appreciated bonds can be sold at any time. Proceeds from defaulted or appreciated bonds are assumed to be distributed to senior debt holders. Other issues, including the transaction's legal structure and tax-paying characteristics, should also be addressed in any cash flow structure.

RECOVERIES

Studies indicate that defaulted bonds trade at an average price of 40 percent of par one month after default. S&P conducted a price review of recently defaulted issues to develop recovery expectations for a cash flow transaction. Although the research seemed to confirm prior work, the actual value of recoveries within six months of default varies greatly by issue. The price range is broad, varying from 4 percent to 96 percent of par, with subordinated debt at the lower end, ranging from 4 percent to 71 percent in the sample. Since the United States has not experienced a recession since the surge in junk bond issuance, none of the statistics includes a recession's effect on the price of defaulted junk bonds with current market stratification. Furthermore, if the dollar amount of defaulted debt increases significantly, the market may assign lower prices to defaulted bonds.

CASH FLOWS STRESSED

S&P expects levels of defaults in the high-yield environment to increase in the future, as very highly leveraged companies are challenged by an economic downturn. Default frequency is higher than previous experience, and cash flows are stressed more by compressing losses into the early years. Historically, losses were more evenly distributed. In addition, recovery assumptions are more conservative than historical performance. Historical experience indicates that recoveries on defaulted subordinated debt would approximate 25 percent—that is, a severity of 75 percent. Therefore, the stress tests are increased significantly from past levels.

Consequently, an A-rated ten-year transaction could withstand more than double historical losses. In addition, stressing the cash flows for losses in the transaction's early years adds about 9 percent further support over average historical performance. However, this level depends on principal repayment characteristics. Table 17-4 shows the historical and A-rated levels for loss calculations.

Table 17-4. Criteria Versus History

	Collateral Default Frequency		*Loss Severity*		*Net Losses*		*Stress Test Benefit*		*Total Credit Enhancement*
Historical experience	25	×	75	=	19		N.A.		N.A.
A criteria	38	×	90	=	34	+	9	=	43

N.A.—Not applicable.

The 43 percent credit enhancement would enable an A-rated pool to withstand losses more than 2.3 times the historical experience of 19 percent.

Appendix: Case Studies

To establish diversification requirements and cash flow stress tests, S&P researched the performance of the high-yield debt market. This included a review of high-yield research to date, two static pool analyses, and prices of recently defaulted issues.

Most studies available measure defaults in terms of actual dollar losses against current dollar outstandings. Although this ratio has not been high on average, default rates may be distorted as the numerator and denominator have both grown rapidly. S&P evaluated two static pools of high-yield bonds as part of its analysis on default expectations (see Figure 17A-1).

Figure 17A-1. Final Distribution of Pool Ratings

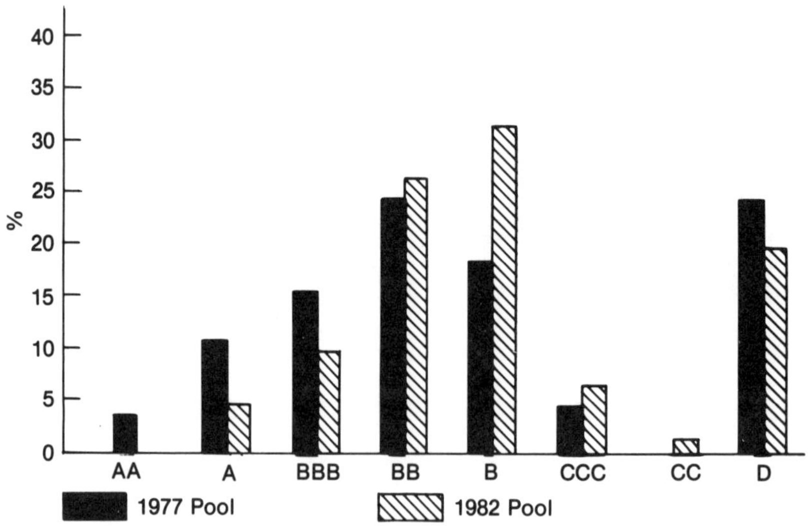

The 1977 Pool

The 1977 pool was composed entirely of bonds of issuers of speculative-grade debt, new and seasoned, with semiannual, fixed coupon, public debt outstanding at July 1, 1977. The 100 issuers in the pool had implied senior debt ratings that ranged from BBB to CC on July 1, 1977. The pool was tracked over 10½ years and had 18 defaults. Exchange offers were considered defaults, as the terms of the original indenture were not met. Default percentages were measured by issuer, rather than by dollar amount of debt outstanding. A rated cash flow transaction includes issuer diversification standards, thereby limiting the effect of default of any one bond on the pool. The 1977 pool included 34 issuers with senior implied ratings of BBB (subordinated debt rating of BB); 6 percent, or 0.56 percent annually, ultimately defaulted. At the time of default, no issuer had an investment-grade rating. Of issuers with implied senior ratings of BB+ or lower on July 1, 1977, 24 percent, or 2.3 percent annually, defaulted. Since the U.S. economy suffered two recessions from 1979 to 1982, when there was a small market for original-issue junk bonds, the 1977 pool includes the performance of primarily "fallen angel" debt during a stressful economic period.

The 1982 Pool

The 1982 pool included debt from 170 different issuers; the majority were original-issue, speculative-grade debt. Defaults on the 1982 pool totaled 18 percent over five and a half years. Of 18 issuers with implied senior ratings of BBB on July 1, 1982, only 1, or 5.6 percent, subsequently defaulted. At the time of default, no bond had an implied senior investment-grade rating. Of issuers with implied senior ratings of BB+ or lower, defaults amounted to 20 percent. The energy industry clearly demonstrated concentration risk, with nearly 70 percent of issuers defaulting. An adjustment was made to conform the pool to a 5 percent industry concentration limit. As a result, the adjusted default rate was 13.4 percent for five years, or 2.4 percent annually. As any transaction rated would meet industry concentration guidelines, the 13.4 percent figure is more relevant than the 20 percent level. The redistribution of ratings in each of the pools is detailed in Figure 17A-1.

CHAPTER 18

Introduction to Mortgages and Mortgage-Backed Securities

K. Jeanne Person
Analyst, Mortgage Research
Salomon Brothers Inc.

INTRODUCTION

The development of securities backed by U.S. mortgage loans has given rise to a huge and highly liquid market. As of June 1988, more than $715 billion of mortgage securities was outstanding, while trading of Government National Mortgage Association (GNMA) pass-throughs alone in 1987 amounted to more than $500 billion, according to GNMA. Spreads between bid and offered prices on many mortgage securities are commonly four thirty-seconds of a point or less.

The market has grown explosively since the first GNMA pass-through was issued in 1970. The annual issuance of mortgage pass-through securities guaranteed by GNMA, the Federal Home Loan Mortgage Corporation (FHLMC), the Federal National Mortgage Association (FNMA) as well as private pass-throughs reached almost $250 billion in 1987, and an increasing volume of derivative instruments, such as collateralized mortgage obligations (CMOs) and mortgage strips, was also being sold.

Figure 18-1. U.S. Credit Market: Debt Outstanding by Type, December 1987

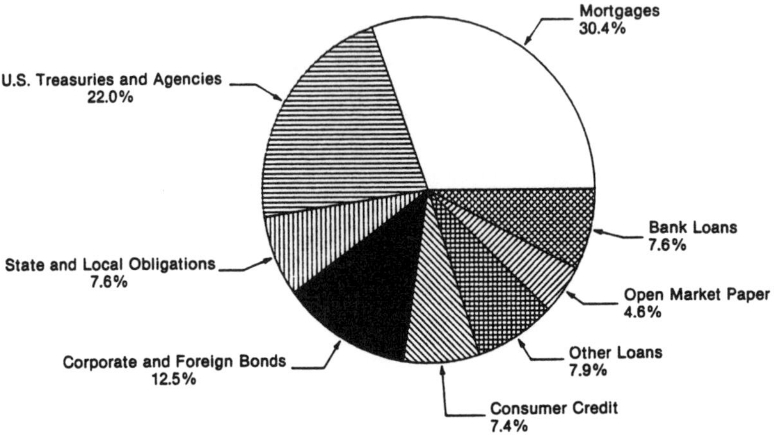

Source: Federal Reserve Board

Notwithstanding this enormous issuance, only a small part of the potential market has been tapped. As of December 1987, outstanding U.S. mortgage debt totaled about $2.9 trillion—or $800 billion more than all privately held U.S. Treasury and agency securities. Mortgages accounted for a third of all borrowing in the U.S. credit markets in 1987 (see Figures 18-1 and 18-2). Yet only about half of the total residential mortgage debt has been securitized.

Mortgage securities are the main vehicle whereby investors who are not mortgage originators participate in the mortgage market. The development of these securities has provided investors with standardized, liquid, and easily financed instruments in a market that formerly offered only nonstandard and illiquid mortgage whole loans. Most mortgage securities enjoy the highest credit standing. GNMA pass-throughs, by far the largest category, are backed by the full faith and credit of the U.S. government. During the past five years, GNMA yields have averaged about 125 basis points above those on comparable U.S. Treasury issues; other types of mortgage securities often provide even higher yields.

The principal investors in the mortgage market have traditionally been institutions with direct mortgage lending experience, largely because they are familiar with the cash flow and credit

Figure 18-2. U.S. Credit Market: Net Borrowing by Type, 1987

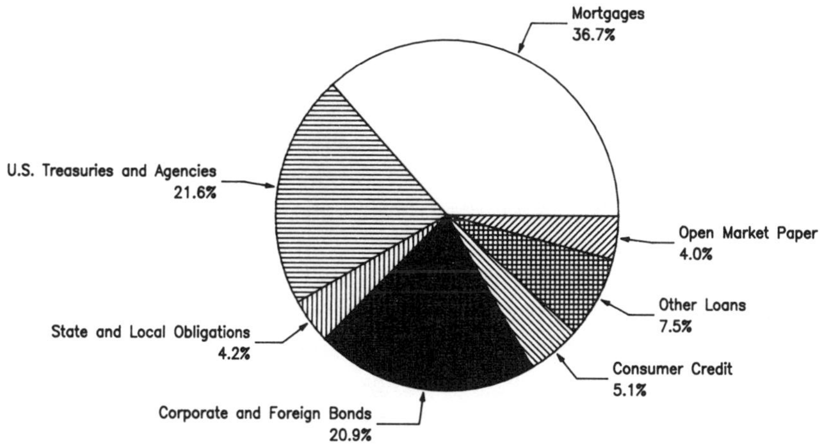

Source: Federal Reserve Board

characteristics of mortgage loans. However, in recent years, innovations in the structuring of mortgage securities have attracted a wide and growing range of new investors, both domestic and international. This chapter provides such newcomers with a basic understanding of U.S. mortgage instruments and the primary and secondary markets in which they are originated and sold.

MORTGAGE INSTRUMENTS

A mortgage is simply a pledge of property to secure a debt. The borrower, or mortgagor, acquires the funds to purchase a property in exchange for a pledge to cede that property to the lender, or mortgagee, should the loan default. The typical residential mortgage in the United States, known as a single-family mortgage, is secured by a one- to four-family dwelling and the land on which it rests. Although there is a growing effort to securitize a wide range of mortgage and related assets, including loans on commercial real estate, single-family residential mortgages back the majority of the mortgage securities issued to date.

Most single-family residential mortgages that are originated in the United States are self-amortizing loans with level, or constant, monthly payments over the life of the loans. Each payment includes a portion of the principal, as well as the interest, and the payment schedule is structured so that the last payment retires the final remaining balance of the loan. The payment schedule of a mortgage contrasts sharply with that of a corporate or government bond, which typically pays interest semiannually and provides a balloon payment of the entire principal amount at maturity.

Although many variants of both balloon and self-amortizing repayment schedules still exist among commercial and multifamily mortgages[1], the government insurance and securitization programs developed since World War II have standardized the payment structure, underwriting procedures, and documentation for a large proportion of the single-family mortgages now being originated. The three most common forms today are the level-payment fixed-rate mortgage, the graduated-payment mortgage (GPM), and the adjustable-rate mortgage (ARM). Together, they make up nearly all single-family mortgage debt.

Level-Payment Fixed-Rate Mortgages

The standard U.S. residential mortgage contract specifies that the principal and interest of the mortgage loan be repaid in equal monthly installments over the term of the mortgage. The vast majority of single-family mortgage securities are backed by level-payment fixed-rate loans with a term of 30 years.

Each installment on a level-payment mortgage includes the interest due, calculated as a fixed percentage of the outstanding balance, and partial repayment of the principal. At the end of the term of the loan, the final payment fully retires the debt. The early payments are primarily interest. As the principal is paid off, the interest payments decline and the principal payments increase (see Figure 18-3). The amount of principal outstanding declines very slowly: Even after ten years, about 90 percent of the original principal on a 9.5 percent mortgage is still outstanding, and the first half of the principal is not repaid until more than 23 years have elapsed (see Figure 18-4).

[1]For example, many multifamily mortgages are partially amortizing loans. The monthly payment is smaller than that required to liquidate the loan at its maturity. Such mortgages call for a final balloon payment of the remaining principal and interest.

Figure 18-3. Level-Payment Fixed-Rate Mortgage—Monthly Payment (9.5% Rate, 30-Year Term, $100,000 Original Balance)

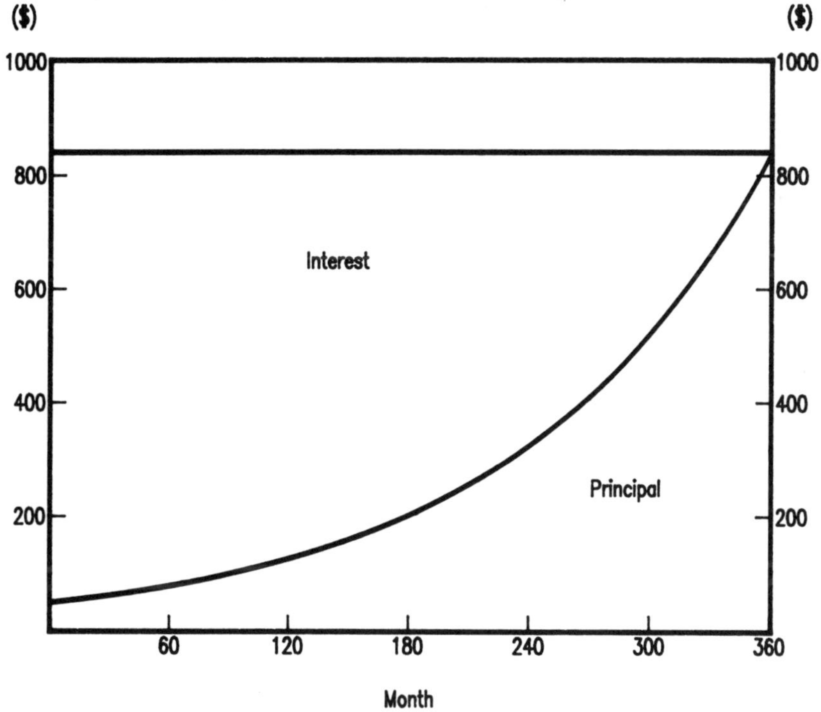

Source: Federal Home Loan Bank Board

Graduated-Payment Mortgages

In the late 1970s, a variation on the standard fixed-rate mort- introduced that called for increasing, or graduated, payments during the first few years of the life of the mortgage: a GPM.[2] GPMs were created when high interest rates forced many potential home owners, especially young and first-time buyers, out of the housing market. GPMs were targeted to younger households whose incomes were expected to rise.

The typical GPM contract provides for low initial monthly payments that increase steadily in the early years of the mortgage until they reach a specified plateau, usually at the beginning of the sixth year (see Figure 18-5). In the first years of the GPM schedule,

[2]See Salomon Brothers Inc., *Analysis of Graduated-Payment Mortgages* (New York: Salomon Brothers Inc., 1984).

Figure 18-4. Level-Payment Fixed-Rate Mortgage—Remaining Principal Balance (9.5% Rate, 30-Year Term, $100,000 Original Balance Dollars in Thousands)

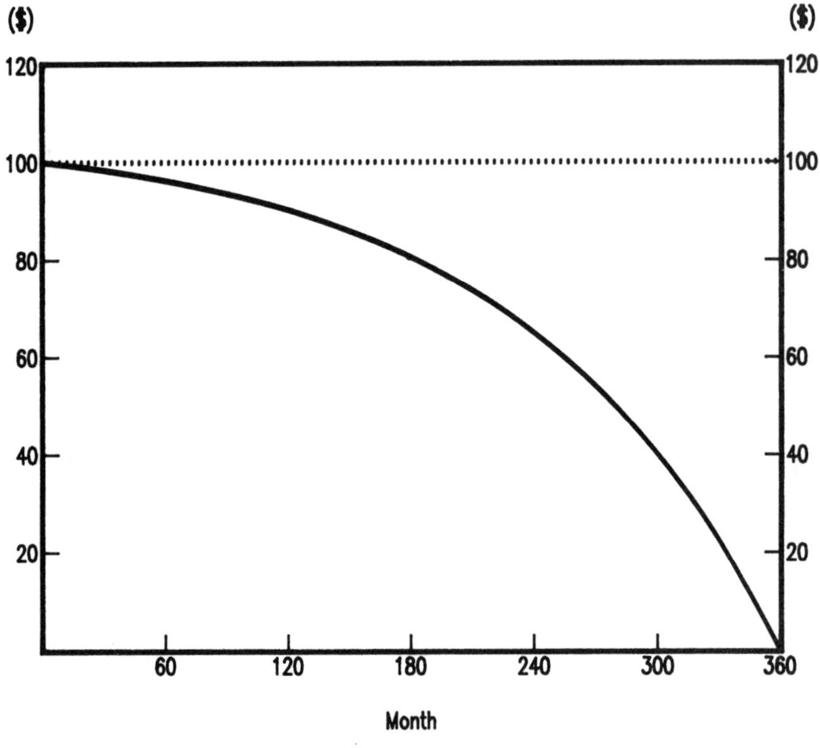

Source: Federal Home Loan Bank Board

the monthly payments do not cover the interest due on the loan; in effect, new credit is extended to the borrower and the outstanding balance rises. The increase in principal balance is called negative amortization. Once the constant-payment phase of the loan schedule is reached, the GPM acts as a level-payment fixed-rate mortgage, in which the payments cover the interest annd amortize the outstanding principal balance over the remaining life of the loan (see Figure 18-6).

The creation of GNMA pass-throughs backed by GPMs in 1979 served to standardize these mortgages. For the most popular type of GPM, the monthly payment increses by 7.5 percent each year for the

Figure 18-5. GPM Monthly Payment (9.5 Percent Rate, 30-Year Term, $100,000 Original Balance, Payment Increase: 7.5 Percent per Year for 5 Years)

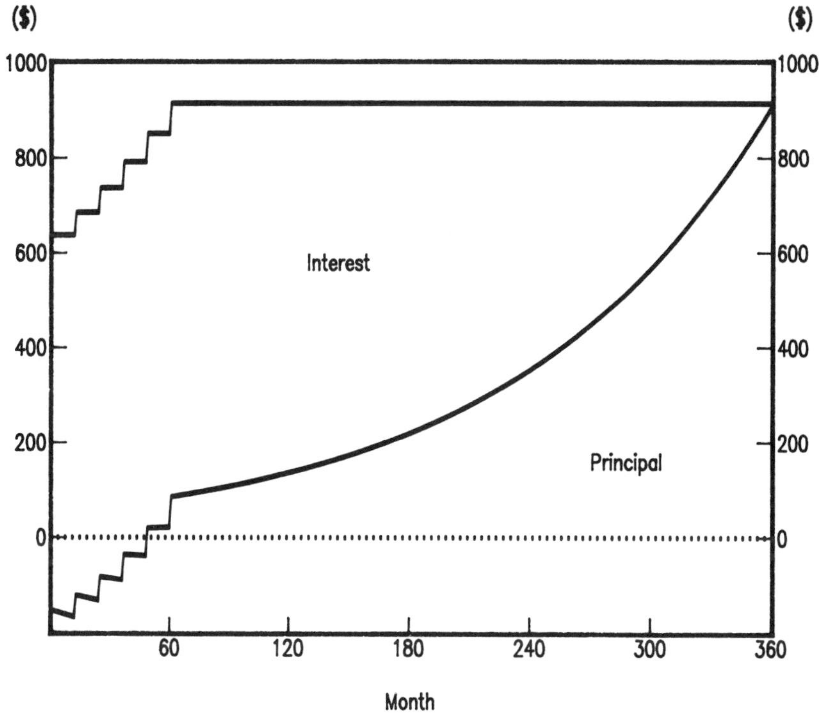

Source: Federal Home Loan Bank Board

first five years and remains constant thereafter. Given this standard increase in payments, the original payment size and the amount of negative amortization vary with the interest rate: Lower–interest rate GPMs amortize negatively for a shorter period and at a slower rate than do GPMs that bear higher interest rates.

Adjustable-Rate Mortgages

ARMs were commonplace in other countries long before they gained widespread acceptance in the United States. Before the steep rise in interest rates in the late 1970s and early 1980s, U.S. borrowers

Figure 18-6. GPM Remaining Principal Balance (9.5 Percent Rate, 30-Year Term, $100,000 Original Balance, Payment Increase: 7.5 Percent per year for 5 Years, Dollars in Thousands)

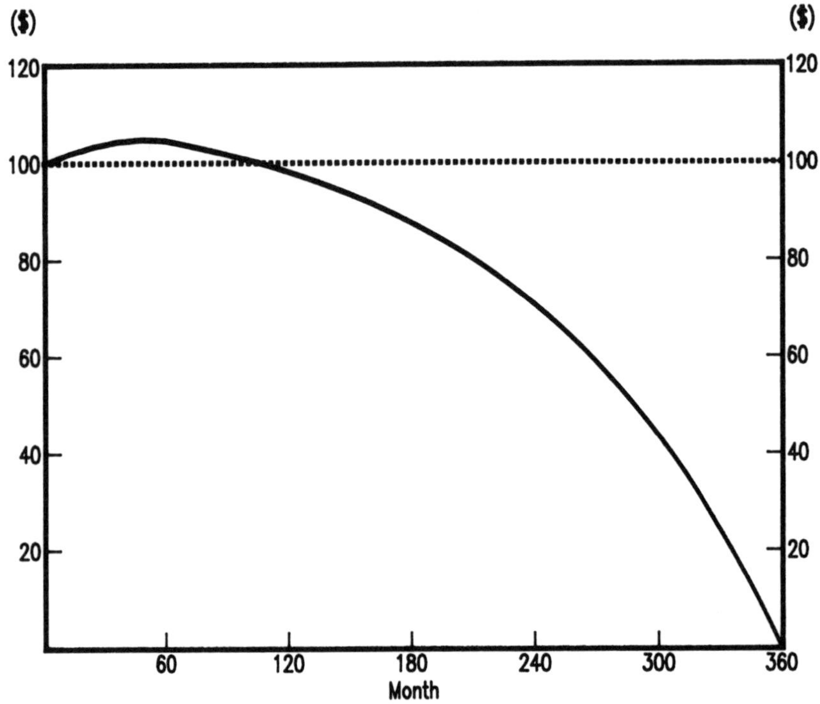

Source: Federal Home Loan Bank Board

preferred the predictable monthly payments of fixed-rate mortgages. In a high-rate environment, however, fixed-rate mortgages present problems for both borrowers and lenders. High mortgage rates at the beginning of this decade began to push the financing cost of the average home beyond the means of many middle-income households. At the same time, portfolio lenders became increasingly conscious of the risk of holding long-term fixed-rate mortgages that are funded with deposits or other short-term liabilities.

ARMs resolved many of these problems. The rates on such mortgages are reset at regular intervals, typically at a spread to a stated short-term interest rate index.[3] Therefore, ARMs help lending

[3]The most common reset indexes are the one-year constant maturity Treasury rate and the weighted-average cost of funds for thrift institution members of the Eleventh District Federal Home Loan Bank (San Francisco).

institutions to reduce the difference in the interest rate sensitivities of their assets and liabilities. With ARMs, some of the interest rate risk is passed on to the borrower, but the lender, in return, can offer a lower rate.

ARMs gained wider acceptance during the first half of this decade because they made it possible for many potential home owners—particularly young families—to qualify for mortgages. By mid-1984, ARMs accounted for roughly two thirds of all conventional mortgage originations—that is, loans not insured or guaranteed by a government agency. The proportion of ARMS among new originations has varied directly with changes in mortgage interest rates: The ARM market share increased when mortgage interest rates rose during the 1983–1984 period and fell when interest rates declined during the 1985–1986 period (see Figure 18-7). It climbed sharply again in 1987, and, most recently, ARMs have represented about half of all conventional originations.

Most ARMs in the United States are originated by savings and loan associations and savings banks, collectively kown as thrifts. Initially, most ARMs were retained by the thrifts as short-term portfolio investments. Consequently, they seldom reached the secondary market, and there was little incentive to standardize the ARM contract. In 1984, however, GNMA and FNMA began securitization programs for ARMs. In 1985, FHLMC followed suit. It is likely that, as the secondary market grows and as lenders seek to originate mortgages eligible for securitization, there will be a tendency for the range of different ARM contracts to narrow.

One of the main differences between U.S. ARMs and those originated in other countries is the inclusion of interest rate or payment caps in U.S. ARMs. Interest rate caps protect the borrower from large increases in the mortgage interest rate. Limits can apply to the rate adjustment on reset dates, the total adjustment over the life of the loan, or both. Payment caps allow the mortgage rate to move with the interest rate index, but limit the amount that monthly payments can change on reset dates.

ARMs shift some or all of the interest rate risk from the lender to the borrower because the interest rate paid by the borrower fluctuates with market rates. For example, for an uncapped ARM that resets once a year, the lender is exposed to interest rate fluctuations

Figure 18-7. ARM Market Share—Percentage of Conventional Mortgage Originations, January 1982–June 1988

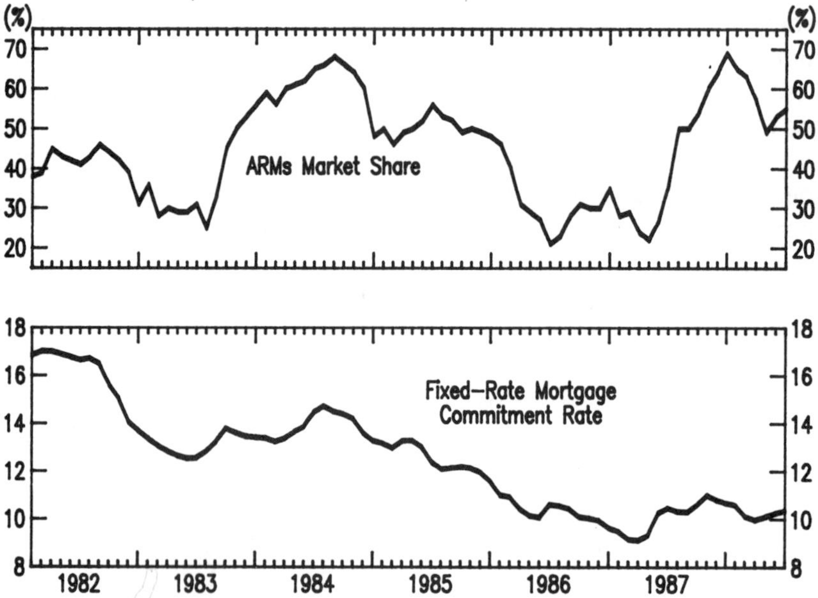

Source: Feder· Home Loan Bank Board.

only between the annual reset dates—instead of being at risk over the entire 30-year term of the mortgage.[4]

THE PREPAYMENT OPTION

One of the most important differences between mortgage investments and corporate and government bonds is the unpredictability of mortgage cash flows, which arises from the borrower's option to prepay. U.S. mortgage agreements typically give the borrower the option to prepay the principal in full or in part at any

[4]For a general discussion of ARMs, see M.D. Youngblood and Judy Hustich-Hoff, *An Introduction to Adjustable-Rate Mortgage Securities: the Market and the Indexes* (New York: Salomon Brothers Inc., 1988). For analysis of the value of Treasury index-based ARMs, see Michael Waldman *A Framework for Evaluating ARMs: Part I: Specific Interest Rate Scenarios* and *Part II: The Salomon Brothers ARM Pricing Model (New York: Salomon Brothers Inc., 1984. Variable-rate mortgages, a forerunner of ARMs, are discussed in The Value of Variable-Rate Mortgage Securities* by Michael Waldman, Javed Saleh, and Mark Gordon (New York: Salomon Brothers, Inc., 1986).

time. Full prepayment can result if the mortgaged property is sold or if the borrower refinances the loan.[5] Partial prepayments take place when the borrower, for whatever reason, pays more than the required monthly installment. The position of the mortgage investor can be described as "long a bond and short an option," where the option is the borrower's right to prepay or to call the loan at par.[6]

The home owner's prepayment option makes it impossible for the mortgage holder to predict with certainty either the cash flows or the average life of the mortgage investment. However, the mortgage investor does not go unrewarded for assuming prepayment risk because mortgage borrowers pay higher interest rates as a premium for the call option.

THE PRIMARY MORTGAGE MARKET

Transactions between borrowers and originators of mortgage loans take place in the primary mortgage market. Home owners are the principal mortgage borrowers in the United States, although businesses, farmers, and nonprofit institutions also employ mortgage financing. Thrifts, commercial banks, and mortgage banks are the principal mortgage originators.

The mortgage originator underwrites the loan, processes the necessary documents, and advances the funds to the borrower. Underwriting entails (1) collecting and verifying information about the borrower's credit and the value of the property securing the loan and (2) evaluating the borrower's ability to meet the monthly mortgage payments. Although lenders adopt a wide range of underwriting standards and some lenders are more flexible than others in applying their standards, lenders typically require mortgage payments to be not more than 28 percent of the borrower's gross monthly income. In addition, lenders generally require down pay-

[5]The sale of the property, however, need not lead to prepayment if the mortgage contract permits the buyer to assume the existing loan. All single-family loans insured by the Federal Housing Administration (FHA) or guaranteed by the Veterans Administration (VA) are assumable. FHA is an arm of the U.S. Department of Housing and Urban Development (HUD); the VA is an independent agency of the federal executive branch.

[6]See Michael Waldman and Mark Gordon, *Evaluating the Option Features of Mortgage Securities: the Salomon Brothers Mortgage Pricing Model* (New York: Salomon Brothers Inc., 1986).

ments of 5–25 percent of the appraised property value. Such a minimum requirement on the borrower's equity serves two purposes: It constitutes an economic penalty to the borrower who defaults on the loan, and it cushions the lender should the borrower default and the property have to be liquidated.

The ratio of the outstanding mortgage principal to the value of the property is called the loan-to-value (LTV) ratio. These ratios on conventional loans typically range from 75 percent to 95 percent. For a conventional loan whose LTV ratio is greater than 80 percent, lenders generally require borrowers to purchase private mortgage insurance, so that the uninsured portion of the loan is no greater than 75 percent of the value of the property.

Insurance programs in the primary mortgage market protect the mortgage security investor because they help ensure payment on the underlying loans. Two federal agencies, the FHA and the VA, provide mortgage insurance intended to serve moderate- and low-income home buyers. FHA and VA loans require smaller down payments than do conventional loans. FHA insurance is available to any borrower, provided that the mortgage meets certain requirements and the pledged structure meets construction standards. FHA requires a down payment of 3 percent on the first $25,000 of the loan balance and 5 percent on the remainder. The maximum insurable loan is $67,500, although a higher limit applies in some high-cost areas. The VA guarantee program is available to eligible veterans and their surviving spouses, and it allows LTV ratios of up to 100 percent. The VA guarantee covers the first 60 percent of the mortgage balance up to a maximum amount of $27,500.

Thrifts, commercial banks, and mortgage banks accounted for 92 percent of all mortgage originations in 1987. Thrifts made the largest share of these loans; they originated 38 percent of all mortgages issued in 1987 and almost half of all single-family mortgages (see Figures 18-8 and 18-9).

Thrift Institutions

Thrifts are insured depository institutions that lend primarily in their own home territories. They are encouraged by both regulatory and tax considerations to hold residential mortgage investments

Figure 18-8. Mortgage Originations by Lender and Property Type, 1987
Dollars in Billions

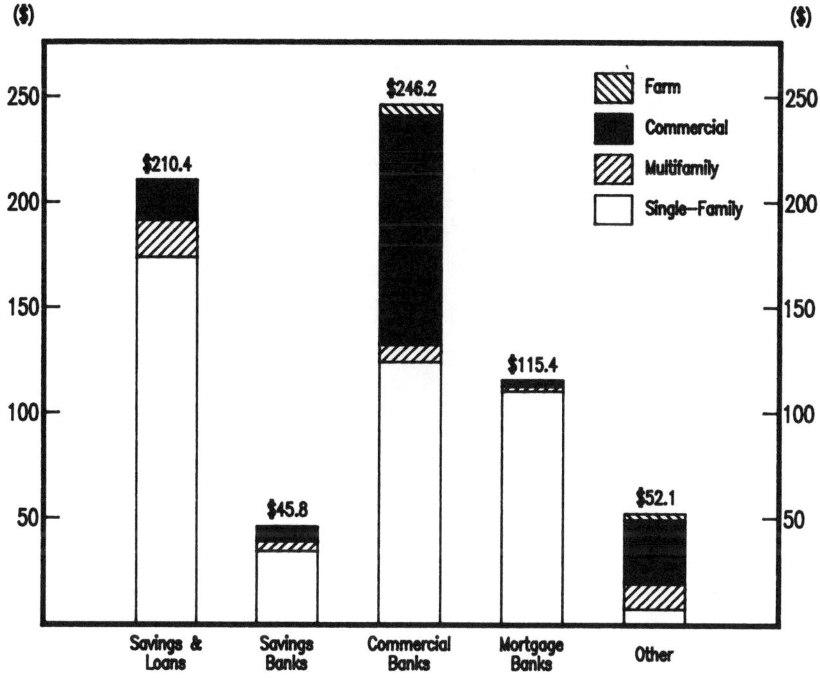

Source: HUD

in their portfolios, either in the form of whole mortgage loans or mortgage pass-through securities. These investments have traditionally been funded with short-term market-rate deposits. However, in periods of rising interest rates, long-term fixed-rate mortgages previously originated at lower interest rates may generate yields below the thrifts' cost of funds. Consequently, thrifts have sought to limit their interest rate exposure by extending their liabilities and by acquiring more short-term interest rate–sensitive assets; in particular, many have concentrated on originating and holding ARMs.

In addition to the interest earned on mortgages and other investments, thrifts derive income from origination and service fees. A loan servicer collects payments and fees from borowers and, if the loan has been sold, forwards the payments to the mortgage holder.

Figure 18-9. Single-Family Mortgage Originations by Lender, 1987

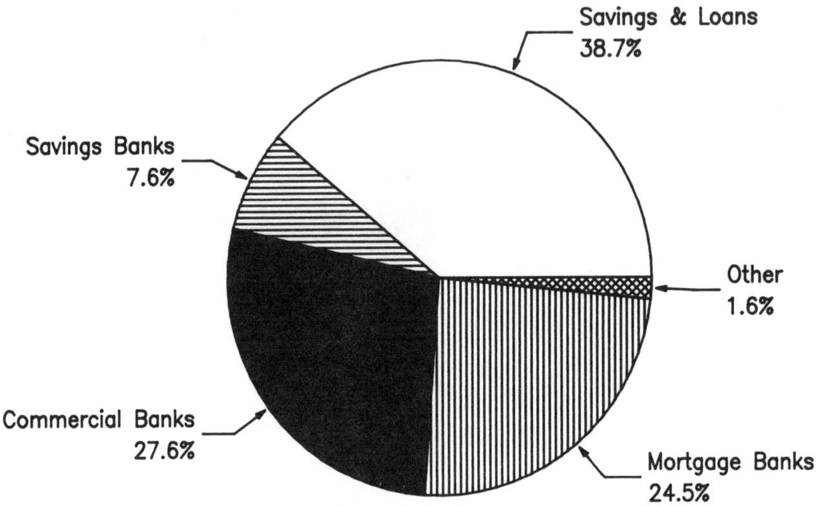

Source: HUD

The servicer also pursues delinquent borrowers and handles default proceedings. The service fee is generally calculated as a percentage—typically 0.25–0.5 percent—of the outstanding loan balance.

Commercial Banks

Commercial banks have significantly increased their participation in the mortgage market during the past two years, both as purchasers of mortgage securities and as mortgage originators. In 1987, commercial banks were the second largest originator of single-family mortgages, capturing a 28 percent market share. Furthermore, these institutions accounted for more than half of all commercial and farm originations. Like thrifts, commercial banks benefit from the interest earned on mortgages relative to funding costs, as well as origination and servicing fees.

Historically, commercial banks had no specific incentives to invest in single-family mortgages, and their share of the primary market was relatively small. However, recent developments in the banking industry have encouraged banks to increase their holdings of mortgage assets. For example, the problems caused by loans to

Third World countries and to real estate developers in economically depressed areas have highlighted the importance of high-quality assets, as well as high-yielding assets.

Of particular significance, in 1988, the Federal Reserve Board adopted risk-based capital standards for U.S. banks and bank holding companies, as part of a historic step by the major industrialized nations to establish a consistent international framework to govern bank capital adequacy. Single-family residential mortgages receive favorable treatment under the risk-based capital guidelines. The capital level for high-quality single-family first mortgages will be only half the capital requirement for many other assets, including commercial mortgages, automobile loans, and credit card receivables. For agency pass-throughs, the risk-based capital levels are even more advantageous; they match those of direct government and government-sponsored agency obligations. The new capital adequacy guidelines create a backdrop for even greater participation in the mortgage market, as commercial banks seek to achieve high earnings while maintaining sufficient capital reserves.

Mortgage Bankers

The postwar evolution of an effective secondary market for mortgages and mortgage-backed securities has enabled mortgage bankers to originate a healthy volume of single-family mortgages. In 1987, for example, they accounted for about a quarter of all single-family mortgage originations. Unlike thrifts, most of which hold large portfolios of mortgage investments, mortgage bankers sell virtually all of the mortgages that they originate—either in the form of whole loans or as mortgage pass-through securities. The earnings of mortgage bankers come from origination fees, service fees, and profits on the sales of the securities.

Historically, mortgage bankers have sought to originate FHA and VA mortgages because of their greater marketability and lower risk of default. Most single-family FHA and VA loans are originated by mortgage bankers, and the vast majority of such loans are packaged into GNMA pass-through securities. However, with the development of FHLMC and FNMA programs that provide secondary markets for conventional mortgages, mortgage bankers have dramatically expanded their originations of conventional loans.

THE SECONDARY MORTGAGE MARKET

Any transaction that involves the buying, selling, or packaging of a mortgage after it has been originated takes place in the secondary mortgage market. This market creates liquidity for loans originated in the primary market; hence, it reduces the risk of holding mortgages and mortgage securities. It also increases the availability of capital market funds to housing and, thus, helps to lower the cost of housing finance. The original function of the secondary market was to move funds among traditional mortgage lenders, such as thrifts. Lenders that faced a demand for mortgages that was greater than their deposited funds could sell their loan assets in the secondary market and use the proceeds to originate more loans; lenders with limited demand for mortgages could buy such loans or securities backed by the loans. In recent decades, for example, population and housing demand expanded rapidly in the southern and western United States, and mortgage demand exceeded the supply of funds. In the northern and eastern parts of the country, the population grew more slowly, and the supply of mortgage funds exceeded demand. The secondary market has enabled funds to flow to where they are needed and has served to keep originators' surplus funds invested in residential mortgages.

A second function of the secondary mortgage market is to channel funds to originators from investors that traditionally have not invested in mortgages. Before the development of GNMA pass-through securities in 1970, this transfer of funds was quite limited. There were some sales of loans or pools of loans—primarily by mortgage banks to insurance companies. In general, however, their illiquidity, their lack of standardization, and the need to evaluate their credit on a pool-by-pool basis made mortgage whole loans unappealing to institutional investors.

Mortgage-Backed Securities

The development of mortgage-backed securities has fundamentally altered the secondary mortgage market. Although securitization does not eliminate the uncertainty of the underlying mortgage cash flows, mortgage-backed securities counter many of the negative investment characteristics of mortgage whole loans. For example, the standardization of the mortgages in a pool and the statistical information provided by the issuer simplify analysis and evaluation of the loans. Securities can be issued with quarterly or semiannual payment schedules, which open the mortgage market to investors that do not have the capability to process monthly payments. The U.S. agency guaranties carried by most mortgage-backed securities remove concerns about the creditworthiness of the borrower or the originator of the underlying loans. For these and other reasons, institutions that would not invest in mortgage whole loans find mortgage-backed securities to be attractive alternatives to government and corporate bonds.

The term "mortgage-backed security" refers to a large and diverse group of instruments. The most important kinds of mortgage securities are pass-through securities; mortgage-backed bonds; cash flow bonds, such as CMOs; and strips.

Pass-Through Securities

The pass-through is by far the most common structure for mortgage-backed securities. The name is appropriate because the servicer of a pool of mortgages collects the borrowers' monthly payments and, after deducting a fee, remits or passes them through to the security holders. A pass-through issuer acquires the mortgages either by originating them or purchasing them in the whole loan market. Many mortgages with similar characteristics are collected into a pool, and undivided ownership interests in the pool are then sold as pass-through certificates. The undivided interest entitles the owner of the security to a pro rata share of all interest payments and all scheduled or prepaid principal payments.

The Federal Housing Finance Agencies

The popularity of the pass-through is due, in large part, to the active role of the U.S. housing agencies in the primary and secondary mortgage security markets. GNMA, FHLMC, and FNMA now account for nearly all pass-through issuances and an even greater portion of the outstanding principal amount (see Figures 18-10 and 18-11). The rest of the issuance is privately backed.

Figure 18-10. Issuance of Agency Pass-Throughts, 1970–1987 (Dollars in Billions)

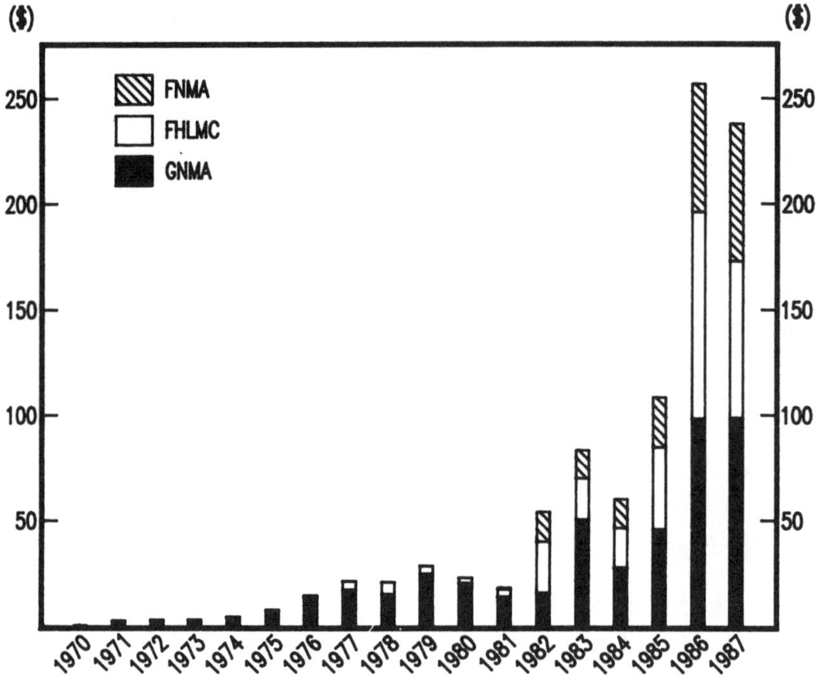

Sources: GNMA, FHLMC, and FNMA

The programs of the three major federal housing agencies reflect the historical development of U.S. housing policy. FNMA was created in 1938 as a wholly owned government corporation. Its charter mandated that it purchase FHA-insured (and, since 1948, VA-guaranteed) mortgages for its portfolio. The intent of Congress was to ensure that mortgage lenders would continue to be able to make residential mortgage loans, even in periods of disintermediation (when withdrawals by depositors are high) or periods of high levels of delinquencies and defaults. FNMA's purchase activities encouraged the standardization of repayment contracts and credit underwriting procedures for mortgages. In 1968, the government's role in the housing finance market was restructured. FNMA was privatized, although it retained its mandate to buy FHA/VA loans for its own portfolio. GNMA was spun off as a separate agency to undertake some

Figure 18-11. Outstanding Mortgage Pass-Through Securities, June 1988 (Dollars in Billions)

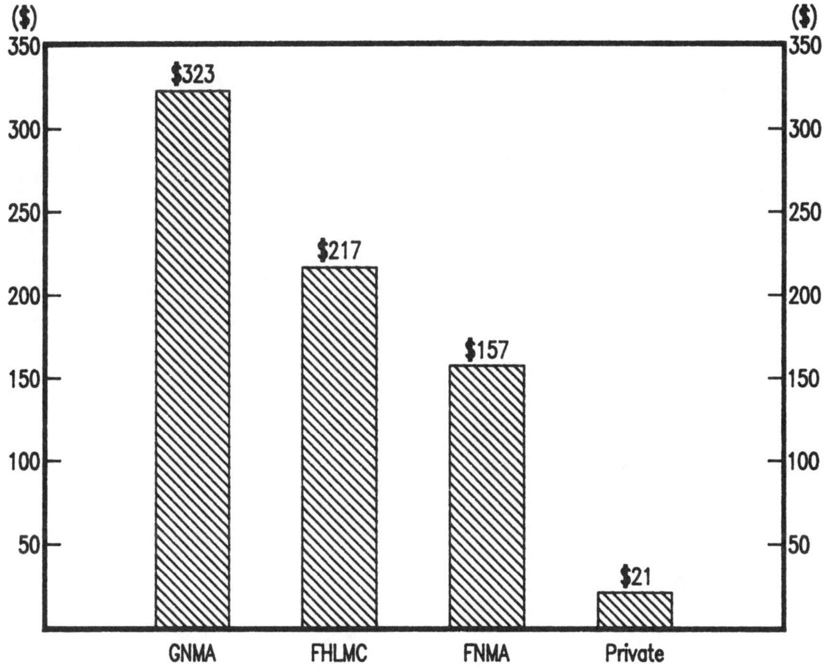

Sources: GNMA, FHLMC, FNMA, and Salomon Brothers Inc.

of FNMA's previous activities; in particular, GNMA took over the financing of home loans not ordinarily underwritten by the established mortgage markets, such as loans to low-income families. GNMA's most important activity has been its mortgage pass-through program, which was instituted in 1970. Under this program, GNMA guarantees the payments of principal and interest on pools of FHA-insured or VA-guaranteed mortgage loans.

The enhanced availability of credit to home owners that qualify for FHA and VA loans led to calls for similar treatment for conventional mortgage credit. In 1970, Congress established FHLMC to develop an active secondary market for conventional loans. In 1972, FNMA also began to purchase conventional mortgages. Thus, by 1972, lenders could sell their newly originated conventional mortgages to either FNMA or FHLMC. FHLMC assembles pools of conventional loans purchased from lenders and securitizes them by issuing pass-through securities called participation certificates (PCs). PCs are then sold at auction to a group of investment bankers that act as primary distributors and secondary market makers for these securities. In contrast, FNMA continued to fund its mortgage purchases throughout the 1970s by issuing debt.

The market for PCs from FHLMC's traditional program, or Cash Program,[7] became well established as an outlet for newly originated loans during the 1970s. Nevertheless, this program did not address the mismatch between seasoned long-term loan assets and short-term liabilities of thrift institutions. To help thrifts increase the liquidity of these seasoned loans, FHLMC introduced its Guarantor Program, or swap program, in July 1981.

Under the Guarantor Program, FHLMC guarantees the payments on a pool of mortgages, much as GNMA guarantees its pass-throughs. Loans in the lender's portfolio are exchanged or swapped with FHLMC for FHLMC-guaranteed securities backed by the same mortgages. The Guarantor Program allows lenders to securitize loans of any age.

In November 1981, FNMA began a similar swap program. Pass-throughs issued by FNMA are called FNMA mortgage-backed secuities. Although FNMA does issue securities backed by mortgages that it has purchased for its own portfolio, the majority of its mortgage-backed securities are issued under this swap program.

Both the FNMA and FHLMC swap programs now encompass both conventional and FHA/VA loans. Thrifts have, thus, been able to convert a significant amount of their seasoned loans into mortgage securities, which can be sold in the secondary market or held in portfolio. The swapping of whole loans for FHLMC or FNMA pass-throughs can be beneficial to lenders even when they do not intend to sell the securities because, unlike whole mortgage loans, agency-guaranteed mortgage securities can readily be used as collateral for reverse repurchase agreements. Hence, by swapping mortgages for securities, thrifts open an important source of short-term financing.[8]

[7]The FHLMC Cash Program is so named because originators receive cash from FHLMC in return for their mortgages. The program is also known as the regular, standard, or baseline program.

[8]See M. D. Youngblood and Irvin Goldman, *The Mortgage Repurchase Agreement, 1980–86: The Evolution of the Instrument and the Market* (New York: Salomon Brothers Inc., 1987).

Agency Pass-Throughs

GNMA, FNMA, and FHLMC mortgage pass-through securities are similar in many ways. Nevertheless, investors should be aware of the differences in the way in which the securities are created and distributed; in the nature of the guaranty to security holders; and in the rules for pooling, payment delay, and delivery.

Creation and Distribution

GNMA pass-through securities are guaranteed by GNMA, but they are issued by a large number of GNMA-approved originators. These originators assemble FHA-insured or VA-guaranteed mortgages into packages (of typically $1 million or more), which are then placed in the custody of a trustee. Upon acceptance of a statement from the trustee that the loan documents are in good order, GNMA provides the originator with a GNMA pool number, which identifies the security to be issued. The mortgage originator then issues pass-through securities, which are ordinarily sold to investment bankers for distribution to institutional investors, regional dealers, and retail investors.

In 1983, GNMA supplemented its original pass-through program with a second program called GNMA II.[9] Under the new program, a central paying and transfer agent (Chemical Bank of New York) consolidates all payments due to the security holder into one monthly check. In contrast, the GNMA I security holder receives a separate monthly check for each security owned. The advantage of receiving one monthly check is offset by the fact that GNMA II securities make monthly payments five days later than GNMA I securities do.

Again, FHLMC and FNMA securities are issued by the agencies themselves, either by pooling mortgages from agency portfolios or by using swap programs. Most of the FHLMC Cash Program pools comprise mortgages purchased from many lenders. By comparison, like GNMA pass-throughs, FHLMC and FNMA swap securities are generally backed by mortgages from a single lender, although both agencies recently instituted multilender swap programs.

Guaranties

The agency guaranties vary in certain respects, but all of them ensure payment of the interest and principal due to the security

[9]The original GNMA pass-through program is now known as GNMA I.

holder. GNMA guarantees full and timely payment of both principal and interest, and this guaranty is backed by the full faith and credit of the U.S. government. As noted, all loans pooled into GNMA pass-throughs are either FHA insured or VA guaranteed, and GNMA securities absorb almost all single-family FHA/VA mortgages.

Most FHLMC mortgage securities carry a guaranty of timely payment of interest and ultimate payment of principal.[10] In 1985, FHLMC introduced a program that guarantees timely payment of principal, as well as interest. Strictly speaking, these guaranties are backed by FHLMC itself; thus, they do not carry the full faith and credit of the U.S. Treasury. On the other hand, FHLMC can use the Federal Home Loan Bank System to obtain funds. Furthermore, the FHLMC board of directors can require the Federal Home Loan Banks to guarantee FHLMC debt, although this authority has never been exercised. Therefore, investors regard FHLMC securities as having the strong credit of a government agency.

Like GNMA pass-throughs, FNMA mortgage-backed securities carry the guaranty of full and timely payment of both principal and interest. Like FHLMC, FNMA backs its own guarantee, and investors perceive it as an agency credit on the grounds that it is regulated by both the HUD and the U.S. Treasury. Moreover, FNMA has a $2.25 billion line of credit with the Treasury, which, to date, has never been used.

Pooling, Payment Delay, and Delivery

In general, the agency programs segregate loans into pools by type of property (single family or multifamily), payment schedule (level, graduated, or adjustable rate), original maturity, and mortgage interest rate.

GNMA requires the greatest homogeneity of mortgages within a pool. Pools may include only one type of loan, such as single-family level-payment mortgages. The loans must be recently originated mortgages.[11] Single-family pools must be made up primarily of either

[10]If a borrower is delinquent or in default, part of the scheduled prinicpal payment to the security holder could be delayed. FHLMC rules provide that all principal must, nonetheless, be passed through to the security holder as soon as it is received by FHLMC from the mortgage lender.

[11]The first scheduled monthly payment on each loan in a GNMA pool must not be more than two years prior to the issue date of the pool.

15-year loans or 30-year loans.[12] Finally, in a GNMA I pool, all mortgage loans must bear the same interest rate; for single-family pools, this interest rate is 0.5 percent higher than the pass-through rate or security coupon. The 0.5 percent spread comprises service fees and GNMA's guaranty fee. Under the GNMA II program, the servicing guaranty spread may vary from 0.5 percent to 1.5 percent.[13]

The mortgages that make up FHLMC and FNMA pools are considerably more heterogeneous. For example, FHLMC single-family pools may include a limited number of multifamily loans.[14] Both FHLMC and FNMA conventional mortgage pools may include seasoned loans, as well as recent originations.[15] Finally, the underlying loans for FHLMC Guarantor Program securities may have coupons that are 2.5 percent above the pass-through rate. FNMA pools can include mortgages with coupons that vary by as much as 2 percent, but the range of loan coupons for FHLMC Cash Program pools is limited to 1 percent.

The agency programs specify different payment schedules after a security is issued. The servicers of mortgage pools must collect payments from many borrowers, process them, and then send pro rata shares to the security holders. To allow time to carry out these functions, mortgage pass-through securities are customarily structured with a payment delay.

For example, for GNMA I securities, security holders receive their first payment 45 days—rather than 30 days—after the security is issued; there is a payment delay of 15 days. Similarly, there are 50

[12]Technically, GNMA requires that 90% of the original principal amount of each pool be either in mortgages with maturities of 20 years or more or with maturities of less than 20 years. For GNMA pools backed by mortgages that have maturities of less than 20 years, at least 90% of the original principal amount of the pool must be in mortgages with the same original term, and that term must be the longest term of any loan in the pool.

[13]For a definitive listing of the eligibility requirements for mortgages in a GNMA I pool, see *GNMA I Mortgage-Backed Securities Guide,* Handbook GNMA 5500.1 Washington, D.C.: U.S. Department of Housing and Urban Development, 19XX). For GNMA II pools, see *GNMA II Mortgage-Backed Securities Guide*, Handbook GNMA 5500.2 (Washington, D.C.: U.S. Department of Housing and Urban Development).

[14]As much as 5% of the principal amount of the pool may be in multifamily loans. Such loans are excluded from single-family GNMA and FNMA pools. GNMA single-family pools may include mortgages on cooperatives, but both FHLMC and FNMA single-family pools exclude them. Each of the agency mortgage-backed security programs allows mortgages on condominium properties to be included in single-family pools.

[15]FHA/VA loans pooled by FNMA must be originated at least 12 months before the issue date of the pool.

days to first payment for GNMA II pools, 54 days for FNMA mortgage-backed securities, and 75 days for FHLMC PCs.

Pass-through securities can be delivered either physically or in book-entry form. Book-entry delivery is now made by registering the transfer of ownership in the electronic records of a central clearing bank. Securities that can be cleared in this way are called wirable securities. Almost all FHLMC and FNMA securities are delivered in book-entry form. Most GNMA pass-thoughs are still delivered physically, although conversion to book-entry clearing is under way.

The basic features of the agency mortgage-backed security programs are summarized in Table 18-1. The various pool categories within each program appear in the appendix to this chapter.

Private Pass-Throughs

Private, or nonagency, pass-through security programs create a secondary market for nonconforming mortgages—that is, conventional loans that fail to meet the size limits or other purchase requirements of FHLMC or FNMA.[16] These programs have grown substantially in recent years: In 1987, issuance totaled $9.4 billion, up sharply from $4.8 billion in 1985. Most private pass-throughs carry AA ratings and typically trade at a yield premium of 30–40 basis points over the agency pass-through market.

In general, these securities have substantial credit safeguards. First, issuers enforce strict underwriting criteria. Second, the risk of substantial credit loss is reduced by diversification: Pools comprise large numbers of mortgages, often from different regions of the country. Finally, to obtain the AA rating,[17] several layers of private insurance are required by the rating agencies.

[16]The maximum size of conventional mortgages eligible for the FHLMC or FNMA programs is set every year, according to a formula specified by Congress; in most parts of the United States, the current maximum for mortgages on single-family units is $168,700.

[17]For example, primary mortgage insurance is required for certain mortgage loans with high LTV ratios. MOrtgage pool insurance covers a certain percentage of loss caused byloan defaults. Additional insurance covers loss due to fraud or misreprresentation in the mortgage loan application. A bankruptcy bond covers certain losses that can result from the reduction by a bankruptcy court of the principal or of scheduled interest and principal payments. Finally, special hazard insurance covers a limited amount of losses due to physical causes, such as earthquakes, mud flows, and floods, that are not otherwise covered.

Table 18-1. Agency Pass-Through Programs

	GNMA I	*GNMA II*	*FHLMC*	*FNMA*
Issuer	FHA-approved lender	FHA-approved lender(s) (single-issuer and multiple-issuer pools)	FHLMC	FNMA
Underlying mortgages	FHA/VA	FHA/VA	Conventional or FHA/VA	Conventional or FHA/VA
Guarantee	Full and timely payment of principal and interest	Full and timely payment of principal and interest	Full and timely payment of interest and eventual full payment of principal, or full and timely payment of principal and interest (separate programs)	Full and timely payment of principal and interest
Guarantor	GNMA (full faith and credit of U.S. government)	GNMA (full faith and credit of U.S. government)	FHLMC	FNMA
Monthly payment	Multiple checks, one for each certificate[1]	One check per investor for all holdings[1]	Federal funds	Federal funds
Delivery	Physical (definitive) certificate; settlement in federal funds[1]	Physical (definitive) certificate; settlement in federal funds[1]	Book entry through Federal Reserve Banks; settlement in federal funds	Book entry through Federal Reserve Banks; settlement in federal funds
Days to first payment	45	50	75	54
Denomination	$25,000 minimum, $5,000 increment	$25,000 minimum, $5,000 increment	$25,000 minimum	$25,000 minimum, $5,000 increment

[1]Conversion to book-entry system through Mortgage-Backed Securities Clearing Corp. now under way. Monthly payments and settlement after conversion are made in federal funds.

Structured Securities

In spite of the dramatic success of the mortgage pass-through market, the cash flow characteristics of pass-throughs still present problems for many institutional investors. To broaden the range of investors, a variety of mortgage-backed instruments has been created.

Mortgage-Backed Bonds

One of the earliest securities that was developed to meet this objective was the mortgage-backed bond, a debt obligation of the issuer that is secured by mortgages. The issuer of a mortgage-backed bond retains ownership of the collateral. In contrast, the issuer of a pass-through security sells investors pro rata shares of the underlying mortgages.

Because a mortgage-backed bond is secured by pledged mortgage collateral, the credit of the issuer is not of major importance in the evaluation of these securities. However, the investor should pay careful attention to the structure of the issue, the type of collateral, and the degree of overcollateralization. Newly issued mortgage-backed bonds are always substantially overcollaterized to ensure that the market value of the collateral does not fall below the value of the bonds. Overcollateralization is necessary because the value of the collateral will fluctuate with changing interest rates and will, in any case, decrease over time as the outstanding principal of the mortgage collateral declines.

The cash flow properties of mortgage-backed bonds are essentially the same as those of traditional corporate or government issues. Interest is paid semiannually at a predetermined rate, and principal is due on a stated maturity date or according to a specified sinking fund schedule. Because the payments of the bonds are not

[17]For example, primary mortgage insurance is required for certain mortgage loans with high LTV ratios. Mortgage pool insurance covers a certain percentage of loss caused by loan defaults. Additional insurance covers loss due to fraud or misrepresentation in the mortgage loan application. A bankruptcy bond covers certain losses that can result from the reduction by a bankruptcy court of the principal or of scheduled interest and principal payments. Finally, special hazard insurance covers a limited amount of losses due to physical causes, such as earthquakes, mud flows, and floods, that are not otherwise covered.

linked directly to the cash flows of the underlying mortgages, the uncertainties of cash flow and final maturity, which are associated with the mortgage pass-through, are absent. The semiannual payment schedule of mortgage-backed bonds also reduces reinvestment risk.

Collateralized Thrift Floating-Rate Notes

The collateralized thrift floating-rate note is a mortgage-backed bond whose rate is reset regularly at a predetermined spread to a stated interest rate index. These issues may also include such features as interest rate caps and collars.[18] Collateralized floating-rate notes became popular as low-cost obligations that enabled thrift issuers to broaden their investor base. In particular, collateralized floating-rate notes tied to the London Interbank Offered Rate (LIBOR) opened a market for thrift debt in Europe. Floating-rate notes have also been sold in the U.S. domestic market.

To date, all publicly issued thrift floating-rate notes have received AAA ratings. To achieve this rating, the issuer maintains collateral on deposit with a trustee; the collateral required is typically 110–200 percent of the principal balance of the notes, plus accrued interest. The type of pledged collateral and the frequency with which it is marked to market determines the collateralization level. Thrift floating-rate notes are usually backed by mortgage securities and U.S. government securities, although the collateral can also include mortgage loans, money market instruments, and cash.

Cash Flow Bonds and CMOs

A mortgage cash flow bond shares properties of both the mortgage pass-through and the mortgage-backed bond. The overcollateralization of a cash flow bond is typically much smaller than that of a mortgage-backed bond because the payments from the cash flow bond are linked more closely to those of the underlying mortgages. However, an issuer of a cash flow bond can modify the stream of interest and principal payments to meet the needs of different investors.

[18]See Jay M. Weintraub and Gioia M. Parente, *Collateralized Thrift Floating-Rate Notes: Structure and Credit Factors* (New York: Salomon Brothers Inc., 1986).

Figure 18-12. CMO Issuance, 1983–1988 (Dollars in Billions)

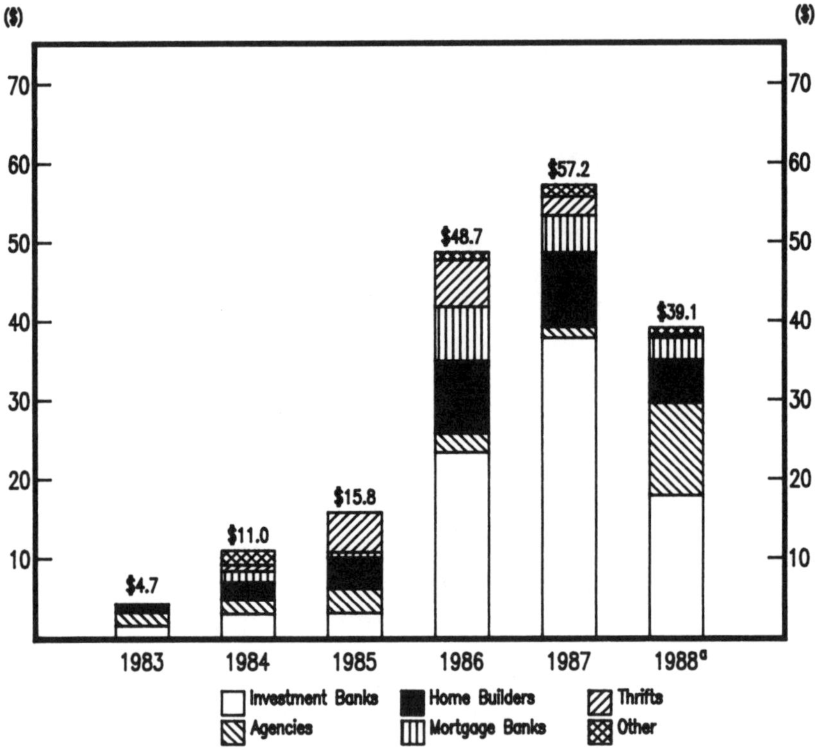

Source: Salomon Brothers, Inc.

The most popular form of cash flow bond to date is the CMO. FHLMC issued the first CMO in June 1983; as of June 1988, more than $175 billion of issues had been brought to market by FHLMC and FNMA, investment bankers, mortgage bankers, builders, thrifts, insurance companies, and commercial banks (see Figure 18-12).

CMOs comprise several classes of bonds issued against a pool of mortgage collateral. A common CMO structure includes four classes: The first three pay interest at stated rates beginning with the issue date, and the final one is an interest accrual bond, or Z bond.[19] The classes, or tranches, of bonds that make up a CMO are retired

[19]The Z bond represents a special CMO class. Z bond investors receive no principal or interest payments while the other classes are outstanding. Instead, the interest earned on a Z bond is added to its principal balance, so that this balance grows on a compound basis at the coupon rate. After all of the earlier classes have been retired, the cash flows from the remaining collateral are directed to make principal and interest payments to the Z bond holders (see Figure 18-13).

Figure 18-13. CMO Cash Flows (CMO Trust 28 167% PSA [1]Dollars in Millions)

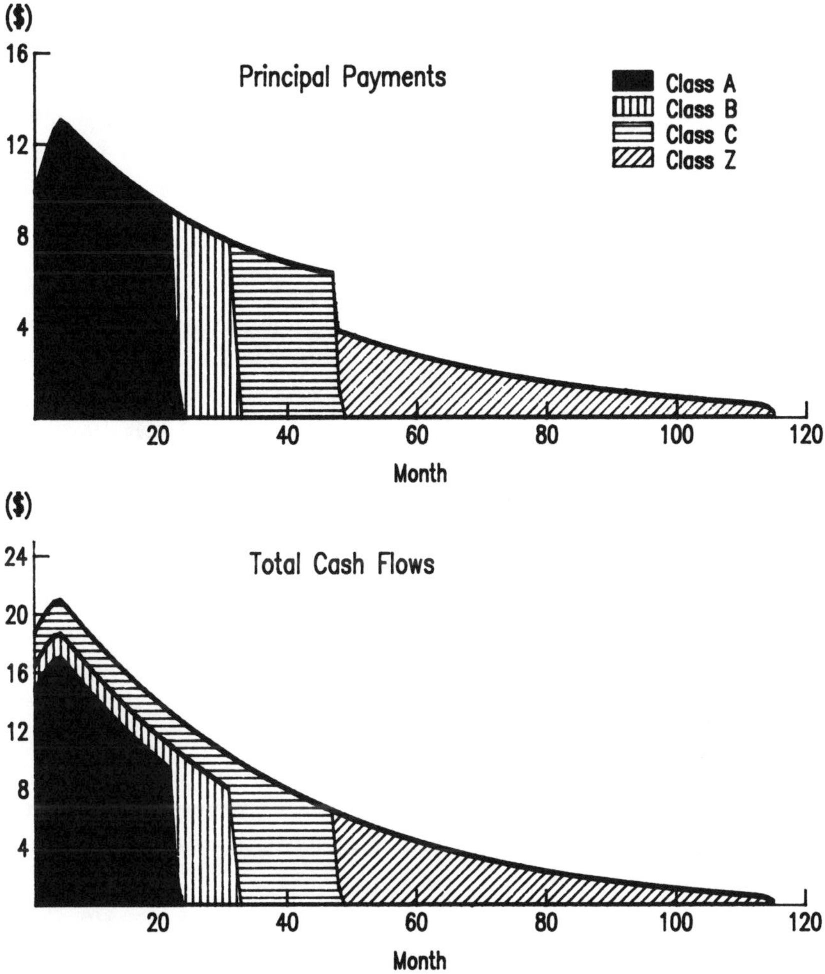

[1]Prepayments assumed at 167 percent of the Public Securities Association Standard prepayment model. See Salomon Bothers Inc., *A New Prepayment Benchmark for CMOs—The PSA Model* (New York: Salomon Brothers Inc., 1985).

sequentially. All principal payments are directed first to the bonds with the shortest maturity—the Class A bonds. When the Class A bonds are retired, the principal payments are directed to the bonds with the next shortest maturity—the Class B bonds. This process continues until all of the bond classes have been paid off. The allocation of cash flows from a pool of mortgages among the classes of a CMO is illustrated in Figure 18-13.

CMOs retain the credit quality and yield advantages of mortgage pass-throughs, while offering investors a variety of payment schedules, a range of maturities, and a limited form of call protection that enables investors to avoid some of the reinvestment risks associated with the early paydown of the underlying mortgages. The development of CMOs has opened the mortgage market to investors that are not equipped to handle monthly payment schedules and irregular mortgage cash flows, as well as to those that seek securities with maturities that are more targeted than those of mortgage pass-throughs.[20]

The CMO structure has also proved to be a flexible tool for designing securities that meet the special needs of particular investor groups. For example, since September 1986, a number of CMOs have been issued with floating-rate classes, whose coupons are reset at spreads over LIBOR. These floating-rate CMOs appeal to many European and Japanese investors.[21]

Two CMO investments, the planned amortization class (PAC) and the targeted amortization class (TAC), were recently introduced to meet investor demand for even more certain cash flows. A PAC bond provides a fixed monthly payment as long as the prepayment rates of the underlying collateral fall within a predetermined range. This cash flow stability is achieved by giving the principal payments of the PAC bonds a higher priority than those of the other CMO classes. TACs also have an assigned redemption schedule, based on the inclusion of support classes in the CMO structure. TACs differ from PACs in that their prepayment protection is asymmetric. TACs enjoy call protection similar to that of PACs, but will lengthen if prepayments are slower than expected.[22]

CMO Residuals

CMO residuals, or equity, are the cash flow available from the underlying collateral in excess of a CMO's required debt service and

[20]For a review of CMOs, see Salomon Brothers Inc., *An Investor's Guide to CMOs* (New York: Salomon Brothers Inc., 1986).

[21]See M. D. Youngblood and Gioia M. Parente, *The Floating-Rate CMO and the Eurodollar FRN* (New York: Salomon Brothers Inc., 1987).

[22]See Robert A. Kulason and Michael Waldman, *Understanding TAC and PAC CMO Structures,* (New York: Salomon Brothers Inc., 1988).

operating expenses.[23] This excess cash flow comes largely from the spread between the interest rate of the collateral and the coupons of the CMO tranches. Other sources of CMO residuals arise from the conservative prepayment and reinvestment assumptions required for AAA ratings. Actual prepayment and reinvestment rates are usually more favorable than the assumed rates, which generates excess cash flows. Finally, cash available from a bond reserve fund can also flow to CMO residual investors.

CMO residuals typically offer high yields as compensation for the variability of their returns and their relative lack of liquidity. In general, most of the return from a CMO residual comes during the first years, when the coupon spread between the collateral and the CMO tranches is greatest—that is, the cash flows to the investor are front loaded. Because CMO residuals are highly sensitive to the prepayment rate of the underlying collateral, their cash flow patterns and rates of return can vary widely under different interest rate scenarios.

The investment features of CMO residuals depend on the structure of the particular CMO. For example, the residual from a fixed-rate CMO generally has a bearish return pattern. Its value rises when interest rates rise and falls when interest rates fall, providing a hedge against the interest rate risk of traditional fixed-income securities. On the other hand, the return from the residual of a floating-rate CMO is typically greatest in a stable market and falls in market moves in either direction. This return pattern reflects the sensitivity of the residual cash flows to changes in LIBOR, as well as to changes in prepayment rates.

Strips

Mortgage strips are created by dividing the cash flows from a pool of mortgages or mortgage securities and allocating specified percentages of interest and principal to each new strip. For example, a FNMA 9 percent pass-through can be stripped to produce two securities—one with a 6 percent coupon and the other with a 12 percent coupon—simply by directing more of the interest from the

[23]See M. D. Youngblood, *A Perspective on CMO Equity* (New York: Salomon Brothers Inc., 1986).

underlying collateral to the higher coupon and less of the interest to the lower coupon. By varying the ratio of interest to principal, strips with a wide range of coupons and performance characteristics can be created.

The performance of a mortgage strip differs markedly from that of a standard pass-through with the same coupon because of the effect of prepayments. A 12 percent strip backed by FNMA 9 percent collateral will have much slower prepayments than a 12 percent FNMA pass-through. Conversely, a 6 percent strip backed by the same 9 percent collateral will have much faster prepayments than a 6 percent FNMA pass-through.

The predominant mortgage strips—and the most elementary—are interest-only (IO) and principal-only (PO) strips.[24] IO strips receive all of the interest payments from the underlying collateral and none of the principal. Conversely, PO strips receive all of the principal and none of the interest.

The price movements of IO and PO strips are extremely sensitive to changes in interest rates. This sensitivity can be explained largely in terms of how prepayments respond to interest rate movements (see Figure 18-14). Falling interest rates lead to faster prepayments because an increasing number of home owners buy new homes or refinance their mortgages. In contrast, rising interest rates result in slower prepayment rates.

Faster prepayments reduce the principal balance of the underlying collateral more rapidly, which leads to smaller interest payments in future periods but returning principal (at par) at a faster rate. Hence, when interest rates fall and prepayments accelerate, IO strips decrease in value and PO strips increase in value. On the other hand, when interest rates rise and prepayments slow, IO strips increase in value and PO strips decrease in value.

The unusual return characteristics of IO/PO strips make them useful instruments for hedging either prepayment risk or interest rate risk. They can also be combined with other strips or pass-throughs to create synthetic securities with certain desired investment features. On the other hand, IO/PO strips are more volatile than other mortgage securities, and investors need to be fully aware of their risks, as well as their benefits.

[24]See Michael Waldman, Mark Gordon, and K. Jeanne Person, *Interest Only and Principal Only STRIPs* (New York: Salomon Brothers Inc., 1987).

Figure 18-14. Projected Price Paths—FNMA 9 Percent IOs and POs, September 30, 1988

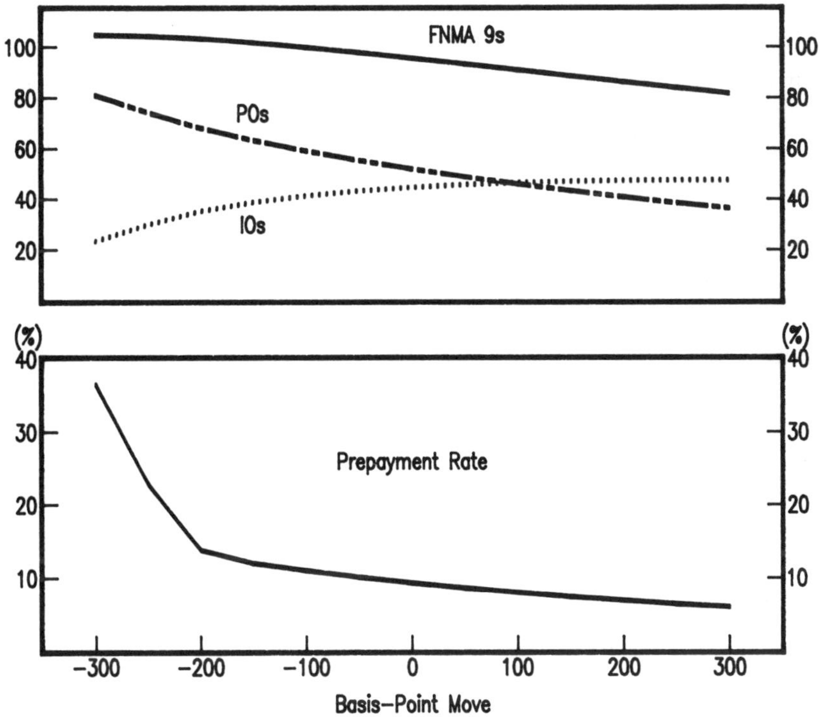

REMICs

The development of derivative mortgage securities led to strong demand for a more flexible legal entity to issue them. In particular, until 1986, cumbersome procedures were imposed on the issuance of CMOs, which had to be structured as debt obligations of the issuer to comply with Internal Revenue Service regulations. Because a debt issue appears as a liability on the issuer's balance sheet, this requirement created accounting and regulatory problems for a number of potential issuers. Moreover, to ensure that CMOs qualified as true debt instruments according to Internal Revenue Service criteria, certain structural inefficiencies were built into CMOs. These inefficiencies limited the amount of CMO bonds that could be issued against a particular pool of mortgage collateral.

The Tax Reform Act of 1986 addressed such difficulties with a new kind of structured financing vehicle, known as a real estate mortgage investment conduit (REMIC).[25] Multiple-class mortgage securities issued as REMICs qualify as asset sales for tax purposes. The new REMIC format also eliminates the need for the structural inefficiencies required for CMOs and provides issuers with considerable flexibility to create new types of mortgage securities tailored to meet specific investor needs.

From the investor's perspective, REMICs offer several advantages over CMOs. For example, REMICs backed by residential loans qualify as mortgage assets for the special thrift bad debt reserve tax deduction. REMICs backed by residential or commercial loans are eligible real estate investments for real estate investment trusts. Furthermore, some investors may consider the credit quality of REMICs structured as multiclass pass-throughs to be superior to that of a comparable CMO. Investors in REMIC multiclass pass-throughs will own a share in the collateral, whereas CMO investors own a bond secured by the mortgages. Finally, investors may now choose from an impressive range of REMIC investments, including fixed-rate securities of various coupons, maturities, and payment frequencies; senior/subordinated issues; floaters, inverse floaters, and super floaters; IO/PO strips and super POs; PAC and TAC bonds, and residuals.

CONCLUSION

The introduction of the mortgage pass-through security was a revolutionary development for the U.S. mortgage market. Pass-throughs have enabled capital market investors that are not traditionally involved in this market to invest in residential mortgages. As a result, the supply of funds available for housing finance has increased, and mortgage interest rates have been lower than would otherwise have been possible.

The annual issuance of mortgage pass-through securities and securities derived from pass-throughs—particularly CMOs—reached record levels during 1986–1987. While the volume of new pass-throughs slowed in 1988, the creation of derivative securities con-

[25]See Kenneth T. Rosen, *The Impact of Tax Reform on the Mortgage Market* (New York: Salomon Brothers Inc., 1986) and Salomon Brothers Inc., *REMICs: The Tax Bill Creates a New Opportunity in the Mortgage Securities Market,* (New York: Salomon Brothers Inc., 1986).

tinued to surge. Indeed, the latter part of the 1980s has become an era of derivative mortgage products. The outstanding supplies of mortgages and mortgage pass-throughs are being repackaged in increasingly sophisticated ways, which provides for an expanding variety of investment applications. Moreover, the concepts developed for residential mortgages are being extended to other kinds of debt. For example, commercial mortgages, automobile loans, and credit card receivables are now being securitized.[26]

Another important trend in the late 1980s has been the internationalization of the mortgage security market. U.S. mortgage securities have attracted growing demand from European and Japanese investors. At the same time, mortgage security markets in other countries—notably Great Britain, Canada, and Australia—are emerging. As new investors are drawn into these markets, increased competition worldwide will accelerate the already rapid pace of innovation.

[26]See K. Jeanne Person, *A Review of Asset-Backed Securities* (New York: Salomon Brothers Inc., 1987); Michael Waldman, *Certificates for Automobile Receivables (CARS)* (New York: Salomon Brothers Inc., 1986); and Michael Waldman, *Introduction to Credit Card-Backed Securities* (New York: Salomon Brothers Inc., 1986). For a discussion of the primary and secondary markets for commercial mortgages, see, David J. Hartzell and Susan Jordan, *Commercial Mortgage-Backed Securities: Investors' Primer* (New York: Salomon Brothers Inc., 1987) and J. Steven Manolis and Gregory A. White, *The Beginning of Commercial Mortgage Securitization: Olympia & York Floating-Rate Notes* (New York: Salomon Brothers Inc., 1985).

APPENDIX: AGENCY PASS-THROUGH CATEGORIES

Code[1]	*Pool Type*[2]
AR	Adjustable-rate mortgages, GNMA II only.
BD	Buy-down mortgages, GNMA I only.
CL	FHA project construction loan, GNMA I only. Construction loan securities pay interest monthly and are generally converted into project loan securities at maturity.
GA	Growing-equity mortgages on which monthly payments increase by 4% annually over the life of the loans.
GD	Growing-equity mortgages on which monthly payments increase annually at any rate for any number of years.
GP	Graduated-payment mortgages on which monthly payments increase annually for five years or less.
GT	Graduated-payment mortgages on which monthly payments increase annually for ten years or less.
MH	Manufactured home loans, GNMA I only.
PL	FHA project loan, level payment, GNMA I only.
PN	FHA project loan, nonlevel payment, GNMA I only.
SF	Level-payment mortgages, maximum 30-year and maximum 20-year (typically 15-year) original maturities.
SN	Serial notes backed by single-family mortgages, GNMA I only.
14, 33, 45, 48	FHA/VA level-payment mortgages, Guarantor Program.
15	FHA/VA level-payment mortgages, Cash Program.
16, 17, 36	Conventional level-payment mortgages, Cash Program.
18, 25-30, 43, 46	Conventional level-payment mortgages, Guarantor Program.
20, 38	Conventional level-payment mortgages, maximum 15-year original maturities, Cash Program.
21, 32, 44, 47, 50	Conventional level-payment mortgages, maximum 15-year original maturities, Guarantor Program.

[1]FHLMC and FNMA use the two-character codes as prefixes to pool numbers.

[2]Underlying mortgages are single-family loans with maximum original maturities of 30 years, unless otherwise noted.

22	Conventional multifamily mortgages, 10- to 15-year maximum original maturities, Cash Program.
23	Conventional multifamily mortgages, Guarantor Program.
24	Conventional multifamily mortgages with final balloon payments, 15-year maximum original maturities, Guarantor Program.
26, 46	Conventional level-payment mortgages, Guarantor Program, FHLMC guaranty for full and timely payment of principal and interest.
31	Conventional multifamily variable-rate mortgages, Guarantor Program.
34	Conventional variable-rate mortgages, Guarantor Program.
35	Conventional adjustable-rate mortgages resetting off the one-year constant maturity Treasury rate, 2% annual rate caps, Cash Program.
39, 42	Conventional adjustable-rate mortgages resetting off the Eleventh District cost of funds index, Guarantor Program.
40	Conventional adjustable-rate mortgages resetting off the one-year constant maturity Treasury rate, 2% annual rate caps, convertible to fixed rate, Guarantor Program.
49	Conventional multifamily mortgages, maximum ten-year original maturities, Cash Program.
60	Conventional adjustable-rate mortgages resetting off the one-year constant maturity Treasury rate, 2% annual rate caps, Guarantor Program.
63	Conventional adjustable-rate mortgages resetting off the one-year constant maturity Treasury rate, 1% annual rate caps, convertible to fixed rate, Guarantor Program.
64	Conventional adjustable-rate mortgages resetting off the one-year constant maturity Treasury rate, 1% annual rate caps, Guarantor Program.
68	Conventional level-payment mortgages, one-time option to reduce the fixed rate beginning on the 12th month and ending on the 60th month of the loan, Guarantor Program.
71	Conventional adjustable-rate mortgages resetting off the one-year constant maturity Treasury rate, 2% annual rate caps, convertible to fixed rate, Cash Program.

77	Conventional adjustable-rate mortgages resetting off the Eleventh District cost of funds index, annual or semiannual rate caps, Guarantor Program.
79	Conventional adjustable-rate multifamily mortgages resetting off the Eleventh District cost of funds index, Guarantor Program.
80	Principal-only strips, conventional level-payment mortgages, Guarantor Program.
82	Principal-only strips, conventional level-payment mortgages, maximum 15-year original maturities, Guarantor Program.
86	Conventional adjustable-rate mortgages resetting off the three-year constant maturity Treasury rate, 2% periodic rate caps, Guarantor Program.
90	Interest-only strips, conventional level-payment mortgages, Guarantor Program.
92	Interest-only strips, conventional level-payment mortgages, maximum 15-year original maturities, Guarantor Program.
A2	Conventional adjustable-rate mortgages resetting off the one-year constant maturity Treasury rate, 2% annual rate caps.
AB	Alaska Housing conventional growing equity mortgages.
AC	Conventional adjustable-rate mortgages resetting off the one-year constant maturity Treasury rate, 2% annual rate caps, convertible to fixed rate any month beginning on the first annual reset date and ending on the fifth annual reset date.
AM	Conventional multifamily adjustable-rate mortgages.
AS	Conventional adjustable-rate mortgages.
AX	Conventional adjustable-rate mortgages resetting off the one-year constant maturity Treasury rate; 2% annual rate caps; convertible to fixed rate on the third, fourth, and fifth annual reset dates.
CA	Conventional level-payment mortgages, assumable.
CI	Conventional level-payment mortgages, maximum 15-year original maturities.
CL	Conventional level-payment mortgages.
CS	Conventional level-payment mortgages, maximum seven-year original maturities.
C3, C4, C5	Conventional growing-equity mortgages on which monthly payments increase by 3%, 4%, or 5% annually; fully amortizing within 8–15 years.

GC	Conventional graduated-payment mortgages.
GG	FHA/VA graduated-payment mortgages.
GL	FHA/VA level-payment mortgages.
MA	FHA level-payment project loans, fully amortizing within 40 years.
MI	Conventional multifamily level-payment mortgages, maximum 15-year original maturities.
ML	Conventional multifamily level-payment mortgages.
MX	Conventional multifamily balloon-payment mortgages.
RL	Conventional reverse buy-down mortgages.
VL	Conventional variable-rate mortgages, fully amortizing within 40 years.

CHAPTER 19

Commercial Mortgage-Backed Securities

Carl Kane

INTRODUCTION

Since the late 1970s, the capital markets have experienced fundamental changes as a totally new kind of debt instrument has emerged: the mortgage-backed security. Until that time, the bond market had grown accustomed to the standard corporate and municipal bonds, with relatively minor variations on a theme. However, in 1977, the Federal Home Loan Mortgage Corporation (FHLMC), in conjunction with several Wall Street investment bankers, succeeded in structuring a security using existing, government-backed FHLMC certificates as collateral. Ultimately, the source of payment on these bonds was thousands of single-family mortgages that had been converted into FHLMC certificates. This became known as a mortgage-backed bond.

With an AAA rating achieved by using government-guaranteed certificates, this instrument was now capable of being sold in the pubilc institutional and retail bond markets. Access to these capital markets provided a vastly increased source of funds for the financing of residential real estate. Now, residential mortgage lenders, builders, and home buyers would not be limited by tight credit caused by inflation, rising interest rates, and the resulting disintermediation experienced by thrift institutions earlier in the decade.

This first and fundamental foray into mortgage-backed securities was possible due to the accumulated experience regarding single-family mortgage loan performance and loss statistics. More important, single-family lending had become highly standardized with relatively similar terms and conditions among the diverse housing markets throughout the country—aided, in no small part, by the efforts of FHLMC, the Government National Mortgage Association (GNMA), and the Federal National Mortgage Association (FNMA) to establish underwriting and documentation standards. Moreover, these agencies were able to provide government guaranties on the payment and timing of principal and interest.

The capital markets continued to satisfy the increasing appetite for funds for residential housing. However, the active players in this market—large lenders, investment banks, and rating agencies—were soon tempted by the accumulated billions of dollars of commercial real estate loans throughout the country. The initial rationale was to follow closely in the footsteps of the residential mortgage–backed security market. Notwithstanding this interest, upon closer inspection, they realized that the commercial real estate and lending markets operated in a fundamentally different manner and that commercial mortgages would require new and innovative securitization techniques.

Income Property Obstacles

The complexities of the commercial mortgage market presented many challenges that inhibited and limited the initial impetus, based on the success of residential securitization:

- No national data base existed regarding commercial mortgage loan performance over a sustained period of time (that is, a complete real estate cycle).
- Long-term delinquency, default, workout, or prepayment statistics could not be readily compiled from the fragmented and inconsistent records maintained by even the largest lenders.
- Within each property and relative to other properties, tenant leases that provide the ultimate source of cash flow in an income property are unique and varied, with no well-established standards.

- Commercial mortgage underwriting and documentation are not standardized; the same lender might use differing terms and conditions on various loans because of the unique situations of each building—tenants, market competition, location, use, owners and their bargaining strength, and soon.
- Commercial property must be actively and continuously managed by professionals to maintain physical condition, competitiveness, and profitability.
- The commercial real estate market is subject to local and regional business cycles that can only be evaluated and understood by detailed analysis of specific supply and demand conditions.
- The market for commercial real estate is fragmented and illiquid, with significant uncertainty about the timing and terms for property sales.
- No government guarantees are available for commercial properties or mortgages, with the exception of certain restricted multifamily situations.

Driving Forces

Despite these obstacles, mortgage lenders and investment bankers persisted in their efforts to find methods to securitize commercial real estate mortgages. The primary attraction was a national portfolio of nearly $500 billion of commercial mortgages, held by all types of lenders as of 1983, as indicated in Table 19-1.

Commercial real estate lenders saw the potential for improved liquidity and profit potential, as well as accounting and tax benefits. Most important, lenders would be free to better manage the durations and terms of their assets and liabilities, while maintaining their lending activity in targeted commercial real estate markets. As a direct result, they would be able to monetize current loan assets and to move strategically in and out of these target markets (defined by geography, loan product, property type, and so on) as the markets and their plans changed.

Developers and owners of commercial real estate also saw the potential opportunities in securitization of commercial mortgages. In general, developers and owners were attracted by a new source of financing for their projects. More specifically, the market for commercial mortgage–backed securities appeared to offer a broader and more stable source of financing, with prospects for lower relative rates and for the ability to fund larger and more complex projects. Some larger developers also foresaw the potential to structure their own securities and tap the capital markets directly.

Rating agencies, especially Standard & Poor's Corporation (S&P), recognized the potential size and opportunity of this new market. Following their experience in the residential market, S&P realized that the development of a true market for commercial mortgage securities traded both publicly and privately would need a rating system to evaluate independently the credit and structural risk of these transactions. This system would have to enable commercial mortgage securities to be compared with and, thus, compete with other rated debt instruments.

Investment bankers also clearly recognized the potential for commercial mortgage securities. Having made a major investment and succeeded in the residential mortgage security business, investment bankers were eager to expand into the commercial market in much the same way. In many respects, commercial mortgage securitization appeared to require the same structuring and distribution capabilities that had already been developed for the residential market.

EVOLUTION AND MILESTONES

The market for commercial mortgage securities first developed late in 1983 and has been evolving ever since. Although growing slower than some had initially predicted, the evolution of the commercial mortgage security market had, by 1987–1988, established all of the fundamental building blocks required to sustain future growth and development. These building blocks include underwriting and rating methodologies, structural alternatives, credit enhancement mechanisms, tax and accounting treatment, and investor awareness, as well as placement and trading capability.

The key milestones in this evolution are shown in Figure 19-1 and discussed following.

First Unrated Commercial Mortgage Security

The first commercial mortgage security was issued in November of 1983 by Olympia & York Equity Corporation. Backed by first

Figure 19-1. Milestones in the Evolution of Commercial Mortgage Securities

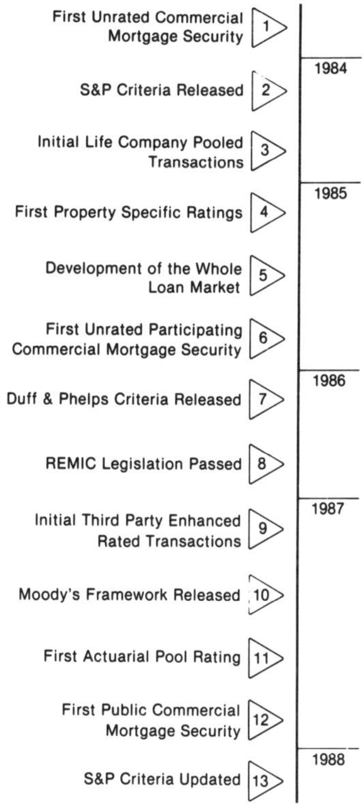

lien positions in three Class A Manhattan office buildings, the issue totaled nearly $1 billion. The 15-year notes were sold on a floating-rate basis tied to the 90-day Treasury bill rates. As a precursor of structures to follow, the transaction was enhanced by the addition of a rated letter of credit and government securities, as indicated in Table 19A-1 in the Appendix.

S&P's Criteria Released

As stated previously, the first and most notable milestone was the introduction, on November 19, 1984, of S&P's two newly developed rating methodologies for single properties and pools of commercial mortgages.

Table 19-1. National Mortgage Debt Outstanding, Mid-1983
Dollars in Billions

	Commercial	*Multifamily*	*Total*
Life insurers	$ 96	$ 19	$115
Commercial Banks	104	17	121
Savings and Loans	18	17	35
Mutual Savings Banks	52	35	87
Federal and Related Agencies	—	12	12
Mortgage pools or trusts	7	9	16
Individuals and others	34	31	65
Totals	$311	$140	$451

Basically, the property-specific technique enabled the rating agency to evaluate a securitized mortgage on large, single-office buildings. Office buildings were chosen as the first target property type because S&P believed they were the least risky and the least subject to rapid physical, economic, and market change. The individual office properties were examined from different perspectives: the property, operations (both past and projected), loan underwriting and servicing, security structure, and participant responsibilities, among others.

S&P attempted to accommodate the needs of large portfolio lenders and their desire to economically securitize pools of commercial mortgages. To this end, S&P developed a separate rating methodology, whereby the past portfolio performance of the issuer was used in an actuarial analysis to determine the ratability and credit support requirements for a large pool of existing loans.

Initial Life Company Pooled Transactions

Soon after the release of the S&P criteria, a series of large pooled transactions was issued, using seasoned portfolio mortgage products. These securities were structured as collateralized mortgage obligations (CMOs) and were funded by the mortgage cash flows. While these transactions were assigned AAA ratings, the ratings were not based on S&P criteria. Instead, the ratings were based on various guaranty mechanisms ultimately supported by the AAA credit rating of the issuers.

The first of these guaranteed transactions was issued on December 20, 1984, by Prudential Insurance Company. This initial transaction totaled almost $1.3 billion and was placed in the Euromarket. Like many of the contemporary residential mortgage securities, this transaction was structured in a three-class CMO, including a zero coupon class (see Table 19A-2 in the Appendix). Shortly thereafter, a number of similar transactions were issued by Penn Mutual, Connecticut Mutual, and others.

Initial Property-Specific Ratings

Early in 1985, several large security transactions were issued that related to individual properties in the New York metropolitan area. In May 1985, American Express initiated the market by the issuance of an AA-rated commercial mortgage security on an unfinished, unoccupied building using a 15-year, no-current-pay, balloon mortgage. This seemed to contradict all the basic requirements of the S&P rating methodology regarding seasoned, stabilized buildings and long-term, self-amortizing mortgage collateral. The unusual structure of this deal was accomplished, due to completion and interim debt service guarantees, zero coupon debt structure, high overcollateralization, and a strong American Express long-term lease (see Table 19A-3 in the Appendix). Other security issues, including Fisher Brothers and Olympia & York, would follow, using various combinations of quality properties, credit tenants, and other types of corporate or lease guarantees to provide credit support.

Initial Development of the Whole Loan Market

During late 1984 and early 1985, an organized market for trading commercial whole loans began to develop in parallel with the development of rated and unrated securities. The whole loan market developed as a way to provide a secondary market for existing and seasoned whole loans that were not directly amenable to rating and structuring. Sellers and buyers in the whole loan market include thrifts, savings and loans, life companies, and pension funds with existing portfolios.

To facilitate their trading function in this market, investment bankers developed "reunderwriting" standards for evaluating and marketing seasoned mortgages in a psuedostandardized form. The whole loans were often packaged in participations backed by the representatives and warranties of the seller. The basic reunderwriting methodologies that were developed in 1985 for whole loans are still used today for whole loan sale and security transactions.

Initial Unrated Participating Commercial Mortgage-Backed Security

All of the preceding mortgage-backed securities issued since late 1983 were structured as securities with standard coupons—whether fixed, floating, or accrued. In December 1985, the first participating commercial mortgage security was brought to market by Lincoln Properties. Backed by two properties under construction, the $146 million issue was structured to provide both a relatively low fixed coupon and a participating interest in excess cash flow, refinancing, and sales proceeds. The participations were capped at a cumulative return of 22.5 percent to qualify as debt (see Table 19A-4 in the Appendix). Few participating mortgage securities have been issued since then, due primarily to the decline in interest rates.

Duff & Phelps' Criteria Introduced

In October 1986, Duff & Phelps (D&P) introduced a rating approach for individual commercial property mortgages and small pools of commercial mortgage collateral. D&P's increased emphasis on more traditional property underwriting techniques enabled it to attract clients relatively quickly and to expand the rated security market. D&P has developed criteria to rate property types other than office buildings, such as multifamily apartment buildings and industrial properties. In August 1987, D&P released rating criteria for large commercial pools.

REMIC Legislation

By 1984, the market for residential mortgage securities was booming. In that year, however, the Treasury issued the "Sears Regulations," which prohibited the tax-free treatment of multiclass pass-through securities. To overcome the impact of the Sears Regulations, complex, burdensome, and costly trust structures were developed, although their ultimate tax treatment was uncertain.

These and other uncertainties regarding the federal tax treatment of mortgage-backed securities were largely eliminated by the creation of the real estate mortgage investment conduit (REMIC) as part of the Tax Reform Act of 1986. REMIC established requirements for ensuring federal tax-free treatment of mortgage-backed securities that applied to both residential and commercial loans.

One feature of the REMIC legislation that had particular significance for commercial mortgage securities was the provision for senior/subordinated structures. The senior/subordinated structure enables the risk of a whole loan or pool of mortgages to be divided into different classes. As a result, the subordinated class enhances the credit quality of the senior class and facilitates rating and marketing.

Initial Third Party-Enhanced Transactions

As indicated, from late 1984 through 1985, a number of commercial mortgage-backed securities were issued and rated, based on the credit rating of the issuer. In 1987, the first mortgage-backed securities with ratings based on third party credit enhancement were brought to market. Because of this enhancement, the rating analysis focused primarily on the credit quality of the enhancer, as opposed to the real estate or mortgages.

The initial third party credit-enhanced transactions were for large, existing, single properties, including both single- and multiple-tenant situations. An example of this kind of transaction involved the famous Chrysler building in Manhattan. The single-class mortgage security was rated AAA, based on an irrevocable guaranty provided by Fuji Bank (see Table 19A-5 in the Appendix).

Moody's Framework Released

Moody's development of a rating approach lagged behind those of S&P and D&P. Not until late 1986 and early 1987 did Moody's release its conceptual framework for the rating of commercial mortgage–backed securities, which differed from earlier rating approaches. Moody's approach focused on a limited number of prime metropolitan areas and studied the real estate fundamentals and market trends within that area to assess the risk and potential worst-case impact on properties securitized within a deal structure. Their analysis was supplemented by research provided by market and appraisal experts in the subject areas. As such, Moody's assigns a numerical rating of 1 to 5 (1 highest, 5 lowest) to each major geographic area as a starting basis for rating an individual property and structure.

First Actuarial Pool Rating

Although first unveiled in 1984 as part of the original S&P rating criteria, no actuarially based ratings were assigned until June 1987. The first such actuarially rated transaction was issued by Capitol Life and was backed by a pool of 600 seasoned mortgages structured into two separate series. Each series included a subordinated class retained by the issuer, which provided the credit support to rate the senior classes (see Table 19A-6 in the Appendix). Unlike earlier life company-guaranteed transactions, the AA rating was based solely on collateral quality and issuer considerations, with no recourse to Capitol Life.

First Public Commercial Mortgage Security

Shortly after the Capitol Life transaction was issued, a similar security was issued by Meritor Savings on December 10, 1987. The Meritor transaction was also structured in a multiclass, CMO-like manner, with a subordinated class supporting the AAA rating of the senior class (see Table A-7 in the Appendix). However, the Meritor transaction was the first commercial mortgage-backed security to be issued in the public markets.

S&P Criteria Revised

Although modified subsequent to 1984 to include multifamily and retail property-specific collateral, the original S&P rating methodology was largely unchanged in concept until April 1988. Although still based on the same principles, the original criteria were revised to streamline and simplify the rating process for both individual properties and smaller pools. The original concept of a national worst-case standard was replaced with a more qualitative and quantitative analysis of local market conditions.

Revision of the S&P rating criteria brings the first epoch of commercial mortgage securitization to a conclusion and completes the circle began in 1984. At the same time, the revised criteria mark the beginning of the next age now that all of the building blocks for the commercial mortgage security market are now firmly in place.

STRUCTURES AND APPLICATIONS

Structures for commercial mortgage-backed securities have undergone significant evolution since the inception of the market in 1983–1984. Other than the early life company pool transactions, the first few years of development were characterized by whole loan participations and simple, single-class bonds. With the advent of REMIC, commercial structures have become more complex and reflect the same structural concepts as those developed previously for the residential market. These features include multiple classes with fast pay, slow pay, and subordination, among others.

The key commercial mortgage security structures and their applications are as follows.

Whole Loans

As mentioned earlier, the whole loan and paticipation loan market was the first market established for trading existing loans among lenders. The initial transactions were typically limited lender-to-lender dealings without intermediaries and involved a complete sale of the loan asset for accounting and tax purposes. In late 1984 and early 1985, investment banks began to operate as intermediaries in these transactions and established a de facto trading market.

The whole loans were of all varieties, including fixed rate, variable rate with a wide range of indexes, graduated payment or step-up mortgages, accrual/partial pay, balloons, and so on. They were written on the full range of property types. As indicated, underwriting and documentation differed significantly from lender to lender and even within a given lender's portfolio.

The usual objectives of the seller were liquidity, restructuring of a portion of its asset base, or accounting gains. The agreement of sale between the parties transferred all the rights to principal and accrued interest payments and all responsibilities to the buyer, usually without recourse to the selling institution. There may be a limited buy-back period if a problem develops quickly on the loan. The only remaining commitment between the seller and buyer was frequently a servicing agreement. The seller may release the servicing or retain it, thereby continuing to earn fees on that activity while staying in contact with the borrowers and the lending market.

Total transfer of responsibility and liability for the loan required extensive due diligence by the intermediaries and the buyers to fully understand the debt. Reunderwriting procedures were developed to gather and analyze the relevant data on existing loans and have provided some level of standardization. These methodologies have been continually refined and are now considered standard practice in both whole loan and existing pooled security transactions.

Participation Certificates

Lenders also used participations for many years prior to securitization to fund large loans above their individual lending capacity. Participations involve a sharing of risk among members of a syndicate—usually on an equal basis. The members often had a preexisting understanding of the underwriting standards of the members and participated in loans as their needs dictated.

The participation form soon became the method preferred by investment bankers to transfer ownership of an existing loan or pool to another buyer. A full 100 percent participation was most commonly used. This was effectively a whole loan sale, although a standard participation and servicing agreement was used. There were two primary reasons for using a 100 percent participation instead of a whole loan sale. First was the ease of closing. The original mortgage, note, and other loan documentation could remain with the seller and eliminate an extensive paper shuffle at closing. Second, the participation certificate (PC) was considered more liquid than the whole loan.

Single-Class Securities

One step beyond the whole loans and the 100 percent PCs is the single-class security. Single-class securities are typically used for new single property originations, but can also be used for existing pools. Usually structured as a simple pass-through, this security enables a larger group of investors to own a share in the collateral cash flow. Consequently, the risks of ownership are spread out and the investment required in any particular mortgage is reduced. Securitizing mortgages in this way permitted smaller lending institutions to participate in larger, higher-quality property loans at an investment level with which they were comfortable.

Single-class securities can be used for a single property, small pools, or larger pools. However, underwriting varies to some extent, depending on the collateral. Larger pools of existing loans are underwritten much as whole loans, except for individual loans with significant loan balances. These larger loans, like individual loans and small pools, are underwritten on a more extensive basis, including market studies, cash flow projections, and appraisals.

Fast Pay/Slow Pay Multiclass Structure

As the market became more familiar with commercial property loans, more sophisticated structures were borrowed and adapted from the residential mortgage security market. The fast pay/slow pay structure, more commonly known as a CMO was introduced late in the commercial market in 1984. Typically applied to pools of loans, a CMO is a cash flow security with multiple classes, each with separate and uniquely defined payment characteristics.

The fundamental concept requires interest to be paid (or accrued) to all of the classes, while principal is repaid to only one class at a time in a sequential order. As principal or cash is received (and not needed to pay interest), the first class is paid down. Then, the next class begins to be paid down after the prior class is paid off.

The different maturities, or durations, of the classes permitted pricing to be based on the Treasury yield curve, which represented the market yield requirements for securities of different maturities. With a typical positively sloping yield curve, the interest cost of the shorter classes would be reduced below that earned by the mortgage, thereby resulting in a lower yield requirement and a higher price for the security. The number of classes and their expected time to maturity could vary considerably, depending on the collateral cash flows, investment climate, and the investors' particular needs.

Senior/Subordinated Multiclass Structure

As described previously, this structure has achieved increasing popularity following REMIC legislation. A variation of multiclass securities, this structure concentrates the inherent default and foreclosure risk in the commercial portfolio on a subordinated class of security bearing the first-loss position and can be applied to individual properties and pools. The subordinated holders may also be required (by responsibilities detailed in the servicing agreement) to make monthly advances of delinquent principal and interest payments. The senior classes have priority interest in cash flow from the collateral and in any distributions from foreclosures. With the removal of the first-loss risk, the senior class or classes become more secure and ratable, which results in a lower cost.

Although allowed by REMIC legislation, an active market has not yet developed for the subordinated class, even though the structure provides a higher potential return to the subordinated investor. The seller's familiarity with the properties and the borrowers enables it to make a more informed decision regarding the risk and expected return than other outside investors would be capable of making. Consequently, the subordinated class is usually retained by the seller.

The seller must also consider tax and accounting treatment when deciding to sell or retain the subordinated class. The decision to retain the subordinated interest may turn a transaction from a desired sale into a financing for accounting purposes. Recourse to the issuer as either a minor subordination interest or a substitution agreement among others may trigger a financing treatment. The trend toward risk-based capital requirements may create market or regulatory problems that could overshadow the benefits derived from the structure, unless a secondary market can be developed for subordinate interests (See the "Accounting and Tax Considerations" section.)

Zero Coupon Security (Class)

A zero coupon bond is a single-class structure in which interest is accrued over time and paid at maturity. A zero coupon class in a multiclass security works in much the same way. While the zero coupon structure has been used for newly originated single-property mortgages, the structure is more commonly used with pools of existing loans in a fast pay/slow pay CMO structure. The new structure accelerates the cash flow available to pay down the early classes, thus increasing their size and reducing the aggregate financing cost. As a result of the timing delay for payment, zero coupon bonds and classes are often required to provide a higher yield than similar current coupon bonds or classes.

Participating Security (Class)

Participating mortgages are multiclass securities that are structured to provide both a stated coupon rate of return and a participating feature. Participations are typically based on gross revenues, net operating cash flow, refinancing proceeds, and sale proceeds, among others. The allocation to the participation is defined in terms of percentage of the component or components to be included in a specific transaction. Some limits may be placed on the cumulative return to a participation to characterize the investment as debt instead of equity.

By providing a participation to a lender, the borrower is often able to obtain a lower rate on the coupon required. This may be especially important when interest rates are relatively high or sustainable cash flow is low. While most often applied to individual mortgages, participations can be aggregated at a pool level.

Hybrid Multiclass Structure

More complex hybrid structures can be created by combining the features of the different fundamental structures. These hybrid multiclass structures could include fast pay/slow pay, zero, and senor/subordinated classes in the same security. As a result, the hybrid multiclass structure allows significant flexibility to respond to a wide range of collateral and investor situations, especially for larger pool transactions.

RATING AND CREDIT ENHANCEMENT

Rating is an essential element in the corporate, government, and asset-backed financial markets. A rating provides an investor with an absolute measure of the risk associated with a specific

Figure 19-2. Rating Process Overview

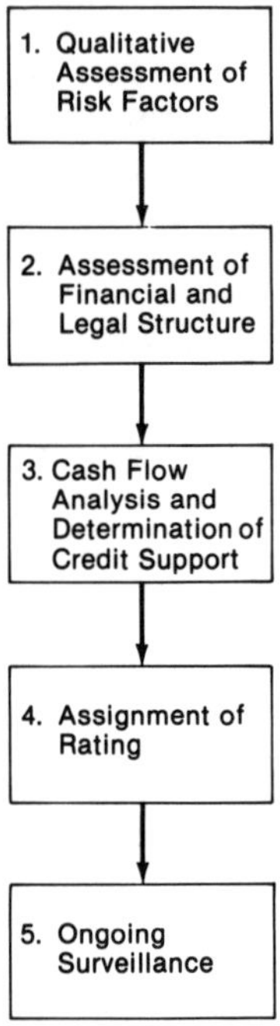

investment. In particular, a rating is a measure of the likelihood that an investor will receive full and timely payment of principal and interest due. Accordingly, investors can use ratings to compare alternative investments in terms of risk and reward.

Methodologies for rating operating companies and governments have been in existence for decades. However, until 1984, no rating criteria were established for commercial real estate mortgages. Since then, S&P, D&P, and Moody's have established criteria for rating commercial mortgage securities. The criteria are applicable to office industrial, retail, and hotel properties, as well as other more specialized properties on a case-by-case basis and in larger pools in which these specialized properties represent a relatively small percentage of the pool's value.

Rating methodologies for commercial mortgages can be divided into three basic types. Property-specific ratings, as the name implies, are for individual properties. Small pool ratings are applicable to pools of up to 50 individual mortgages. Actuarial criteria apply to larger pools of at least 50 mortgages with which statistical analysis can be employed. Use of actuarial criteria is restricted to larger issuers with long-term historical experience that covers significant portfolios. Although the specific methodologies used by the three rating agencies are similar in basic principles, they do contain differences. Moreover, as indicated, these rating criteria have been and will continue to evolve over time.

All of the existing rating methodologies share a common rating process, which consists of five essential steps, as shown in Figure 19-2:

- Qualitative assessment of risk factors
- Assessment of financial and legal structure
- Cash flow analysis and determination of credit support
- Assignment of the rating
- Ongoing surveillance

Property-Specific Rating

Qualitative Assessment of Risk Factors

A detailed market analysis approach is used to assess the local economy, supply/demand situation, and competitive position of each property in terms of potential future performance. The analysis focuses on a variety of areas, as described in Table 19-2, to which the various rating agencies assigned different priorities and weightings.

Assessment of the Financial and Legal Structure

The terms of the underlying mortgages are analyzed to determine prepayment and repayment risk. Security positions are evaluated by title and lien searches and by analysis of any ground lease provisions. A loan that does not fully amortize within the term of the security will be subject to refinancing risk, which must be quantified. The potential ability to refinance prior to the balloon maturity date is assessed using conservative growth and rate assumptions. A similar analysis is performed for zero coupon bonds.

The legal analysis of the bond structure considers three major issues: bankruptcy remoteness, the flow of funds, and the responsibilities of the transaction participants. Bankruptcy remoteness is generally established by the creation of a single-purpose entity that is administered by a third party bond trustee. The rating agencies review all of the agreements between and among the various parties to the deal to evaluate the responsibilities of each and to judge the probability of timely payment of principal and interest to the bond holders.

Cash Flow Analysis and Determination of Credit Support

Cash flows for individual properties are created based on the market, bond, and loan structure analyses. Various stress tests (for example, high vacancy rates, depressed lease rates, inflated operating expenses, and tenant bankrupcy) are applied to the initial cash flows to evaluate the property's ability to meet debt service requirements in a market downturn. In addition, loan size and seasoning and loan-to-value (LTV) ratios are reviewed to identify potential high risk.

The results of the stress tests include a projected cash flow from each property. Cash flow under stress is then used to quantitatively evaluate both debt source coverage and the LTV ratio under these circumstances. In the event that debt service coverage falls below 1.0 or the LTV ratio increases beyond a stated value for a specific rating, the rating agency imputes the need for additional credit support. The rating agency also adds a liquidity reserve for short-term disruptions in cash flow. See Figure 19-3.

Assignment of the Rating

This is the final step in rating a security. However, the issuer generally approaches the agency with a desired rating level. As the analysis proceeds, credit enhancement levels and bond structure are modified to achieve the desired result. The final rating is assigned once all of these issues and the related documentation are completed.

Ongoing Surveillance

The agencies continue to monitor a transaction on an annual basis to ensure that significant problems that would cause a down-

Figure 19-3. Application of Worst Case Cash Flow Analysis

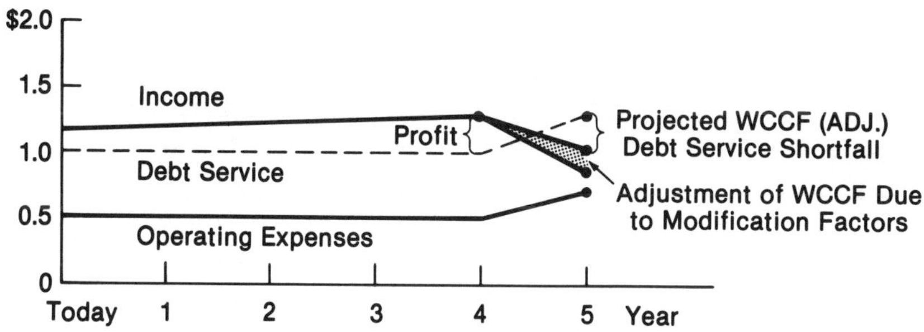

grade in the initial rating have not developed. Surveillance is based on financial and tenant information, as well as site inspections.

Table 19-2. Property Risk Factor Analysis

Property Factor	*Key Issues*
Local economy	Diversity, historic trends
Local real estate market	Volatility created by supply/demand imbalance or government regulation
Property location	Pros and cons of specific location
Tenancy	Diversity, turnover, and credit risk
Leases	Pass-through and escalation provisions for inflation protection
Property history	Past performance in down economic cycles
Payment history	Past default or late payments
Property management	Expertise and track record
Ownership	Financial condition and past performance
Construction quality	Operating efficiency and capital improvement requirements
Hazards	Casualty (e.g., fire), special (e.g., flood, earthquake), and substance (e.g., asbestos)

Small Pool Rating

The rating of small pools is based on the same fundamental principles as the rating of a single property. That is, each property in a small pool undergoes the property-specific evaluation, as required for a single property. The results of the individual property-specific analysis are then aggregated to determine the gross credit enhancement requirements for the pool as a whole.

However, the small pool credit enhancement gross requirements may be reduced, based on the property type and geographic diversity of the pool's component mortgages. In a pool of at least ten mortgages that satisfy these diversification criteria, the total cedit support required may be reduced up to 10 percent, depending on the specific criteria of each of the rating agencies.

Large Pool Rating (Issuer Specific)

Qualitative Assesement of Risk Factors

A detailed evaluation of the issuer is conducted. The evaluation includes a variety of factors relevant to the issuer's ability to originate and finance commercial mortgages on an ongoing basis. Some of the key factors considered include underwriting criteria, documentation standards, organization and staff, and servicing, as indicated in Table 19-3.

In addition, a basic statistical profile of the mortgage portfolio is compiled to ascertain key factors, such as average LTV ratios, loan size, seasoning, and geographic diversity. The pool to be issued is assessed to ensure that the mortgages included do not reflect adverse sampling "cherry picking." Representations by the issuer are also required to ensure that the pool to be securitized reflects the overall portfolio composition.

Assessment of the Financial and Legal Structure

Assessment of the financial and legal structure for a large pool transaction is basically the same as that for individual properties and small pools. Documentation and the key attributes of each loan are analyzed accordingly. As with the individual property and small pool transactions, the bankruptcy remoteness of the issuer entity, cash flow from the individual mortgage to the security holders, and notes and responsibilities of the participants are all assessed.

Cash Flow Analysis and Determination of Credit Support

The cash flows of the individual mortgages are projected to determine the aggregate cash flow available to support debt service on the security. Any deficiencies are calculated and included in the credit support requirements. In addition, a potential pool loss analysis is conducted on an actuarial basis. The potential pool loss is calculated as the product of the adjusted foreclosure experience, multiplied by the presumed foreclosure severity. As in the property-specific and small pool criteria, a liquidity reserve is established to cover potential short-term disruptions in cash flow.

Assignment of the Rating

The rating assignment for a large pool follows the same process as discussed for individual property and small pool ratings.

Ongoing Surveillance

Issuers are required to provide the rating agency with ongoing performance information regarding the rated pool collateral. As with single-property and small pool transactions, the rating of large pool transactions may be adjusted downward, based on adverse results.

Table 19-3. Issuer-Specific Risk Factor Analysis for Large Pools

Risk Factor	*Key Issues*
Underwriting criteria	Definition, documentation, standardization, and criteria
Documentation standards	Standardization, terms, and conditions
Organization and staff	Structure, position descriptions, qualifications, tenure, experience, and controls
Servicing	Systems and procedures, operating control, early warning and problem detection, and default and foreclosure policy

Credit Enhancement Methods

As indicated, there are three key areas of concern in the rating of commercial mortgage securities, in which problems could develop. In these cases, credit enhancement is required by the rating agencies to support a given rating.

- Maintenance of collateral value so that the property and mortgage have a realizable economic value at least as great as the bond principal outstanding.
- Protection against cash flow shortfall to ensure sufficient cash to pay operating needs of the property, as well as the mortgage (and, ultimately, the bond).
- Protection against refinancing risk (balloon loans) to ensure that the debt can be refinanced or paid off at the time of maturity.

There are a variety of mechanisms for providing the required credit support. Each mechanism is ultimately evaluated by the rating agencies in terms of creditworthiness, liquidity, and duration. The most commonly used techniques are summarized in Table 19-4 and are discussed as follows.

Collateral Value

Several mechanisms have been used to provide credit support for collateral value. Sufficient value in the underlying mortgage collateral has been ensured by overcollateralization, whereby a predetermined excess of mortgages is pledged as security. The excess or overcollateralization is equal to or greater than the rating agency's expected worst-case loss in value.

A second effective method is the substitution agreement. If the issuer or a related party with a suitable credit rating has a large lending or portfolio capacity, it may offer to substitute or replace nonperforming assets in the collateral pool. Certain REMIC restrictions permit this substitution only in the first six months of a security's life.

Contain guarantees or surety bonds may also be used to support collateral value deficiencies. These guarantees may be provided only by rated guarantees.

Cash Flow Shortfall

Many mechanisms can be used to ensure cash flow adequacy:

- Optional/mandatory delinquency advances by the servicer
- Reserve funds established at origination or accruing over time
- Revolving line of credit with a rated institution

- GIC; eligible investment account
- Letter of credit from a rated institution
- Surety bond from a rated entity
- Master lease from a credit tenant
- Lease payment guarantee from a rated source
- Net worth guarantee of the issuer
- Senior/subordinated structure with sufficient subordination to cover shortfall

Table 19-4. Potential Credit Enhancement Mechanisms

Mechanism	*Risk Application*		
	Collateral Value	*Cash Flow Shortfall*	*Refinancing*
Overcollaterization	X	X	X
Substitution	X	X	X
Advance payments		X	
Reserve funds	X	X	
Revolving credit line	X	X	X
Guaranteed investment credit (GIC)	X		
Letter of credit	X	X	X
Surety bond	X		
Master lease	X	X	
Lease payment guarantee		X	
Net worth guarantee	X		
Senior/subordinated	X	X	
Liquid assets facility			X
Principal/purchaser guarantee	X		X

Refinancing Risk

To guard against the possibility of not obtaining refinancing for a balloon loan, letters of credit and corporate guarantees have been used.

Another method adopted by the rating agencies is called a liquid assets facility. As such, the issuer must commence the process and obtain a refinancing commitment from one to three years before the maturity of the balloon loan. This allows some time for business cycle fluctuations to be resolved and for financing to be arranged.

ACCOUNTING AND TAX CONSIDERATIONS

Accounting treatment for commercial mortgage securities has evolved over several years and is based on specific generally accepted accounting principles (GAAP) and the pervasive GAAP standards of form over substance. The ultimate responsibility for the application of GAAP to the transaction rests with the preparer of the issuer's financial statements. Relevant GAAP issues are currently undergoing reassessment, due in part to the impact of securitization. The key accounting issues related to most transactions are:

- Sale versus financing treatment
- Accounting for security issuance
- Residual accounting

Sale versus Financing Treatment

Many commercial mortgage security transactions involve the transfer of a single mortgage loan or pool of loans with recourse in the event of default. The GAAP for such a transaction is Statement of Financial Accounting Standards (SFAS) No. 77, *Reporing by Transfers for Transfers of Receivables with Recourse.* A transfer of receivables with recourse is recognized as a sale if all of the following conditions are met:

- The transferor (issuer) surrenders control of the future economic benefits embodied in the receivables. Control has *not* been surrendered if the transfer has an option to repurchase the receivables at a later date.
- The transferor's obligation under the recourse provisions can be reasonably estimated. Lack of experience with receivables similar to those being transferred or other factors that affect a determination at the transfer date of the collectibility of the receivables may impair the ability to make a reasonable estimate of the probable bad debt losses and related costs of collections and repossessions. A transfer of receivables is not recognized as a sale if collectibility of the receivables and related costs of collection and repossession

cannot be reasonably estimated. This is a particular problem with commercial collateral, in which these results may be difficult to determine.

- The transferee cannot require the transferor to repurchase the receivables, except pursuant to the recourse provisions.

SFAS No. 77 further states that if any of the conditions are not met, the amount of the proceeds from the transfer of receivables shall be reported as a liability (and, accordingly, shall be treated as a financing transaction). Although generally negating sale treatment, maintaining a material interest in the future economic benefits of the mortgage loan may not necessarily overcome the substance over form considerations, as discussed in Accounting Principles Board Statement No. 4. The practice for commercial mortgage transactions has generally been to record the event as a financing when a material continuing interest in the receivable has been retained by the Issuer (for example, a subordinated interest, overcollateralization, contingent liability, or a letter of credit).

Accounting for Security Issuance

The issuance of a bond or security involves underwriting fees, issuance expenses, and discount or premium (based on price to investor). The GAAP for the bond issuance costs and treatment of discount or premium is set forth inn SFAS No. 91, *Accounting for Nonrefundable Fees and Costs Associated with Originating or Acquiring Loans and Initial Direct Costs of Leases.*

SFAS No. 91 requires that loan (underwriting) fees, certain direct issuance costs, and purchase premiums or discounts be recognized as an adjustment of yield by the interest method based on the contractual terms of the loan, assuming prepayments in certain specified circumstances. Generally, commercial mortgage security transactions would assume no prepayments for accounting purposes.

Paragraph 18 of SFAS No. 91 defines the interest method (sometimes referred to as the level yield method) as a method "to arrive at periodic interest income (including recognition of fees and costs) at a constant effective yield on the net investment in the receivable (that is, the principal amount of the receivable adjusted by unamortized fees or cost and purchase premium or discount)." The difference between the periodic interest income determined and the stated interest on the outstanding principal amount of the receivable is the amount of periodic amortization.

Both issuers and investors should apply this methodology to the bond classes (if the transaction is accounted for as a financing by the issuers). The assumption of no prepayments requires the use of the contractual terms of the bonds to calculate the effective yield. Prepayments would trigger recognition of the related discount or premium, so that the effective interest rate on the remaining portion of the loans continues unchanged.

Residual Accounting

Accounting for the residual interest in a commercial mortgage security transaction depends on the type of transaction (sale or financing) and viewpoint (issuer or investor). If the transaction was accorded sale treatment, the issuer would record any gain or loss at the completion date of the transaction. The purchaser of the residual would have to determine the nature of the accounting treatment required on its financial statements by asking questions that would be the same as those facing the issuer for a transaction accorded financing treatment by the issuer. The questions relate to whether the residual owner should consolidate or use the equity method or the cost method of accounting, as follows:

- *Consolidation.* If the residual owner holds more than 50 percent of the residual, GAAP requires consolidation. To the extent that the residual owner has an investment in excess of net equity in the commercial mortgage security transaction, such investment should be evaluated as to recoverability based upon future cash flows.
- *Equity method.* If the residual owner holds between 20 percent and 50 percent of the residuals, GAAP requires use of the equity method. This would require the residual owner to record a pro rata share of the reported net income of the transaction as an increase to the investment and cash distributions received as a reduction of

the investment. In applying the equity method, the residual owner must test for overall recoverability of the investment.

- *Cost method.* If the residual owner holds less than a 20 percent interest in the transaction, the investment should be accounted for by the cost method. This would allow the residual owner to record income only to the extent of cash distributions actually received.

REMIC

REMIC is the most visible recent development that affects both residential and commercial mortgage securitization. As such, REMIC eliminates much of the uncertainty regarding the federal tax status of mortgage securities. In general, REMIC treatment enables the related mortgage security to be taxed once at the investor level without any taxation at the issuer level. REMIC also provides a standard investment vehicle with two generic classes of investors—regular and residual—each with specified tax treatment.

From the perspective of developers, owners, lenders, and other issues, REMIC specifically allows the use of certain structures that had previously been limited by the Sears Regulations. In particular, REMIC allows multiclass pass-through and senior/subordinated structures to be issued and transferred. Both structures—especially the senior/subordinated structure—are readily applicable to commercial mortgage securities, as previously discussed.

Moreover, REMIC provisions allow these structures to be treated as sales or financings for GAAP purposes, while treated as sales only for tax purposes. As a result, issuers can structure these transactions most effectively for economic and accounting purposes, without suffering any adverse tax consequences. Also, REMIC allows complete freedom in establishing the legal form of the securities to suit specified business objectives.

From an investor's perspective, REMIC provides several special benefits. Regular REMIC interests are treated as qualifying mortgage assets for thrifts and other REMICs, as well as qualifying real estate assets for real estate investment trusts (REITs), as long as the underlying collateral qualifies. For foreign investors, regular REMIC interests in pre-July 1984 mortgages are not subject to 30 percent withholding tax on interest income. Also, as indicated, all investors are afforded more clearly defined and more certain tax treatment as a result of REMIC legislation.

CONCLUSION

Conduits and New Originations

The market for new originations will advance beyond the premier properties in top national markets and into the second tier of large cities and strong regional developers. Prime deals will continue to be underwritten and sold by the top investment banks. However, many lesser or regional investment banks, merchant banks, commercial banks, and insurance companies are carefully watching this market and may enter on a selective deal basis.

One method that institutions are actively pursuing is the commercial mortgage conduit. In concept, the conduit would operate in much the same way as residential lender conduits to enable relatively small properties and issuers to participate in the commercial securitization process. In practice, an effective structure for a commercial mortgage conduit has been in development for several years, with limited results. Even so, the likelihood is that many such conduits will be formed in the longer term to focus on the specific needs of the different participant groups.

Structure

For the most part, future transactions will be structured in senior/subordinated or multiclass pass-through formats, and most will elect or reserve the right to elect REMIC status. The whole loan market may begin to get more active as a by-product of the trend toward the senior/subordinated structures. As ratings become more prevalent and surety programs become established in commercial securities, even issues sold to retail investors may become popular and may further expand the range of this market.

Beyond the next few years, the underlying structures are likely to increase in complexity and track more clearly with residential security developments. This will result in a trickle-down effect, with residential securitization leading the way. The techniques employed in the residential market, such as interest-only strips, principal-only strips, and planned amoritization classes, are expected to be used on the commercial side. Also, hybrid debt/equity structures in the form of participating mortgages may satisfy developers' need for more cash up front and the capital market's need for conservative LTV and debt service coverage ratios.

The emergence of third party guaranty programs from surety companies may significantly change the transaction structure from reliance on the projected property cash flow to examination of the responsibilities and debt-paying ability of the surety company. However, there is a limited capacity of the companies for guaranties of this type, and nonguaranteed senior/subordinated structures and partially guaranteed transactions will still prevail.

Rating

Significant changes in the rating methods used by the agencies is not expected. Instead, their requirements will gradually evolve, as they become more familiar with commercial mortgage transactions, as structures evolve, and as they gain more experience from past rated deals. The current criteria could expand to include other property types, such as industrial, speciality property types, and lodging facilities. However, the fundamental rating concepts are expected to be much the same.

With the first actuarially rated commercial mortgage-backed securities issued in 1987, others may soon follow from insurance companies and large thrifts. Furthermore, as the rating agencies gain more experience with the actuarial rating, reliance may shift more toward prospective criteria relying on underwriting, servicing, and related operations as key rating criteria instead of portfolio lending experience.

APPENDIX: TRANSACTION TERMS SHEETS

Table 19A-1. Premium Quality, Unrated, Commercial Morgage–Backed Security

Issue date	November 1983
Issuer	Olympia & York Equity Corporation
Underwriters	First-lien mortgages on three major Class A Manhattan office buildings with master leases on unleased space and additional collateral in government securities or letter of credit from AA-rated New York City bank to ensure 1:1 debt service coverage ratio
Securities	$1 billion floating-rate first mortgage notes 15-year term due 1998 Accrual rate floating 175 by over 90-day Treasury bill Cap and floor at 17% and 7%, respectively
Rating	None

Table 19A-2. Credit Enhancement Through Maintenance of Net Worth of Guarantor

Issue date	December 20, 1984			
Issuer	Prudential Realty Securities III, Inc.			
Guarantor	Prudential Funding Corporation, owned jointly by Phibro-Salomon Inc. and the Prudential Insurance Company of America, whereby the Prudential agrees to maintain guarantor's tangible net worth at a minimum of $1			
Underwriters	Salomon Brothers Interntional Limited Credit Suisse First Boston Limited Prudential-Bache Securities			
Collateral	Unsecured general obligation ranked equal with all other unsecured and unsubordinated indebtedness of the issuer and guarantor; bonds paid by cash flow from commercial mortgages contributed by Prudential to the issuer.			
Securities	*Amount*	*Coupon*	*Maturity*	*Type*
	$386,049,000	11.875%	1/15/92	Sinking fund bond
	545,691,000	12.125	1/15/95	Sinking fund bond
	365,216,000	0	1/15/99	Zero coupon bond
	$1,296,956,000			yielding 11.84%
Other terms	May be sold only in Europe or through private secondary sales in the United States Fixed maturity with mandatory sinking fund redemption Optional redemption at specified price, plus premium			
Rating	AAA by S&P			

Table 19A-3. Corporate Payment Guarantee and Credit Tenant Leases

Issue date	May 14, 1985
Issuer	American Express Company American Express International Banking Corp. American Express Travel Related Services Co., Inc. Shearson Lehman Brothers Inc.
Guarantors	American Express Company guarantees payment of accrued value of note prior to delivery of mortgage note to bond trustee
Underwriters	Salomon Brothers International Shearson Lehman Brothers International
Collateral	First lien on leasehold interest of American Express corporate headquarters in the World Financial Center, New York City
Securities	$450 million zero coupon Euronotes due 2000 First public-rated commercial mortgage bond First rated commercial mortgage bond using balloon mortgage
Other terms	No liquidity reserve needed because no debt service until maturity Accreting bond value is sufficiently overcollateralized by value of property over the term of the bond One-year refinancing requirement for liquid asset facility
Rating	AA by S&P

Table 19A-4. Participating First Mortgage Bonds

Issue date	December 13, 1985
Issuer	Lincoln Property Associates Limited, as managing general partner of two partnerships, each owning a separate office building and related facilities
Underwriters	Drexel Burnham Lambert Inc.
Objective	To provide permanent mortgage loans on two projects upon their completion
Collateral	Two participating first mortgages (one against a fee simple interest and the other a leasehold interest) on two separate commercial office buildings under construction as of the issue date with a cost to complete of $109,500,000 and an appraised value at stabilization of $182,500,000

Securities	$146,000,000 participating first mortgage bonds due 2000 Earning interest at 1.5%, payable semiannually, with variable interest in the amount of 50% of the net cash flow from each project, and additional interest in the amount of 50% of residual value of the projects at maturity, subject to a maximum yield limitation of 22.5% annually
Other terms	Operating cash reserve funds Agreements provided by the affiliated general partners to: • Contribute additional funds to cover cost overruns • Redeem the bonds if not completed as scheduled • Loan funds to cover negative cash flow in excess of the operating reserve funds • Provide for other conditions of financial and management nature No recourse against other assets of the project partnerships No joint responsibility between project partnerships
Rating	None

Table 19A-5. Third Party Credit Enhancement Security

Issue date	April 21, 1987
Issuer	Chrysler Building of New York Inc.
Underwriters	Salomon Brothers Inc.
Credit enhancement	Irrevocable letter of credit issued by the Fuji Bank, Limited
Collateral	Mortgages on the Chrysler Building (a leasehold interest), an adjacent office building, and four contiguous retail buildings
Securities	$250 million of 9.125% notes due May 1, 1999, payable semiannually
Other terms	No investor recourse to the issuer
Rating	AA by S&P

Table 19A-6. Multiclass, Senior/Subordinated, AA-Rated Private Offering with REMIC Election

Issue date	June 1987
Issuer	Capitol Life Insurance Co., subsidiary of Integrated Resources Inc.
Underwriters	Drexel Burnham Lambert Inc.
Objective	Yield a higher sale price for the loans by using a multiclass structure, rather than a whole loan sale
Collateral	Two pools of commercial mortgages, consisting of about 300 mortgages each

Securities	$180 million approximate transaction value
Other terms	Cash reserves of approximately 12.5% of the value of pool 1 and approximately 14% of the value of pool 2
	No investor recourse to the issuer
Rating	AA by S&P

Table 19A-7. Multiclass, Senior/Subordinated, AAA-Rated Public Offering with REMIC Election

Issue date	December 10, 1987
Issuer	Meritor Mortgage Securities, a subsidiary of Meritor Savings Bank
Service	Meritor Savings Bank
Underwriters	Goldman, Sachs & Co. (lead manager)
	Salomon Brothers Inc.
	Drexel Burnham Lambert Inc.
Objective	To shorten duration of asset mix
	To downsize the loan portfolio
	To provide liquidity for operations and investment
Collateral	Seasoned, first-lien mortgage loans on 141 properties throughout the United States

Number of Loans	*Loan Balance*	*Property Types*
42	$ 73,910,507	Office Buildings
39	69,648,166	Multifamily apartments
25	54,105,758	Retail and shopping centers
32	41,380,836	Industrial and warehouse buildings
3	3,818.486	Other property types
141	$242,863,753	

Classes	*Amount*	*Maturity*	*Coupon*	*Price*
Senior A-1	$ 87,079,000	8/1/92	8.75%	99.922%
Senior A-2	71,847,000	12/1/94	9.40	99.472
Senior A-3	54,000,000	6/1/99	9.40	97.095
Total	$212,926,000			

Subordinate Class B: 11.75% of underlying collateral value retained by Meritor

Other terms	Reserve fund of $1,016,000
	Expense reserve fund
	Voluntary advances of late monthly payments by service
Rating	AAA by S&P and Moody's

CHAPTER 20

Ratings of Real Estate Mortgage Securities for the Hospitality Industry

Daniel J. Smith

INTRODUCTION

Analysis of real estate securities that are collateralized by loans on hospitality properties focuses on the credit quality of two key elements: the real estate and the business operation. This analysis studies the quantitative and qualitative features of the collateral, as well as the financial and legal structure of the security. When assigning a public or private rating, rating agencies determine the likelihood of timely payment of principal and interest.

RATING CRITERIA

Consistent with Duff & Phelps Credit Rating Co.'s (DEP's) analysis of other income-producing property types, its approach to evaluating hospitality properties focuses on various qualitative characteristics, such as the real estate hotel market, the site location, the area economy, the construction quality and appearance, the franchise operator or management company, the owner, and seasoning. It also includes the quantitative property analysis. In addition, an evaluation of potential hazards, such as asbestos or toxic waste, and the effect of balloon mortgages is considered critical to the analysis.

Consistent with D&P's approach to rating other types of income-producing real estate, a weighting and blending of these qualitative and quantitative factors determines the appropriate rating. If an evaluation indicates that some of the qualitative factors should be stressed more in a particular situation, these factors will carry more weight than other factors in the determination of an overall rating.

PROPERTY TYPE

For purposes of our analysis, the U.S. hospitality market is divided into various categories: luxury, upper-market, middle-market, economy, all suite, and destination resorts.

Luxury hotels have the most expensive room rates in the market and provide extensive personalized service to guests. Luxury hotels typically have a very high ratio of employees to guests. These properties may be independent (with no chain affiliation), or they may be in the top price and service segment of a nationally recognized hotel chain. These hotels can have a development period of over 24 months.

Although at a somewhat lower level than luxury hotels, upper-market hotels also offer personalized service and have a high ratio of employees to guests. The development period for upper-market hotels is generally 18 to 24 months, due to size and location. Upper-market hotels are generally affiliated with a major franchise management company; this company may also be the owner or operator of the hotel.

In a middle-market hotel, personalized service is considered average compared with luxury and upper-market properties, there are usually no bellhops, valet parking, or other comparable personal services. These hotels typically have amenity packages that include a restaurant, lounge, meeting space, and swimming pool. Total development time for middle-market hotels is usually 12 to 18 months.

Budget/economy motels are limited-service hotels that offer a limited amenity package. Some economy hotels may not have a swimming pool, restaurant, or meeting space. Typically, these hotels are marketed toward the more transient business and pleasure guest with a one- or two-night stay. Guests may include salespeople with calls in the area or travelers on limited per diem expense accounts. Due to limited facilities, economy motels usually have a development period of 6 to 12 months.

All-suite hotels, the newest product addition to the hospitality market, can be developed within all of the categories described earlier. All-suite hotels are typically marketed to extended-stay guests and families, who are attracted by the larger rooms and expanded amenities.

Unlike guests at a center city or suburban hotel, guests who stay at a destination resort hotel are vacationers or business groups who plan to spend the vast majority of their time at the resort. Personalized service in terms of group activities and an expanded amenity package is mandatory at a resort hotel. These hotels generally have golf and tennis facilities, spas, several swimming pools, saunas, and jacuzzes; they may even have a marina and a beach. Destination resorts are marketed as a high-quality hospitality service. Yet, due to their vacation atmosphere, they are tyically informal in style.

OPERATING PERFORMANCE

The historic and current room rates, occupancy ratios, and revenue/expense relationships for the property, as well as competitive properties, are reviewed. In any hotel market, the relationship between existing supply and proposed construction is critical. A rapid expansion of hotel rooms within a market is viewed with concern, unless demand statistics support this growth. Trends for the subject, as well as the market, are important indexes; specifically, occupancy and room rates should show growth or, at least, stability during the past three years. The market demand for other facilities, including banquet halls and convention meeting rooms, is also reviewed. Advance bookings of conventions and meetings are analyzed to determine their impact on the hotel's projected performance and profitability.

Recent property changes, such as renovations or a shift in marketing efforts to attract new market segments, are also analyzed to determine the effect on operations. For example, an existing hotel that has recently changed its market position from a middle-market hotel to an economy hotel must demonstrate the effect of the change in their projected occupancy and operating margins. The hotel may expect increased occupancy at the expense of decreased room rates. The net effect on gross operating profit is adjusted to reflect higher or lower projected expense margins.

The marketing plan of the operator is also reviewed. Hotels that have an established presence in the market and maintain a strong relationship with a national chain are viewed favorably in our analysis. A long-term franchise agreement that is seasoned and has been profitable to all parties is the strongest evidence of this relationship.

The hotel's relationship with neighboring properties and the strength of the surrounding commercial market are also reviewed. It is also determined if the hotel is attracting the intended guest profile. The guest profile is defined as a breakdown of the types of guests anticipated to stay at the hotel. It could include tourists, conventioneers, business travelers, and extended-stay clientele. Prebooking reviews, corporate-rate user counts, and guest questionnaires are some of the ways in which hotels determine their guest profile.

Location within the competitive market is often an important market consideration. Accessibility and visibility are key factors in determining the strength of the location. Accessibility to transportation centers, such as airports and rail and public transportation, is considered important, as well as proximity to demand generators, such as local offices and entertainment attractions. If the hotel is located near a business park and is dependent on business travelers that meet with companies within the park, the occupancy and tenant mix of the business park is analyzed, along with potential growth within the park. Banquet facilities and meeting space are analyzed in terms of size compared with competitive properties and demand within the market.

The location of the hotel will also have an impact on the guest profile. With the exception of resorts, locations are primarily divided into downtown, suburban office park, airport, and highway locations. Each may cater to the business traveler, but will meet different needs and will be marketed to different groups within the business traveler category.

The impact of other on-site facilities, including restaurants, banquet facilities, and meeting space, is also analyzed to determine trends and varieties of income sources that will assist the hotel in maintaining income levels during times of economic stress.

Analysis of both the real estate and guest profile is critical to the overall rating process. While historical operating results are important, the effect of current and projected market conditions on the hotel's performance is considered vital to the success of the financing.

MANAGEMENT

Key factors examined when assessing the quality of the operator are effective management of employees, employee turnover rates, properly targeted guest services, marketing plans and programs, operating budgets, financial forecasts, and established capital replacement schedules.

Franchise and management companies play a major role in the success of a hotel. A hotel may be independently managed or may have a formal management agreement with a local or national company. In addition, the hotel may have a limited agreement with a franchise company to use its name, reservation system, centralized purchasing, and national advertising. Employees at the hotel will be employees of either the management company or the franchise company.

An experienced operator that has demonstrated a record of success at the property or in other facilities is considered vital. Additionally, the manager's success in maintaining appropriate staffing levels for the hotel and in providing adequate services targeted to meet the needs of the hotel's guest profile indicates a familiarity with the needs of the market that is crucial. Turnaround time for replacement of the operator or manager in the event of performance failure is essential in our analysis.

Effective service to the guest is essential to the business operations of the hotel. Even amenities for economy hotels, which do not provide extensive amenity packages, are analyzed in terms of their relative services to guests. Regardless of the amenity package offered, management's attention to guest services must be demonstrated.

D&P analyzes the structure (incentive based versus volume based) and the reasonableness and affordability of the management fees charged. Management fees are analyzed to determine if they are subordinate to debt service, return on equity, or other expenses of the hotel. Potential incentive fees are analyzed to determine their effect on gross operating profit and net operating income (provided that they are subordinate to debt service).

Management must have a specific marketing plan and be able to demonstrate an ability to properly budget the income and expenses of a hotel. A scheduled plan for replacement of furniture, fixtures, and equipment must be demonstrated. Furniture should be replaced every five to seven years and carpeting should be replaced every four to five years at a maximum. Heating and cooling systems should regularly undergo repair, maintenance, and replacement.

Because the hospitality industry generally has a high employee turnover ratio, the training program for new employees is reviewed. In addition, expansion plans for new hotels run by the same operator are reviewed for potential overextension of resources.

The long-term viability of the management company and the track record of the hotel, along with that of other hotels in the chain, are reviewed. Conference bookings, prebookings, and a demonstrated ability to raise room rates while controlling expenses and maintaining occupancy are also analyzed. A working relationship with airlines, rental car companies, and other travel-related corporations can be effective in raising occupancy; promotional activities must be strategically targeted and cost effective.

AREA ECONOMY

Examination of the economy includes a review of economic and demographic influences on the region, the metropolitan statistical area, and the city. If a market for the hotel is influenced strongly by a cross-section of the national economy, this is analyzed as well.

Political climates within the economy that will affect future development, such as zoning restrictions and moratoriums, are reviewed. Zoning of areas for possible redevelopment activities that may produce long-term competition, particularly from older hotels, is considered.

The area's tourist attractions and their impact on the hotel are analyzed as well. The historical performance of various tourist attractions is studied to determine their impact on the performance of the property. Hotels that depend on the tourist business may be seasonal in nature; if applicable, cash flow projections need to reflect the seasonality inherent in the monthly cash flows.

The area's business climate is analyzed to determine the strengths and weaknesses within the business community. A hotel that depends on business travelers should be located in an economically diverse region with signs of stability and economic growth. Dependence on one industry or one company is a concern to D&P's analysts, due to the volatility of future economic conditions.

The hotel's age, physical and functional status, structural condition, and usage of space can affect the property's cash flow. In addition to the rooms, the condition of the property's public areas is reviewed. This includes pools, exercise rooms, meeting facilities, restaurants, lounges, and so on. Analysis of the condition of the furniture, fixtures, and equipment is incorporated into the overall analysis of construction quality. Also, overall architectural features of the hotel, including design, parking, landscaping, safety, and security, afect the overall success of the hotel.

The functional design and floor plan of the hotel are reviewed. Traffic patterns should allow for convenient access to meeting rooms, restaurants, and guest rooms. Bottlenecks in traffic patterns should not occur. Work areas should be functional. They should be out of high traffic areas, yet convenient to employees who work in these areas on a daily basis.

Guest safety is considered extremely important. This includes a review of the amount and condition of fire sprinklers, emergency exits, and other safety-related systems. Adherence to local zoning requirements and current safety codes is examined. Hazards such as toxic waste and asbestos are specifically addressed.

Maintenance of the exterior and common areas is important. Proper signage and upkeep of the entrances are important. The architectural design should also be functional, with monitoring systems in place for heating and cooling, temperature controls for banquet and meeting space, adequate water pressure throughout the property, and electrical outlets conveniently placed in various meeting rooms for visual presentations, computer installation, and other uses.

SEASONING

As with other income-producing real estate, seasoning of both the mortgage loan and the property is considered important. Property seasoning refers to the historical operations of the property after reaching a stabilized occupancy level. D&P will analyze less seasoned mortgages and new originations. However, if the loan contains seasoning, a good payment history, and principal reductions, it will be viewed more favorably.

In fact, seasoning of a hotel can be a blessing or a curse for the mortgage loan. Although D&P views the seasoning of the property as important, we recognize that aging may be a deterrent to increasing operating income if the property has not been updated. Hotels should be seasoned to the point of having a stable history, but should still be new enough that, with proper maintenance, total obsolescence will not occur for at least 20 to 30 years.

OWNERSHIP

Although ownership of the property may be in the name of a single-purpose limited partnership or other corporate entities, analysts look beyond the partnership or corporate structure to the general partners to evaluate the track record and current financial condition of the ownership entity. However, unless the hotel is managed by the owner, an owner may not be actively involved in the day-to-day decision-making process of running the hotel.

In any case, the owner should have the ability to advance temporary cash flow shortfalls and to provide adequately for both normal and unexpected capital replacements during the life of the debt issue. Financial statements of the owner and general partner should reflect their liquidity and should highlight asset value for all owned properties, sources of funds, and reserves for capital expenditures. All contingent liabilities must be disclosed and will be reviewed by D&P's analysts.

CONCLUSION

Public and private ratings for hospitality properties have opened up a new avenue of financing for this property type. Ratings are sought by developers, owners, and lenders as a way to finance and manage cash flow. The various quantative and qualitative factors considered in hotel analysis provide investors in rated securities with a thorough evaluation of both the business and the real estate factors that affect an investment in a hospitality property.

CHAPTER 21

The Securitization Market Meets the Second Mortgage Loan

Peter J. Travers and Victor M. Lopez-Balboa

INTRODUCTION

For many years, the second mortgage loan was the last-resort source of liquidity for troubled individual debtors. Fixed-rate second mortgage loans were originally extended in the late nineteenth century—primarily to finance down payments. They nearly ceased to exist as a viable product during the Great Depression, due to high rates of default. Finance companies began to market second mortgage loans again during the prosperity of the post-World War II real estate boom. The floating-rate home equity line-of-credit second mortgage appeared in the mid-1970s, but was not originated in any volume until the mid-1980s.

With the passage of the Tax Reform Act of 1986, the second mortgage loan market exploded. Over a five year period, the tax bill eliminates the deductibility of consumer loan interest of all types, except for that of loans secured by residential real estate. Savvy consumers, aware of the compelling after-tax cost advantages of borrowing against the value of their homes, flocked to the second mortgage market. During the last two years, this loan has completed its metamorphosis from a mortgage-type loan used for down payments and home improvements to a consumer-type loan used for education, automobile purchases, vacations, and consumer debt consolidation. In 1982, fixed-rate second mortgage loans outstanding were approximately $70 billion, and home equity loans outstanding were only about $1 billion. By the end of 1987, traditional second mortgage loans outstanding totaled approximately $130 billion, and home equity loans outstanding totaled approximately $70 billion.[1] As auto loans, credit card loans, and installment loans are repaid with the proceeds of tax-deductible second mortgages, this high rate of growth is likely to be sustained.

The development of the second mortgage market generally and of home equity loans in particular coincided with another development of fundamental importance to consumer banking: the emergence of securitization as a practical and capital-efficient funding vehicle. Issuers have begun to recognize that second mortgage loans are suitable collateral for asset-backed securities and that the same benefits that accrue from securitizing auto loans and credit card accounts are available through second mortgage securitization. As this consumer product continues its exceptional and disproportionate growth, the availability of effective securitization vehicles to fund that growth will become critical. In fact, in late 1988 and early 1989, there were several private placements of securities backed by traditional fixed-rate second mortgages.

THE SECOND MORTGAGE MARKET

Home Equity Loans and Traditional Second Mortgages

There are two major types of second mortgage loans: fixed-rate, closed-end loans (traditional second mortgages) and variable-rate, open-end loans (home equity loans). "Closed-end" refers to a fixed borrowed amount; "open-end" refers to a variable borrowed amount in the form of a line of credit. As noted earlier, traditional second mortgage loans earned their name because, for nearly a century, they were the only kind of second mortgage loan available. The home equity line of credit is primarily a phenomenon of the past four years. There are also fixed-rate, open-end and floating-rate, closed-end

[1]SMR Research Corportion, *Second Mortgage & Home Equity Loans: 1988* (Budd Lake, N.J.: SMR Research Corportion, 1988).

Figure 21-1. Estimated Second Mortgage Outstandings by Institutional Holder, 1987

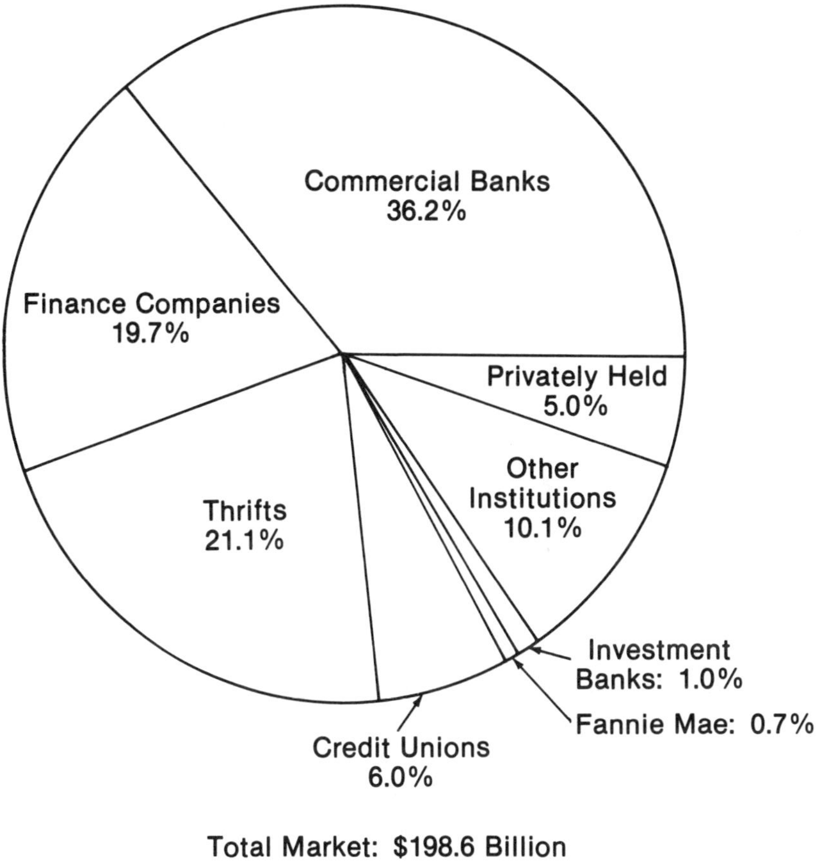

second mortgages, but the amounts outstanding of each are minimal.

Size of the Market

Home equity loan outstandings are still smaller than those of traditional second mortgages (see Figure 21-1). The total market for second mortgages is estimated to be $225 billion dollars, with approximately $100 billion outstanding in home equity loans and $125 billion in traditional fixed-rate second mortgage loans.[2] The

[2]*Ibid.*

Figure 21-2. Estimated Second Mortgage Outstandings, 1982–1988

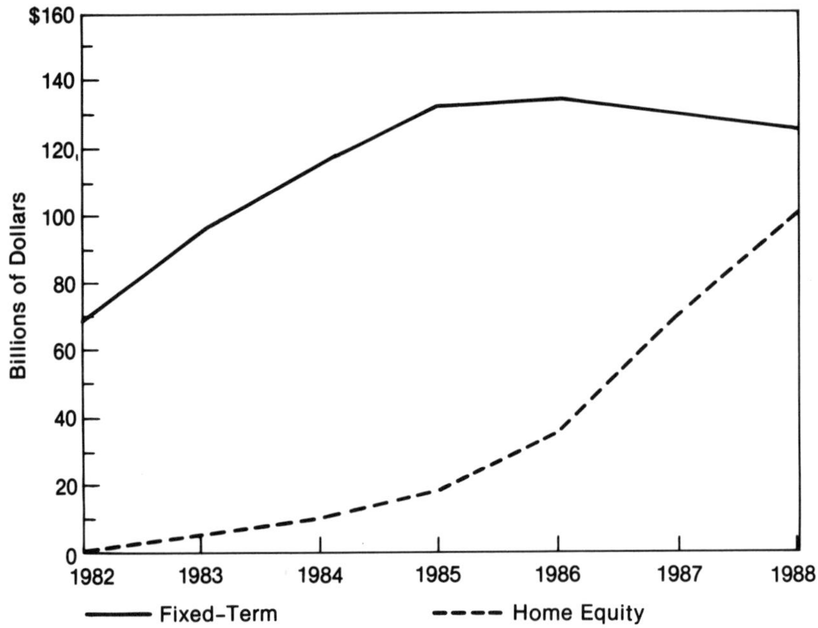

growth in the overall second mortgage market since the early 1980s has come almost entirely from home equity loan originations.

However, the pattern of growth for 1989 is difficult to predict. Certainly, many borrowers view the home equity loan as a less expensive alternative to credit cards. The flexibility of access by check or credit card to $30,000 in credit, as needed, during a 15-year repayment horizon would suggest that home equity loan growth should continue to outstrip that of traditional second mortgage loans. However, several factors may cause traditional second mortgages to have a robust year as well. First, in the current inverted yield curve environment, home equity loans (which are typically priced at a 150- to 350-basis-point spread to the prime rate) may be as expensive as traditional second mortgage loans (which are typically priced at a 250- 300-basis-point spread to intermediate or long-term Treasury securities). Second, if borrowers expect rising short-term rates in the future, fixed-rate loans become more attractive. This effect may be strong because the prime interest rate has risen two and a half points since early 1988. Third, second mortgage lenders—especially commercial banks and thrifts, which must reserve expensive capital against the nonearning portion of home equity loans—

frequently find traditional second mortgage loans more profitable than home equity loans. Closed-end second mortgage loans earn money for the originator immediately, whereas open-end loans cannot be profitable until they are drawn on and remain outstanding for a period of time. Consequently, lenders may structure second mortgage marketing programs to steer consumers into the fixed-rate product.

Originators and Holders

Commercial banks are the largest holders of second mortgages, with approximately $75 billion outstanding at year-end 1987 (see Figure 21-2). Their dominance stems from their overall size and their muscle in marketing consumer debt-type products. Thrifts are also strong competitors in the second mortgage market, with approximately $42 billion outstanding at year-end 1987.[3]

Although third in holdings, finance companies have the longest track record in the second mortgage market. Indeed, two independent finance companies, Household Finance Corporation and Beneficial Corporation, are among the top originators of seconds. It is not surprising that a finance company was the first company to publicly securitize second mortgages—particularly since the average finance company leverage is 6 to 1, whereas a depository institution may leverage itself 16 or 17 to 1. The strict constraints that the rating agencies impose on finance company leverage should provide these firms with a special incentive to fund their second mortgages off balance sheet, through securitization. Relatively modest leverage also means that finance company second mortgages are typically more expensive than those of banks and thrifts. Nonetheless, the finance companies will remain strong competitors for several reasons. First, the finance companies will continue to attract consumers who perceive that finance companies offer a level of personal service that depository institutions do not. In addition, second mortgage borrowers may be, to a limited extent, insensitive to interest rates because of the relatively small average size of the mortgages. For example, the monthly payments on a $20,000, 15-year fully amortizing second mortgage rise only $13 for each percentage point difference in interest rates.

Neither the Federal National Mortgage Association (FNMA) nor the Federal Home Loan Mortgage Corporation (FHLMC) are signifi-

[3] *Ibid.*

cant participants yet in the second mortgage market. Their absence from the market can be attributed to several factors. These agencies have been impeded from swapping their guaranteed mortgage-backed securities for fixed-rate whole loan second mortgages because second mortgages normally amortize on the simple interest method. On the other hand, FNMA and FHLMC securities amortize on the actuarial method. However, the agencies have indicated flexibility on this point, and are willing to analyze substantial pools for purposes of arranging such a swap. With respect to outright purchases, FNMA has erratically purchased traditional second mortgages since 1981, in an aggregate amount of approximately $6 billion. Currently, neither agency is actively purchasing pools, although they are willing to look at pools brought to them. With respect to home equity loans, the agencies are faced with a lack of homogeneity in programs and underwriting practices, together with limited historical data. They have stated that they currently have no plans to purchase or swap for home equity loans. Any change in FNMA and FHLMC securitization policies would significantly alter the landscape of the second mortgage market.

Underwriting Characteristics

To understand second mortgages and their potential for securitization, a review of the key indicators of underwriting quality is essential. In doing so, it is worth emphasizing that second mortgages are hybrid instruments, neither entirely consumer loans nor mortgage loans. A purely collateral-based approach to second mortgage lending is probably not appropriate in light of the subordination of the lender's recourse to property. The collateral is less likely to bail the institution out of underwriting mistakes than it is for first mortgage loans. On the other hand, the value of the collateral that secures the loan is still a central underwriting concern. Both mortgage lending and consumer lending underwriting practices are relevant.

There are roughly seven major underwriting characteristics of second mortgage loans, as follows.

Loan-to-Value Ratio

The typical maximum loan-to-value (LTV) ratio of a home equity loan, when combined with the balance of the first mortgage, is

75 percent of the property's appraisal value for commercial banks and thrifts and 85 percent for finance companies. The impact that this ratio can have is indicated in the guidelines published by Standard & Poor's Corporation (S&P) for fixed-rate, closed-end second mortgages. They have suggested that a 23 percent loss coverage will be required to achieve an AAA-caliber pool composed of nonpurchase money loans with an LTV ratio of 80 percent. A 45 percent loss coverage is required if the loans have a 90 percent LTV ratio. These guidelines reflect the substantial impact of LTV ratios on the collateralization levels required for credit support. Note that the calculation of an LTV ratio requires some monitoring of the underlying first mortgage.

Ratio of First to Second Mortgage Loan

Credit enhancers and the rating agencies place enormous importance on the size of the second mortgage relative to the size of the first mortgage. The smaller the first mortgage is in relation to the second, the more likely it is that the second mortgagee will recover value in foreclosure. This is not surprising because the smaller the claim of the senior loan compared with that of the second mortgage, the more credit protection will be available from the mortgage collateral. Second mortgage originators are well advised to capture these data on their systems when the second mortgage is made.

Appraisals

The usefulness of the LTV ratio depends largely on the soundness of the estimate of value. A majority of second mortgage loans are originated on the basis of full appraisals, whereas a smaller percentage is originated on the basis of "drive-by" appraisals and is based on tax assessments. Full appraisals are important because a second mortgage loan is almost always made other than when the property is sold in an arm's-length transaction. Drive-by appraisals can be supplemented with an adjustment to the estimated value, based on a property appreciation index for the neighborhood or area that is applied to the last available sale price.

Debt Service to Income

Most originators use a median debt service-to-income ratio as a guideline when approving credit lines. A typical minimum ratio would be between 35 percent and 40 percent. Many institutions that use such a formula can relate it to one that they use generally in other areas of their consumer lending businesses.

Purpose of Loan

Identification of the purpose of the loan, although difficult to monitor, can be helpful when assessing the credit quality of the pool. Home improvement and debt consolidation are the major uses of second mortgage proceeds, and these are more desirable than loans whose proceeds are used for vacations and other consumer expenditures. The question of usage is linked closely to the type of property that constitutes the collateral and whether the borrower occupies that property. Loans made against single-family, owner-occupied real estate are, of course, considered the safest.

Method of Access

Access to the line by checks will be preferable to credit card or automatic transfer because checks imply less impulse, consumption-oriented use.

Monitoring the First Mortgage

When underwriting a second mortgage, second mortgage originators should try to collect certain data on the underlying first mortgage. For example, the amortization schedule of the first mortgage is necessary to compute an accurate combined LTV ratio and to determine the size of the first mortgage relative to the size of the second mortgage; both factors are important in assessing credit risks. In addition, such data as first mortgage seasoning and payment history provide the lender with further insight into a mortgagee's repayment characteristics.

MAJOR HURDLES TO SECOND MORTGAGE SECURITIZATION

A number of obstacles are in the path of a second mortgage securitization transaction. These include the uncertain character of the cash flows, doubt regarding their credit quality, and the novelty of various legal issues. Historically, the chief obstacle has been the immaturity of the consumer loan securitization market. However, the large volume and diversity of securitized assets have permitted investors to become familiar with a wide variety of cash flow patterns and collateral characteristics. An entire infrastructure of investors, rating agencies, credit enhancers, lawyers, and accountants has been built. Legal and accounting issues have been addressed, resolved, and routinized. Systems capabilities have been developed to permit sophisticated cash flow modeling for purposes of tranching securities and constructing cash flow configurations. As a result of these developments, the market is more than ready to absorb novel asset-backed securities.

Uncertain Cash Flow

Cash flow uncertainty has always posed difficult questions for the securitization market, particularly with respect to 30-year, fixed-rate first mortgages. Originators of first mortgages have had two advantages in confronting this problem that originators of second mortgages do not possess. First, large amounts of data on prepayment rates in different interest rate environments have been gathered in the past several decades. Data for second mortgages will not be available in the same volume for many years. Second, the long-term, purchase money character of the first mortgage makes analysts more comfortable in assuming that first mortgagors will behave in an economically rational manner. For example, if interest rates rise, it seems reasonable to believe that prepayments will slow significantly; the data have borne this out. As a result of this relative predictability, it is easier to model the relationship between fluctuations in interest rates and prepayments. On the other hand, second mortgage borrowers more frequently make prepayment decisions independent of interest rate movements and expectations. These borrowers often have a specific need in mind and view the loan as an unusual and, perhaps, unfortunate event. They may tend to pay off their loan whenever they are able to do so.

The uncertainty of second mortgage cash flow takes a slightly different form for each of the two types of loan. With home equity loans, there are three cash flow problems. First, home equity lenders offer a dazzling variety of programs and amoritization options. A typical program requires the borrower to pay a monthly fixed percentage of the outstanding amount (for example, 2 percent) regardless of the interest rate. Such a provision precludes a high degree of predictability in principal amortization and can cause negative amortization in high interest rate environments. There are also programs that do not require principal payments or that delay such payments for several years. The resulting balloon obligation is unattractive to rating agencies, credit enhancers, and the market.

Second, there is a dearth of information on prepayment rates and, hence, on the average lives of home equity loans. Many industry experts believe that a typical home equity loan has an average life of three to four years. However, the average life that results in any particular case depends heavily on the percentage of the line that is drawn down at the outset, as well as the required payment of principal, if any. Lines that are largely drawn at the closing will tend to amortize more predictably, since relatively little additional borrowing power will be available.

Third, the interest rate on home equity loans typically floats with the prime rate. Because investors perceive prime as a managed—rather than a market—rate, they will generally not purchase prime-based securities. A home equity loan–backed security must bear interest on another index.

Traditional second mortgages pose similar cash flow problems. They are fixed-rate, level-pay obligations that avoid the floating-rate and amortization uncertainties of home equity loans. Unfortunately, the fixed interest rate makes the absence of reliable prepayment data a formidable marketing problem.

Average life uncertainty causes fixed-rate buyers to demand a hefty yield premium, especially because securities backed by second mortgages may be priced at a 3- to 4-year average life, while the final maturity is normally 15 years. This "extension" risk is far more severe than that found with other consumer loan–backed securities.

Fortunately, there are several reasons that the cash flow uncertainty of second mortgage loans does not pose an insurmountable obstacle to securitizatioon. First, second mortgages have much shorter average lives and final maturities than traditional first mortgages. The value of securities backed by these assets will be affected relatively less by uncertainty regarding average life. Second, prepayment history for both fixed-rate, closed-end and variable-rate, open-end second mortgage loans is beginning to build. Originators, as well as industry research groups, have developed consistent—

though meager—prepayment data. The quality and usefulness of this information will improve in the next few years. Third, different securitization structuring techniques can reduce the effect of uncertain cash flow by segmenting the risk and allocating it to the parties that are best suited to absorb each portion. Finally, home equity loan–backed securities have an advantage in addressing cash flow uncertainty because, as with other floating-rate instruments, they would tend to trade close to par given sufficiently high–interest rate caps. This feature significantly reduces the yield premium demanded by investors for securities that amortize unpredictably. Furthermore, there is a reasonably good correlation between prime, on the one hand, and the London Interbank Offered Rate (LIBOR) and commercial paper rates, on the other. As a result, it is possible to issue securities linked to a market rate index, even though the collateralizing assets are based on prime.

Credit Quality

In light of their tarnished history, it is probably not suprising that considerable doubt exists among investors regarding the credit quality of second mortgages. From a rating agency perspective, second mortgages exhibit several negative characteristics. Because second mortgages amortize more slowly than other consumer debt, the agencies are especially concerned about the risk to investors that long amortization "tails" on the assets pose. Some think that losses on second mortgages may increase—rather than decrease—with seasoning, as relatively good credits prepay their loans quickly. If this suspicion is true, the tail assets will tend to be of low quality.

The rating agencies also believe that the high rate of growth of the second mortgage market and the relative immaturity of many products (especially home equity loans) preclude a well-founded judgment regarding their credit quality at this time. This growth has occurred in the last six years, since the last national economic recession. Home equity loans, in particular, pose difficult credit issues because they do not have scheduled amortization of principal and could even experience negative amortization, as noted earlier. Balloon mortgages, by their nature, are nearly impossible to analyze from a credit perspective.

Despite these negative perceptions of second mortgage loans, there are various positive factors. Most important is the outstanding charge-off and delinquency rates that these loans have experienced to date. Traditional second mortgages appear to have net charge-off rates of approximately 25 basis points and delinquency rates (over 60 days) of between 1.5 and 1.75 percent. Credit data for home equity loans are even more impressive. Consumer Bankers Association data suggest that charge-offs on home equity loans averaged less than three basis points for the six months ended June 1988. Approximately 0.76 percent of home equity loans were delinquent during this period. By comparison, delinquency rates during 1987 were estimated at 2.33 percent for credit cards and 1.72 percent for auto loans. These data are impressive, even after factoring in the relative prosperity prevailing when these assets were originated and home equity loans' potential to draw down to avoid delinquencies.

The agencies are beginning to appreciate the upscale and sophisticated profile of home equity borrowers. The Federal Reserve reports that holders of home equity accounts are typically younger and have had more years of education than other home owners have had. Families with home equity accounts had median 1986 family incomes of $42,000, compared with $27,000 for home owners without such accounts. For home owners with home equity accounts, the median amount of equity in the home was $64,000; for home owners without such accounts, it was $46,000. Similar data are not available for traditional second mortgages, but many originators believe that similar observations could be made about their customers.

Finally, recent studies suggest that a significant percentage—between 10 percent and 30 percent—of second mortgage loans actually represent first liens on the underlying real estate. This phenomenon results primarily from amortization or prepayment on the underlying first mortgage.

The consideration of all of these factors—both positive and negative—leads knowledgeable observers to take a cautiously favorable view of the quality of second mortgage loans. However, it seems clear that until several more years of data, including data gathered during a recession, are available, the rating agencies and the market will demand more credit support for second mortgage pools than might be expected. Among other consequences, this attitude gives third party credit enhancers a special opportunity to add value in a securitized financing. The history of the transactions done to date suggests strongly that a portfolio of either type of second mortgage loans can achieve remarkably low levels of overcollateralization or recourse if it is analyzed by a sophisticated and knowledgeable credit enhancer.

Legal Issues

A variety of generic legal issues must be resolved in any securitization transaction. In addition, several of these issues are specific to second mortgages. These latter include enforcement of liens, preservation of security interests, recordation of the transfer of the security interest, usury limits, and regulatory accounting treatment.

Generally speaking, the procedures for enforcing a second mortgage are the same as those for a first mortgage. A payment default under a second mortgage will not normally be a default under a first mortgage, but the foreclosure on a second mortgage may lead to a default under a first mortgage that contains a due-on-sale provision. As a result, the holder of a second mortgage may be forced to pay off the first mortgage to take title to the property and avoid a total loss, in case the bidding by third parties at a foreclosure sale is not high enough to repay both the first and second mortgages.

One of the fundamental legal questions relates to the security interest of the home equity lender with respect to advances subsequent to the closing on a home equity credit line. Traditionally, future advances under a credit line secured by a mortgage take priority over intervening loans secured by the same property, as long as the future advance on the credit line was obligatory. If additional advances are subject to conditions in which a borrower cannot be reasonably assured at the outset of meeting, the priority of future advances will be unclear. However, many states have eliminated the distinction between voluntary and obligatory advances and provide, instead, that future advances under a credit line mortgage made within 20 years from the date of the mortgage relate back to the recording date of that mortgage. From the standpoint of securitization, drawdowns under the home equity line should be automatic, at least in states without the new type of statute.

The rating agencies require sellers of first mortgage loan pass-throughs to transfer mortgage documentation to the trustee for the transaction and to re-record the first mortgages in the name of the trustee. The rating agencies require such transfer and recordation to ensure the validity of the trustee's security interest in the mortgages. In the absence of such a transfer, the interest of the trustee in the mortgages may be defeated by creditors of the seller or by subsequent transferees of the mortgages by the seller. Transfer of documentation and re-recording title to the mortgages, therefore, permit the loan-backed securities to be rated higher than the rating of the seller.

In the Household transaction, the rating agencies relaxed their rule requiring document transfer and title recordation in the trustee's name. Instead, they permitted the loan documentation to remain with the selling Household affiliates, as long as Household's long-term ratings remained BBB+ or higher. This departure from established rating precedent for first mortgage pass-throughs specifically accommodated the logistical nightmare of securitizing 26,500 loans with an average size of approximately $28,000. In contrast, first mortgage pass-throughs often have fewer than 1,000 loans in the pool. It appears likely that this type of accommodation by the rating agencies will be necessary in most second mortgage securitization transactions, in which the seller is not a federally regulated depository institution. In other cases, the accommodation may be available only to investment-grade-rated sellers.

State usury laws also present a structuring issue. Although the asset-backed securities will not violate any usury law restrictions (since they are likely to be governed by New York law), the loans, themselves, could become subject to usury restrictions by virtue of their transfer to the trust, if their exemption from the state usury law was based on the originator's status (for example, as a national bank). A borrower could then raise usury as a defense in collection proceedings, although the success of such a defense is doubtful. Nevertheless, this point of state law will need to be researched when a loan pool is cut.

Another significant legal question, which relates to structuring flexibility, is how to achieve a "sale" for purposes of regulatory accounting practices. An accounting sale will allow the originator to take the loans off of its regulatory balance sheet and to free up the required capital associated with those assets. The regulatory analysis for purposes of the accounting sale depends on whether second mortgage loans are deemed to be residential mortgages under the instructions and glossary to the bank call report forms. If they are not deemed to be residential mortgages, no recourse to the originator will be permitted. If they are so deemed, recourse of between 5 percent and 10 percent may be permitted. Federal regulators have informally indicated that second mortgages do qualify as residential mortgages, although nothing has been put in writing. In either case, securitization structures can incorporate an escrow arrangement for excess interest that will address this problem. To the extent that counsel can be satisfied that some direct recourse is permitted, the credit support that the agencies require can be reduced.

SECOND MORTGAGE SECURITIZATION TRANSACTIONS

For many years, the origination of second mortgages has generally been undertaken by firms that have easy access to the capital markets on an unsecured basis or that have assiduously built up a private network of buyers that have come to appreciate their safety and yield. This whole loan market has been reasonably efficient for small amounts, but clearly cannot absorb the substantial volume of new second mortgage origination. There is hardly any whole loan secondary market for home equity loans. By separating the origination from the funding of second mortgages, securitization will allow smaller firms to compete more evenly with well-capitalized originators. Mortgage bankers will also benefit from securitization because, although they may possess a competitive advantage in origination, they may not have the resources to finance their originations on the balance sheet.

The securitization secondary market for second mortgages began to take shape in 1988, with several small fixed-rate, closed-end pass-through transactions. The securitization market for home equity loans was launched in early 1989, with the $746 million public offering of home equity loan–backed securities by Household. These precedents, together with other potential structures, should give issuers confidence in the ability of the securitization market to create and distribute attractive securities backed by illiquid second mortgages.

Home Equity Loans—Household Finance Corporation

In January 1989, Household issued the first home equity loan–backed security. These securities, known as home equity loan asset-backed certificates, were sold as pass-through certificates that evidenced undivided interests in a pool of 26,500 home equity revolving credit loans secured by first (12 percent) and second (88 percent) liens on residential property. The underlying home equity loans float predominantly at spreads of 350 to 550 basis points above prime and were originated in 30 states. They have a combined LTV ratio of 68 percent and have an average utilization rate of 91 percent.

Using a REMIC tax election, Household issued these certificates in two classes. The Class A certificates, whose interest floats at a 35-basis-point spread to the one-month commercial paper composite, are rated AAA by S&P and Aaa by Moody's on the basis of subordination of cash flow from the Class B and Class C certificates. The Class B certificates, which float at a spread of three eighths over one-month LIBOR, are rated AA– by S&P and A1 by Moody's on the basis of a 100 percent guarantee from Household. The Class C certificates, which are unrated and retained by Household, represent (1) the excess yield from the pool after payment of interest on the Class A and B certificates and (2) compensation to Household for servicing and guaranty fees. The interest rates on the Class A and Class B certificates are capped at weighted-average loan rates of the home equity loan pool, less servicing fees. At the cutoff date, this cap corresponded to an interest ceiling for the first month of approximately 13 percent and a 22 percent lifetime cap.

Several aspects of the transaction are noteworthy. First, the structure borrowed heavily from technology developed in the first mortgage securitization market. The certificates imitated a sequential pay CMO, in which the Class B certificates are entitled to receive principal only after the entire principal of the Class A certificates is retired. Second, although only the drawn-down portion of the home equity loans was transferred to the securitized pool, principal payments on both the initial amounts drawn down and subsequent advances on the same account were used to retire the securities. Consequently, subsequent advances on the home equity loans will be funded by Household on balance sheet and will have a longer average life than that of the certificates. Finally, as noted above, the rating agencies rated the Class A certificates AAA/Aaa, even though the second mortgages were not re-recorded in the name of the trustee.

Other Home Equity Loan Structures

The Household transaction is a variation of the basic floating-rate pass-through structure. Two other structures exist that seem likely to be deployed in the second mortgage securitization market. The first is home equity loan auction rate certificates (ARCs). Drawing on the precedent set by the auction preferred stock market, ARCs are a means of raising inexpensive floating-rate funds while rendering irrelevant the prepayment risk inherent in home equity loans. With the auction rate structure, a trust would purchase home equity loan balances and fund the purchase with the ARCs, which could be credit enhanced by either subordination, letters of credit, or surety bonds. The ARCs would be auctioned every 30 days, in an amount determined by the remaining balance of the underlying pool. Because ARC investors have only a 30-day horizon (until each auction), they are indifferent to the average life uncertainty of the ARCs. In addition, the amortizing nature of the auction should also lead to a downward pressure on reset rates, especially in light of adjustable preferred stock (APS) data that suggest that as many as two thirds of all orders submitted at each auction are hold orders.

Currently, the market for ARCs or auction rate notes is limited, due to Investment Company Act restrictions against investments by money market funds in securities whose final maturity is greater than one year. However, certain structures would enable money market funds to purchase ARCs and auction rate notes. With an expanded investor base, ARCs could rapidly become a popular vehicle for securitizing floating-rate assets.

A collateralized commercial paper program is also a funding alternative for home equity loans. The home equity loan lender would sell a pool of loans to a nominally capitalized, third party–owned special-purpose corporation. The special-purpose corporation would then issue commercial paper to fund the home equity loans over time, rolling over its commercial paper position to fund the underlying home equity loans. A liquidity facility would be available to the special-purpose corporation in the event that its access to the commercial paper market was interrupted. Attractive financing rates are attainable under this structure, as borne out in precedents for conduit trade receivable financings by Citibank, Chase, and First Chicago, among others. However, to the extent that the liquidity facility is ever drawn on, the financing cost will rise significantly.

Traditional Fixed-Rate Second Mortgages

The securitization of fixed-rate second mortgages has evolved from occasional whole loan placements to small private placements of single-class pass-through certificates. Recent transactions by Advanta Corp. and The Money Store have taken the latter form. The transactions were $50 million or less in size and were insured by the Financial Guaranty Insurance Company. Generally, the sellers have retained recourse in the form of a 4–6 percent subordination of cash flow to Financial Guaranty. In turn, satisfied with the credit quality of the senior certificates, Financial Guaranty has wrapped the transaction with its AAA surety bond. As single-class pass-throughs, the transactions unloaded the prepayment uncertainty of the traditional second mortgages onto investors.

Alternative structures have been developed to allocate the prepayment risk of the assets more efficiently. Second mortgage lenders are best situated to assess the prepayment rate of their portfolio. As a result, structures that segregate risk components between the securitization market, which can efficiently evaluate and price certain cash flow components, and originators, which are experienced in repayment characteristics, can substantially reduce the re-offer spread on second mortgage securities. One such structure involves a fixed-rate second mortgage pass-through certificate with a maturity guaranty—for example, at six years. Although traditional second mortgages may exhibit average life variability, the extension risk displayed by extremely slow prepayment risks is truncated at the maturity guaranty point. Having made arrangements up front to insulate itself from funding and interest rate risk, the guarantor may be willing to charge a reasonable premium for the guaranty.

CONCLUSION

During the next several years, the pace of securitization activity is likely to be brisk. Securitization, has, in effect, received the imprimatur of the federal banking authorities, through their adoption of the risk-based capital guidelines. As a result, the cheapest source of new capital for banks will be the internal reallocation of assets away from the highest risk-weighted categories and toward lower categories. Thus, there will be a substantial capital incentive to securitize second mortgages and other consumer loans in the 100 percent risk-weight category in off-balance-sheet financings. If the proceeds are invested in mortgage securities or other assets with a lower risk weighting, the selling bank will have created new regulatory capital. The securitization market is also rapidly becoming more mature and refined. As investors become more comfortable with the cash flow and credit characteristics of a wider variety of assets, reoffer spreads will narrow, and execution will become less time consuming and onerous.

The potential for structural improvements in securitization financings is especially clear with second mortgages. Securitization structures for these assets are still in their first generation. Additional developments adapted from other assets and fostered by the availability of more and better information on portfolios will allow second mortgages to play a prominent—if not predominant—role in this market in the years ahead. New techniques for cutting the tail on securitization pools and better acceptance of the credit quality of these assets will reinforce this phenomenon. Furthermore, the flexibility and tax-advantaged character of second mortgages will allow them to garner a progressively larger share of the consumer loan market, as borrowers pay down loans with the proceeds of second mortgages. In fact, the second mortgage loan may become the staple of consumer loan securitization in the 1990s.

CHAPTER 22

Farmer Mac: The Federal Agricultural Mortgage Corporation

Philip A. Brooks

INTRODUCTION

Joining the Federal National Mortgage Association (FNMA), the Federal Home Loan Mortgage Corporation (FHLMC), and the Government National Mortgage Association (GNMA) is the newest entrant in the quasigovernmental real estate industry markets: Farmer Mac. Formally known as the Federal Agricultural Mortgage Corporation, it was created in January 1988 as part of the Agricultural Credit Act of 1987 (P.L. 100-233). Farmer Mac is scheduled to go into full operation by middle to late 1989.

Farmer Mac's congressional charter is to provide a guaranty for securities backed by agricultural real estate and rural housing mortgages. It will not deal in loans for implements, tractors, harvesters, or other operational equipment. This provision of guaranty or credit enhancement should make loans on farm real estate easier to originate, pool, and sell to investors. Farmer Mac's mandate is to increase the availability of long-term credit at fixed rates to farmers and ranchers and to help people in rural communities to buy moderately priced homes.

Farmer Mac was created as an outgrowth of the federal

government's efforts to address the deep financial woes of the agricultural industry. Congress had turned its attention to aiding the financially strapped Farm Credit System, which originates the vast majority of the nation's farm loans, by pumping in huge amounts of money to keep it solvent. Private agricultural credit lenders, such as insurance companies, commercial banks, and savings and loan associations, were also squeezed, as farm profits blew away and foreclosures increased. They, too, needed relief.

Born in the aftermath of the farm crisis, which saw more farmers go bankrupt than during the Great Depression, Farmer Mac is too late to save farmers from their wrenching economic experiences of the late 1970s and early 1980s, when accelerating variable-rate mortgages stripped profits. By making available long-term fixed-rate credit, Farmer Mac could help prevent such disruption in the future. Some agricultural credit experts say that if a similar program had been in existence in the early 1970s, America's farm crisis may not have been so harsh.

FARMER MAC'S RESPONSIBILITIES

Farmer Mac's duties are straightforward and simple. In addition to its guaranty authority, they include developing uniform underwriting, security appraisal, and repayment standards for loans—in this case, fee simple, first mortgages on agricultural real estate. Mortgages on single-family dwellings in rural areas, with populations of less than 2,500 people, may qualify as well. The biggest loan that Farmer Mac will guarantee is $2.5 million, while the smallest is $50,000. Loan-to-value ratios for all mortgages cannot exceed 80 percent.

Farmer Mac's focal point is its ability to provide a repayment guaranty. Its mandate is to ensure investors of the timely payment of principal and interest on securities issued by certified poolers of qualified agricultural real estate mortgages. Like GNMA, Farmer Mac is restricted only to guaranteeing mortgage pools; however, its guaranty does not constitute the full faith and credit of the United States. Unlike FNMA or FHLMC, it cannot buy whole loans or issue securities. Another important difference is that Farmer Mac will provide only a 90 percent guaranty—not 100 percent like GNMA.

To build the 90 percent guaranty reserve, Farmer Mac will assess security issuers an initial guaranty fee of not more than 50 basis points of the outstanding principal amount of each loan pool. Farmer Mac can also assess these issuers an annual fee of 50 basis points, beginning in the second year after the date on which the guaranty is issued. The remaining 10 percent guaranty is put up by lenders in a reserve pool. This pool must be exhausted before Farmer Mac will pay off any loan pool that goes bad. These reserve funds may be invested only in federal security instrumentalities.

The 10 percent guaranty of the poolers should be enough of a buffer to prevent triggering of the Farmer Mac guaranty. According to 1987 statistics that Congress considered when studying the Farmer Mac legislative proposals, then-current data on farm mortgage delinquencies indicated that the 10 percent coinsurance reserve would have been adequate without resorting to abnormally stringent appraisal and underwriting standards. These statistics also revealed that recent loan performances of farm lenders showed net charge-offs well below 10 percent in 1985 and 1986. For example, 1985 commercial bank net charge-offs on farm production loans as a percentage of total farm production loans outstanding were 3.1 percent. Of course, these statistics reflect general economic trends when the financial status of the agricultural economy was at its worst since the Great Depression. Since that time, that economy has shown stability and is beginning to improve.

Should its reserve fund become depleted, Farmer Mac is authorized to borrow up to $1.5 billion from the U.S. Treasury to cover guaranties. The guaranty authority of Farmer Mac will be implemented over a period of several years. During the first year of operation, the maximum aggregate amount of Farmer Mac's guaranty is limited to 2 percent of the total agricultural real estate debt outstanding at the close of the prior calendar year, excluding the debt of the Farm Credit System institutions and the Farmers Home Administration. Calculation of this debt is to be determined by the Federal Reserve Bank. During the second full year of Farmer Mac's operation, that aggregate percentage is increased to 4 percent. In the third year, it increases to 6 percent. Unused authority from the first and second years may be carried forward to the second and third years. After the third year, no limitation is placed on Farmer Mac's guaranty authority.

ELIGIBLE SECURITIES

The types of securities that Farmer Mac will guarantee can vary, but the most probable vehicle is the collateralized mortgage obligation (CMO) structured as a real estate mortgage investment conduit (REMIC). Unlike FNMA and FHLMC mortgage-backed securities, securities backed by Farmer Mac will not be exempt from registration and reporting requirements of the Securities and Exchange Commission (SEC). Farmer Mac CMOs could be rated in a two-tier fashion: one for the 10 percent at-risk portion, another for the 90 percent guaranteed portion.

The REMIC structure will allow investors to have multiple classes with differing maturities. Investors may have a regular interest, which has a set term on a startup date for a specific principal amount of a fixed interest rate, or they could have a residual interest representing contingent cash flows of the extent of prepayments or contingent payments on underlying mortgages.

The interest charged to the borrower will depend on the pricing of the securities. Such pricing will be based, in part, on fees paid to originators, Farmer Mac, the SEC, and investment banks. For optimal marketing, standardized payment features must be formalized. Loans paying annually or semiannually will probably carry higher loan rates than monthly paying loans.

STANDARDS AND REQUIREMENTS

Detailed borrower standards are still being worked on, but they will probably be similar to those for other types of mortgage loans. Each borrower will be required to show enough cash flow to service the mortgage. Lenders will be required to adhere to documentation and appraisal standards. Borrowers in states with borrowers' rights statutes cannot be refused a Farmer Mac guaranty, but lenders may assess them additional fees to cover costs and expenses.

Qualified lenders can be member institutions of the Farm Credit System or corporations, associations, or trust organizations chartered under U.S. law or state law. Obviously, one of the lender's purposes must be the sale or resale of securities that represent interests in or obligations backed by pools of qualified loans that have been guaranteed by Farmer Mac. However, there are many other requirements. Among them, a lender must show acceptable managerial ability with respect to agricultural mortgage loan underwriting, servicing, and marketing. The lender must also open its books to Farmer Mac's scrutiny. Originators will have the right to service the loan. After all of the requirements are met and the application is made, Farmer Mac has 60 days to approve a lender.

Pooling must be prudent, which requires lenders to diversify their mortgages. Geographic diversification is mandated, as are varying principal amounts. No loan greater than 3.5 percent of the aggregate pool amount may be included in a pool, and no two loans from the same borrower can be included in any one pool. Finally, no pool can consist of more than 50 loans.

If a default occurs, the originator must absorb any loss up to the total amount it contributed to the 10 percent reserve, and others in the pool must do the same. Only after this has occurred would Farmer Mac provide payment to cover any additional loss. If a lender fails to make the payment of principal or interest on a security, Farmer Mac is required to make the payment to the security holder.

THE BEGINNING OF OPERATIONS

Farmer Mac is on a congressionally mandated schedule to begin its operations. An interim board of directors was named in the summer of 1988. The temporary board's job was to raise $20 million from the sale of common stock. In November 1988, Farmer Mac completed its first public offering of the sale of common stock to be used to capitalize the corporation.

This Farmer Mac stock was divided into three classes: Classes A and B are voting stock, while Class C is nonvoting. Class A stock was available to be purchased by, transferred to, or held by banks, other financial institutions, and insurance companies. Class B stock can be held only by Farm Credit System institutions. The initial public offering price was $20 per share. Class C stock was issued to purchasers of Class A or B stock, but was not allowed to be traded and has not been offered to the public.

The interim board of directors set minimum ownership requirements for four categories of Class A shareholders. Small institutions with less than $50 million of assets had to purchase at least 250 shares to be considered as originators. Intermediate-sized institutions with more than $50 million and less than $100 million of assets had to purchase at least 500 shares to be considered as originators. Large institutions with between $100 million and $500 million of assets had to purchase at least 1,250 shares to be considered as originators, while major institutions with over $500 million of assets had to purchase over 5,000 shares.

To be eligible to act as a pooler of Farmer Mac–approved agricultural real estate mortgages, institutions had to purchase at least 12,500 shares of Class A common voting stock. Because of an oversubscription of offers to purchase Class A stock, the number of shares required to be owned by institutions in these categories was reduced proportionally. The common voting stock of Classes A and B and the nonvoting common stock of Class C are not transferable from the owners to other entities for five years from the anniversary date of the circular offering or one year after Farmer Mac makes its first public offering of Class C nonvoting stock, whichever occurs first.

A 15-member permanent board of directors will be named by the interim board of directors when the capitalization process is completed. Five members will be elected by the stockholders, which are represented by insurance companies, banks, and other financial institutions. Another five members will be elected by Farm Credit System institution representatives holding common stock. Five politically appointed directors have already been nominated by the President, and four of those were confirmed by the Senate in 1988. The fifth political appointee will be nominated by the President in 1989.

CONCLUSION

If the promise of Farmer Mac is upheld, renewed economic vitality in agriculture should be the payoff. If the success of FNMA and FHLMC are any indication, Farmer Mac should do a splendid job down on the farm.

CHAPTER 23

Pass-Through Certificates Backed by Lease Payments for Commercial Aircraft

Karl P. Essig

INTRODUCTION

In October 1987, American Airlines issued $92.6 million of equipment note pass-through certificates. The proceeds from the offering were used to refinance the debt component of the leveraged leases for six McDonnell Douglas DC-9-82 aircraft acquired by American in 1986.

The issue was noteworthy because it represented the first public debt offering securitized by the cash flow from multiple leveraged leases. In addition, the issue (a pass-through issue) achieved more favorable pricing and nonmoney terms than would have been available for an issue of conventional equipment trust certificates (ETCs) placed in either the public or private market. Given these advantages and the favorable reception of investors, American concluded its second pass-through issue in September 1988. Other issues are expected to follow.

STRUCTURE

The structure of this transaction evolved from discussions in late 1986 between American and Morgan Stanley. American was

Figure 23-1. Equipment Note Pass-Through Certificates

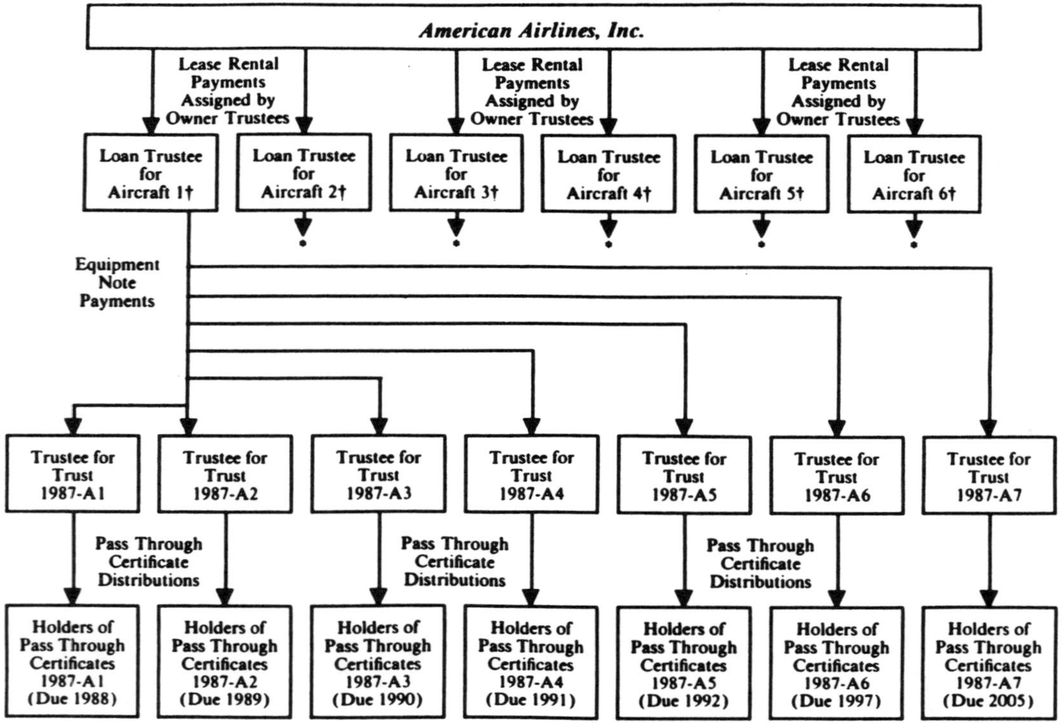

(†) Payments of the balance of the Lease rental payments to the Owner Participants for Aircraft 1 through 6 are not shown on the diagram.

(*) Payments related to Aircraft 2 through 6 flow in the same manner as the payments related to Aircraft 1.

interested in finding the most cost-effective way to refinance the debt portion of six leveraged leases. Using an understanding of the asset-backed security market and leveraged leasing, Morgan Stanley developed a structure that pools the debt associated with multiple leases and creates a series of debt tranches that simultaneously capitalizes on the shape of the yield curve and permits the optimization of individual leases.

American established seven trusts, each of which is associated with a specific tranche of the issue. Each trust issued certificates that pass through to certificate holders all cash flows received by the particular trust. Each trust uses the proceeds from the debt issue to purchase equipment notes from equity owner/participants in leveraged leases of the individual aircraft.

The equipment notes are debt obligations secured by lease streams from the individual sale/leaseback transactions. Each trust holds an equipment note for each of the six aircraft, and each trust has defined principal distribution dates and a specified interest rate. In this manner, cash flow from each plane is used to service a portion of the principal and interest of each of the seven tranches (see Figure 23-1).

To determine the optimal number of tranches and the specific maturity of each, Morgan Stanley analyzed the pooled debt service cash flows of the leveraged leases completed on the six aircraft. We determined that given a steep yield curve, superior economies could be achieved by dividing these cash flows into five bullet tranches, ranging from 0.2 years to 4.2 years, and two sinking fund tranches, with average lives of 8 years and 13.8 years. Each tranche was priced off a relevant benchmark, which, in aggregate, yielded a lower all-in cost to American than if the entire issue were priced off a single index (see Table 23-1).

Prior to final pricing, we ran a number of sample lease optimizations to ensure that the tranching would not vary given limited movements in interest rates. Once the actual coupon rate was set for each tranche, the lease cash flows were reoptimized, and cash flows were allocated among the tranches to preserve the financing cost to American and the economic return to the investor.

**Table 23-1. American Airlines 1987-A Grantor Trusts—
October 2, 1987
Equipment Note Pass-Through Certificates ($92,621,770)**

Trust	Maturity	Principal Amount	Coupon	Price	Spread at Pricing	Average Life (years)
1987-A1	1/1/88	$ 3,447,770	8.96%	Par	+20 (3 mo. LIBOR)	0.228
1987-A2	1/1/89	6,523,000	9.13	Par	+85 (15 mo.)	1.228
1987-A3	1/1/90	9,928,000	9.42	Par	+80 (2 yr.)	2.228
1987-A4	1/1/91	7,881,000	9.65	Par	+75 (3 yr.)	3.228
1987-A5	1/1/92	1,705,000	9.97	Par	+85 (4 yr.)	4.228
1987-A6	7/1/92	1,039,000				
	7/1/93	1,594,000				
	7/1/94	1,751,000				
	7/1/95	3,964,000				
	1/1/96	2,065,000				
	7/1/96	4,112,000				
	1/1/97	5,424,000				
	Total	$19,949,000	10.52	Par	+85 (10 yr.)	7.990
1987-A7	1/1/98	$ 1,547,000				
	1/1/99	4,023,000				
	1/1/2000	5,407,000				
	1/1/2001	7,093,000				
	1/1/2002	7,901,000				
	7/1/2002	162,000				

**Table 23-1. American Airlines 1987-A Grantor Trusts—
October 2, 1987
Equipment Note Pass-Through Certificates ($92,621,770) (Continued)**

Trust	*Maturity*	*Principal Amount*	*Coupon*	*Price*	*Spread at Pricing*	*Average Life (years)*
	1/1/2003	8,452,000				
	1/1/2004	4,092,000				
	1/1/2005	4,511,000				
	Total	$43,188,000	11.11	Par	+135 (14 yr.)	14.091
		$92,621,770	10.80%	Par	+113 (10 yr.)	8.977

ADVANTAGES TO THE AIRLINE

Significant economic benefits accrue to an airline with the pass-through structure. Typically, the debt portion of a leveraged lease for an individual aircraft is sold in the private market to one or more purchasers as a sinking fund issue with a single interest rate. By comparison, the pass-through structure accommodates a multiple number of aircraft with different equity owner/participants. Therefore, it eliminates the need to negotiate individual financings for each aircraft and allows an airline to amortize fixed issuance costs over a larger principal amount.

In addition, if the airline desires call flexibility, as American did, the cost of financing to the call date is considerably lower for tranches of debt with ascending coupons than for a sinking fund issue with a single coupon. With an upward sloping yield curve, the airline pays a lower interest cost on tranched debt in the early years. The size of the savings is a function of the length of time to call and the difference between the early coupons and the weighted-average interest cost.

Furthermore, the pass-through structure generally provides nonmoney terms that are superior to those available to the airline in the private market. For example, a pass-through issue does not provide for cross-acceleration among tranches in the event of default. Such a covenant would likely be required in a private placement.

As an alternative to the private market, some airlines have accessed the public market through a series of ETCs. Similar to a private placement, public ETCs finance the debt portion of a leveraged lease that is associated with a single aircraft. In general, public ETCs are structured as a series of small debt issues, each of which has restrictive call provisions. The American issue provides the airline with considerably greater call flexibility, since longer tranches can be callable at the issuer's option after a limited period.

The American issue provides pricing superior to both the private placement and the public ETC structures because the tranches are viewed as more liquid investments and are, therefore, priced relative to public market spreads. In addition, the pooling of the debt component of several aircraft leases provides greater flexibility in structuring the cash flows, given a particular yield curve.

Finally, because the issue is structured to resemble a corporate bond with a known maturity, relatively stable cash flows, and sinking fund, this lease debt is attractive to the more traditional buyers of corporate debt. As a consequence, there is a wider market for this form of debt, which includes mutual funds, bank trust accounts, pension funds, and insurance companies.

ADVANTAGES TO INVESTORS

This security is attractive to investors for a number of reasons. Many of the tranches are large enough to provide the investor with liquidity, while offering a yield advantage to similarly rated corporate paper. In addition, the tranches exhibit cash flow stability and provide the investor with some call protection. There is a low risk of early termination, and the security benefits from additional bankruptcy protection.

The larger size of a pass-through issue attracts a greater number of investors than does a typical ETC for a single aircraft. These securities offer the investor an opportunity to buy highly rated debt with a somewhat higher yield than similarly rated corporate paper.

Pass-through certificates exhibit little repayment risk when compared with other securitized financings, such as mortgage- and automobile loan–backed issues. Prepayments occur only in certain limited circumstances—principally the loss of the aircraft or the termination of its use by the airline due to obsolescence. There is a relatively low risk of early termination due to obsolescence, as these planes are a small portion of American's planned 250-plane fleet of McDonnell Douglas MD-80s.

Finally, the rating agencies award pass-through certificates, as well as ETCs, a higher rating than that of the airline's senior debt, due to special protection under Section 1110 of the U.S. Bankruptcy Code. This section excludes the equipment notes from an automatic stay-of-creditor claim in the case of default. In other words, the airline must continue to make interest and principal payments on the debt or forfeit the use of the airplanes.

FUTURE TRENDS IN AIRCRAFT FINANCE

A number of factors suggest that this type of structure will have an increasingly important place in the future of aircraft finance. Collectively, domestic U.S. airlines have aircraft financing needs that exceed the capacity of the private market; changes in tax legislation have increased the importance of the debt component of leveraged leases; and the structure has the capacity to accommodate specific airplane, airline, or market nuances.

The Tax Reform Act of 1986 reduced the benefits associated with equipment ownership. As debt becomes a more important aspect of equipment financing, equity investors will be relatively less important than they were in the past.

CONCLUSION

The pass-through structure provides a method of financing the combined debt of a multiple number of leveraged leases. As such, it does not depend on the type of aircraft being financed. Nor must all of the aircraft in the pool be of the same type. In addition, not all of the aircraft must be delivered or subjected to a lease at the time of financing. Thus, the structure can eliminate the time, expense, and market risk inherent in bridge financing. Finally, the equity investors need not be the same.

Similarly, the structure is sufficiently flexible to include bullet maturities or sinking fund tranches. The final structure chosen will be a function of the objectives of the airline and the equity participants, the pooled cash flows, and the steepness of the yield curve.

The pass-through structure can be used for any type of equipment and for foreign or domestic lessees. With respect to a foreign lessee, the equity component can be structured to be consistent with local practices, while a pass-through structure can be used to obtain the lowest cost of debt in the U.S. or international market.

CHAPTER 24
Case Study: The U.S. Department of Education Loan Asset Sales Program

Pat Cooper

INTRODUCTION

The U.S. Department of Education's (ED's) sale of loans from its college housing and academic facilities portfolios was one of the three federal government loan asset sales successfully achieved by two federal agencies in fiscal year 1987. ED's loan sale met its objectives of maximizing total proceeds, meeting the budget targets on time, and complying with the Federal Credit Policy Working Group's Guidelines for Loan Asset Sales. ED's innovative transaction has several unique features that illustrate its precedent-setting contributions to the privatization of government programs.

The most important result of that loan asset sale was the unique blend of cooperation between the public sector and the private sector, which should serve as the bedrock for future loan sales. Selling loans without recourse meant selling loans in accordance with private sector standards—not government standards. Differences in procedures and practices familiar to public and private sector parties require both sides to negotiate to reach reasonable compromises. The public sector had to adapt quickly and demonstrate a high degree of flexibility, while the private sector had to accept certain constraints on the authority of government agencies and individuals. This extraordinary joint effort of both the public and private sectors is embodied in the success of ED's 1987 Loan Asset Sales Program.

Proceeds of the Sale

On September 29, 1987, the College and University Facility Loan Trust One acquired from ED a portfolio of 324 loans to postsecondary educational institutions, aggregating $237,248,552 in principal amount. Simultaneously, the trust issued $126,995,000 of secured bonds, which were sold to the public, and certificates of beneficial interest, which are currently held by ED. ED realized net proceeds of $120,492,693 (after issuance expenses and funding the liquidity and expense funds), plus certificates estimated to be worth $10.8 million (assuming a present value discount rate of 14 percent). The secured bonds were sold at an average spread of 93 basis points over U.S. Treasuries, which represented the nonrecourse cost of government loan asset sale. In other words, ED was able to realize approximately 95 percent of the amount that the U.S. Treasury would have received through the sale of bills, bonds, and notes of comparable maturities.

Structure

The loan sale transaction used a senior subordinated overcollateralization structure, which enabled the bonds to be rated AAA by both major rating agencies. The senior/subordinated structure dedicates all repayments on the 324 loans first to payments due on the bonds and second to the certificate holder(s). The cash flow of all repayments from the loans exceeds the payments due on the bonds by an overcollateralization level of 108 percent on a cash flow basis, with a liquidity fund of $2.6 million. The structure provided the highest overall return to ED, given the nature of the loans, market conditions, and ED's objectives. Five unique aspects of the structure were:

- *Use of a structured transaction.* This permitted access to efficient markets for the bonds, achieved a high degree of credit strength due to diversification, minimized the time necessary to complete the loan sale, and eliminated the passing on of the tax exemption to investors.

- *Aaa/AAA ratings.* These provided the most aggressive pricing for the bond issue and broadened the market for the trust's bonds and for future ED loan sales.
- *Overcollateralization as credit enhancement.* This provided greater net proceeds to ED when compared with third party enhancements, such as bond issuance.
- *Regulated investment company statutes.* This permitted the trust to avoid federal and state taxation, including alternative minimum tax, and increased the value of the cash flow. A favorable revenue ruling was given by the Internal Revenue Service (IRS), and a favorable exemptive order was granted by the Securities and Exchange Commission (SEC) for this transaction.
- *Noncallable serial and term bonds.* These created yield advantages by providing investors with certainty as to the timeliness of the prepayment of principal.

Loan Portfolio

The impressive economic result was due not only to structuring, but also to the strong credit quality of many of the loans themselves. The portfolio of loans to be sold was on average of investment-grade quality, with low default rates and timely payment histories. This fundamentally sound credit quality met the high standards of the most efficient market sectors.

Selling the loans without recourse required a massive document reconstruction effort to bring the loans up to acceptable commercial standards. By January 1987, only two thirds of the loan files had been located; those files were substantially incomplete. Before the sale of the 324 loans, all documentation was complete. Only seven loans were replaced due to inadequate legal documentation. Financial information on the borrowers was an even more important issue at the outset; yet, by sale time, only 6 of the 147 loans rated for this loan sale had incomplete information. A staff of over 40 people from ED and Chemical Bank completed this massive effort at a reasonable cost. Henceforth, a new computer system will inventory files, generate reports on loan information, and implement detailed aspects of the ongoing program.

Marketing

The investment community was generally unfamiliar with loans to colleges and needed to be educated about ED's loan programs. Investors buying the bonds required familiarity with the types of loans, their credit quality, the trust's structure, over-collateralization, the protections offered to investors, and the default history of the portfolio. ED provided this critical information for the prospectus, which enhanced the marketing effort and met disclosure requirements under security laws. To provide this information, ED and Chemical Bank jointly managed the information-gathering and verification process.

Marketing of the bonds occurred in September 1987, when the issue sold in a technical rally in an otherwise weak market. Although not all of the bonds were sold immediately, the entire issue was placed with investors by mid-October.

The fiscal year 1988 sale, currently expected to be two and a half times the size of the 1987 sale, will require more extensive investor familiarity with the bonds to achieve the level of interest necessary to improve initial sales.

Parties to the Loan Sale

Establishment of a stand-alone trust that could run itself for the next 37 years required the involvement of a number of parties. Although the trust is a passive investment vehicle, it must perform numerous routine detailed tasks on an ongoing basis to ensure that investors receive proper payments. Service providers were required to be retained to perform those tasks. These functions include those of a loan servicer (transferred to the private sector, in accordance with the guidelines), bond trustee, owner trustee, manager, accountants, and auditors. Service providers were solicited competitively and were chosen based on their abilities to provide quality service at a reasonable cost. The relatively large number of service providers was necessary to permit a division of responsibilities among those firms specializing in performing the required duties.

Other services typical to securitized loan sales of this type were performed before the closing by underwriters, legal counsel, auditors, printers, and the rating agencies.

Overall Evaluation

ED's successful 1987 loan sale was the result of a combination of four factors: an efficient sale structure, a portfolio of generally high credit quality, an enormous amount of cooperation between the public sector and the private sector, and the absence of significant legal problems. Legal problems significant enough to break deals can be routine in similar complexly structured transactions; in this case, legal concerns required decisions, but did not jeopardize the transaction. The 1987 loan sale established the mechanisms for the loan sale process, and preparations are already well under way for the 1988 loan asset sale.

PROGRAM IMPLEMENTATION AND MANAGEMENT

ED's three primary objecives in conducting its 1987 Loan Asset Sales Program were:

- To maximize net financial benefit to the federal government
- To meet ED's budget targets on a timely basis
- To comply with the Guidelines for Loan Asset Sales, dated July 8, 1986, established by the Federal Credit Policy Working Group

The key requirements of the guidelines were:

- To reduce the government's cost of administering credit by transferring servicing, collection, and other administrative activities to the private sector
- To provide an incentive for agencies to improve loan origination and documentation
- To determine the actual subsidy of a federal credit program

As ED's financial adviser, Chemical Bank created and implemented a structure that met the Loan Asset Sales Program's objectives and was an economically efficient way to sell the college housing and academic facilities loans. The unique requirements that these objectives imposed demanded that the sale structure be custom-tailored to the characteristics of the loans and to the ramifications of the objectives.

Because approximately half of all loans in the portfolio were tax exempt and one of the requirements of the guidelines was to remove this benefit to private sector investors, Chemical Bank developed a structure that required substantial effort to implement, similar to first-time securitized transactions in the marketplace. To meet the 1987 timetable, numerous activities were undertaken on parallel tracks. The following review points out the highlights of the transaction.

In early 1987, ED determined that it would meet its budget targets from two sources: (1) the Loan Discounting Program, which would be available to colleges and universities from January to June, and (2) a subsequent Loan Asset Sales Program. The total amount to be raised was $579.2 million.

Preparatory Activities

While the Loan Discounting Program was still in effect, Chemical Bank and ED began work on the Loan Asset Sales Program by developing a management plan and a loan sale structure. Beginning in February, Chemical Bank undertook to inventory all loans and to establish a filing system. Since many loans were missing a substantial amount of documentation, Chemical Bank mounted a massive effort to obtain originals or certified copies of needed documents. During this time, on the transaction structuring side, substantial legal work was accomplished to ensure that structuring options were analyzed and that the recommended structure complied with appicable tax and security laws. At the same time, Chemical Bank began discussions with the rating agencies to gain their acceptance of a senior/subordinated structure, with the credit rating based on a statistical sampling of loans. As a result, the structure for the loan asset sale was solidly in place by the end of the Loan Discounting Program.

Sizing of the Loan Asset Sale

Prior to defining the pool of loans available for sale in 1987, final results of the Loan Discounting Program were needed to establish the portfolio of loans remaining that would be available for sale. In mid-July, these results were compiled and the 1987 loan sale pool was randomly selected from the portfolio of 1,928 loans. The Loan Discounting Program raised $499 million, leaving approximately $80 million to be raised through a loan asset sale. Practical and market factors determined the size of the trust's offering of bonds to the private sector. In light of rating agency requirements, a minimum sale of 300 loans was determined to be most economically efficient. A lesser number would have necessitated greater overcollateralization, which would have reduced net proceeds to ED. Additionally, an offering of bonds in excess of $100 million was strongly recommended to attract the attention of investors (for whom a large bond issue ensures liquidity in secondary market trading) and of bond salespeople (who earn commissions based on volume). For these reasons, it was decided in July to offer bonds in the range of $125–130 million.

Selection of Service Providers

The use of a special-purpose trust as a loan sale vehicle was a result of tax and security law considerations and required that the following service providers be retained by or on behalf of the trust: owner trustee, bond trustee, loan servicer, auditors, accountants, bond printer, financial printer, and independent evaluator. In addition, managing underwriters were solicited competitively to purchase the trust's bonds.

Selection of the three firms that served as managing underwriters was accomplished at the end of June, based on four main criteria. The most important criteria were the amount of the expected net proceeds to ED and the security distribution capabilities of each firm. The process of selection and the performance of the three firms selected are discussed later.

Other service providers were selected in July and August by criteria that included their respective abilities to complete the required tasks in the given time frame at the most reasonable price. The selection of a loan servicer was particularly critical, given the cash flow–based nature of the transaction and the number of loans expected to be sold.

Development and Documentation

Concurrent with the selection of the remaining service providers, work began on the loan sale transaction. The working group was divided into teams according to their technical expertise. The working group met as a whole and in specialized teams to negotiate specific terms of the transaction, to define roles of the parties, and to draft specific language to document the agreed-on arrangements. Frequent meetings of the working group as a whole were held to (1) force all members to focus on the key aspects of the transaction, (2) share knowledge, and (3) define the specific duties of the parties to the transaction. To meet the timetable, it was necessary to run a number of large meetings simultaneously to maintain the pace of the transaction and to keep all parties at the same level of understanding. Each party had to reach its own independent understanding of the loan assets and of the transaction structure.

As a result, by the end of August, all members of the working group had the same level of involvement in the transaction, which resulted in the completion of work in time for the September 1987 sale. Specialist teams finalized individual documents. Transaction documents were completed in less than three months. Typical structured loan sale transactions involving a similarly high degree of new product development normally require six to eight months to complete transaction documents by a more conventional process of drafting and review. By forcing groups into overlapping roles, the time frame involved was significantly compressed. It is expected that time spent in negotiations and drafting will be reduced even further for the second loan sale, if the structure of the first sale is followed.

Throughout the entire process, refinements were made quickly to incorporate comments from rating agencies and regulatory authorities. For the most part, these included additional tests that would monitor future cash flows, as well as the establishment of reserve and liquidity funds. Sizing of the overcollateralization and flow of funds were the major topics of continual discussion with the rating agencies.

Pricing was set for Friday, September 18, 1987. Because a new stress test was requested by one of the rating agencies (a test ultimately revealed a valid cash flow concern), pricing was delayed until Monday, September 21, 1987. The timing proved fortunate. The window of opportunity remained open, with prices of long Treasury bonds firm to strengthening following weeks of price declines. The rally was shortlived, and, following ED's pricing on Monday, bond prices again dropped. ED's decision to accept pricing on Monday proved timely because, at the end of the day, the benchmark long U.S. Treasury bond had dropped over one-half percentage point (or almost $6 per $1,000 bond). Monday was also the last day on which ED could have priced and reasonably expected to close prior to the fiscal year-end on September 30. Closing occurred on the morning of September 29, as scheduled.

Conclusion

The implementation and management of the Loan Asset Sales Program achieved ED's stated objectives for the 1987 sale. The structure of the transaction, as originally conceived and recommended, was successfully implemented in less than half the time required for comparable private sector transactions.

STRUCTURE ANALYSIS

College and University Facility Loan Trust One issued $126,995,000 of secured bonds and certificates of beneficial interest in the net assets of the trust. The trust acquired from ED a pool of 324 loans to postsecondary educational institutions, aggregating $237,248,552 in outstanding principal amount in return for the net proceeds of the bonds of approximately $120,492,693 (net of the payment of bond issuance expenses and the funding of the liquidity fund and the expense fund) and the certificates of an estimated value of $10,770,424 (assuming a present value discount rate of 14 percent).

The bonds were issued as serial bonds (or bonds of an issue in which some bonds mature in each year over a period of years) with bullet maturities (maturing on December 1, 1989, 1991, and 1993) and term bonds with mandatory sinking fund redemptions (maturing on June 1, 2002, and December 1, 2014). The bonds are noncallable, other than mandatory sinking fund redemptions. The availability of a guaranteed investment contract issued by the Federal National Mortgage Association (FNMA) allowed for the reinvestment

Figure 24-1. Loan Asset Sale Structure

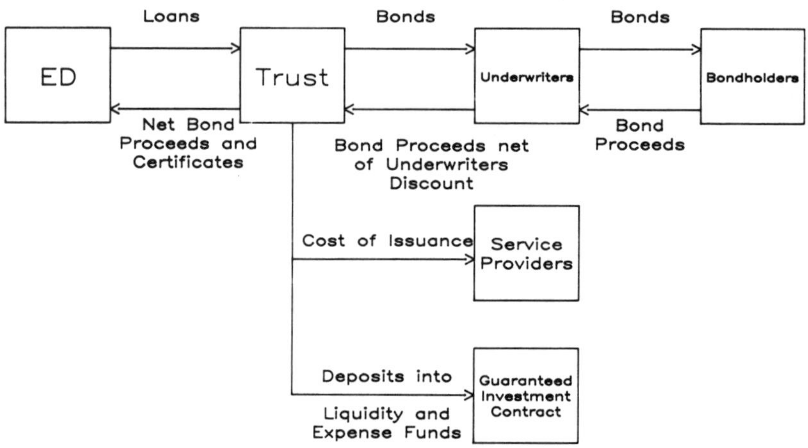

of prepayments and any other early payments on the loans in the reserve fund at a rate of 5 pecent. This ability to reinvest prepayments at a rate above the highest rate on the loans was a fundamental requirement to ensure the cash flow sufficiency of the noncallable structure.

The trust uses a senior/subordinated structure (bonds/certificates) to provide overcollateralization sufficient to achieve Aaa/AAA ratings from the two major rating agencies. By allocating the loan default risk primarily to the Certificate holders, an internal credit enhancement structure is created; its only cost is the interest rate pricing differential between the bonds and the certificates. The transaction structure is described graphically in Figures 24-1, 24-2, and 24-3.

Figure 24-2. Cash Flow Structure

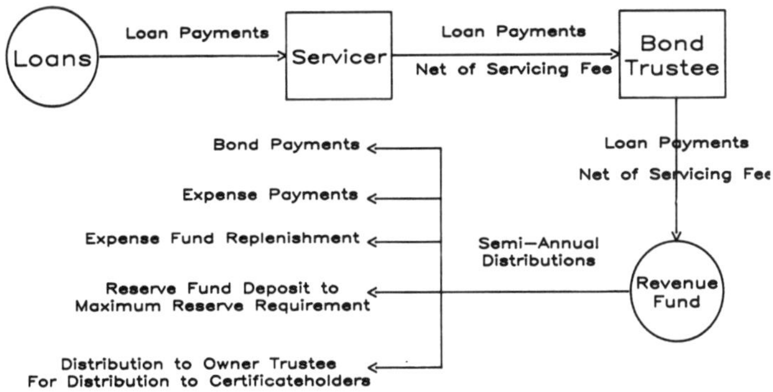

Figure 24-3. Funds Flow Structure

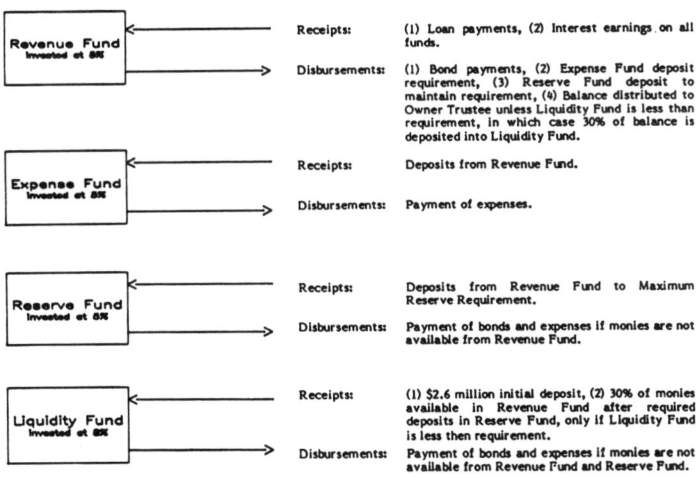

Objective

The structure proposed and implemented was developed to maximize the net financial benefit to the federal government for a loan sale in accordance with the Federal Credit Policy Working Group's Guidelines and ED's budget target and within ED's time frame. The total return to ED was derived from a combination of net proceeds received from the bonds and the value of the certificates. The objective of the strategy implemented was to achieve the highest possible price for the bonds—first, by creating securities that could be sold into a market with enough buyers and sellers to provide efficient pricing, and, second, by creating securities with the highest credit quality and maximum certainty as to predictability of payment through call protection (that is, the right to redeem outstanding bonds before the scheduled maturity). The strategy was for the underwriters to market the bonds as an AAA corporate bond issue to obtain more aggressive pricing relative to securities sold in the mortgage- and asset-backed security markets. Securities in the latter two markets yield a premium (lower price) relative to corporate issues because of the prepayment uncertainty that characterizes debt backed by pools of loans.

The certificates representing the subordinated interest were structured to allow for their eventual sale to the public. ED expects to hold the certificates until a certain amount of seasoning has taken place to establish a performance record. A sale of certificates without such a performance record would require a substantial yield premium—possibly creating a windfall return to investors for assuming greater uncertainty. Whether ED gains the most value by selling the certificates as a whole, selling in two pieces (that is, preferred certificates and common certificates), or holding the certificates will depend on market conditions when the sale of the certificates is contemplated.

Analysis

The structure implemented provided the highest overall net financial benefit to ED, given the nature of the assets, market conditions, and ED's objectives. Following is a description of the highlights of the sale structure, with the rationale behind each decision.

Use of a Special-Purpose Entity (the Trust) to Issue Multiple Classes of Senior Bonds and Subordinated Certificates

The pooled loan sale approach, such as the approach used, had a number of advantages over whole loan sales or other pool approaches. Specifically, these advantages included:

- The ability to eliminate tax exemption associated with certain individual loans
- Timing advantages that enabled investors and the rating agencies to analyze the portfolio as a whole rather than as individual parts
- The credit value created for investors through pooling diversification
- Multiple classes of bonds (that is, serial and term bonds) that allowed for the debt to be tailored to different investor requirements
- The senior/subordinated structure, which achieved greater cash flow certainty for bond investors than the pass-through approach does.

Overall, the use of the special-purpose entity as the issuer of bonds and certificates allowed ED to access markets in which sufficient efficiency in pricing existed. Also, certain structuring aspects, such as those detailed earlier, gave investors greater value without significant cost to ED, while at the same time meeting ED's objectives.

Aaa/AAA Ratings

Except for the trade-offs described later, use of Aaa/AAA ratings was most attractive because this rating:

- Provided for the most aggressive pricing of the bonds
- Created quality perception for the bonds which limited the effect on bond pricing of the negative disclosure under the special considertions section in the prospectus
- Broadened the potential investor community interested in the bonds, which created more market awareness for the initial sale and for subsequent sales

Certain trade-offs were created by using the Aaa/AAA ratings. The main disadvantage was the need to overcollateralize to 108 percent on a cash flow basis with a 2 percent liquidity fund. Presumably, for an A rating, overcollateralization may have been as low as 104 percent. In that case, the lower rating allows more of the cash flow to be available to support more bonds, creating more up-front proceeds. However, when analyzed on a total return basis (bond proceeds, plus value of certificates), the lower rating is less advantageous because of the lower price paid for lower-rated bonds and the loss of cash flow to the certificates, which decreases the certificate value. This aspect of the rating decision was discussed in detail during the underwriting selection process, in conjunction with discussions of ED's overall objectives regarding up-front proceeds versus total return, including the value of certificates. The result of these discussions was the selection of AAA/Aaa ratings to maximize the total value to ED.

Selection of Method of Credit Enhancement

The options available to ED for enhancing the credit quality of the bonds were either overcollateralization or third party credit enhancement in the form of either bond insurance or a letter of credit. As outlined in the structuring report, the key points were:

- Overcollateralization was a relatively efficient way to enhance the creditworthiness of debt securities because the cost is directly related to the future experience of the portfolio if the certificates are not sold. If the subordinated interest is sold, the cost is equal to the pricing differential between the discount rate used to price the bonds and the discount rate used to price the certificate.
- The viability of a letter of credit as enhancement for the bonds was limited, given the long maturities of the bonds.
- Prior to closing the bonds, ED should proceed down parallel tracks with regard to using bond insurance, since its use would depend on pricing of the insurance, market conditions regarding how insured bonds would trade vis-a-vis noninsured AAA bonds, and the minimum overcollateralization that the bond insurer would require.

The decision on whether to use overcollateralization to a AAA level or use bond insurance was straightforward, given the events at the time that the decision was made (in late August/early September):

- The bond insurer quoted a preliminary insurance premium of .375 percent per annum, based on the outstanding balance of the bonds.
- The bond insurer would require at least 104 percent overcollateralization to qualify the issue for insurance. This was subject to change, based on further inspection of the transaction and based on the rating agencies' final overcollateralization requirements.
- Salomon Brothers Inc. indicated that an insured issue would carry a market premium (vis-a-vis noninsured AAA bonds) or approximately 10–20 basis points because of the market's negative perception of the underlying credit when bond insurance is used.

The decision not to use bond insurance was based on comparison of the additional cost of approximately 50 basis points per annum (insurance premium, plus market premium) with the possible benefit of reducing overcollateralization by about 4 percent (assuming that the rating agencies would agree that 104 percent overcollateralization, by itself, would provide a rating of at least Baa/BBB). On an overall return basis, ED would receive greater total proceeds without bond insurance.

Overcollateraliztion Levels

The overcollateralization was implemented through a combination of excess scheduled cash flow and a liquidity reserve fund, which are as follows:

- *Excess cash flow.* When combined with projected interest income, the amount of cash flow available from the scheduled payments on the loans is 108 percent of the amount necessary to pay debt service on the bonds and projected expenses, as of each bond payment date. This 108 percent overcollateralization is available to absorb defaults and nonpayments on the loans. Additionally, if loans are delinquent in payment for six months or more, excess current cash flow, which would otherwise flow out to certificate holders, is retained by the trust in the reserve fund to the extent necessary to maintain the 108 percent overcollateralization.

- *Liquidity fund.* As further protection for the bonds, a liquidity fund equal to $2.6 million (approximately 2 percent of the original bond amount) is available to pay debt service on the bonds and to pay expenses if the excess cash flow and amounts held in the reserve fund are fully depleted.

The amount of cash flow overcollateralization and the size of the liquidity fund were based on the rating agencies' view of the credit quality of the loans and how the loans would perform in a worst-case scenario (that is, a hypothetical Great Depression). A cash flow overcollateralization rate of 108 percent, in conjunction with a 2 percent liquidity fund, was sufficient to satisfy the rating agencies' stress tests. This was 4 percent less than the 112 percent overcollateralization that was originally projected at the outset of the transaction. This significantly increased the proceeds to ED.

Both Moody's Investors Service (Moody's) and Standard and Poor's Corporation (S&P) rated a sample of 147 loans randomly selected from the portfolio. The ratings of the sampled loans were used to develop estimates of the rating category distribution of the entire portfolio and of the 324 loans sold to the trust. S&P's estimates of the overall rating distribution of the portfolio are shown in Table 24-1.

Chemical Bank verified S&P's estimates of the rating distribution by using a statistical methodology for developing the average

Table 24-1. S&P's Rating of the Portfolio

Rating Category	*Estimate (% of Portfolio)*
AAA	7.76%
AA	15.48
A	22.95
BBB	36.38
BB	9.67
B	3.08
CCC	4.70

rating as provided by statisticians. Moody's did not provide detailed information on the ratings of the sampled loans. As provided in its municipal credit report on the bonds, dated September 29, 1987, Moody's conclusions were that 11 percent of the portfolio was of high-grade credit quality (Aaa and Aa), 72 percent of medium-grade credit quality (A and Baa), and 17 percent of below-medium-grade quality (below Baa).

Based on the underlying credit quality of the portfolio, both rating agencies developed stress tests that were intended to measure to a high degree of certainty the projected performance of the loans in a worst-case scenario. To receive the Aaa/AAA ratings, the trust must be able to continue to pay the debt service on the bonds and to pay estimated expenses in a timely manner, even after subjecting the cash flow to the stress tests. The trust was able to meet the stress tests at the least cost, through the combination of both the 108 percent cash flow overcollateralization and the $2.6 million liquidity fund.

S&P's stress test assumed that, starting in the beginning of year 2, 13 percent of the loans would default over the following three years (30 percent in year 2, 30 percent in year 3, and 40 percent in year 4) and defaulted loans would not pay for a period of five years. At the end of five years, only 50 percent of the defaulted loans would resume payment. Additionally, S&P was concerned about cash flow concentration in only a few large loans, particularly later in the life of the issue (after 15 years), and required that the $2.6 million liquidity fund not decrease over time.

Moody's stress test combined an economic stress test and an ongoing stress scenario, based on the past performance of the loans. The economic stress test spanned a period of nine years, peaking in the fifth year at a default rate of 16.48 percent. At the end of the ninth year, all but 1.66 percent of the defaulted loans would resume payment. The trust must be able to pass the economic stress scenario, assuming that it started in any year (that is, Moody's needed to see 28 different stress scenarios). The ongoing stress scenario assumed that 3.7 percent of the loans default in year 1 and that ongoing defaults thereafter create cumulative defaults of 4.7 percent through year 9, 5.6 percent defaults through year 15, 6.2 percent defaults through year 23, and 6.95 percent defaults to the end of the transaction. Combining these two stress tests, Moody's stress test projected that between 21 percent and 23 percent of the loans could be in default at any one point in time.

Noncallable Serial and Term Bonds Versus Sequential Pay CMO-Type Structures

The selection of a noncallable serial and term bond structure was based on the yield advantage created by providing investor certainty as to the repayment of principal. Callable bonds would have demanded a yield premium of as much as 50 basis points more on the bonds, depending on market conditions.

Noncallable bonds created some cash flow inefficiencies that needed to be analyzed. With callable bonds, the ability to redeem high coupon bonds early, instead of investing the money in the reserve fund earning only 5 percent, would have created much greater value to the certificate holders to the extent that there were loan prepayments. The greater the likelihood of loan prepayments, the greater the economic inefficiencies created by noncallable bonds. The important assumption about ED's loan portfolio is that prepayments are unlikely. The borrowers would not be likely to prepay after being given an excellent opportunity to prepay at a substantial discount in the first half of 1987 under the Loan Discounting Program. Also, as the coupon rates on the loans average only 3.16 percent, the likelihood of prepayment due to interest rate movements is highly unlikely. Under these circumstances, the inefficiences of noncallable bonds, which were not great, were outweighed by the yield benefit created in the marketplace.

Regulated Investment Company Status

To avoid the detrimental economic effect of double taxation (that is, income tax payable by the trust, in addition to income tax payable by the investors), the structure as originally recommended and as implemented was to register the Trust as an investment company under the Investment Company Act of 1940 (1940 Act), so as to qualify as a regulated investment company (RIC) under the Internal Revenue Code. Detailed preliminary discussions with representatives of the SEC regarding the 1940 Act and with representatives of the IRS clearly indicated that this approach was viable.

RICs are exempt from federal taxes, taxes imposed by most states, and alternative minimum taxes in recognition of a long-standing policy against the imposition of an entity-level tax on passive investment vehicles similar to the trust. If the trust were not registered under the 1940 Act and ED were to sell more than 50 percent of the certificates, the trust would potentially be subject to the alternative minimum tax until 1989. Thereafter, if ED were to sell the certificates, the trust would continue to be subject to the alternative minimum tax. The amount of tax resulting from such a sale of the certificates was reasonably estimated to be $2 million, with substantial risk that the amount of tax could be sharply higher over the life of the trust, due to the possibility of changes in loan prepayment behavior, due to the tax recurring upon subsequent resales, and due to unforeseen changes in the tax laws. Proposed legislation by the House of Representatives would double the alternative minimum tax now in effect.

The decision to obtain RIC status was the result of ED's firm decision to structure the transaction so the certificates could be sold to maximize total proceeds. To support ED's decision, RIC status eliminated tax risks and its potentially severe negative cash flow risk impact. Aside from the direct effect of the tax on the trust, the rating agencies would have required a substantial reserve fund to protect investors from the effect of the tax, which, in turn, would have substantially reduced net proceeds. As a result, RIC status had significant economic benefits to ED and resulted in a much more economically stable transaction.

Disadvantages of RIC status under the Internal Revenue Code were twofold: (1) increased reporting requirements due to registration requirements under the 1940 Act and (2) compliance with diversification and other requirements of maintaining RIC status. These requirements were built into the duties of the trust's manager.

An additional factor in maintaining the trust's RIC status was the use of a guaranteed investment contract (GIC) from a federal agency—namely, FNMA—to satisfy the diversification requirements. As a RIC, the trust could not have more than 25 percent of its assets invested in any one issuer, unless such amounts were invested in federal government or agency obligations. In effect, the use of a private investment contract would have necessitated changes in the structure if, for any reason, the amount in the GIC was greater than

25 percent of the trust's assets. In the last analysis, FNMA's investment contract bid was more competitive than any other offer and, therefore, became the most economical means of meeting this diversification requirement.

As an aside, it should be emphasized that the use of a federal agency GIC does not constitute or imply recourse to the federal government for this loan sale. In this case, the GIC is used solely for the reinvestment of payments received from the loans. Moreover, FNMA commonly provides GICs for similar transactions in the private sector.

MARKETING ANALYSIS

As reviewed earlier, ED sought to achieve consistency with the Federal Credit Policy Working Group's guidelines. Sales of the loans to the private sector established a fair market price to be paid for loans sold without recourse.

A solicitation for underwriters was drafted for a negotiated firm commitment underwriting, as opposed to a competitive offer or best-efforts private placement. The purpose of establishing this type of underwriting was to maximize the efficiency of the process so as to meet ED's aggressive timetable even if adverse conditions arose. A private placement transaction was not considered because a fair market value would not have been established.

Sixteen responses were received, and five firms were invited to give oral presentations. From those five, Salomon was chosen as the lead underwriter, and Shearson Lehman Brothers Incorporated and First Boston Corporation were chosen as comanagers. Presentations of all three underwriters selected contained different structures; however, both the Salomon and Shearson structures returned the highest total net proceeds. Because of the expected benefits of the noncallable structure, Salomon was chosen over Shearson as lead underwriter. By closely tracking the U.S. Treasury rate curve, a higher return was expected to be achieved. While the underwriters maintained philosphical differences of opinion on structuring the transaction (which were consistent with individual firm proposals), all parties worked toward the successful completion of the agreed-on structure.

Market Conditions

During the course of the summer, while loan documents were being collected and the transaction was being formulated, credit markets were reacting globally to the falling value of the dollar in foreign exchange markets. Inflation fears in the United States were confirmed by the Federal Reserve Bank's raising of its discount rate in early September. The main concerns about the U.S. economy centered on the trade and budget deficit. During the week of September 7, 1987, the July trade deficit was announced. Although the deficit was higher than expected, the main reason for its size was an increase in petroleum imports. Announcements by U.S. Treasury officials that they would not seek a lower dollar somewhat moderated fears of inflation. During the week of September 14, a sizable inflow of corporate tax receipts occurred as a result of the new tax bill. There was uncertainty about the federal debt ceiling, and no announcement of anticipated U.S. Treasury borrowing was made. Expectations of rising inflation were moderating, and, at the end of a week, a technical rally in the bond markets occurred.

Against this background, the bonds were priced on September 21 in a volatile, nervous market. A technical rally began on Thursday, September 17, and lasted through Monday, September 21. As this rally began, a number of corporate issuers that had waited on the sidelines came to market, which raised the weekly volume of corporate issues to the highest level seen in eight weeks. New-issue volume continued to be heavy into the following week, with volume again reaching near-term highs. The technical rally saw interest rates on U.S. Treasury obligations decline after a steady increase throughout the summer. Following the rally, the steep increase of interest rates continued into October (see Figure 24-4). Because liquidity in the market was tight, new issues that were brought into the market just prior to the pricing of the bonds had spotty performance records.

Spreads for the Trust's Issue

To compensate investors for risk, a spread over the comparable U.S. Treasury rate is added and is expressed in basis points. (One hundred basis points are equal to one percentage point.) During

Figure 24-4. Interest Rate Comparison: 10-Year versus 30-Year Treasuries

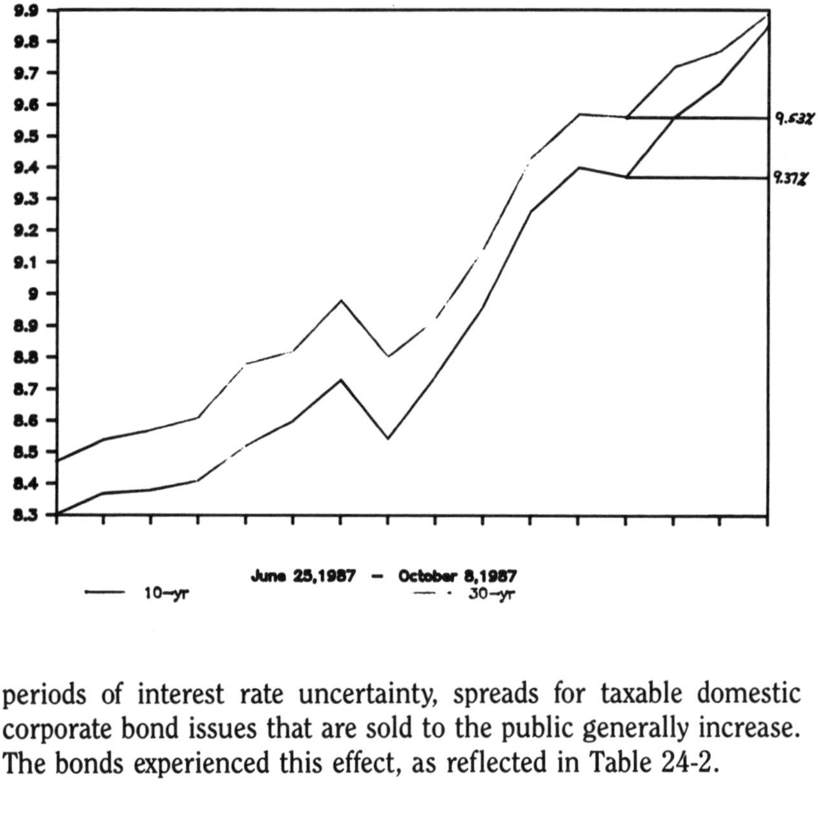

periods of interest rate uncertainty, spreads for taxable domestic corporate bond issues that are sold to the public generally increase. The bonds experienced this effect, as reflected in Table 24-2.

Table 24-2. Spreads to U.S. Treasury Securities

Year	*Salomon Proposal*	*7/23*	*8/18*	*9/14*	*9/20*	*Final Pricing*	*Current Pricing*
2	15	15	20	30	35	35	75
4	25	25	35	40	45	50	80
6	30	30	40	50	65	75	90
10	45	40	60	75	85	95	100
20	65	60	80	—	—	—	—
30	—	65	—	90	100	110	115

Pricing movements were a result of the underlying economic and financial realities in the market during the months in which ED's loan sale transaction was being negotiated. Interest rate levels were rising and liquidity was very tight.

Pricing the Bonds

Although price and interest rate movements at the time of pricing were somewhat disappointing, factors governing their movement were out of the control of the syndicate. Relatively speaking, pricing was clearly superior to AA or A corporate issues in the market at the time. The following points regarding the pricing of each of the five tranches should be emphasized:

- The first tranche (8.50 percent, due December 1, 1989) of ED's issue was priced at 35 basis points over U.S. Treasuries, 11 to 25 basis points lower in spread than comparable actual issues of December 1, 1991) AA or A corporate bonds.
- The second tranche (9.20 percent, due December 1, 1991) was priced 50 basis points over U.S. Treasuries and about 25 basis points over FNMA securities and was judged reasonable in light of the supply in the market at the time.
- The third tranche (9.70 percent, due December 1, 1993) was priced 75 basis points over U.S. Treasuries. By interpolation, the pricing was spread about 35 basis points over FNMA securities of comparable maturity.
- The fourth tranche (10.20 percent, due June 1, 2002) was priced 95 basis points over U.S. Treasuries and approximately 35 basis points over FNMA issues. Given the weak book of business in this maturity (only $10 million in orders from investors at pricing time) and the general widening of spreads that occurred in this maturity range on Thursday and Friday of the previous week, this was judged an acceptable spread level.
- The final tranche (10.55 percent, due December 1, 2014) was priced at 110 basis points over U.S. Treasuries. This was a significantly lower spread than that prevailing for pass-through securities. This fact, together with the absence of orders in this maturity, led to the conclusion that 110 basis points was a reasonable amount.

The weighted-average spread over U.S. Treasury securities for the trust's issue was 93 basis points. The average life of the issue was approximately 11 years, and the weighted-average coupon was 10.22 percent. A rough calculation reveals that, if the bonds had been sold at no spread over U.S. Treasuries, the proceeds would have been about $7.6 million higher than those realized at the average spread of 93 basis points. In other words, through its nonrecourse sale of the senior debt, ED realized 95 percent of the amount that the government would have realized through a sale of its own Treasury bonds with full recourse.

A summary of the net proceeds that ED received is shown in Table 24-3.

Table 24-3. ED's Net Proceeds

Loans sold to the trust	$237,248,551	100.000%
Net bonds sold to the public	126,272,954	53.224
Expenses[1]	3,106,928	1.310
Net proceeds[2]	120,492,693	50.788
Present value of certificates (discounted at 14%)	10,770,424	4.540
Total estimated proceeds	$131,263,117	55.328%

[1]As per Schedule I of escrow agreement.

[2]Net proceeds after funding the liquidity fund at $2,600,000 and the expense fund at $73,333.

The average interest rate differential between ED's portfolio of loans, which carry an interest rate of 3.16 percent, and the price that the Trust is paying on the bonds represents the largest single determinant of the net proceeds. While transaction costs associated with the privatization effort diminished proceeds, these were very small when compared with the effect of overall interest rate movements. ED retains additional value from the loans, as evidenced by the certificates. These certificates have value currently estimated to be $10.8 million in terms of present value; however, the exact value can only be determined when the certificates are sold. ED must add the realized amount of the certificates to the amount received as a result of the sale of the bonds to definitively review the total proceeds, or cents on the dollar received for the 1987 loan sale.

Underwriter's Compensation

With respect to the underwriting spread, the following gross numbers applied:

- *two years.* $4.00 per $1,000 face value of bonds.
- *four years.* $5.50 per $1,000 face value of bonds.
- *six years.* $6.25 per $1,000 face value of bonds.
- *ten years.* $6.75 per $1,000 face value of bonds.
- *thirty years.* $8.75 per $1,000 face value of bonds.

Components of the spread are shown in Table 24-4.

Table 24-4. Spread Components

Management fee	20%
Underwriting fee	20
Selling commission	60
	100%

It was agreed that the management fee would be split, with 50 percent going to Salomon, 25 percent to Shearson, and 25 percent to The First Boston. The underwriting commitment would be evenly split among the underwriters.

Distribution

Several aspects must be considered in analyzing distribution performance. The size of the issue gives investors an initial impression about what they may expect in secondary market trading. This is important because the more active the secondary market, the easier it will be for that investor to sell at a price that is market driven. An inactive secondary market in an issue means that the issue is salable (usually to the original underwriters that make a market), but at a price more influenced by the underwriter that purchases the bond than by investors.

Volatile markets, an oversupply of corporate issues being brought to market, and an unpredictable interest rate environment were all factors that determined the final price and the success of the sale effort of the underwriters. Time pressures entered into the equation, as a compressed sale effort between pricing and closing left some bonds unsold after closing. One of the criteria used in choosing the underwriters was their individual capital positions and their ability to stabilize new issues in a volatile market. This requires each firm to inventory the issue, rather than sell any piece at a cheaper price, which possibly raises the spread over U.S. Treasuries for subsequent issues. The spreads shown in Table 24-5 prove that all firms worked to hold the issue at its initial offering price after the syndicate broke on September 29.

A breakdown of sales by geographical distribution and type of investor is shown in Table 24-6.

Although it was disappointing to have bonds remain unsold at closing, all bonds were eventually placed by the underwriters. The reasons that bonds remained in underwriter inventory at the time of closing were the compressed marketing period, the delayed pricing of the issue (from September 18 to September 21,), and, most important, the volatile market conditions at the time of pricing. In addition, investor and institutional interest may have been focused on the Farm Housing Authority (FmHA) Rural Housing Trust being priced later in the week. The FmHA issue was far larger in size and attracted more attention. Although the sale of earlier maturities of the trust's bonds was active, the 10- and 30-year maturities were placed on October 1, 1987, and October 2, 1987, in their entirety. Given that these two tranches represented 72 percent of the issue, it was important that placement be successful at spreads to Treasuries that did not significantly exceed original pricing. This is important because subsequent issues may be priced against the spreads at which the bonds were actually placed previously, in addition to market conditions then prevailing.

ROLE OF LEGAL COUNSEL

Given the complex nature of the transaction, a review of the interests represented by the various legal counsel is useful.

Table 24-5. Summary of Spreads over Treasuries in Basis Points

Tranche	*9/21*	*9/22*	*9/23*	*9/24*	*9/26*	*9/28*	*9/29*	*9/30*	*10/1*	*10/2*
A	35	36	31	16	14	38	42	39	47	44
B	50	50	45	30	31	55	58	59	58	58
C	75	72	75	64	55	83	82	81	79	81
D	95	96	93	78	80	101	100	101	100	100
E	110	111	108	93	95	115	115	115	115	116

Tranche	*10/05*	*10/06*	*10/07*	*10/08*	*10/09*	*10/12*	*10/13*	*10/14*	*10/15*
A	42	41	42	44	44	46	46	45	44
B	57	56	56	60	60	60	61	63	61
C	80	82	82	81	85	86	84	85	87
D	102	102	100	100	101	101	102	101	100
E	115	114	115	116	114	116	116	116	115

Table 24-6. Distribution by Geographic Area and Investor

By state	
Massachusetts	3%
Pennsylvania	3
Georgia	4
Tennessee	6
Connecticut	25
New York	20
Other	39
	100%
By type of investor	
Insurance companies	66%
Banks	13
Retirement fund	8
Money managers	3
Others	10
	100%

Issuer's Counsel

In reviewing the role of counsel to the trust, in the trust's capacity as issuer of the bonds, it is important to keep in mind that, while the trust is technically the purchaser of the loans from ED, it only does so for the benefit of the bond holders (which own a security interest in the loans). As a result, the trust does not have an independent commercial interest. Accordingly, the chief interest of counsel to the trust, as issuer, is ensuring that the transaction is properly structured and documented.

It is important to emphasize that the role of issuer's counsel is passive only in a commercial sense—that is, it does not involve advocacy of commercial or proprietary interests in the negotiation of the transaction. However, issuer's counsel plays an active role in coordinating the preparation of transaction documents, registering the bonds under the applicable security laws, obtaining rulings from the IRS, and establishing the legal existence of the trust. Indeed, the commercial neutrality of the issuer trust makes issuer's counsel an appropriate legal representative to deal with the SEC, the IRS, and, to some extent, the rating agencies.

Seller's Counsel

ED's commercial and programmatic interests were independently represented by ED's Office of the General Counsel (OGC). Such interests of ED were appropriately represented and negotiated primarily by OGC. OGC's role included conducting extensive due diligence of the loans for the benefit of ED; resolving questions that arose concerning the applicability to the transaction and to ED of various federal laws, other than tax and security laws (for example, the Higher Education Act and the Government Corporation Control Act); negotiating the terms and contents of transaction documents; and drafting and reviewing documents governing the transfer and assignment of the loans.

In advocating the commercial and programmatic interests of ED during negotiation of the transaction, OGC was able to draw on legal counsel (both internal and outside) to Chemical Bank as financial adviser.

Underwriter's Counsel

The underwriters, as purchasers and sellers of the bonds issued by the trust, are in the position of representing the interests of the bond holders. That is not to say that underwriters do not serve any interests of the trust and ED, as they take the bonds to the financial markets and, subject to market conditions, seek to obtain the best price and widest distribution available. However, in the preparation and negotiation of the transaction documents, underwriters and their counsel represent the structural and, to some extent, economic interests of the bond purchasers. Accordingly, although underwriter's counsel is generally not in conflict with issuer's or seller's counsel about satisfying the requirements of the security laws, they do represent a commercial and proprietary interest in opposition to the interests of ED.

Counsel to Other Service Providers

The ongoing service providers to the trust—that is, the owner trustee, the bond trustee, and the servicer—do not have independent commercial interests in the transaction beyond the fees that they receive for the work performed and potential liability arising from their acts or failure to act. Accordingly, while each of these parties was represented by legal counsel during the documentation of the transaction, the role of such counsel was limited, in each case, to ensuring that the respective parties' obligations and compensation were clearly defined and documented and that the party was adequately protected against undue liability.

Recognition of this limited role is particularly important when distinguishing the owner/trustee's counsel from issuer's counsel. While the owner/trustee is the active participant in the trust, the role of counsel to the owner/trustee is limited to protecting the interests of the owner/trustee and does not include representing the trust with respect to security and tax law requirements for issuing the bonds.

SECURITY AND TAX LAWS ISSUES

RIC Election

One important objective in structuring the transaction was to ensure the tax-passive nature of the trust, since tax liability at the entity level for the trust would have a negative impact on the price of the certificates sold and would reduce the return to ED. Although certain of the tax rulings sought and obtained from the IRS largely ensured avoidance of such tax liability for the trust, ED's business decision to sell the certificates in the future raised the likelihood that the alternative minimum tax rules under the Internal Revenue Code would result in an alternative minimum tax liability upon such a sale. On the basis of cash flow projections for the first sale, such potential alternate minimum tax liability was estimated at between $2 million and $15 million on a net present value basis.

To avoid potential alternative minimum tax liability, it was decided to qualify the trust as a RIC, which, under the relevant provisions of the Internal Revenue Code, is exempt from federal taxation, including the alternative minimum tax. This required registering the trust as an investment company under the 1940 Act—subject, however, to seeking exemptions from certain provisions of the 1940 Act [see the "6(c) Exemptive Order" section]. RIC status also exempts the trust from taxation in Massachusetts (the state in which the trust, as a Massachusetts business trust, is located), which avoided subjecting the transaction to uncertainty regarding the timing and availability of any Massachusetts state tax ruling, as well as the representations necessary to obtain such a ruling.

Another requirement for RIC status was to ensure diversification of the assets and investments of the trust (no single asset or loan of the trust and no single investment—unless an investment in U.S. government or agency securities—could exceed 25 percent of the trust's assets and investments). This requirement obviously affects the investment of payments received on the loans (whether prepayments or merely payments received in between the payment dates of the bonds) prior to the distributions to the bond holders. In the first sale, this was satisfied by obtaining a GIC from FNMA. Another straightforward way to address this issue would be to use loan prepayments to pay bonds.

Qualifying the issuer as a RIC in any future sale may continue to be the best alternative to resolve the potential alternative minimum tax liability, particularly since the precedent has been set and this approach has been accepted by the IRS and the SEC. However, this conclusion may change if either (1) the current requirements for RIC status are unable to be satisfied—that is, there is diversification of assets (including any GIC), (2) the requirements for RIC status under the Internal Revenue Code are changed and become more onerous, (3) the alternative minimum tax provisions of the Internal Revenue Code change to diminish or eliminate any potential alternative minimum tax liability, or (4) ED decides, as a matter of policy, to retain permanently the subordinated interest in the trust. In view of the fact that present proposals before Congress would double the impact of the alternative minimum tax provisions, it is unreasonable to assume that the effect of the alternative minimum tax provisions would diminish.

IRS Revenue Ruling Request

Rulings were obtained from the IRS to obtain certainty regarding the tax status of the trust. In other contexts, an opinion from Skadden, Arps would probably have been sufficient. However, in view of the highly visible nature of the transaction and, particularly, the fact that a comparable federal government asset sale program was seeking similar rulings, it seemed more prudent to obtain rulings on certain issues. An additional factor that favored obtaining rulings was the practical necessity of consulting with the IRS in any case and its willingness to be helpful in providing rulings. The ruling obtained was proposed by Skadden, Arps in the early stages of structuring the transaction and was first implemented for ED's loan asset sale.

6(c) Exemptive Order

The trust that was used in the transaction structure is, by definition, an investment company under the 1940 Act. However, sections of the 1940 Act restrict or prohibit aspects of the transaction structure that was recommended as the most advantageous for the Loan Asset Sales Program. Accordingly, it was necessary to seek an exemption (under Section 6(c) of the 1940 Act) from either the 1940 Act itself (a blanket exemption) or from provisions of the 1940 Act that restricted certain aspects of the proposed structure. Given the strong financial reasons for the trust to be an RIC under the Internal Revenue Code (discussed earlier), it was decided to take the latter approach—that is, register as an investment company but seek a section-by-section exemption. During the course of the transaction, the SEC appeared to give conflicting guidance regarding its ability to grant such an exemption (particularly since the SEC had not previously granted exemptions from certain sections of the 1940 Act from which the trust needed to be exempt). When the SEC ultimately indicated its willingness to favorably consider such exemption requests, this approach was followed.

If, for any reason, it was determined not to qualify the trust in any subsequent sale as an RIC for tax purposes, the advantages to obtaining a section-by-section 6(c) exemption—rather than a blanket exemption—would disappear. Furthermore, the SEC might be less willing to grant another section-by-section exemption if RIC status was no longer a necessary part of the transaction.

TRANSACTIONAL ISSUES

Representations and Warranties

Perhaps the most difficult subject of the structure and document negotiation in the first sale was the representations and warranties given by ED as seller of the loans. A great deal of time and thought had to go into the negotiation of their exact wording, length of duration, and remedies available for breach. In hindsight, this was probably unavoidable, as representations and warranties involved the most direct conflict between the government's interest in selling the loans without recourse and the expectations of the private sector (represented by underwriters, their counsel, and the rating agencies) to have the representations and warranties that have become standard in private sector underwritten structured financings.

The important distinction that grew out of the extensive negotiation over representations and warranties was between credit risk and legal risk. Credit risk refers to the risk to the holder of the loans that borrowers will continue to be financially able to pay their debt and that the value of collateral will diminish due to applicable market conditions or actions of the borrower. On the other hand, legal risk refers to the risk that the enforceability of any loan will have been or will be diminished as a result of any deficiencies (1) in the documentation of the loan or of any security interest or lien on any collateral or (2) in the record retention or servicing practices of ED.

These concepts are not mutually exclusive, and ED was concerned that assumption of certain legal risks necessarily included acceptance of some credit risk as well. At some point, agreement was reached over this distinction in principle. After weighing the costs and benefits of doing so and consulting with other government agencies that either conduct or review loan asset sales to ensure consistency of approach, ED excluded the retention of certain aspects of legal risk from the definition of recourse. Of course, application of that principle to the actual language of the representations, warranties, and remedies continued to be a difficult task.

ED's decision to retain certain aspects of legal risk can also be viewed as ED's willingness to state in the documents—as a factual matter—that the loans being sold are what they purport to be.

The representations, warranties, and remedies for a breach that were finally agreed on are sufficiently complex that a detailed analysis is beyond the scope of this report. However, it is important to emphasize that the representations and warranties that were negotiated in the first sale presumed ED's policy decision that it would accept certain legal risk based on the conclusion that the risk of having to take back and replace loans (or, at ED's option, to make cash payments) outweighed the cost of significantly reduced proceeds from the sale if the investors were required to assume all legal risks as well.

Loan Selection and Replacement

In the course of establishing a cost-efficient method of rating each portfolio of loans sold, agreement was reached with the rating agencies that a randomly selected and statistically significant number of loans, taken from the entire portfolio of loans held by ED to be sold over the course of the loan sale program, would be reviewed by the rating agencies. On the basis of such review, the rating agencies would determine an overall rating for ED's portfolio, which the agencies would apply to any individual pool of loans selected from the portfolio for sale, provided that the pool, as well as any loans taken from the overall portfolio for any reason, is selected in a manner consistent with the agreed-on statistical methodology. As a result, any loan selection—whether for purposes of creating a new pool to be sold or for replacement of a loan or loans in a pool already sold (pursuant to the representations and warranties)—must adhere to the accepted statistical methodology.

The methodology is designed to ensure the random distribution at all times of the remaining portfolio held by ED and of any given pool selected for sale. As a result, loans cannot be subjectively selected (again, whether for a pool or for replacement). Furthermore, any actions taken that would require removing loans from ED's remaining portfolio by any process other than the approved statistical methodology (for example, another loan discount program) would nullify the establishing rating for the portfolio and necessitate a new rating process.

Adherence to the methodology added to the complexity of the remedies available under the representations and warranties, and, of course, to the procedures to be followed in the event that any loan must be replaced. However, the rating agencies' acceptance of the statistical methodology resulted in a very significant savings to ED, both in time and fees otherwise payable to the rating agencies, by avoiding the necessity of having all loans reviewed by the agencies for each sale.

Legal Opinions

Since the authority and right of ED to sell loans are a matter of legal interpretation, the purchaser of the loans required that appropriate legal counsel opinion such matters. However, because legal opinions by ED officials can, themselves, be a means of recourse against ED, the requirement that the loans be sold without recourse presented a problem.

The solution was for OGC to address its opinions to the officers of ED that were conducting the loan sale, with an express recognition that copies may be provided to other parties to the transaction. However, the OGC opinion also expressly disclaimed any intention to create any additional financial obligation on the part of ED, its offices, or officials. In addition, certain opinions initially requested of OGC were, after some negotiation, satisfactorily provided by issuer's counsel instead.

OPERATIONS ANALYSIS

Loan Documentation

Activities that relate to the collection of loan documentation were a critical part of the Loan Asset Sales Program. The file reconstruction effort, which enabled ED to sell the loans without recourse, was necessary for the loan servicer to carry out its duties in accordance with standard commercial practice. The purchaser would also demand that the documentation meet reasonable standards of servicing. Over 40 people worked on the loan documentation activities.

In January, when Chemical Bank first looked at the loan files in Washington, D.C., only approximately two thirds of the files could be found. Of those that were found, many were incomplete or contained few documents. The goal of the document collection activity was to complete as many files as possible prior to the actual sale, thereby minimizing replacement of loans after the sale. This objective was successfully achieved. Documentation was completed for virtually all of the loans in the first sale. Only seven loans in the initial pool of loans could not be sold due to lack of documentation.

A second major objective of the loan documentation reconstruction was to collect the information required by the rating agencies to rate a sample of loans and to present it in a format for quick review. Much less financial information was initially available in ED's Washington, D.C., files than loan documentation. Ultimately, information was sent to the rating agencies to allow them to assign a rating category to 147 loans, of which only 6 did not have complete financial information.

Table 24-7 indicates the status of loan documentation at three points during the collection process: (1) after the initial review of ED's files (taken from a Chemical Bank inventory report on June 9, when 94 percent of ED's files had been inventoried); (2) intermediate results, after the initial trustee mailing and ED's search of the federal regions; and (3) the final result just prior to when loans with incomplete primary documents were replaced in the pool of loans that was sold in the 1987 loan sale.

Table 24-7. Percentage of Documents in Loan Files

	Primary Documents[1]	Loan Agreements	Legal Opinions	Fiscal Year 1986 Financials
Initial review	56%	68%	35%	23%
Intermediate review	83	76	74	55
Final review	98	94	94	96

[1]Includes indentures, bond resolutions, and note documents.

Documentation Collection Process

In February 1987, Chemical Bank established a team in ED's offices in Washington, D.C., to inventory, audit, and copy the loan files for the total portfolio and then ship them to Chemical Bank's offices in New York. All documents were copied and sent to New York by the end of September. Also in February, Chemical Bank sent an initial mailing to all trustees, under a joint letter from Chemical Bank and ED. Chemical Bank received at least partial documentation from approximately 30 percent of the trustees. ED contacted federal regions around the country and located files that had not been shipped to Washington, D.C., when the U.S. Department of Education was established in 1980. These files were also shipped to New York. A team of documentation specialists was established in New York, and the auditing of files commenced.

At the beginning of June, the first 80 loans from among the schools that did not participate in the Loan Discounting Program were randomly selected for sale. Chemical Bank began to collect missing documents and to prepare the files for the rating agencies' review. When the results of the Loan Discounting Program were tallied in the middle of July, 320 additional loans were randomly selected. The effort to collect documents for the loans in the rating sample intensified.

In the third week of July, three teams were established to complete a financial and credit analysis on the loans in the rating sample:

- A team of financial analysts and senior Chemical Bank accountants compiled spreadsheets on each school, detailing the school's financial health over the past three to five years for the rating agencies.

- A second team of credit analysts provided the rating agencies with credit information that the agencies required on each loan.
- A third team compiled enrollment and other related statistical data for each loan.

The first of the 147 loans was sent to the rating agencies on July 30. All of the financial and credit analyses were completed, and the last of the 147 loans was sent to the rating agencies by August 25.

By the end of July, Chemical Bank established a team under a manager from General Electric Credit Corporation to collect documents for all loans in the loan sale, but not in the rating sample. In addition, contact people were appointed, and procedures were established jointly with ED to establish document collection procedures for documents that were difficult to obtain.

To identify problems with the perfection of security interests, a lien search on Uniform Commercial Code (UCC) filings was initiated. A team of Chemical Bank paralegals and lawyers analyzed the results of the search to identify any obvious problems with perfection. Legal counsel from ED then looked at the results to determine which loans should be replaced.

For three weeks in August, ED undertook its verification of the loan information. A team of analysts was sent to New York to complete a case file audit form for each loan.

During the first week of September, the pool of loans to be sold was finalized. All loans with problems were removed from the sale pool. During the last week in August and the first week in September, the deliquency report was completed. Statistics required for the prospectus were compiled on the loans during this period.

Final preparation of the loans required Chemical Bank to make copies of all of the loan files, to send one copy to the servicer and one copy to the bond trustee, and to certify that the copies were exactly the same.

Loan Replacement Criteria

ED developed the loan replacement criteria with the advice of Chemical Bank to satisfy ED's obligations under the loan sale agreement. The loan sale agreement called for the replacement of loans that did not conform to certain warranties made by ED. To minimize any replacement of loans after the closing date, Chemical Bank and ED performed a thorough review prior to the sale. Loans that met the criteria were replaced prior to the sale.

The following were the criteria for replacement:

- All primary documents not in the file
- Loans that do not have a perfected UCC filing and have a third party with a prior UCC claim
- Loans that do not have a recorded mortgage and have a third party with a prior lien
- A borrower that is in litigation with ED
- A borrower that is insolvent (the proxy for insolvency used in the 1987 loan sale was having an outstanding performance bond or not having a clean opinion from the borrower's auditor)
- Loans that were delinquent for 30 days or more at some time during the 12 months prior to closing

Table 24-8 gives a breakdown by reason for replacement of the loans that were replaced from the pool of loans selected for the 1987 loan sale.

Table 24-8. Loans Replaced from the 1987 Loan Sale

	Replaced Loans
Insolvency	22
UCC	11
Documentation	7
Litigation	1

Also, a loan to a borrower on Guam was replaced because the loan servicer was not capable of servicing it.

Additionally, 239 delinquent loans were identified and removed from the portfolio eligible for sale. Fifty-nine of these loans were delinquent 30 days or more between September 1986 and June 1987. One hundred eighty loans were delinquent 30 days or more on June 30, 1987.

The same replacement criteria used for the first loan sale should be applied to the second loan sale. A header sheet will be developed to address each of the criteria. A lien search analysis will also be performed, as in the first loan sale.

ED's Loan Verification Process

ED's verification of the loans is critical for a successful loan sale. The process must be thorough and accurate. The objectives of the verification process are (1) to generate and verify the information on the loans included in the prospectus, (2) to fulfill ED's responsibilities under the representations in the loan sale agreement, and (3) to identify loans for replacement. This last item may be the most important because failure to identify loans for replacement prior to pricing can cause major replacement problems after closing.

For the first loan sale, a team of analysts from ED spent three weeks in New York to verify the loans. They prepared case file audit forms on 400 loans, which included potential replacement loans. The primary problem that the team encountered was that the scope of the effort could not be fully defined in the beginning. New requirements, which resulted from negotiations among the various parties and concerns expressed by the rating agencies, came up in the middle of the process and forced the team to analyze many of the loans again, in accordance with additional criteria. Given the prototypical nature of an extraordinarily complex transaction, the problem was unavoidable.

The second loan sale will have over twice the number of loans as the first loan sale. It will require the same number of people (approximately six) for at least a six-week period. To minimize the amount of time spent on this review, particularly in light of the large number of loans, the case file audit form should be thoroughly reviewed and revised. All important requirements should be identified at the outset. More important, the form should be streamlined so that only questions directly related to the information in the prospectus and to ED's responsibilities under the loan sale agreement are included. Furthermore, ED should coordinate with the document collection agent, Chemical Bank, prior to the start of the process. Afterward, it should discuss its findings with Chemical Bank concerning loans identified as potential replacements. This will serve to improve the quality of the processes for both the selection of loans and the generation of information included in the prospectus.

Document Procurement Procedures

A variety of methods were used to obtain loan documentation. Because of the time pressures involved, some of the measures were costly. For example, beginning in the third week of July, Federal Express was used to gather documents. A letter was mailed overnight to the borrower or local trustee, with a return overnight envelope. Although expensive, this method ensured timely collection of documents.

When Chemical Bank had problems in persuading a borrower or trustee to release a document, the problem was referred to ED. A phone call from ED often had a positive effect. As a final alternative, it was offered to have someone from ED or from Arthur Andersen & Co. travel to the borrowers to pick up the documents. The level of cooperation among all of the parties involved was very high. Staff from ED traveled in a few instances; however, Arthur Andersen personnel were never used for travel. In most cases, ED and Chemical Bank personnel together were able to persuade the institutions to forward the documents.

ADP/Computer Support

As part of the Loan Asset Sales Program, Chemical Bank provided substantial support for ED's data processing needs. The following requirements rose during the course of the program and were successfully met: generation of a portfolio description; development of a system to randomly select pools of loans; development of a loan documentation inventory system; generation of data on the loans for the prospectus, including the delinquency report; and assistance of ED in providing support for the data processing needs of the underwriters, servicers, and accountants.

After meeting several times with the automatic data processing (ADP) support team of ED, Chemical Bank decided to structure the flow of computer data in the following way. The FRB would generate a monthly data tape for ED's College Housing and Academic Facilities Loan Portfolio and would send this tape to ED early in the first week of every month. ED would proceed to edit and conform (unpack all fields, standardize the school name field, and so on) this tape and would send the tape to Chemical Bank upon request. Upon receipt of the tape, Chemical Bank would download the raw data to a personal computer and convert the data to dBase III. After conversion of the data, Chemical Bank would be in a position to begin data reporting and analysis. A graphic description of this process appears in Figure 24-5.

Figure 24-5. Data Flow Diagram

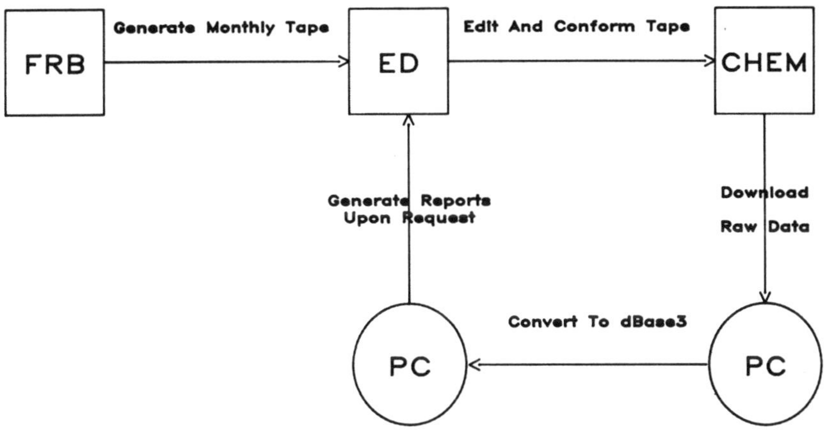

Chemical Bank received the initial tape (as of January 31, 1987) in early February. Chemical Bank proceeded to download the tape and convert the data to dBase III. Once converted to dBase III, several programs were written to produce the description of portfolio dated May 27, 1987, which was sent to prospective underwriters and servicers.

Simultaneously with production of the description of portfolio, the computer support team worked on an input screen with appropriate edit checks to facilitate the document collection effort by Chemical Bank's document collection team.

In addition, Chemical Bank researched and input other data to the data base. These data consisted of identifying loans made to public or private institutions, as well as identifying prior ratings stated by Moody's or S&P about each of the borrowers to whom the loans were issued.

Updating of Data Base

After downloading the initial computer tape in February, Chemical Bank developed several programs to test the validity of the data. Through the use of these programs, Chemical Bank was able to identify discrepancies in data and notify either the FRB or ED of these discrepancies. To ensure the accuracy of this process, Chemical Bank downloaded an additional tape as of May 31, 1987, and performed the same validity tests on these data to screen for discrepancies. Discrepancies were again reported to the FRB and ED.

By performing these data checks, Chemical Bank was able to minimize the amount of data discrepancies that still existed on the final tape, which was downloaded in July (containing data as of June 30, 1987). This increased the efficiency of the final concerted effort made by Chemical Bank and ED to ensure that no data discrepancies existed on the final computer tape.

Sampling Methodology: Design and Implementation

The computer support team worked many hours with the statisticians—first, to develop the plan for the sampling methodology and, then, to design a system to implement the methodology.

This actually entailed the following:

- Several meetings were held with the statisticians until a mutually agreed on sampling scheme was determined. The portfolio was stratified into parts (strata), based on the outstanding balance of each loan and whether the loan had been made to a public or private institution. After being segmented in this fashion, the portfolio was further divided into two groups: a group of loans ineligible for prepayment and a group of loans with the potential of being prepaid by June 30, 1987. This further division, which resulted in nine strata, was made because the eligibility for sale of loans that were in the Loan Discounting Program was not known prior to June 30, 1987.

- The next stage was to develop a computer system to implement the sampling methodology. This system comprised several interrelated dBase III programs, as well as a program to randomly sequence loans by using both Lotus 1-2-3 and dBase III software. The unknown status of the loans eligible for prepayment led to the additional calculation of a minimum and maximum number of loans to be drawn from the group of loans ineligible for prepayment; this calculation was necessitated by the need for the document collection team to begin collection of documents prior to June 30, 1987.

Preparation of Information for the Prospectus

Due to intense time pressure, all data needed for the prospectus were generated by Chemical Bank from the tape supplied by ED and were verified by both ED and Arthur Andersen over a 48-hour period (September 2, 1987–September 3, 1987). This was possible because Chemical Bank had tested all programs prior to this peak period.

Loan Eligibility

Loans were declared ineligible for sale if they met any of the following criteria:

- If the loan had been prepaid.
- If the loan had been in default for 30 or more days between September 2, 1986, and September 1, 1987. In addition, if one or more loans issued to a borrower were in default on principal, interest, or both for 30 or more days between September 2, 1986, and September 1, 1987, all loans for that borrower were declared ineligible for sale.
- If the loan matured prior to January 1, 1989.
- If the loan was originated after June 30, 1987.

Definition of a Loan

Another question that Chemical Bank addressed was the definition of a loan for sale purposes. All loans to one borrower could have been sold as a unit, all loans in a bond series could have been sold as a unit, or a lower level of detail could have been used. This was further complicated because the FRB's computer system treated loans with semiannual principal payments or multiple interest rates as multiple loans. It was finally agreed that a loan would be defined as a note or any individual bond within a series; multiple loans that existed due to semiannual principal payments or multiple interest rates would be treated as one loan. Each loan would have distinct and independent collateral or, in the case of a series, would be issued in parity with the other loans of the series. This definition was used because, given the random sampling criteria, it was desirable to spread the loans of one borrower as widely as possible among the loan sale pools so as to spread the credit quality of each borrower among the various pools.

Loan Discounting Program Coordination with Loan Asset Sales Program

The Loan Discounting Program proved to be very successful for ED. By reoffering the program to college and university borrowers, ED promoted goodwill with borrowers that might not have wished that their loans be sold. In addition to promoting goodwill, the Loan Discount Program gave ED a high monetary return (63¢ on the dollar) and substantially achieved most of ED's budget target for fiscal year 1987. (See the "Comparison of Loan Discounting Program and Loan Asset Sales Program" section.)

Despite being highly successful for ED, the Loan Discounting Program presented some coordination issues for the completion of the first loan asset sale, as follows.

Document Collection

The Loan Discounting Program had both positive and negative effects on the document collection effort. The significant amount of money received through the Loan Discounting Program substantially decreased the amount of money needed from the first loan asset sale, thereby reducing the number of loans that required reconstructed documents. Since loan documentation was in less than satisfactory condition, this avoided a potential serious bottleneck for the 1987 loan sale.

However, if the Loan Discounting Program had ended a few months prior to the final eligibility date of June 30, 1987, the loans to be sold in the first pool could have been identified much earlier. This would have allowed the document collection team to start its collection effort earlier and to have obtained complete documentation on a greater number of loans.

In conclusion, the Loan Discounting Program acted as both a positive and negative influence on document collection. To maximize the benefit to ED, any future plans for loan discounting or loan asset sales should be made using the knowledge gained from the documentation collection effort put forth in the first loan sale.

Rating Agencies

The Loan Discounting Program created the need for lengthy discussions with the rating agencies regarding the sampling methodology.

For the document collection team to have documents ready for review by the rating agencies in the required time frame, collection efforts had to begin prior to June 30, 1987. For this reason, part of the sample to be used by the rating agencies to generate an average rating had to be drawn before the end of the Loan Discounting Program. Thus, a sample had to be drawn from the portfolio before the portfolio was finalized.

Needless to say, this concerned the rating agencies. To alleviate their concerns, Chemical Bank held several meetings with the statisticians to formulate a sampling methodology to gain the approval of the rating agencies. Lengthy discussions regarding the mechanics of sample generation were needed to accommodate the Loan Discounting Program.

The rating agencies wanted to ensure that if loans that were withdrawn from the Loan Discounting Program had different credit characteristics than loans that had never applied to the Loan Discounting Program, these credit characteristics were accurately represented in the sample to be rated. To ensure this, the sample to be rated would contain loans drawn proportionately by the dollar value of each stratum as a percentage of the dollar value represented by the total portfolio. This approach eliminated concerns about inaccurate representation of the portfolio in the sample to be rated.

In conclusion, nothing could have been done to finalize the

universe of loans eligible for sale prior to June 30, 1987. To achieve the efficiencies of the recommended structure, considerable extra effort was required to ensure the integrity of the sampling methodology. For other loan sales in which a statistical sampling methodology is to be used, it would be beneficial to finalize the portfolio eligible for sale well in advance of beginning the sale effort.

Comparison of Loan Discounting Program and Loan Asset Sales Program

Although a superficial review of both programs will indicate that ED received a certain percentage of the par value of its loans from the Loan Discounting Program and the Loan Asset Sales Program, a direct comparison is difficult for several reasons. Both programs used vastly different approaches to achieve a similar end result.

During a six-month period, from January to June 1987, the Loan Discounting Program offered colleges and universities the opportunity to prepay their obligations at a BBB corporate discount rate, which was set at the beginning of each month by using a combination of U.S. Treasury rates and BBB spreads in effect for the specific maturity of each loan to be prepaid.The decision to use BBB rates was based on an earlier anlaysis of the portfolio during 1986, which estimated the average rating of the portfolio of loans to be BBB. The Loan Discounting Program generated the results shown in Table 24-9 upon its conclusion on June 30, 1987.

Table 24-9. Loan Discounting Program Results

Loans Repaid	*Principal Value*	*Net Proceeds Received*	*% of Principal Value*
1,182	$791,853,405	$499,058,935	63%

The Loan Asset Sales Program commenced immediately after the Loan Discounting Program ended. Pricing of the bond issue took place on September 21, 1987, with closing one week later. The 1987 loan sale generated the results shown in Table 24-10 upon closing September 29, 1987.

Table 24-10. 1987 Loan Sale Results

Loans Sold	*Principal Value*	*Net Proceeds Received*	*% of Principal Value*
324	$237,248,551	$120,143,950	50.6%
		10,770,424[1]	4.5
		$130,914,374	55.1%

[1]Present value of certificates at closing, assuming a 14% discount rate.

To compare the Loan Discounting Program with the Loan Asset Sales Program, two key factors must be considered: the interest rate environment and market penetration, as discussed in the conclusion.

Interest Rate Environment

The interest rate environment during the past year has been volatile, and, therefore, timing is a critical factor in the analysis of any return achieved on a portfolio. The Loan Discounting Program benefited from the fact that general interest rate levels were lower when it was implemented than the interest rate levels in effect at the time of pricing for the 1987 loan sale (September 21, 1987). To compare the two interest rate environments, an average of the U.S. Treasury rates used during the six-month Loan Discounting Program was computed for maturities similar to those of the bonds and was compared with the actual rates at which the bonds were offered. The same calculation was performed for the BBB spread during that period. To complete the analysis, BBB spreads in effect when the bonds were priced are also presented. Table 24-11 depicts the differences.

Table 24-11. Comparison of Two Interest Rate Environments

	Average, January–June		*Actual, September 21, 1987*		
Years	*U.S. Treasury Rates*	*BBB Spread*	*U.S. Treasury Rates*	*Trust Spread*	*BBB Spread*
2	6.78%	90	8.24%	35	95
4	7.11	102	8.74	50	104
6	7.34	110	9.03	75	110
10	7.62	123	9.37	95	119
30	7.89	153	9.53	110	168

Two aspects of this comparison are readily apparent. First, the general level of interest rates rose by an average of 160 basis points from the time that the Loan Discounting Program was offered to the time of the bond pricing. Second, spreads on BBB corporate bonds are significantly wider than those that the trust achieved. Had the Loan Discounting Program commenced in September, the proceeds that ED received would have been significantly reduced.

To best show how the volatile interest rate environment would have affected the Loan Discounting Program, two examples are analyzed:

Assumptions: The weighted-average maturity of the loans is 19 years. Since ED used the final maturity date of each loan to detrmine the discount rates used in the Loan Discounting Program, this analysis uses the 19-year average maturity of the loans. The cash flows used in this analysis are the same cash flows used in the prospectus.

Example 1:

Example 1 calculates a value for the loans by assuming that the loans were prepaid at a discount between January and June 1987. The discount rate is computed by taking an average 19-year U.S. Treasury rate (simple average of 19-year Treasuries between January and June 1987) and adding to it an average 19-year BBB spread above Treasuries (simple average of 19-year BBB spreads above Treasuries between January and June 1987). After inputting the monthly cash flows of the loans, the cash flows are discounted back, using the rate described earlier after adjustment to a monthly equivalent basis. This calculation yields a present value of $154,751,966 to ED on the total par amount of $237,248,522 (a return of 65¢ on the dollar).

Example 2:

Example 2 calculates a value for the loans by assuming that the loans were prepaid, using a discount rate in effect during the week of pricing. The discount rate used was the 19-year U.S. Treasury rate, plus the corresponding 19-year BBB spread above this Treasury rate. The monthly cash flows of the loans were discounted at the calculated discount rate adjusted to a monthly equivalent basis. This calculaton yielded $136,320,853 to ED on the total par amount of $237,248,552 (a return of 57¢ on the dollar).

The difference between the value generated in Example 1 and the value generated in Example 2 ($18,431,114, or 8¢ on the dollar) can be attributed solely to a volatile interest rate environment. This significant difference in return shows how sensitive the value of low interest rate loans is to the higher general level of interest rates.

This analysis should be viewed for illustrative purposes only, and the results should not be directly compared with results achieved in the Loan Discounting Program. The loans used in this analysis were loans actually sold in the first loan sale pool—not loans sold in the Loan Discounting Program. The loans used in this analysis could have had different characteristics (such as weighted-average maturity and weighted-average life) than the loans prepaid under the Loan Discounting Program. These characteristics are critical to the analysis; thus, no direct comparison can be made. In addition, an average maturity rate was used to discount all of the loans in this analysis. To truly replicate the Loan Discounting Program, each loan would have to be discounted individually at an appropriate rate.

Conclusions

The Loan Discounting Program was offered to 100 percent of the institutions that were in ED's portfolio and were not in default as of October 1, 1986, for an extended period of time (January 1987–June 1987). Any institutions interested in prepaying their loans at a BBB spread over Treasuries had the option to do so. Therefore, if ED wanted to raise a high volume of net proceeds received through a future loan discounting program, significantly higher discount rates would need to be used (perhaps a B-rated spread over Treasuries). The use of these higher discount rates would greatly reduce the percentage return to ED from this program.

If another loan discounting program were to be employed, it would carry with it the following two negative effects:

- *Added difficulty in conducting future loan asset sales.* Since another loan discounting program would significantly change the portfolio, the sampling methodology implemented for the first sale would become invalid. Therefore, no future sale could be made using the existing methodology. To achieve any future sales, a new methodology would have to be formulated, and discussions with the rating agencies would have to begin again.

- *Loss of goodwill.* Were ED to reoffer a loan discounting program that used a higher loan discounting rate, some negative reactions from schools that participated in the previous program could be expected, due to economics. Had they waited several months, they could have saved a significant amount of money as a result of the higher discount rate required to induce repayment.

Although the Loan Discounting Program was highly successful, any future discounting programs would bring unpredictable dollar results to ED, while also having the complications discussed previously. Access to private sector investors effectively allows ED a tertiary funding source apart from the U.S. Treasury Department and the schools themselves. In addition, any future loan asset sales—with known costs associated with the transaction—will be able to generate a predictable amount of proceeds for ED.

Loan Origination and Servicing

Loan Origination: Office of Postsecondary Education

As financial adviser for the Loan Asset Sales Program, Chemical Bank worked closely with the origination and servicing areas of the Office of Postsecondary Education. An initial review and comparison of ED's origination policies to private sector practices indicate that they are similar in many ways. The loan documentation required at origination and many of the review practices have parallels in the private sector. However, there is one significant difference: ED's decision to award a loan is based primarily on policy considerations (school need, interest rates capped by legislation, and so on), with credit review of secondary importance. These policy considerations are a part of the legislative rationale for originally authorizing the loans. On the other hand, a private sector lender typically grants a loan with the goal of realizing a maximum return, and credit decisions play a critical role. The two most important variables in setting a loan's interest rate are market interest rates and the credit quality of the borrower. This difference in approach is readily apparent in the deep discount at which ED sold the loans.

The private sector attempts to standardize as many procedures as possible to keep independent judgments to a minimum. The first step of this process is usually the creation of a loan origination manual that sets forth lending standards and the key provisions to be negotiated for all transactions. Examples of standardized documentation are usually given. When securitizing loan assets, rating agencies find that review of such standardized procedures gives them an understanding of the lending philosophy and practices behind granting the loans. With this understanding, they are better able to understand the underlying credit of an issue that is supported by the underlying loans.

Whether or not such a procedure manual exists, an elaborate control process is typically followed when making credit decisions. The process involves multiple layers of documentation review and decision analysis, including review by legal counsel. The process of review by different areas acts, in itself, as a control to ensure that the lender's interests are protected in the event of a default. For example, a breakdown in ED's review process was apparent in one instance in which the rating agencies assigned a CCC rating to a loan (which would otherwise have been A or better) because the loan was secured by a pledge of marketable securities without a pledge and trust agreement. While this was only a single instance, it indicates the importance of thorough review procedures.

Loan Servicing: Institutional Receivable Branch

A comparison of ED's servicing practices with standard commercial practices reveals that ED's policies tend to be reactive, while commercial practices tend to be more proactive. In the past, ED focused solely on collecting delinquent payments, but not until many months after the first delinquency; also, ED did not attempt to rectify loan covenant breaches or analyze the financial health of the institution. Conversely, commercial servicers monitor the loans more closely and develop trigger mechanisms to indicate a borrower's deteriorating financial health. Depending on the type of loan, there is close coordination between origination and servicing; a lender typically establishes and manages an ongoing relationship with the borrower.

Sampling Methodology

Given the time constraints placed on the 1987 loan sale, it was not possible for the rating agencies to rate each loan individually.

Even if it had been possible, the cost to ED would have been substantial. Thus, an approach had to be developed that would allow the rating agencies to generate an average credit rating for the portfolio within the required time frame, while also minimizing the cost. The only viable approach was the use of a statistical sample, from which the rating agencies could determine an average credit rating for the portfolio.

Chemical Bank hired two independent statisticians to assist in the development of a sampling methodology. After several meetings, it was decided to use a stratified sampling approach. This entailed dividing the portfolio into segments based on the following criteria:

- Participation in the Loan Discounting Program
- Outstanding Balance of each loan
- Whether the loan was issued to a public or private institution

The methodology is outlined as follows. The portfolio eligible for sale as of June 30, 1987 (the end of the Loan Discounting Program), was divided as follows.

Loans Ineligible for Prepayment

- *Stratum 1.* Loans made to public institutions with a curent outstanding balance (as of January 31, 1987) less than $1,000,000.
- *Stratum 2.* Loans made to public institutions with a current outstanding balance (as of January 31, 1987) greater than or equal to $1,000,000 and less than or equal to $5,000,000.
- *Stratum 3.* Loans made to private institutions with a current outstanding balance (as of January 31, 1987) less than $1,000,000.
- *Stratum 4.* Loans made to private institutions with a current outstanding balance (as of January 31, 1987) greater than or equal to $1,000,000 and less than or equal to $5,000,000.

Loans Eligible for Prepayment That Have Been Withdrawn from the Discounting Program

- *Stratum 5.* Loans made to public institutions with a current outstanding balance (as of June 30, 1987) less than $1,000,000.

- *Stratum 6.* Loans made to public institutions with a current outstanding balance (as of June 30, 1987) greater than or equal to $1,000,000 and less than or equal to $5,000,000.
- *Stratum 7.* Loans made to private institutions with a current outstanding balance (as of June 30, 1987) less than $1,000,000.
- *Stratum 8.* Loans made to private institutions with a current outstanding balance (as of June 30, 1987) greater than or equal to $1,000,000 and less than or equal to $5,000,000.

Other

- *Stratum 9.* Loans with a current outstanding balance (as of June 30, 1987) greater than $5,000,000.

Use of Methodology

A methodology was formulated to use each of these nine strata to draw a sample to estimate the portfolio's average credit rating, which would be the basis for determining overcollateralization levels. Since the creditworthiness of the portfolio was the point of concern, extra emphasis was put on large loan balances in this sample. The rationale was that a default on a large loan has a greater impact on the cash flows than a default on a smaller loan does. Therefore, each stratum was represented by a sample of loans proportional to the current outstanding balance of loans in that stratum of the portfolio.

A slightly different methodology was formulated to draw a sample for each loan sale pool. This methodology differed because the goal in drawing this sample was to construct a pool that was representative of the loan sale portfolio—not to estimate an average rating. Therefore, the emphasis was not placed on large loan balances, but on the premise that each stratum must be equally represented in the pool. To satisfy this objective, each stratum was represented on a sample of loans that was proportional to the number of loans in that stratum of the portfolio.

In conclusion, the sampling methodology was highly efficient. After lengthy discussions, the rating agencies accepted the methodology in its entirety. Thus, the rating agencies were able to act expeditiously to determine an average credit rating for the portfolio. The overall goal of cost effectively achieving an average credit rating for the portfolio was realized.

Comparison of Loan Sales on a Taxable Basis and a Tax-Exempt Basis

To approximate the difference in value between selling the loan portfolio on a fully taxable basis and selling on both a taxable and a tax-exempt basis, the following hypothetical analysis has been developed. Results from this analysis should not be compared with actual sale results, as factors such as transaction size and structure would be dramatically different. Additionally, the cash flow differences that result from additional variables specific to the loan sale in September preclude any direct comparison.

1. Approximately 51 percent of the loans could have been eligible for sale as tax-exempt loans, while the remainder could have been sold on a taxable basis (percentages are of outstanding principal balance as of September 2, 1987). The monthly cash flows of the loans were multiplied by 51 percent (to represent monthly tax-exempt cash flows) and by 49 percent (to represent monthly taxable cash flows).
2. Using 2-, 4-, 6-, 10-, and 30-year AAA tax-exempt rates as of the week of pricing, a weighted-average interest rate was computed by multiplying the rates for each respective maturity by the percentage of bonds allocated to each tranche (this information was taken from Salomon's final cash flow report). This annualized weighted-average rate was adjusted to a monthly equivalent to discount each monthly tax-exempt cash flow. This calculation produced a present-value amount for the tax-exempt portion of the portfolio.
3. Using the same methodology outlined in (2), a weighted-average taxable rate was computed by multiplying the 2-, 4-, 6-, 10-, and 30-year U.S. Treasury rates, plus the corresponding trust spreads on these rates, by the percentage of bonds outstanding for each of the maturities that these rates represented (all information was taken from Salomon's final cash flow report). After adjustments, the monthly equivalent of this weighted-average rate was used to discount each monthly taxable cash flow. This calculation produced a present-value amount for the taxable portion of the portfolio.
4. The addition of the values generated in (2) and (3) provided a total present-value return on the loans sold that equalled $162,435,094.

This amount was divided by the total par amount of the assets sold—$237,248,552—to provide a percentage return on the dollar that equalled 68¢.

5. For comparison, the total monthly cash flows of the loans sold in the first pool (tax exempt plus taxable) were discounted at the taxable rate determined in (3). This produced a total present-value return on the portfolio that equalled $145,573,988, assuming that the entire portfolio was sold on a taxable basis. Dividing this amount by the total par amount produced a percentage return on the dollar that equalled 61¢.
6. Subtracting the value obtained in (5) from the value obtained in (4) provided the additional amount of money gained if the portfolio was sold on both a taxable basis and a tax-exempt basis: $16,861,106. This value was also divided by the total par amount to provide a percentage return on the dollar. This amounts to 7¢ on the dollar.

This analysis produced a larger return to ED than that produced by the actual Loan Asset Sales Program because transaction costs and several other variables were not assumed and an average rate approach was used. The present-value difference of 7¢ reflected the hypothetical opportunity loss in not selling eligible loans on a tax-exempt basis. In reality, this loss would be reduced, as a result of a different structuring approach and the resultant variable costs associated with it. Also, the analysis does not give any effect to increased tax revenues generated by structuring the transaction as taxable bonds. The hypothetical opportunity loss would be narrower if these revenues were factored into the equation.

Index

A

G

H

I